SUSTAINING THE STATES

The Fiscal Viability of American State Governments

American Society for Public Administration
Series in Public Administration & Public Policy

David H. Rosenbloom, Ph.D.
Editor-in-Chief

Mission: Throughout its history, ASPA has sought to be true to its founding principles of promoting scholarship and professionalism within the public service. The ASPA Book Series on Public Administration and Public Policy publishes books that increase national and international interest for public administration and which discuss practical or cutting edge topics in engaging ways of interest to practitioners, policy makers, and those concerned with bringing scholarship to the practice of public administration.

RECENT PUBLICATIONS

Sustaining the States: The Fiscal Viability of American State Governments
by Marilyn Marks Rubin and Katherine G. Willoughby

Using the "Narcotrafico" Threat to Build Public Administration Capacity between the US and Mexico
by Donald E. Klingner and Roberto Moreno Espinosa

Environmental Policymaking and Stakeholder Collaboration: Theory and Practice
by Shannon K. Orr

Organizational Assessment and Improvement in the Public Sector Workbook
by Kathleen M. Immordino

Challenges in City Management: A Case Study Approach
by Becky J. Starnes

Local Economic Development and the Environment: Finding Common Ground
by Susan M. Opp and Jeffery L. Osgood, Jr.

Case Studies in Disaster Response and Emergency Management
by Nicolas A. Valcik and Paul E. Tracy

Debating Public Administration: Management Challenges, Choices, and Opportunities
by Robert F. Durant and Jennifer R.S. Durant

CRC Press
Taylor & Francis Group

ASPA
American Society for
Public Administration
ADVANCING EXCELLENCE IN PUBLIC SERVICE

American Society for Public Administration
Series in Public Administration and Public Policy

SUSTAINING THE STATES

The Fiscal Viability of American State Governments

Edited by
Marilyn Marks Rubin • Katherine G. Willoughby

CRC Press
Taylor & Francis Group
Boca Raton London New York

CRC Press is an imprint of the
Taylor & Francis Group, an **informa** business

CRC Press
Taylor & Francis Group
6000 Broken Sound Parkway NW, Suite 300
Boca Raton, FL 33487-2742

Printed on acid-free paper
Version Date: 20140618

International Standard Book Number-13: 978-1-4665-5541-9 (Hardback)

Visit the Taylor & Francis Web site at
http://www.taylorandfrancis.com

and the CRC Press Web site at
http://www.crcpress.com

Contents

Preface

The United States provides a classic example of a bottom-up system of federalism. It was created in 1787 when representatives of the then-thirteen colonies convened to ratify a constitution under which both the central government and the states would be sovereign entities. Within certain constitutional and statutory constraints, state governments thus (1) develop and execute their budgets without review and modification by the federal government, (2) determine their own revenue structures and levels and types of expenditures, and (3) borrow and manage debt. The U.S. system stands in contrast with nearly all other top-down nation-states in which the established central government constitutionally or legislatively assigns expenditure responsibilities and revenue raising authority to subnational units of government.*

State fiscal decisions have a significant impact on this nation's economy. Together, with their more than 90,000 local governments, states account for almost 12 percent of gross domestic product (GDP) and 60 percent of all government expenditures.† Taken together, subnational governments in the United States employ more than one out of every eight workers and provide the bulk of all basic governmental services consumed by individuals and businesses.

The purpose of this book is to provide a comprehensive and timely knowledge base of trends in, the current status of, and future prospects for the fiscal sustainability of state governments. Upon reading the following chapters, you should come away with a comprehensive view of the very broad reach and multiple contributions of state governments to individuals and communities across the nation. You should be well versed in the resources that states generate and use to conduct the business of government. You will be exposed to the very real and significant constraints on

* Kincaid, J., The Constitutional Frameworks of State and Local Government Finance, in *The Oxford Handbook of State and Local Government Finance*, ed. Robert D. Ebel and John E. Petersen, New York, Oxford University Press, 2012, pp. 45–82.

† Calculated by authors using data from the U.S. Census Bureau and the U.S. Bureau of Economic Analysis.

state ability to fulfill their responsibilities, and you will be introduced to several key challenges that state governments face and actively address to reach and maintain fiscal sustainability. Hopefully, you will gain a clear, realistic understanding of state operations and financing in the United States, as well as a sense of optimism for the capacity of these governments to move forward.

Editors

Marilyn Marks Rubin is professor of public administration and economics at John Jay College of City University of New York and director of the college's MPA program. She has authored several publications on fiscal policy and budget-related issues and was an advisor to the Korean Women's Development Institute on gender budgeting. Professor Rubin is a fellow of the National Academy of Public Administration and a past chair of the Association for Budgeting and Financial Management.

Katherine G. Willoughby is professor of public management and policy in the Andrew Young School of Policy Studies at Georgia State University. Her areas of expertise include state and local government budgeting and financial and performance management. She has trained government officials and staff from numerous countries in public budgeting, management, and reform. Professor Willoughby is a fellow of the National Academy of Public Administration and a past chair of the Association for Budgeting and Financial Management.

Contributors

John R. Bartle is dean of the College of Public Affairs and Community Service at the University of Nebraska, Omaha. He is coeditor of *Management Policies in Local Government Finance*, coauthor of *Sustainable Development for Public Administration*, and editor of *Evolving Theories of Public Budgeting*. Bartle is a fellow of the National Academy of Public Administration and a past chair of the Association for Budgeting and Financial Management.

Carolyn Bourdeaux is associate director for research of the Fiscal Research Center in the Andrew Young School of Policy Studies at Georgia State University and associate professor in the school's Department of Public Management and Policy. She served as director of Georgia's Senate Budget and Evaluation Office, worked as a legislative aide to the U.S. Congress, and consulted for local and regional transportation and economic development agencies. Her areas of expertise include state budget and tax policy, education, and administrative reform.

Can Chen is a doctoral candidate in the School of Public Administration at the University of Nebraska, Omaha. His primary research interests are transportation finance, capital budgeting, and innovative infrastructure financing.

Sean P. Corcoran is associate professor of educational economics at New York University's Steinhardt School of Culture, Education, and Human Development, and an affiliated faculty of the Robert F. Wagner School of Public Service and NYU Institute for Education and Social Policy (IESP). His research focuses on human capital in the teaching profession, the economics of school choice, and state and local public finance.

Sarah A. Cordes is a doctoral candidate at the New York University Robert F. Wagner School of Public Service. Her research and teaching interests include education and urban policy, housing, public finance, and applied statistics and econometrics. Cordes is also an Institute for Education Sciences–Funded Predoctoral Interdisciplinary Research Training (IES-PIRT) fellow, serving as a graduate assistant in the Institute for Education and Social Policy at NYU.

William R. Darnell is a securities pricing analyst at a global asset management firm and has worked at a Fortune 25 company as a financial analyst in the wealth management division. Darnell is a federally commissioned officer in the U.S. Army National Guard, Infantry.

Dwight V. Denison is professor of public and nonprofit finance at the Martin School of Public Policy and Administration at the University of Kentucky. He is the current director of graduate studies for the master's degree programs in public administration and public policy at the University of Kentucky. His areas of expertise include bond finance, financial management, debt management, and tax administration. Denison is a past chair of the Association for Budgeting and Financial Management.

Robert D. Ebel is a consultant on public financial management for the World Bank and member of the staff of Local Governance Innovation and Development. Prior to his present roles he was chief economist and deputy chief financial officer for the Washington, DC, government, as well as a senior fellow at the Joint Urban Institute/Brookings Institution Tax Policy Center (TPC).

Robert A. Greer is assistant professor in the Department of Public Administration and Policy at the University of Georgia, specializing in public budgeting and finance. His research focuses on state and local government debt, municipal bond markets, and issues of fiscal federalism. He teaches public financial administration, public budgeting, and research methods.

Merl Hackbart is Provost's Distinguished Service Professor of Finance and Public Administration and interim director of the Martin School of Public Policy and Administration at the University of Kentucky. He served as budget director for the Commonwealth of Kentucky. Hackbart is a fellow of the National Academy of Public Administration and a past chair of the Association for Budgeting and Financial Management.

Roy T. Meyers is professor of political science and affiliate professor of public policy at the University of Maryland, Baltimore County (UMBC), and was founding director of UMBC's Sondheim Public Affairs Scholars Program. He authored *Strategic Budgeting*, which received the Lewis Brownlow Book Award from the National Academy of Public Administration. Meyers edited the *Handbook of Government Budgeting* and has published several articles on the federal budget process.

John L. Mikesell is Chancellor's Professor of Public and Environmental Affairs at Indiana University. His areas of expertise include sales and property taxation and budget processes. He has worked on the Indiana state revenue forecast since the mid 1970s. Mikesell's textbook *Fiscal Administration* is widely used in graduate public administration programs. He is a past chair of the Association for Budgeting and Financial Management.

Scott Pattison has served as the executive director of the National Association of State Budget Officers (NASBO) in Washington, DC, since 2001. Prior to coming to NASBO, Pattison served as Virginia's budget director, and before that headed the Regulatory and Economic Analysis section of the Virginia Department of Planning and Budget. Pattison is a fellow in the National Academy of Public Administration and a past chair of the Association for Budgeting and Financial Management.

Shanna Rose is a political economist with expertise in government budgeting and health policy. She is an associate professor of government at Claremont McKenna College. Her book *Financing Medicaid Federalism and the Growth of America's Health Care Safety Net* examines the role of fiscal federalism in driving the growth of public spending on health care for low-income Americans. Her research has appeared in the *Journal of Politics*, *Public Administration Review*, and *Public Choice*, among others.

Irene S. Rubin is professor emerita at Northern Illinois University. Her areas of expertise include the politics of public budgeting and fiscal stress of federal, state, and local governments. She has authored several books, including *The Politics of Public Budgeting: Getting, Spending, Borrowing, and Balancing*; *Balancing the Federal Budget: Eating the Seed Corn or Trimming the Herds*; and *Class, Tax, and Power: Municipal Budgeting in the United States.*

Amy Ellen Schwartz is professor of public policy, education, and economics at the New York University Robert F. Wagner School of Public Service and director of the NYU Institute for Education and Social Policy. Her areas of expertise include applied econometrics, urban policy, education policy, and finance. Schwartz has consulted with nonprofit organizations and government agencies about issues related to economic and tax policy, including the impact of business improvement districts on property values.

Cynthia S. Searcy is assistant dean for academic programs at the Andrew Young School of Policy Studies at Georgia State University, as well as assistant professor in the Department of Public Management and Policy. Her areas of expertise include public budgeting and financial management, education, and health policy. She recently investigated revenue trends for Georgia's public school districts and the financial health of charter schools, and the responses of State Children's Health Insurance Program participants to program copayments.

Sally Coleman Selden is associate dean for academic programs and professor of management at Lynchburg College. Her areas of expertise include public and nonprofit management, organizational behavior, human resources management, and leadership. Selden is currently involved in two research projects: High Performance Work Systems in Nonprofit Organizations and the State Government Workforce Project in collaboration with the National Association of State Personnel Executives.

David L. Sjoquist is Dan E. Sweat Distinguished Chair in Educational and Community Policy and professor of economics in the Andrew Young School of Policy Studies at Georgia State University. He is editor and/or author of numerous books and articles about public finance, taxation, and urban and regional economics. Sjoquist has also conducted extensive funded research for governments at every level in the United States.

Michael C. Walker is associate professor and coordinator of criminal justice studies at the Passaic County Community College in Paterson, New Jersey. He served 32 years with the Paterson Police Department, attaining the rank of captain prior to retiring and returning to serve as Paterson's police commissioner. He is a member of the FBI Uniform Crime Reporting Subcommittee and has lectured internationally on police leadership and police training.

Chapter 1

Sustaining the States: An Introduction

Scott Pattison
National Association of State Budget Officers

Katherine G. Willoughby
Georgia State University

Contents

State Roles and Fiscal Sustainability

The 50 state governments in the United States play a dominant role in the delivery of a wide range of public services (see Figure 1.1). States spend approximately $1.7 trillion annually and, together with local governments, account for close to 12 percent of the nation's gross domestic product (GDP). States are engaged in educating and protecting their residents, caring for natural resources, building and maintaining infrastructure, and promoting economic development. States help to keep millions of people

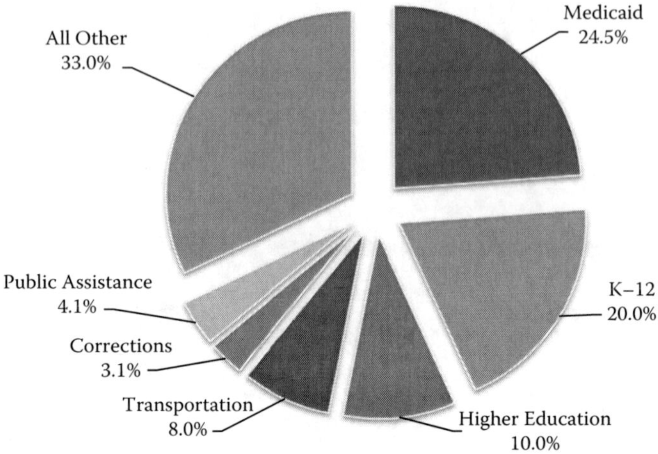

Figure 1.1 Total state expenditures, FY2013 estimated. Total state expenditures are all federal and state funds. (From NASBO State Expenditure Report, State Expenditures by Function, Estimated Fiscal 2013, November 21, 2013, 2. Available at: http://www.nasbo.org/sites/default/files/State%20Expenditure%20Report.Summary_0.pdf.)

healthy through massive health care expenditures, including Medicaid, and by way of nutritional support programs. Although almost entirely funded by the federal government, other health-related programs such as the highly utilized Special Supplemental Nutrition Program for Women, Infants, and Children (WIC) would not be available without the involvement and service infrastructure provided by state governments. WIC alone provides benefits for 9 million people each month.

States also play a critical role in keeping the public safe by funding state police and correctional facilities. More than 85 percent of the nation's inmates are the responsibility of state governments, and millions more are monitored by states after their release. One of the most basic ways an individual in this country shows identification is through a driver's license, with licensing generally handled by state motor vehicle agencies. In terms of education, the largest public support of universities and community colleges comes from state government, as does a major portion of the funds for K–12 education.

Especially in light of these critical responsibilities, the states face significant challenges as we near the midpoint of the second decade of the 21st century. The biggest concern is the new "fiscal normal" following the most dramatic economic downturn experienced in this country since the Great Depression—the Great Recession that lasted from December 2007 to June 2009 (NBER 2012). This new normal is characterized by modestly growing state revenues, but growth that is insufficient for meeting the spending demanded by politicians and voters. Federal Reserve Chairman Ben Bernanke explained it well when he said that we are facing "the still-moderate underlying pace of economic growth."* Modest growth in state revenues means modest growth of state budgets prospectively, at least compared to the decades prior to the Great Recession.

The states have weathered recessions in the past, attesting to state government resiliency. There were 11 business cycles in the latter half of the 19th century and 22 more since 1900 (NBER 2012), two of which occurred in the first decade of this century. Boyd (2003) writes that the bull economy of the 1990s, followed by the first recession of the 21st century in 2001, contributed to the weaker position of states for weathering the Great Recession.

State income and sales tax receipts especially benefited from the run-up of the economy in the 1990s, as did state pension investment returns. Conversely, "state spending pressures were minimal" during the period (Boyd 2003, 324). Restructured federal funding to states for public welfare and new tobacco settlement monies† provided an added fiscal cushion for states, allowing many to expand programs, cut taxes, enrich pension benefits for employees, and fill reserve funds. Total state government revenue at the start of the 21st century stood at $1.26 trillion, spending equaled $1.08 trillion, and indebtedness, $548 billion (Wulf 2002).

The stock market slump of 2000 and the recession that began in March 2001 reduced the growth of state revenues. The downturn ended in November 2001 but had a much longer-lasting impact on state finances than was recognized at the time (Boyd 2003). Unrealistic forecasts related to both tax receipts and pension investment return rates, the timing of the decline in state revenues, and in many cases, following the path of least resistance in terms of engaging fiscal management solutions, hampered the ability of states to react quickly and to plan for recovery.

On the expenditure side, continually growing Medicaid costs, increasing education needs, and widespread losses in pension portfolio values resulted in significant state budget gaps. Table 1.1 shows state deficits as a percent of national GDP, indicating the severity of the 2001 recession compared with the one preceding it that ran from July 1990 to March 1991 (NBER 2012). State deficits as a percent of GDP in 2002, the year following the end of the 2001 recession, are almost twice the size of those in 1992, the year following the end of the 1990–1991 recession.

The states recovered slowly after the 2001 recession, but the basis of recovery was both insubstantial and fleeting. State surpluses and rainy day funds grew into the mid-2000s, and state reserve balances peaked at $69 billion in fiscal 2006. But, these reserves provided little protection for states when faced with the looming deficits resulting from the 18-month Great Recession.

---

* Chairman Ben S. Bernanke, *Semiannual Monetary Policy Report to the Congress*, before the Committee on Banking, Housing, and Urban Affairs, U.S. Senate, Washington, DC, February 26, 2013, available at http://www.federalreserve.gov/newsevents/testimony/bernanke20130226a.htm.

† In the 1990s, tobacco companies settled a lawsuit brought by state governments and agreed to pay billions of dollars in fines to states to compensate for state expenditures related to smoking.

Table 1.1 Impact of Recession on State Budget Deficits during Most Recent Downturns

	State Deficits (Billions of $)	*National GDP (Billions of $)*	*State Deficits as % of GDP*	*State Deficits as % of State–Local Spending*
Fiscal Year				
Downturn of 1990–1991				
1991	–8	5,896	–0.14	–1.16
1992	–13	6,167	–0.21	–1.79
Downturn of 2001				
2002	–40	10,464	–0.38	–3.15
2003	–75	10,892	–0.69	–5.64
2004	–80	11,506	–0.70	–5.79
2005	–45	12,254	–0.37	–3.10
Downturn of 2007–2009				
2009	–110	14,244	–0.77	–6.16
2010	–191	14,390	–1.33	–10.73
2011 estimated	–130	14,930	–0.87	–7.25
2012 estimated	–112	15,500	–0.72	–6.20

Source: Ebel, R., Estimated Deficits: 1991–1992 (NASBO annual surveys), 2002–2005 and 2009–2012 Estimated (Center for Budget Policy and Priorities), GDP (Bureau of Economic Analysis, National Income Accounts), Table 1.1.5; estimated for fiscal years by using average of adjacent calendar years.

The NBER (2012) determined that the recession ended in June 2009. But, the unemployment rate that stood at 4.4 percent in 2007 spiked to over 10 percent in 2010, and the poverty rate increased to 15.9 percent in 2011, the highest since the early 1960s (Bishaw 2012). State constant dollar revenues were at about the same level as those a decade earlier (Ward 2010). Referring to Table 1.1, state deficits as a percent of GDP indicate heavy fallout in the first full year after the official end of the recession—state budget gaps as a percent of GDP stood at 1.3 percent; state deficits as a proportion of total state and local spending reached almost 11 percent.

Since 2009, with one exception, the annual state budget growth rate has averaged about 4 percent—less than half the 9.4 percent rate as late as 2007.* The sustained fiscal stress brought about by the Great Recession is perhaps evidenced most clearly by gubernatorial "funnel vision." For several years after the recession was officially declared to be over, the number of issues discussed by governors in their state of state addresses declined. For example, in 2007, at least two-thirds of governors discussed eight issues in these speeches: education, health care, natural resources, taxes, jobs, public safety, performance, and budget balance. But, in 2012, just three issues were addressed by at least 66 percent of state chief executives: education, jobs, and taxes (Willoughby 2012). Even with revenues growing slowly, governors are still shy of turning to new or increased taxes for budget solutions. "Governors recommended fewer revenue increases in fiscal 2014 compared to 2013," and they were as likely to push for decreases as increases (NASBO 2013a, 40).

While the recent 4 percent annual state budget growth is positive, it is lower than the average 5.5 percent annual increase in state budgets from 1977 until the start of the Great Recession. This slowdown is significant given that voter desires for state services coupled with ongoing pressures for tax cuts far surpass a 4 percent budget growth rate. For example, state governments' share of spending on Medicaid is growing at about 6 percent annually. If state revenues are growing at 4 percent annually, but Medicaid spending is increasing at 6 percent annually ... well, you do the math!

To a certain extent, state revenue changes during and immediately following the Great Recession pale in comparison to the continued hammering on expenditures by states to solve their budget problems. Spending cuts have been a staple throughout the recovery period. By far, the top strategy used by states for reducing or eliminating budget gaps remains targeted, then across-the-board spending cuts. In 2013, there were 21 states that made targeted cuts; 9 made across-the-board expenditure cuts. For 2014, there are 16 states recommending targeted, and 4 across-the-board cuts; targeted and across-the-board cuts are recommended by 8 states for 2015. Increasing expenditures on health care, including for Medicaid, continue to crowd out spending for everything other than education.

To address an impending budget imbalance today, a state would have to cap parts of Medicaid services and programs, cut spending for other state functions, raise revenues, increase borrowing, or engage a combination of some or all of these strategies. Some states have already started to take extreme actions. For example, in 2009, Arizona stopped Medicaid funding of organ transplants because state

* NASBO reports 4.9 percent growth in state general funds in 2008, 3.8 percent growth in 2009, and a decline of 5.7 percent in 2010. The growth rate rebounds to 3.8 percent in 2011 and an estimated 4.1 percent by 2014. See National Association of State Budget Officers, *The Fiscal Survey of the States*, Spring 2013, p. 2, available at http://www.nasbo.org/sites/default/files/Spring%202013%20Fiscal%20Survey%20of%20States.pdf.

revenues were dropping so rapidly. For a variety of reasons that will be examined throughout this book, a state may be hindered from implementing any of these strategies. Also, cutting services, raising taxes, and increasing borrowing all have consequences that negatively impact individuals, businesses, and institutions.

The modest postrecession recovery could morph into a robustly performing economy in which states realize higher revenues to support budget growth, although most economists are not optimistic about such a scenario. The nation's GDP would have to grow by 4 percent annually for several years to advance the economy in this way. Since the end of the Great Recession, however, GDP has averaged closer to a 2 percent increase annually. On the state level, many budget officers forecast healthy economic growth in 2015 and 2016, but foresee slower growth for the 2010 to 2020 decade than has been experienced in the past. In fact, state governments already provide some evidence of adjusting to the new fiscal normal. A recent NASBO (2013b) report shows that in fiscal year 2012, spending by the states declined for the first time in 26 years.

California presents a prime example of what states will have to do in the future. The state's economy performed fairly well until the 1980s, but then growth slowed. State spending policies and behavior, however, remained unchanged from when economic growth was strong. Spending initiatives were passed by voters that required funds to be earmarked for specific purposes such as K–12 education, but revenue increases were not often approved concurrently. The mismatch was evident when the state entered the Great Recession with a $7 billion budget deficit and no rainy day funds. Consequently, significant budget cuts to education and health care were made and voters passed a $6 billion annual tax increase in November 2012.

Management in the States

States have been at the forefront of the performance and results movement, engaging performance data and evidence of effectiveness to inform management and budget processes. While the results may be hard to achieve and difficult to quantify, there are examples of exciting initiatives being undertaken by states across the nation. Michigan, for instance, increased funding for its universities in 2012 but tied the additional funds entirely to performance outcomes. The state is establishing benchmarks and targets for selected performance indicators, such as the increase in the number of degrees awarded.

Performance information is being used in other states to inform the budgeting process. Virginia, for example, has formulated performance measures for all areas of government. To illustrate, environmental quality measures include how many old landfills need to be closed and how many wetlands are being lost; this information is being used in the budget process for making allocation decisions. States such as Utah and Colorado are using performance information to assess the efficiency of all their processes and activities. And Georgia and Idaho have implemented aspects of zero-based budgeting in which select agency budgets are being examined in their entirety to determine spending results and if reallocation of resources is necessary.

There are constraints on states that impose the fiscal discipline necessary to address budget and other fiscal problems. For example, all states but Vermont have a constitutional or statutory balanced budget requirement. Although there are a variety of definitions of balance evidenced in state constitutions and statutes, the very existence of such a constraint impacts budget decisions. States (and local governments) are often referred to as revenue-driven entities, given budget balance requirements. In effect, these governments cannot spend more money than is available to them through their taxes, non-tax revenue sources, and borrowing. Also, there are often limits placed on revenue generation, and there are always limits as to how much subnational governments can borrow. Suffice it to say, the federal government does not have a balanced budget requirement.

In another difference from the federal government, many states have budget stabilization, rainy day, or contingency funds to help navigate through fiscal storms. Immediately prior to the Great Recession, state governments had over 10 percent of their general funds in reserves. Few national or local governments around the world have the same level of reserves. The budget and management benefits to states for shoring up their reserves were starkly evident during the recession. They helped to prevent service and program cuts from being as painful as they could have been absent the reserves, and kept tax increases to a minimum. Without a doubt, assistance from federal government stimulus funds (American Recovery and Reinvestment Act or ARRA) helped as well.

States started to replenish their rainy day funds when the recession ended in 2009. Massachusetts, for example, took $375 million in one-time tax settlements from 2012 and deposited these funds into the state stabilization fund rather than using them to balance the budget. Even with modest growth, states today have nearly 5 percent of their general funds in reserves, again preparing for a future economic slump.

Still, state governments do not have the same tools as national governments to manage fiscal volatility, even though some, like California, have larger populations and economies than many countries around the world. States do not control their own money supply and cannot control interest rates—they are at the mercy of the Federal Reserve and markets for that. Also, even though economic development has become an important, even expected, function of states and a top policy issue for governors for the last decade, states lack the economic powers given to national governments.

States do, however, have powers over their revenue systems, even though they rarely use them to the fullest extent possible. States can levy personal and corporate income taxes and sales taxes, and they can decide what tax rates to impose. They can raise revenue through lotteries, gambling, and in numerous other ways. They can impose fees and earmark revenues from these fees for specific activities. They can, for example, use fees for fishing licenses to pay for game and inland fisheries departments, or fees for camping sites at state parks to cover the costs of parks and recreation services. For instance, Louisiana raised state park fees for fiscal year 2013 to make up for budget cuts.

Unfortunately, most state tax structures do not reflect changing demographic, economic, and technological changes. Consider the sales tax. In the 1950s, nearly two-thirds of sales were for goods, and state sales taxes captured significant amounts of these transactions. Individuals paid taxes on purchases like food and clothing, refrigerators, and chairs. Today, services make up close to half of all economic transactions in the United States, and most of these sales are not taxed. E-commerce has been on the rise for several years, but states do not fully capture revenues from this shopping modality either.

The highly elastic personal income tax has become a predominant revenue producer in most states. Unfortunately, personal income tax receipts tumble more than sales tax receipts during an economic downturn. On the business tax side, many corporations pay little or no corporate income taxes to the states, partially as a result of tax incentives provided by state governments. For example, New York State provided close to $2 billion in tax incentives to businesses in tax year 2013 (Rubin and Boyd 2013). It is thus not surprising that the corporate income tax is no longer an important state revenue source.

The Federal Link

Even with a strong vision for the future, careful budgeting, and some innovation, states face significant budget and financial management challenges. Some result from state actions taken over decades, but many problems are the consequence of the evolution in fiscal federalism. In the last 30 years, the constant dollar value of federal grants to state and local governments has tripled—from $221 billion in fiscal 1980 to $606 billion in fiscal 2011 (U.S. Government Accountability Office 2012).*

Today, the typical state receives about one-third of its revenues from the federal government, although this varies widely among states, as illustrated in Table 1.2. In 2012, for example, in Wyoming, federal funds accounted for 18 percent of total state governmental revenues, while in Mississippi, federal dollars made up 49 percent of total state governmental revenues. As indicated, in some states, tax receipts comprise a larger share of governmental revenues than do federal funds (Wyoming, Wisconsin, Texas, and Rhode Island); in others, shares of state taxes and federal dollars are close or about equal (Maine and Georgia); and in still others, federal funds overshadow state taxes as a share of total state governmental revenues (Mississippi).

About 44 percent of federal funds to states are for Medicaid and other programs in which the states are given mandates regarding the types of spending and

* Values in 2011 constant dollars.

Table 1.2 Selected States, State Taxes, and Federal Revenue as Percent of Total State Governmental Revenues, Fiscal Year 2012

State	*Total Governmental Funds (FY2012) from*				*Total Governmental Funds ($ in billions)*
	State Tax Receipts ($ in billions)		*Federal Revenue ($ in billions)*		
Wyoming	($2.0)	43%	($0.8)	18%	$4.6
Wisconsin	($14.9)	55%	($9.5)	35%	$27.2
Texas	($44.2)	45%	($38.2)	39%	$97.5
Rhode Island	($2.8)	48%	($2.4)	41%	$5.9
Maine	($3.5)	48%	($3.2)	44%	$7.2
Georgia	($15.9)	46%	($15.3)	44%	$34.7
Mississippi	($6.2)	40%	($7.6)	49%	$15.6

Source: State Comprehensive Annual Financial Reports, for the year ending June 30, 2012, Statement of Revenues, Expenditures, and Changes in Fund Balances for each state; see below.

State of Georgia, Comprehensive Annual Financial Report, Fiscal Year Ended June 30, 2012, prepared by State Accounting Office, p. 28. Available at http://sao.georgia.gov/sites/sao.georgia.gov/files/related_files/site_page/Final%20CAFR%202012%20Secure.pdf.

State of Maine, Comprehensive Annual Financial Report for the Fiscal Year Ended June 30, 2012, prepared by the Office of the State Comptroller, p. 26. Available at http://www.maine.gov/osc/pdf/finanrept/cafr/cafr2012.pdf.

State of Mississippi, Comprehensive Annual Financial Report for the Fiscal Year Ended June 30, 2012, prepared by Department of Finance and Administration, p. 32. Available at http://www.dfa.state.ms.us/Offices/OFR/BFR%20Files/CAFR%20Files/2012%20CAFR.pdf.

State of Rhode Island, Comprehensive Annual Financial Report, Fiscal Year Ended June 30, 2012, prepared by Department of Administration, Office of Accounts and Control, p. 37. Available at http://controller.admin.ri.gov/documents/Financial%20Reports/114_Comprehensive%20Annual%20Financial%20Report_06-30-2012.pdf.

State of Texas, Comprehensive Annual Financial Report, Fiscal Year Ended August 31, 2012, prepared by Texas Comptroller of Public Accounts, p. 44. Available at http://www.window.state.tx.us/finances/pubs/cafr/12/pdf/CAFR-2012.pdf.

State of Wisconsin Comprehensive Annual Financial Report for the Fiscal Year Ended June 30, 2012, prepared by the State Controller's Office, p. 44. Available at ftp://doaftp1380.wi.gov/doadocs/2012%20CAFR_Linked.pdf.

State of Wyoming Comprehensive Annual Financial Report for Fiscal Year Ended June 30, 2012, prepared by CAFR Division of State Auditor's Office, p. 38. Available at http://sao.state.wy.us/cafr/2012_Report/cafr2012.pdf.

activities allowed. Federal funds often come with matching requirements—states must contribute a certain percentage of total funding for specified programs and particular services. Given that states must balance their budgets, if they decide to accept the federal money, they must make trade-offs between spending money for the federally funded programs and other state spending priorities. Further, once federal funds have been accepted, states must grapple with the uncertainty that occurs with a federal budget process that is dysfunctional—the recent federal government shutdown providing an extreme example. With gridlock at the federal level, at best, the timing of state receipt of funds is impaired, or at worst, the funds (but not the mandate to provide the service) may be cut entirely.

Ongoing Challenges

In addition to a growing dependency on federal funds and obsolete tax structures, substantial infrastructure needs of the states are a growing concern when juxtaposed with realistic fiscal sustainability. State spending for capital outlays that reached almost a quarter of total state expenditures in the late 1950s stands at 6.5 percent today.* Across the nation, bridges, roads, highways, transit systems, and buildings need maintenance, upgrading, or replacing, and the list of infrastructure needs is gargantuan in size and expense.

These capital needs fall into all categories of state functions—primary and secondary education, university systems, corrections, law enforcement, health care, natural resources, and even the arts. For example, the Texas Commission on the Arts requires that its facilities have special access for people with disabilities to arts events and programs, and the Virginia Department of Historic Resources oversees funds to protect historic properties throughout the state.

Despite some pretty dire predictions about the financial demise of the states, these governments have weathered numerous economic downturns in the past, though they must continually implement policies to maintain and advance their fiscal viability.

While most states are experiencing some level of fiscal stress concerning the challenges noted here, there is no right way for all states to address any of the attendant problems. State contexts and priorities differ. Residents of some states may want a low-taxing and -spending environment. Others may want higher levels of services that necessitate higher state revenues, meaning taxes.

* U.S. Bureau of Census, Annual Survey of State Government Finances via State Government Finances Access Database, QQ02 (all records in 1942–1950 format). The database provides limited data for even-numbered years between 1942 and 1950 until 2008. State totals for 1959 exclude Hawaii, and for 1958 and earlier, exclude Alaska and Hawaii. Public safety includes corrections and police.

States have made great strides in managing through the Great Recession and in the years since its official end. These accomplishments have often gone unheralded, with media coverage instead focused on the more egregious failures of state government, whether it is the mismanagement by an Illinois governor who ended up in prison or the problems that plagued Florida's election system. In fact, states have been at the forefront of grappling with problems like pension liabilities and currently are taking fiscally prudent actions such as replenishing rainy day funds—even with significant pressures for other spending or tax cuts.

From 2009 to 2012, the states collectively closed budget gaps of $500 billion, primarily through dramatic expenditure cuts—and they are still making them. Georgia, for instance, attempted to become the first and only state among 50 to close down its state archives to the public. This action was averted in July 2013 when the state transferred the archives from the Secretary of State's Office to the Board of Regents (Millsaps 2013).

What's Ahead in This Book

The following chapters examine the broad range and depth of state revenues, responsibilities, and activities. The book opens with an assessment of executive budgeting in the states. Chapter 2 presents the experiences of states with strong executive-driven systems and the various rules and institutions that impact state government budget discipline. The next several chapters consider state revenue sources and structures and the prospects for state tax equity and efficiency in the future. State borrowing and the challenges associated with debt types and levels are reviewed. The realities of state pension liabilities and prospects for the sustained fiscal health of these promised benefits to employees are illuminated. Focused examination of state spending overall and on critical functional areas and including state work forces then follows. The conclusion presents an assessment of four challenges that will surely test the fiscal vibrancy of the states going forward: vulnerability to future economic downturns, growing dependence on an increasingly austere federal government, the obsolescence of state tax systems, and an ever more coercive system of federalism.

References

Bishaw, A. (2012). Poverty 2010 and 2011: American Community Survey Briefs. U.S. Census Bureau. Available at http://www.census.gov/prod/2012pubs/acsbr11-01.pdf.

Boyd, D.J. (2003). State Fiscal Conditions: 2003 and Beyond. *The Book of the States, 2003*. Lexington, KY: Council of State Governments, pp. 321–328.

Millsaps, J. (2013, June 20). State Archives Join University System. University System of Georgia Newsroom. Available at http://www.usg.edu/news/release/state_archives_join_university_system (accessed July 30, 2013).

National Association for State Budget Officers (NASBO). (2013a). *The Fiscal Survey of the States*. Available at http://www.nasbo.org/sites/default/files/Spring%202013%20 Fiscal%20Survey%20of%20States.pdf.

National Association for State Budget Officers (NASBO). (2013b). *State Expenditure Report: Examining Fiscal 2011–2013 State Spending*. Available at http://www.nasbo.org/sites/ default/files/State%20Expenditure%20Report%20%28Fiscal%202011-2013%20 Data%29.pdf.

National Bureau of Economic Research (NBER). (2012, April 23). U.S. Business Cycle Expansions and Contractions. Cambridge, MA. Available at http://www.nber.org/ cycles/US_Business_Cycle_Expansions_and_Contractions_20120423.pdf (accessed September 20, 2012).

Rubin, M.M., and Boyd, D. (2013). *New York State Business Tax Credits: Analysis and Evaluation*. Report prepared for the New York State Tax Reform and Fairness Commission.

U.S. Government Accountability Office. (2012, September). *Grants to State and Local Governments: An Overview of Federal Funding Levels and Selected Challenges*, GAO-12-016. Washington, DC.

Ward, R.B. (2010, April 15). *State Fiscal Trends and the Federal Role: Testimony to the Subcommittee on Commercial and Administrative Law, Committee on the Judiciary, U.S. House of Representatives*. Albany, NY: Nelson A. Rockefeller Institute of Government.

Willoughby, K.G. (2012). The State of State Addresses: The New Normal Fosters Gubernatorial Funnel Vision. In *The Book of the States*, ed. Audrey S. Wall. Lexington, KY: Council of State Governments, pp. 193–202.

Wulf, H.S. (2002). Trends in State Government Finances. In *The Book of the States*, ed. Audrey S. Wall. Lexington, KY: Council of State Governments, pp. 269–274.

Chapter 2

Political Institutions for Sustainable State Budgets

Irene S. Rubin
Northern Illinois University

Roy T. Meyers
University of Maryland, Baltimore County

Contents

Introduction

The Richard Ravitch–Paul Volker State Budget Crisis Task Force concluded that the finances of the states are unsustainable (State Budget Crisis Task Force 2012). The study focused on six states—California, Illinois, New Jersey, New York, Texas, and Virginia—but suggested that other states are confronting similar problems. Expenditures are growing too quickly and revenues too slowly. The effects of prior underfunding of long-term obligations are coming home to roost. Further, the study argued that state budget laws and practices hinder fiscal stability and mask imbalances.

What institutional arrangements or budget rules might be most helpful in restoring or maintaining sustainability? Among many possibilities, this chapter examines only two: stronger budgetary powers for the governors and supermajority requirements to pass a tax increase. We explore the extent to which they have enhanced budgetary sustainability in places where they have been adopted. We conclude with some suggestions about how political institutions can lead to more sustainable budgets.

The research question requires a historical perspective, to track effects over time. The richness and detail required here limit the scope of our study of governors' powers; we have focused on three states with some of the strongest gubernatorial powers. For the states with supermajority requirements to pass a tax increase, we looked primarily at states that passed their requirements a number of years ago and whose laws cover a range of revenue sources and not just one. For both governors' powers and supermajorities, we picked the more extreme cases that should have had the most obvious outcomes. That is, if the expected positive outcomes have not occurred in these states, then the suggested reforms are not likely to work in other states either. We have relied on a variety of sources, including referenda results, tax analyses, opinion surveys, studies by advocacy groups and think tanks, news stories, law cases, and reform proposals. Though most of the academic studies on governors' powers and supermajorities have not dealt explicitly with sustainability, where they were relevant, we have included them in the discussion.

The Meaning of *Sustainable Budget*

The analysis turns initially on what is meant by *sustainable* (Schick 2005; Chapman 2008; Dothan and Thompson 2009; Ward and Dadayan 2009; Ward 2012; Bifulco et al. 2012). State governments have long had sustainable budgets, if that term means states fulfill their promises to bondholders; the last state that lacked the ability to do so was Arkansas in 1933. That only one state reached this nadir during the Great Depression implies that state budgets can handle a level of economic stress that is much greater than that of the recent Great Recession.

Yet there is more to sustainability than being able to pay back borrowing in a timely fashion. Sustainability requires that over the long run, the growth of spending does not exceed the growth of revenues. Over the business cycle, it means that states save enough during good times to cover financing gaps during recessions. Debt service should not increase over an extended period faster than the growth of the state's tax base. Borrowed funds should be dedicated to effective infrastructure investments, and long-lived liabilities should be substantially prefunded.

Unfortunately, not all states have followed widely recognized practices of good budgeting, and their budgets are unsustainable as a result. Many states have failed to adequately fund postemployment benefits such as pensions and retiree health insurance, and have cut taxes below what is needed to finance future spending for Medicaid. Many states have also failed to build sufficiently large rainy-day funds, and then responded to recessions by adopting policies that pushed obligations into future years, thus worsening their structural deficits.

The concept of budget sustainability should also include more than financial balance. Balancing a budget by failing to make necessary investments, allowing roads to deteriorate, failing to fund public education, or cutting public health spending may reduce productivity and make the state unattractive to residents and businesses, as well as increase future costs. A budget that relies on taxes or fees that are heavier than citizens or businesses can afford, or an unproductive tax system that does not match the changing economy, is ultimately unsustainable as well.

Strong Governors

The colonial experience in the United States left the new country with a profound mistrust of strong executives. State constitutions gave legislatures budgetary powers, and executives were intentionally weak. This pattern began to change around the time of the Civil War, as a perception emerged that stronger executive control could temper the excesses of legislative bodies. At first, the reform thrust was to arm state governors with strong veto powers, so that legislatures proposed, but executives disposed. However, in the early 1900s, a second approach was utilized, called executive budgeting, which reversed the pattern, so that executives proposed and legislatures disposed.

Executive budgeting means that the chief executive and his or her budget agency gather spending proposals from the departments and programs, review them, trim them back, possibly adding some expenditure or revenue, and then present the combined proposals to the legislature. A particularly strong form of executive budgeting was adopted by Maryland in 1916 and New York in 1927. In this form, the governor reviews and adjusts agency budget requests before the legislature considers them, and the legislature can reduce but not increase proposed amounts.

Adoption of executive budgeting in many other states left more room for legislative discretion, and in some cases, for public participation. In California, the progressive governor Hiram Johnson set in motion a movement that led the state in 1922 to give future governors a weaker form of executive budgeting power. But California was also one of the many noneastern states that implemented direct democracy approaches such as the initiative and referendum. Widespread concern that the economic elite already had too much control over state government limited the extent to which centralization of budgetary powers in the governor's office would be acceptable.

The main argument for giving the governor the power to propose budgets was that states would realize more prudent budgetary outcomes. Instead of a diverse legislature often at odds with itself, one person would be in charge. Concentrated power would enable rapid decision making in times of crisis. The governor, relying on a staff in the executive budget office, was expected to have more expertise and could be held accountable by the public if the budget got out of control. The governor was supposed to act for the public at large, while it was expected that the legislature would act on behalf of individual districts and narrow interest groups.

Those arguments from a century ago can be heard today, for some contemporary budgeting experts have supported the idea that further centralization in the executive is a prerequisite for good budgetary decision making (Poterba 1996; Poterba and von Hagen 1999). On the other hand, their opponents have observed that governors also have constituencies, and may favor selected interest groups rather than the general public. And while executive budgeting advocates assert that budget transparency is guaranteed by putting one person in charge, executive decision making often takes place behind closed doors, whereas legislative decision making is often more visible and open to the public. Moreover, unlike during the early 20th century, when spending was almost entirely discretionary and thus subject to gubernatorial proposal and veto powers, the majority of state spending today is considered mandatory—it takes legislation to change the path of spending. Even in strong executive budgeting states, governors cannot realistically control this spending simply by requesting less and imposing those levels on legislatures. Instead, they must propose complicated changes to, for example, maintenance-of-effort and equity formulas for elementary and secondary education.

There have been no definitive studies that have validated the arguments made by proponents of stronger gubernatorial budgetary powers. Much academic work has been about who wins between the governor or legislature based on incumbents' preferences rather than on any measure of policy effects, such as sustainability (e.g., Kousser and Phillips 2012; Rosenthal 2013). Other research has suffered from problems of measurement, shortcomings in available data, and underspecified models. For example, Sharkansky's (1968) widely cited study of agency acquisitiveness—whether agencies asked for and received large budget increases—found that gubernatorial support for agencies' ambitious requests helped to predict legislatively approved levels. This was the flip side of the executive budgeting argument that strong governors are needed to control excessive spending.

The utility of the research was compromised by the sampling procedure, as it included only those states that published agency budget requests. That is, in most strong governor states, such requests were not published, but rather sent to the governor's budget office for review and likely reduction.

Another challenge is how to accurately measure gubernatorial budget power. Numerous studies have constructed index variables composed of measures drawn from the *Book of the States* published by the Council of State Governments (CSG) and from *Budget Processes in the States* published by the National Association of State Budget Officers (2008; e.g., Beyle 1992; Barrilleaux and Berkman 2003). The value of these indexes has been limited given the changes made to index composition over time, inclusion of powers that appear tangential to gubernatorial power, or inability to capture potential interactions between a diverse range of powers available to governors across the 50 states.

Since the executive budgeting model relies heavily on the assumption of electoral accountability over state finances, one relevant finding is that voters, upset with poor economic conditions, have a record of punishing governors (Hansen 1999). Governors thus have a motive for obscuring fiscal stress. Recessions lead to state revenue declines, necessitating spending cuts that are more easily made by strong governors, but also exposing them to blame from those who bear the brunt of cuts. Research suggests that stronger governors are more likely to be viewed by voters as responsible for the economic condition of the state (Rudolph 2003, 204–206). Strong governors also bear the implicit responsibility for proposing taxes, adding another count to potential indictments from voters. Accountability in practice may make it *more difficult* to raise taxes or cut spending to resolve a financial crisis, because the public holds the governor responsible for such actions, and the more powerful the governor, the more likely he or she is to be held accountable in this manner.

Alt and Lowry (1994, 2000; Lowry et al. 1998) have made the accountability argument richer and subtler by adding the different expectations voters have of Democratic or Republican governors. Republican governors are punished by voters if the budget increases, and Democratic governors are punished for cuts. A drawback of this study for our purposes is that Alt and Lowry used no measure of the variance in governors' institutional powers. One can only guess that a stronger Republican governor would be punished more severely than a weaker one for raising taxes, while a stronger Democratic governor would be punished more severely for cutting programs. To the extent that this guess is accurate, strong governors are more accountable to the public, as reformers argued, but the effect may be to narrow the options available for budget balancing, making balance more difficult to achieve.

For a more complete understanding of gubernatorial budgetary powers and sustainability, it is necessary to draw as well on case studies (Stonecash 1991). The best sources are two edited books from Clynch and Lauth (1991, 2006). With chapters written by budgeting scholars with strong local knowledge, these cases provide many examples of how gubernatorial and legislative budgeting powers and behaviors have changed over time. Our conclusion after reading these essays is that the diversity of state practices cannot be summarized with law-like statements about the impact of formal budgetary powers.

Study States with the Executive Budgeting Model

We focus here on three states that adopted most or all of the executive budgeting model at the beginning of the reform era, roughly a century ago: Illinois, New York, and Maryland. Our intent is to apply something approaching an acid test to the assertions of advocates of strong executive budgeting. If budgetary outcomes in these three states do not meet the model's expectations, then the model deserves doubt.

Recent events in these three states suggest that strong gubernatorial powers can help states manage their fiscal problems. Each current governor proposed tax increases and pension savings that were adopted by the legislature. But a closer look reveals that many of the financial problems these states addressed resulted not just from the most recent Great Recession, but were structural, that is, at least partially created by or at least not prevented by strong governors in the past. Sometimes programs were adopted or expanded without sufficient revenue to finance them over the long term, or taxes were cut far below expected spending. Structural deficits were often covered up for years by internal and external borrowing and by misleading accounting practices.

Illinois

In Illinois, the governor has strong veto powers, but the legislature can increase the governor's budget or cut it. If the legislature adds to the governor's budget, the governor can reduce the extra spending through various forms of the veto: regular, line item, reduction, and amendatory. For the latter, however, the governor must resubmit the legislation to the legislature. Legislative threats to cut the governor's proposed budget give legislators the power to force negotiations.

Illinois could be a poster child for bad budgeting and chronic fiscal crisis, despite relatively strong executive budgeting powers. General fund deficits have been common and chronic. Some governors have behaved exactly the opposite of the executive budget movement's hopes. For example, former governor Rod Blagojevich (the most recent of four Illinois governors to end up in prison) used the amendatory veto to force the legislature to accept his proposal that the Chicago mass transit system provide free rides to seniors, despite the lack of funding for this benefit. The larger problem is that absent gubernatorial leadership, the state failed to modernize its tax structure, and instead financed structural deficits through explicit borrowing in the bond market, implicit borrowing through underfunding of pensions, and delayed payments to vendors for services rendered (Bunch 2010).

New York

In New York, the governor also has strong veto powers. The legislature can add to the governor's budget proposals, but only if each addition appears separately, which the governor can then veto. The legislature rarely passes the budget by the April 1 start of the state's fiscal year. The legislature uses budget delay as a tool to force the governor to negotiate; such negotiations are generally successful from the legislature's perspective.

The New York State legislature is rated as one of the most dysfunctional in the nation. Rank-and-file members have relatively little say in legislation, or over the budget. The governor and the leaders of both houses together make most of the important decisions. According to an insider account from a senate backbencher, these three officials sort through the various budget proposals and come to decisions with little public debate (Lachman 2006). One goal of executive budget reforms was to make it clearer who was responsible for what, but given that New York's budget has often been determined behind closed doors in negotiations between the governor and legislative leadership, the goal of transparency has not been met (Bifulco and Duncombe 2010).

New York has experienced structural deficits for years. According to one author, "for decades, regardless of the strength of the economy, recurring revenues have been insufficient to sustain ongoing spending" (O'Cleireacain 2010). The state's fiscal problems stem from spending expansions adopted during periods of economic growth that were unsustainable when the economy declined. These expansions were sponsored by or approved by the governor, and the state made routine use of techniques for obscuring the size of the resulting deficits. These included one-time revenues, internal and external borrowing, delaying of payments into the following year, pushing up revenues from future years to the present one, and other manipulations. These supposedly temporary solutions made the next year's budgets even harder to balance (Brecher et al. 1994). The state's comptroller, quoted by Ward (2010, 2012), said: "This 'deficit shuffle' reduces budget transparency, creates funding instability for critical State programs and allows the State to avoid making the difficult decisions needed to effectively align spending with available revenue."

When Governor Andrew Cuomo took office in 2011, the picture changed, with some real reforms to bring spending and revenues back in line. But, a strong governor able to make positive changes in the finances of the state has been the exception, not the rule, in New York.

Maryland

Maryland's fiscal condition is considerably better than that of Illinois and New York. In 1916, prompted by a deficit after a period of spending growth, Maryland's constitution was amended to create the first state-level executive budget in the

United States, and the nation's strongest one. The legislature could reduce but not increase the governor's budget proposals (Meyers and Pilkerton 2003). But in fact, the legislature was not as radically disempowered as it appeared. If the legislature chooses to reduce an item, or to condition how an agency may spend the funds, the governor can neither add the item back nor easily ignore legislative directions on how the money may be spent. Legislators' threats to cut the governor's budget are thus a real source of power in negotiations with the chief executive about what will go into the budget. Legislators may also initiate spending appropriations if they include a source of revenues. Most important, a 1978 constitutional amendment clarified that the legislature may propose mandatory spending in bills that, if passed, require the governor to fund these programs in future budgets (Friedman 2006). This legislative adaptation to constitutionally strong gubernatorial budgetary power thus encourages dedicating funds and spending mandates. As a consequence, the state budget is far less flexible and transparent than would have been expected by proponents of executive budgeting.

While financial management in Maryland has been better than in most states, that has not prevented the state from incurring structural imbalances. The Democratic governor Parris Glendening approved a massive expansion of local education aid at the same time income tax cuts were implemented, even though this would produce a structural deficit. These policies were ratified by his successor, Republican Robert Ehrlich. And while Maryland has avoided excessive borrowing, it has significantly underfunded its pension plans in the past. The state is now addressing these structural deficits, with leadership from both the governor and legislature; the legislative leadership's Spending Affordability Committee has required a three-year plan for eliminating the deficits.

Based on the experiences of Illinois, New York, and Maryland, we doubt that additional gubernatorial strengthening in other states—in the forms of stronger veto powers, less authority for legislatures to modify gubernatorial budgets, less time for legislative consideration, and extensive reprogramming powers for governors—would improve state budget sustainability. Legislatures have not been the sole engines of increased spending with chief executives guarding the public purse. Importantly, giving governors more formal powers does not guarantee that such powers will be used or used well. Also, empowering governors does not preclude adaptations to these powers by legislatures. When formal budgetary power becomes too one sided, dysfunctional countermeasures begin to be implemented, which can then distort state finances and make budgeting less transparent and accountable (see also Abney and Lauth 1989, 1998).

Supermajority Requirements

Executive budgeting reforms address the balance of power between the legislature and the governor; supermajority requirements to pass a tax increase often shift decision-making power from legislative majorities to minorities because minorities can block a tax increase. Sixteen states now have some kind of supermajority requirement.* Advocates claim that a supermajority requirement limits the scope of government by "starving the beast"—that capping revenues prevents spending expansions that could create structural imbalances. The states generally have requirements for annual balance and are disciplined by the credit markets, so holding down revenue growth might, in fact, result in slower growth of spending.

Study States with Supermajority Track Records

Some state supermajority requirements are relatively recent, so they do not have a track record of consequences, and others have supermajority requirements that apply only to selected revenues or only for emergency bills. One would not expect to see slow revenue growth or more sustainable budgets as a result of such rules. Consequently, we focus on the 12 states with supermajority requirements that apply to several major tax and revenue sources and that have had such limits for a number of years. If supermajority requirements have a positive effect on sustainability, it should be apparent in these cases. The states with a three-fifths requirement are Delaware, Kentucky, Mississippi, and Oregon. The states that have, or in Washington State's case had, a two-thirds requirement are Arizona, California, Louisiana, Missouri, Nevada, South Dakota, and Washington. Oklahoma is the only state that requires a three-fourths majority.

The first question about supermajorities is whether they work to keep taxes lower than would otherwise be the case. In a widely cited study, Brian Knight (2000) concluded that supermajority requirements do keep down the level of taxes, though he did not address the impact of these rules on fiscal sustainability. However, according to the Tax Foundation (Drenkard 2013), two of the top five highest sales tax rates in the country were supermajority states (California and Mississippi). Also, of the five states that had the highest combined state and local sales tax rates, four of them were supermajority states (Arizona, Louisiana, Washington, and Oklahoma) (Drenkard 2013). For income taxes, the effect was split—two of the supermajority states had the highest top brackets in the country, but three had no income tax at all. Regarding state and local taxes as a percentage of personal income, the averages for supermajority states and simple majority states are close over time (Leachman et al. 2012).

Part of the reason for the similarity of tax burdens between supermajority and ordinary majority states is that states without supermajority requirements have

* This number recently decreased from 17 to 16 when Washington State's Supreme Court struck down its two-thirds majority requirement in February 2013. For more information on differences in these requirements among the states, see Center on Budget and Policy Priorities, "State Supermajority Rules to Raise Revenues," April 22, 2013, available at http://www.cbpp.org/files/PolicyBasics-StateSupermajorities-4-22-13.pdf (accessed June 25, 2013).

many other reasons not to raise taxes (Jordan and Hoffman 2009). Some states have legislative or constitutional revenue limits. Many elected officials are ideologically committed to not raising taxes and have publicly pledged not to do so. Most importantly, fear of getting kicked out of office makes elected officials hesitant to raise taxes. Who needs a supermajority requirement when a simple majority cannot be mustered for a tax increase?

It is not only that simple majority states are reluctant to increase taxes, but also that some supermajority states raise taxes despite the procedural hurdle. When there is a supermajority of support for revenue increases—as when Democrats dominated Delaware and Oregon in 2009—the hurdle is not restrictive. And in some states that have supermajority requirements, the legislature may refer a tax measure to public referendum with passage by a simple majority vote. Both Arizona and Arkansas increased taxes in this manner.

An important limitation of supermajority requirements is that it has been difficult to define *tax* and *increase* in a sufficiently airtight way to avoid evasions. In some of the 12 states, fee increases do not require a supermajority. California relied on changing fees until a 2010 citizen initiative defined *fee increases* as *tax increases.* States have also bent the rules by reinterpreting them, such as in 2011, when California changed the tax code's definition of merchants so Internet sales could be included in the tax base without invoking the supermajority requirement for a change in taxes.*

Getting around the rule is not just a matter of redefining revenue so it does not count against the rule. It also depends on how the rule is worded. In 2007, Washington State voters had passed Initiative 960, which required a two-thirds vote of the legislature to raise taxes or approval of the public by referendum. But after two years, the legislature could rescind this initiative by a simple majority vote. In February 2010, desperate for new revenue, the legislature did so, making it legal to pass a tax increase with a simple majority, which subsequently happened on a party-line vote.

Supermajority requirements do not prevent tax increases. Seljan (2011) found that while states with supermajorities are less likely to raise taxes in boom times, they are more likely than other states to raise taxes during recessions. It may be that raising taxes in a down economy is especially needed because of the effects of supermajority requirements during economic growth; starving the beast during good times may make service levels so threatened during recessions that voters are willing to support tax increases to preserve them.

---

* The 2011 law, Assembly Bill 155, expanded the definition of out-of-state retailers that are "engaged in business in this state," requiring them to register with and collect and remit tax payments to the California Board of Equalization. For more information, see California State Board of Equalization, "Use Tax Collection Requirements for Out-of-State Retailers Operative September 15, 2012," available at http://www.boe.ca.gov/sutax/abx1-28faq.htm (accessed June 25, 2013).

While supermajority states do raise taxes during recessions, the barriers to raising taxes slow down the response and often take some options off the table. The result may be longer and deeper recessions and more profound service cuts than would otherwise be the case. The Pew Center on the States (2009) reported that 6 of the most severely stressed 10 states in the nation were those with supermajority requirements (California, Arizona, Nevada, Florida, Michigan, and Oregon).

Supermajority requirements affect not only the timing of revenue increases, but also the choice of which revenue sources to increase. States with supermajorities are somewhat more likely to have tax systems that are burdensome on the poor—5 of the top 10 most regressive state tax systems are supermajority states (Davis et al. 2009). Supermajority requirements may contribute to the degree of tax regressiveness because states find it easier to muster a supermajority for tobacco and liquor taxes, and because fees are sometimes exempted from supermajority requirements. Both fees and so-called sin taxes typically fall more heavily on the poor.

Supermajority requirements can also inhibit efforts to improve the efficiency and effectiveness of public spending when they define elimination or reduction of tax breaks as tax increases. In Washington State, for example, the Joint Legislative Audit and Review Committee reviewed 120 of its tax expenditures, recommending 6 for termination because they failed to accomplish their goals and 29 for modification because there were no stated goals for them. However, because of the supermajority requirements to eliminate tax breaks, the state was unable to eliminate a single one.

As critics have charged, supermajority requirements do empower legislative minorities to hold tax increases hostage until they get what they want. This form of pressure can be costly. Passing legislation is often about building a sufficiently large coalition, which may require sweeteners to win some support. The larger the majority required in a split legislature, the more sweeteners are required. If, on the other hand, the minority uses the supermajority requirement to prevent any tax increases, states must choose how to cut spending when a majority (but not a supermajority) of the legislature wants spending to be higher than revenues allow. The burden is often concentrated on dependent populations.

An alternative is to capture revenues previously received by local governments or to pass state responsibilities down to them. For example, in 2012, Arizona shifted costs for highway patrol, corrections, and park services onto local governments. Since Proposition 13, California has often used local government revenue to balance the state budget, and the localities have responded by advocating propositions to prevent what they portray as raids on their resources. The state's tradition of direct democracy, when it combines a revenue supermajority requirement with spending mandated by numerous propositions, has made the state's budget process unworkable.

The pressure from supermajority requirements on spending may also be released by internal borrowing, such as underfunding pension commitments, or the use of other financing and accounting gimmicks, such as rushed sales of state assets. While other states experiencing fiscal stress also engage in such tactics, the supermajority states were more likely to experience severe and prolonged fiscal stress and may have relied on such tactics more heavily. By making it relatively harder to raise revenues, supermajorities likely encourage structural imbalances and these counterproductive responses.

In sum, supermajority requirements do not seem to reduce the burden of taxation compared to simple majority states. In fact, the supermajority states are disproportionately represented among the most fiscally stressed of states. Some of these states cut their revenues during the good years, and found it more difficult to respond to the recession. Most raised taxes in some way, but were influenced by the wording and coverage of their supermajority requirements. These states generally found it impossible to eliminate wasteful tax breaks. Constraints on raising revenues resulted in deeper service cuts than necessary, on the one hand, and additional borrowing and budget gimmicks of many sorts, on the other. Supermajority rules empower minorities to extract concessions for their support to reach the required supermajority, increasing costs, on the one hand, and threatening democratic budget procedures, on the other. Our conclusion is that supermajority requirements do not enable more sustainable budgeting.

Conclusions

In this era of extreme partisan polarization, it is common for advocates to argue that there is one best way to promote policy goals. Not only do the opposing strong claims usually die together, but the claims are rarely correct, and that is the case here as well. Fiscal sustainability in the American states has not been guaranteed by centralizing budgetary powers in governors' hands or by giving any legislative minority the right to block tax increases.

Producing fiscal sustainability is hard work. It requires looking beyond the current budget and the next election, by using medium- to long-term projections of spending and revenues, and acknowledging the inevitable uncertainties in such projections. Decision makers must avoid underfunding pensions and mortgaging future revenue sources. They often need to revise policies that over time turn out to be more costly than the state can afford.

Strict interpretations of balanced budget requirements, which are often intended to promote sustainability, can perversely have the opposite effect. States can pay too much attention to the short-term cycle and not enough to long-term trends. For example, a state can mistakenly assume that growth in revenue during boom years will continue. Cutting taxes then, or using the above-average revenues to fund new spending, exposes the state to the next recession, making more significant spending cuts and tax increases necessary. This prevents the state from acting even in a limited way as a countercyclical force in the state's economy, and encourages inefficient large and rapid changes in service delivery and tax rates. The better approach is to calculate balance over the business cycle, build large balances in rainy-day funds during good years, and rely heavily on them as supplemental revenues during lean years. The federal government could help here by creating a more effective and automatic countercyclical assistance program, one that would provide supplements to adequately funded state rainy-day funds.

We are not arguing here against fiscal rules, but rather that such rules need to be based on a nuanced understanding of sustainability. Rather than empower a blocking minority, as supermajority requirements do, useful fiscal rules set limits or targets for central fiscal concerns of the states, such as for debt capacity. Bond rating firms and credit markets effectively punish states that exceed certain debt capacity ratios. When budget projections show such policy limits in danger of being exceeded, these limits then serve as useful signals that policies should be changed. To be credible, such limits need to be developed through a process of careful deliberation and analysis.

It is similarly helpful when thinking about the desirable balance of powers between state political institutions to not merely assume that a formal shift in powers will have immediate and positive effects. Empowering governors works only when the individuals elected as governors are responsible leaders. Placing strong accountability expectations on governors for financial problems will give bad governors the incentive to "paper over" real problems. And state legislatures, aware of their central roles in American government, understandably react to excessive grants of power to governors, sometimes in ways that reduce sustainability. A more even distribution of power between the legislature and governor may increase accountability and contribute to sustainability as each branch curtails the excesses of the other.

Each of the 50 states has a complicated mix of institutional features specific to it. Thinking about how an individual state can improve its fiscal sustainability requires an understanding of that state's historical trajectory and the specific institutional features now in place—those that appear to work well and those that do not. When unacceptable outcomes threaten or occur, then the poorly performing features of that state's institutions should be targeted for reform. It is highly unlikely that a uniform solution will apply to all 50 states.

We also believe that it is a mistake to look exclusively at the formal powers of state institutions and the formal rules applied to budgeting. For states to reach fiscal sustainability, norms supporting that ideal are necessary. Such norms would expect politicians to have wide-ranging disagreements over budget policies, but also meet their responsibilities to address revenue adequacy and spending growth on a timely basis using accurate numbers. Developing and protecting such norms is central to the hard political work of making state budgets sustainable. No single institutional power or fiscal rule will produce them.

References

Abney, G., and Lauth, T.P. (1989). The Executive Budget in the States: Normative Idea and Empirical Observation. *Policy Studies Journal*, 17, 829–840.

Abney, G., and Lauth, T.P. (1998). The End of Executive Dominance in State Appropriations. *Public Administration Review*, 58, 388–394.

Alt, J.E., and Lowry, R.C. (1994). Divided Government, Fiscal Institutions, and Budget Deficits: Evidence from the States. *American Political Science Review*, 88, 811–828.

Alt, J.E., and Lowry, R.C. (2000). A Dynamic Model of State Budget Outcomes under Divided Partisan Government. *Journal of Politics*, 62, 1035–1069.

Barrilleaux, C., and Berkman, M. (2003). Do Governors Matter: Budgeting Rules and the Politics of State Policymaking. *Political Research Quarterly*, 56, 409–417.

Beyle, T.L. (ed.). (1992). *Governors and Hard Times*. Washington, DC: CQ Press.

Bifulco, R., Bunch, B., Duncombe, W., Robbins, M., and Simonsen, W. (2012). Debt and Deception: How States Avoid Making Hard Fiscal Decisions. *Public Administration Review*, 712, 659–667.

Bifulco, R., and Duncombe, W. (2010). Budget Deficits in the States: New York. *Public Budgeting and Finance*, 30(Spring), 58–79.

Brecher, C., Horton, R., and Mead, D.M. (1994). Budget Balancing in Difficult Times: The Case of the Two New Yorks. *Public Budgeting and Finance*, 14(2), 79–102.

Bunch, B. (2010). Budget Deficits in the States: Illinois. *Public Budgeting and Finance*, 30(Spring), 105–129.

Chapman, J.I. (2008). State and Local Fiscal Sustainability: The Challenges. *Public Administration Review*, December Special Issue, S115–S131.

Clynch, E.J., and Lauth, T.P. (1991). *Governors, Legislatures, and Budgets*. New York: Greenwood Press.

Clynch, E.J., and Lauth, T.P. (2006). *Budgeting in the States: Institutions, Process, and Politics*. New York: Praeger.

Council of State Governments. *The Book of the States*. Available at http://www.csg.org/policy/publications/bookofthestates.aspx.

Davis, C., Davis, K., Gardner, M., McIntyre, R.S., McLynch, J., and Sapozhnikova, A. (2009). *Who Pays? A Distributional Analysis of the Tax Systems in All 50 States*, 3rd ed., technical report. Institute on Taxation and Economic Policy. Available at http://www.itepnet.org/whopays3.pdf.

Dothan, M., and Thompson, F. (2009). A Better Budget Rule. *Journal of Policy Analysis and Management*, 28, 463–478.

Drenkard, S. (2013, February 11.). State and Local Sales Tax Rates in 2013. Available at http://taxfoundation.org/article/state-and-local-sales-tax-rates-2013.

Friedman, D. (2006). *The Maryland State Constitution: A Reference Guide*. Westport, CT: Praeger.

Hansen, S.B. (1999). "Life Is Not Fair": Governors' Job Performance Ratings and State Economies. *Political Research Quarterly*, 52, 167–188.

Jordan, M., and Hoffman, K. (2009). The Revenue Impact of State Legislative Supermajority Voting Requirements. *Midsouth Political Science Review*, 10, 1–16.

Knight, B. (2000). Supermajority Voting Requirements for Tax Increases: Evidence from the States. *Journal of Public Economics*, 76, 41–67.

Kousser, T., and Phillips, J. (2012). *The Power of American Governors: Winning on Budgets and Losing on Policy*. New York: Cambridge University Press.

Lachman, S.P., with Polner, R. (2006). *Three Men in a Room: The Inside Story of Power and Betrayal in an American Statehouse*. New York: The New Press.

Leachman, M., Johnson, N., and Grundman, D. (2012). *Six Reasons Why Supermajority Requirements to Raise Taxes Are a Bad Idea*, technical report. Center for Budget Policy and Priorities.

Lowry, R.C., Alt, J.E., and Ferree, K.E. (1998). Fiscal Policy Outcomes and Electoral Accountability in American States. *American Political Science Review*, 92, 759–774.

Meyers, R.T., and Pilkerton, T.S. (2003). *How Can Maryland's Budget Process Be Improved?*, technical report. Maryland Institute for Policy Analysis and Research, University of Maryland, Baltimore County.

National Association of State Budget Officers. (2008). *Budget Processes in the States*. Washington, DC.

O'Cleireacain, C. (2010). *Hidden in Plain Sight: New York's Unbalanced Budgets*, technical report. Rockefeller Institute of Government, State University of New York, Albany.

Pew Center on the States. (2009). *Beyond California: States in Fiscal Peril*, technical report. Philadelphia.

Poterba, J. (1996). Budget Institutions and Fiscal Policy in the U.S. States. *American Economic Review*, 77, 395–400.

Poterba, J.M., and von Hagen, J. (eds.). (1999). *Fiscal Institutions and Fiscal Performance*. Chicago: University of Chicago Press.

Rosenthal, A. (2013). *The Best Job in Politics*. Thousand Oaks, CA: CQ Press.

Rudolph, T.J. (2003). Institutional Context and the Assignment of Political Responsibility. *Journal of Politics*, 65, 190–215.

Schick, A. (2005). Sustainable Budget Policy: Concepts and Approaches. *OECD Journal on Budgeting*, 5, 107–126.

Seljan, E. (2011). Supermajority Limits to Fiscal Policy. Paper presented at APSA, 2011, available from the Social Science Research Network.

Sharkansky, I. (1968). Agency Requests, Gubernatorial Support, and Budget Success in State Legislatures. *American Political Science Review*, 26, 1220–1231.

State Budget Crisis Task Force. (2012). *Report of the State Budget Crisis Task Force*, technical report. Available at http://www.statebudgetcrisis.org/wpcms/wp-content/images/Report-of-the-State-Budget-Crisis-Task-Force-Full.pdf.

Stonecash, J.M. (1991). Observations from New York: The Limits of 50-State Studies and the Case for Case Studies. *Comparative State Politics*, 12, 1–9.

Ward, R.B. (2010). *Gubernatorial Powers to Address Budget Gaps during the Fiscal Year*, technical report. Rockefeller Institute.

Ward, R.B. (2012). Achieving Fiscal Sustainability for State and Local Governments. In *The Oxford Handbook of State and Local Government Finance*, ed. R.D. Ebel and J.E. Petersen. New York: Oxford University Press, pp. 917–936.

Ward, R.B., and Dadayan, L. (2009). State and Local Finance: Increasing Focus on Fiscal Sustainability. *Publius*, 39, 455–475.

Chapter 3

Changing State Revenue Strategies

John L. Mikesell
Indiana University

Contents

Introduction

States face two basic choices in creating their revenue systems. The first is the extent to which the cost of government will be paid primarily by direct consumers of government services rather than being distributed generally through the tax system. If direct consumers pay, the state sells services and the tax system is not used to finance the service. A pricing system must be developed so that users pay and nonusers do not. This requires there to be identifiable direct customers and no substantial external beneficiaries from the service being provided. Many state services cannot be effectively or efficiently financed with charges, but many can.

The second choice is in regard to which taxes are to be included in the portion of the revenue system not based on charges. The concerns here relate to what tax base will be used, what tax structure will be applied to that base, and how that structure will be administered. Options are wide. There is no necessary reason why a particular set of state services must be financed with only one revenue system. Rather, tax systems should be designed to reflect revenue system objectives—yield, equity, economic neutrality, low collection cost, and transparency—and these objectives are independent of what services are financed. Taxes are always a feasible option, even for services that could be supported with charges, although that is seldom the best alternative when a service meets the criteria necessary for such charges.

This chapter examines the choices that states have made in developing their revenue systems. It first examines the structure of state systems in comparison with those used by the U.S. federal and local governments, giving particular attention to revenue diversification. The next section considers the constraints placed on state revenue choices. A third section examines how diversified state revenue systems have developed, followed by analysis of non-tax revenue sources that states use. The conclusion highlights some important challenges that state revenue systems must overcome if they are to continue covering the costs of state services.

State Revenue Systems: Growth and Diversification

State tax collections in fiscal 2010 exceeded $702.2 billion; own-source general revenue (including taxes, charges, and miscellaneous revenues) exceeded $988 billion.* The tax total is roughly 5 percent of gross domestic product, and own-source revenue roughly 7 percent of gross domestic product. As service responsibilities of state governments have increased over the years, so too have state own-source revenues and tax collections. Figure 3.1 traces the path of state real per capita own-source revenue and tax collections from 1932 to 2010. The average annual rate of growth over this period for real per capita taxes was 3.1 percent, and for own-source revenues, 3.4 percent. These robust growth rates for such an extended time period reflect the increased revenue needs of state governments as their scope of responsibilities has increased. Figure 3.1 also shows how state revenues were impacted by the two most recent recessions in 2001 and 2007–2009.

States account for the largest component of subnational government revenues in the United States. They currently account for about 60 percent of total tax

* U.S. Bureau of Census, Governments Division, *State Government Finances in 2010*, www.census.gov.

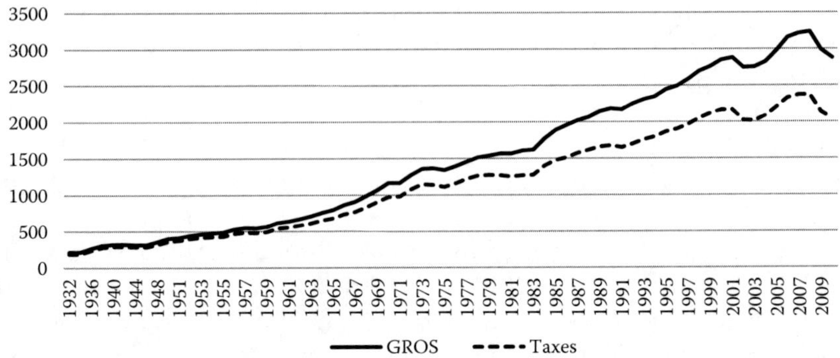

Figure 3.1 State real per capita own-source revenue and taxes, 1932–2010. GROS is own-source general revenue, meaning revenue raised by the taxing and charging actions of the government itself, and excluding revenues transferred from another government. (From U.S. Bureau of Census, Governments Division, *State Government Finances*, various years.)

collections and about 55 percent of total own-source general revenues of subnational governments.* These shares increased from slightly more than 40 percent in 1940 to close to their current levels by 1980. Since World War II, the greatest increase in state shares was from 1960 through 1980, a period of substantial decline in the role of the property tax in local revenue systems. Without substantial change in utilization of the property tax, a major increase in federal transfers, or a major realignment of underlying fiscal responsibilities, state shares are not likely to change dramatically in the future. State revenue systems will continue to bear lead responsibility for financing government services at the subnational level.

State revenue systems are structured differently from those of the federal government or local governments, both of which rely primarily on a single tax base. The federal government relies almost exclusively on the income base, levying the broad-based individual income tax and the corporate income tax for general operations and the payroll tax to support social insurance systems. These income-based taxes combined account for 96.7 percent of total tax revenue and 90.7 percent of total revenue for the federal government.† The individual income tax dominates, yielding 50.4 percent of total tax revenue and 47.4 percent of total federal revenue in 2011. Excise taxes on production or consumption contribute the remainder of federal tax revenues.

* Own-source general revenue includes taxes, current charges, and miscellaneous revenues collected by state government. They do not include revenues for state insurance or retirement programs (unemployment compensation systems, for instance), from state liquor stores, or from any state utility systems.

† Executive Office of the President, *Budget of the United States Government, Fiscal Year 2013: Historical Tables*, http://www.whitehouse.gov/omb/budget/Historicals.

This personal income tax dominance emerged in the late 1930s before which time federal excise tax collections exceeded combined income tax collections (individual, corporate, and payroll). Total excise tax collections exceeded those from either individual or corporate income taxes until 1942. Corporate income tax collections exceeded those for individual income taxes until 1944. From then on, the major federal tax has been the tax on individual income. While there was much discussion about use of a federal general sales tax to finance World War II, that alternative was rejected in favor of converting the then-limited individual income tax into a tax paid by the masses (Zelenak 2010). Federal reliance on the income base has not been seriously challenged since. Discussions about a flat tax, a value-added tax, a national retail sales tax, and other consumption-based taxes have ebbed and flowed but have come to nothing. In spite of concerns about complexity, economic distortions, and perverse burden distributions, reform of federal income taxes appears to be a topic for discussion and political campaigning rather than action.

On the local government level, the property tax dwarfs all other bases, as it has done since the early days of the nation. In 2010, for all local governments taken together, the property tax generated 74 percent of tax revenue and 46.9 percent of general revenue raised by local governments.* Because local governments employ user charges and receive intergovernmental assistance to a greater degree than do the states, the property tax share of general revenues is much lower than its share of tax revenues. The only other tax yielding as much as 10 percent of local tax revenues is the general sales tax (11.2 percent).

Property taxes are seldom highly regarded by the general public, and many states have acted to control and constrain their use by local governments. The difficulty is finding alternatives to the property tax. Other local taxes lack the stability, controllability, and reliability of the property tax.† Increased state transfer payments bring their own problems. States face their own fiscal challenges, making satisfactory transfers to local governments chancy. States may choose to mitigate their own budget problems by reducing transfers, thus moving their problems to the localities. Furthermore, state transfers often involve greater state control over local choices because state lawmakers do not want to risk the possibility that state money will be misused in local hands. Replacing the property tax is not easy for local governments, and as a result, local government tax systems remain heavily reliant on that source in spite of its unpopularity.

While there is considerable discontent with both federal income taxes and local property taxes, actual movement to significantly diversify either system has been modest. Property tax reliance did diminish from an average of 86.9 percent of local

* U.S. Bureau of Census, Governments Division, *State and Local Government Finances in 2010*, www.census.gov.

† The property tax did not, however, provide fiscal stability or reliability for local governments during the Great Depression, but that was an extreme exception to normal behavior. Collections were generally stable during the Great Recession.

tax revenue in the 1960s to an average of 74.9 percent in the 1980s, but it has not significantly declined since then. Dominance of the income base in the federal tax system has continued since it was increased to finance World War II. In fact, in the absence of state general sales tax and local property taxes, the national revenue system would be completely dominated by the income base, with the problems of distortion, inequity, and incentive for avoidance and evasion that extraordinarily heavy use of a single tax base would bring.*

As shown in Table 3.1, states have a more balanced tax system than either the federal government or local governments. In 2010, for the states taken together, 31.7 percent of tax revenue was generated by general sales taxes and 33.6 percent by individual income taxes. While these two taxes dominate, the states collectively received more than 5 percent from corporate net income taxes and from motor fuel taxes. No non-income tax in the federal system yields as much as 5 percent of total tax revenues, and no non-property tax in local use yields as much as 15 percent of total local tax revenue.

Shaping State Revenue Systems from the Top

States diversify because they have considerable flexibility in what sources they may employ. They operate with fewer federal constraints on state revenue choices than are found in some other federations.† The U.S. Constitution neither prescribes nor assigns the revenue options for the states, and it is largely silent about what revenues are forbidden to the states, the prohibition against taxes on international trade and on printing their own money being the primary exceptions.‡ This flexibility for states is inherent in the 10th Amendment to the Constitution: "The powers not delegated to the United States by the Constitution, nor prohibited by it to the States, are reserved to the States, respectively, or to the people." Revenue authority is one of these residual powers held by the states so that states have great flexibility in tax choices. They are limited by politics, economics, competition with surrounding states, and their own creativity rather than any national revenue prescription.§

* Diversity can make it more difficult for taxpayers to comprehend the full cost of government services, so diversified revenue structures are not without their problems.

† Local governments might show greater diversity in revenue choices if they had greater flexibility. However, as creatures of their state governments, they have available only the options allowed them by their states, and states tend to be rather restrictive.

‡ There are a number of constitutional principles within which states must operate. For example, the states may not tax in a manner that unduly burdens interstate or international commerce (the Commerce Clause), they must provide equal protection and due process, and they may not use payment of taxes as a requirement for voting. But these are applicable to all state policies, not just those involving taxation.

§ This is in contrast to the situation for local governments. These units, as creatures of their states and lacking sovereignty granted by the federal constitution, have only the taxing powers granted by state actions.

Table 3.1 State General Revenue in the United States, Fiscal Year 2010

Type of Revenue	*Total ($K)*	*National Share of Tax Revenue*	*National Share of Own-Source Revenue*
General revenue	1,562,962,875		
Own-source general revenue	987,401,192		100.00%
Total taxes	701,555,688	100.00%	71.05%
Property taxes	14,264,321	2.03%	1.44%
Sales and gross receipts taxes			
General sales and gross receipts	222,542,958	31.72%	22.54%
Selective sales taxes			
Insurance premiums	15,826,938	2.26%	1.60%
Motor fuels	36,636,267	5.22%	3.71%
Public utilities	14,759,377	2.10%	1.49%
Tobacco products	16,831,613	2.40%	1.70%
Casino/racing excises	7,406,300	1.06%	0.75%
Licenses			
Corporation	9,925,276	1.41%	1.01%
Motor vehicle	20,865,522	2.97%	2.11%
Occupation and business, NEC	12,749,807	1.82%	1.29%
Income taxes			
Individual income	235,994,401	33.64%	23.90%
Corporation net income	36,739,534	5.24%	3.72%
Other taxes			
Death and gift	3,891,096	0.55%	0.39%
Documentary and stock transfer	4,249,924	0.61%	0.43%

Table 3.1 (*Continued*) State General Revenue in the United States, Fiscal 2010

Type of Revenue	*Total ($K)*	*National Share of Tax Revenue*	*National Share of Own-Source Revenue*
Severance	11,200,886	1.60%	1.13%
Current charges	169,575,319	n.a.	17.17%
Miscellaneous general revenue	116,270,185	n.a.	11.78%
Lottery proceeds available	17,752,773	n.a.	1.80%

Source: U.S. Bureau of Census, Governments Division, *State Government Finances, 2010*, www.census.gov.

Wildasin (2007, 651) sums up the revenue-raising authority available to states in the United States: "Indistinct though its boundaries may be, the residual taxing authority of the states granted by the Constitution evidently accommodates non-trivial diversity in state and local revenue structures." States have used this authority to devise revenue systems as they see fit.

Similarities across states in their revenue systems are largely the product of successful experimentation being copied and not the result of a national standard or requirement. For instance, Mississippi and West Virginia demonstrated that retail sales taxes could yield significant revenue even in the Great Depression. By the start of World War II, there were 19 more states (plus the territory of Hawaii) that had permanently added the tax to their revenue systems. In another example, the success that New Jersey had with the lottery that it adopted in 1970 led to lottery operations in "all states north of the Mason-Dixon line from Illinois to the Atlantic, excluding Indiana and Vermont" by the end of 1975 (Mikesell and Zorn 1986, 311).* Lotteries implemented in the mid-1960s in New Hampshire and New York were not seen as successful and did not lead to copying.

States also value their capacity to design their taxes as they choose. For instance, when the federal government offered to administer state individual income taxes at no cost to the states as part of the general revenue sharing program in 1972, no state accepted the offer. To participate, states would have had to piggyback their income tax on the federal tax. Most states tended to use the federal income tax structure in defining their taxes already, and all states had information sharing agreements with the federal government, thus allowing them to implicitly piggyback on

* Maryland, just south of the line, was the only other lottery state by 1975.

federal administration. However, the formal linkage, even with free administration, was too much loss of control for the states. The offer expired unused when the revenue sharing program was terminated.

Competition for economic activity almost certainly shapes state revenue choices. States are reluctant to tax in ways that might put their businesses at a competitive disadvantage with neighboring states and are eager to make their systems comfortable for their firms. For instance, states have flocked to restructure their corporate income taxes by switching the profit apportionment formula across states from one that averages the shares of property, sales, and payroll within the state to a formula that gives low weight to payroll.* That reduces the share of a firm's profit that would be taxable in states in which the business has high employment, thus giving businesses with large in-state payrolls a tax advantage. States have rather quickly switched to apportionment formulas with lower payroll factor weights. In 1978, of 46 states with apportioned corporate income taxes, 40 used a formula that gave payroll a weight of one-third; by 2012, only 11 states did (Bernthal et al. 2012). Competition among the states, not a nationally prescribed template, brought the structural shift. Whether the change made much difference in economic activity is not clear, but states thought it would and that was all that mattered (Goolsbee and Maydew 2000).

The federal government does implicitly encourage certain state taxes over others by limiting deductibility in calculating federal individual income tax liability to some taxes but not others, thus resulting in the federal government absorbing part of the tax burden of these deductible taxes. For the individual taxpayer, state and local taxes on real and personal property may be deducted by those who itemize, as may either tax on individual income or retail sales (sales tax deductibility provisions have changed in recent years), but no other state taxes.† That reduces the net tax burden from these taxes and gives a federal incentive for their use, rather than nondeductible user charges and selective excises. Although the impact is not as strong as might be anticipated, it is apparent that deductibility and changes in deductibility as a result of the Federal Tax Reform Act of 1986 did impact the use of income and sales taxes by states and local property tax rates (Gade and Adkins 1990; Holtz-Eakin and Rosen 1990; Metcalf 1993).

* The alternatives that lower the weight on payroll are the single-sales factor (giving no weight to payroll paid in the state) and double-weighted sales factor (reducing the impact of payroll from one-third to one-fourth of the apportionment factor). With lower weight to payroll, a firm with considerable employment (and hence payroll) in a state will not have a high share of its total profits allocated for taxation to that state. The firm can expand its employment in the state without that state capturing a higher share of profits for taxation there.

† The alternate minimum tax blunts the impact of deductibility, just as does the use of the standard deduction. Deduction requires that the taxpayer not take the standard deduction, and the AMT may cause the value of the deduction to be lost entirely.

State Tax Systems: Getting to System Diversity

Individual states make diverse choices about how they distribute the cost of services. While the general sales tax and the individual income tax are the dominant tax options, the extent to which individual states rely on each varies considerably. Theindividual income tax yielded more revenue than any other tax in 30 states in 2010, the general sales tax was most productive in 18 states, and the corporate income tax and the severance tax were each most productive in one state. Table 3.2 summarizes the diversity of state revenue systems across the states.

For the general sales tax, individual state reliance ranges from 43.3 percent of total own-source revenue to 0 percent in five states (Alaska, Delaware, Montana, New Hampshire, and Oregon). For the individual income tax, reliance ranges from 41.1 percent of own-source revenue to 0 percent in seven states (Alaska, Florida, Nevada, South Dakota, Texas, Washington, and Wyoming). For the corporate net income tax, reliance ranges from 15.8 percent to 0 in four states (Nevada, Texas, Washington, and Wyoming). The motor fuel tax is levied in all states, but the relatively small share it contributes to total tax revenue varies widely, from 5.8 percent to 0.4 percent. Other taxes show variation, but these are the only ones with national yields above 5 percent of total tax revenue.

Some taxes that are modest in overall state revenue collections are important for individual states. For example, the severance tax yields 41.5 percent of own-source revenue in Alaska, far higher than the 1.6 percent in national totals, and the corporate license tax yields 14.8 percent of own-source revenue in Delaware, much more than the 1.01 percent in national totals. Because states can design their tax systems to accommodate their own economic, political, demographic, competitive, and social situations, this diversity is not surprising.

The relative importance of tax sources in state revenue systems changed considerably through the 20th century with regard to the role of particular taxes and the degree of tax diversity. Table 3.3 provides the history of state tax reliance since 1902, showing tax shares for general sales, individual and corporate net income, property, license, and the "big excises" (motor fuel, alcohol beverages, and tobacco product) taxes. These taxes constituted 87.5 percent of state tax collections in 2011 and 87.3 percent in 1902, and similar shares of the total for the years in between. However, the relative role that individual taxes have played in covering the cost of government has changed over the years.

State tax policy before the Great Depression was simple. The property tax was the principal state tax source, just as it was for local governments. The tax produced 36.8 percent of total state tax revenue in 1921, and high reliance on the tax continued through the 1920s, although the share had declined to 28.5 percent by 1929. While 11 states levied an individual income tax by 1922, total yield was only a little over 5 percent of tax collections. Four states (North Dakota, Colorado, New Mexico, and Oregon) adopted a motor fuel tax in 1919, and its yield grew as more states followed and motor fuel sales increased, reaching 18.1 percent of

Table 3.2 Diversity of State Revenue System Choices, Share of General Own-Source Revenue across Individual States, Fiscal 2010

	Individual States, Fiscal 2010				
Type of Revenue	*Mean Share*	*Median Share*	*Highest State Share*	*Lowest State Share*	*Number of States with No Collections*
Property taxes	0.0222	0.001	0.277	0	13
Sales and gross receipts taxes					
General sales and gross receipts	0.214	0.208	0.444	0	5
Selective sales taxes					
Insurance premiums	0.017	0.015	0.04	0.006	0
Motor fuels	0.04	0.041	0.06	0.0036	0
Public utilities	0.012	0.006	0.069	0	0
Tobacco products	0.019	0.02	0.061	0.00264	0
Casino/racino excises	0.012	0	0.118	0	29
Licenses					
Corporation	0.01	0.002	0.158	0	0
Motor vehicle	0.021	0.019	0.051	0.0005	0
Occupation and business, NEC	0.013	0.009	0.057	0	0
Income taxes					
Individual income	0.208	0.226	0.425	0	7
Corporation net income	0.033	0.03	0.128	0	4

Table 3.2 (*Continued*) Diversity of State Revenue System Choices, Share of General Own-Source Revenue across Individual States, Fiscal 2010

	Individual States, Fiscal 2010				
Type of Revenue	*Mean Share*	*Median Share*	*Highest State Share*	*Lowest State Share*	*Number of States with No Collections*
Other taxes					
Death and gift	0.003	0	0.017	0	0
Documentary and stock transfer	0.004	0.001	0.028	0	1
Severance	0.029	0.001	0.415	0	14
Current charges	0.1836	0.185	0.327	0.058	0
Miscellaneous general revenue	0.122	0.107	0.371	0.056	0
Lottery proceeds available	0.018	0.011	0.09	0	7

Source: U.S. Bureau of Census, Governments Division, *State Government Finances, 2010*, http://www.census.gov; American Gaming Association, *State of the States, 2010*, http://www.americangaming.org.

tax collections by 1927. Various licenses such as motor vehicle and motor vehicle operator licenses, general business licenses, and corporate licenses generated up to 30 percent of total tax revenue, but no single type of license dominated. The dominant state property tax was, in effect, piggybacked on the local tax, with property valued by local property assessors and otherwise administered by local officials. State government responsibilities were modest, the economy was agrarian, and property tax revenue was reliable.

Property tax dominance began to change in the late 1920s and early 1930s with the decline in the property tax and rise of the motor fuel tax. From 1927 to 1932, state property tax collections fell by 12 percent, a fall-off that continued through the first half of the 1940s, with collections recovering to their 1927 level only in 1952. No longer was the tax a stable and reliable source of revenue, as both households and businesses failed to pay their property tax bills when they were received. Tax sales to collect amounts owed on delinquent parcels failed to recover the expected liabilities, and finances of both state and local governments were stressed. After its Great Depression collapse, the property tax never returned to a significant role in state government tax systems. Currently, the tax barely yields 2 percent of state tax revenues. The fiscal

Table 3.3 State Tax Reliance, 1902–2010

Year	*Total Reported Taxes ($K)*	*Property Tax Share (%)*	*General Sales and Gross Receipts Share (%)*	*Motor Fuel Tax Share (%)*	*Tobacco Tax Share (%)*	*Alcoholic Beverage Tax Share (%)*	*Individual Income Tax Share (%)*	*Corporate Net Income Tax Share (%)*	*License Tax Share (%)*
1902	132,889	61.71%	0.00%	0.00%	0.00%	0.00%	0.00%	0.00%	25.59%
1913	254,889	54.93%	0.00%	0.00%	0.00%	0.78%	0.00%	0.00%	27.86%
1922	831,889	41.83%	0.00%	1.56%	0.00%	0.00%	5.17%	6.97%	31.25%
1932	1,685,889	19.46%	0.42%	31.26%	1.13%	0.00%	4.39%	4.69%	29.06%
1942	3,903,386	6.77%	16.20%	24.09%	3.33%	6.57%	6.39%	6.88%	18.14%
1948	6,743,149	4.10%	21.91%	18.67%	5.00%	6.31%	7.41%	8.67%	14.83%
1950	7,929,881	3.88%	21.06%	19.48%	5.22%	5.29%	9.14%	7.39%	15.48%
1955	11,588,993	3.56%	22.75%	20.31%	3.96%	4.07%	9.44%	6.36%	15.74%
1960	18,026,371	3.37%	23.87%	18.50%	5.12%	3.61%	12.26%	6.55%	13.84%

1965	26,117,456	2.93%	25.70%	16.46%	4.92%	3.51%	14.00%	7.39%	12.32%
1970	47,956,015	2.28%	29.56%	13.10%	4.81%	2.96%	19.15%	7.79%	9.62%
1975	80,154,888	1.81%	30.92%	10.30%	4.10%	2.45%	23.48%	8.29%	7.85%
1980	137,075,178	2.11%	31.49%	7.09%	2.73%	1.81%	27.06%	9.72%	6.34%
1985	215,893,155	1.85%	32.25%	6.18%	2.02%	1.40%	29.60%	8.17%	6.38%
1990	300,488,565	1.95%	33.18%	6.45%	1.84%	1.06%	31.97%	7.24%	6.27%
1995	399,147,005	2.38%	33.13%	6.37%	1.84%	0.90%	31.47%	7.28%	6.53%
2000	539,655,337	2.04%	32.33%	5.55%	1.55%	0.76%	36.06%	6.03%	6.04%
2005	650,629,485	1.74%	32.73%	5.31%	1.99%	0.72%	34.06%	5.95%	6.55%
2010	701,555,688	2.03%	31.72%	5.22%	2.40%	0.78%	33.64%	5.24%	7.19%
2011	757,254,745	1.84%	30.96%	5.27%	2.28%	0.76%	34.22%	5.31%	6.85%

Source: U.S. Bureau of Census, Governments Division, *State Tax Collections*, http://www.census.gov.

problems of the Great Depression induced states to implement the three taxes that continue to dominate state tax systems into the 21st century: the personal income tax, the corporate income tax, and the general sales tax.

By 1940, much of the current state tax structures were in place: 30 had personal income taxes, 32 corporate income taxes, and 32 retail sales taxes. A number of these broad-based taxes were also adopted in the 1960s, but by the end of that decade, the most productive components of state tax systems were generally in place. Almost all states (45) adopted motor fuel taxes in the 1920s and distilled spirits taxes in the 1930s (47), the former likely related to the increasing use of the automobile and the latter certainly driven by the end of Prohibition. More states adopted cigarette taxes in the 1930s and 1940s than in any other decade, but adoptions are generally scattered across the decades. Five or more states adopted casino excises in the 1980s, 1990s, and 2000s. However, casino tax adoptions do not show the concentration that was shown to be the case for the broad-based taxes, and the tax yields minimal revenue (less than 1 percent of state own-source revenue in 2010). The pace of adoptions is shown in the distributions in Figures 3.2 and 3.3. The revenue-productive, broad-based tax system upon which state finances are typically based is the result of state tax legislation during the Great Depression and during the 1960s. There have been few substantial tax restructurings since that decade.

The adoption patterns have left states with diverse revenue systems. Figure 3.4 provides a graphical representation on how this state tax diversity has developed using the Herfindahl index of concentration for total state tax collections. Higher values of the index indicate a greater degree of concentration.* The index shows that state tax structures became more diversified through the 1930s and into the mid-1940s, the period in which the property tax was lagging and general sales and motor fuel taxes were becoming more important. From that point, systems became more concentrated and the concentration index returned to roughly the same degree of diversity as was in place in the early 1930s. The index has stood at about 0.25 since the turn of the 21st century.

Figure 3.2 also displays the share of total tax revenue to the states from general sales and individual income taxes combined. This share, after a dramatic increase in the 1930s, increased consistently from the 1940s through the next 60. It has diminished slightly in the 2000s, but the two taxes continue to yield over 60 percent of total state tax revenues. The general diversity of state tax revenue and the moderate increase in concentration since the mid-1940s result from these two broad-based

* The Herfindahl index of concentration equals the sum of the squared shares of total tax for each component tax in the tax system. Individual taxes in this computation are property tax, individual income tax, corporate net income tax, general sales tax, motor fuel tax, tobacco tax, alcoholic beverage tax, license taxes, amusement tax, pari-mutuel tax, insurance premium tax, public utilities tax, other selective excise taxes, death and gift taxes, documentary and stock transfer taxes, severance tax, and all other taxes. With this division of taxes, the index can range from 0.059 (equal distribution among sources) to 1.0 (total concentration).

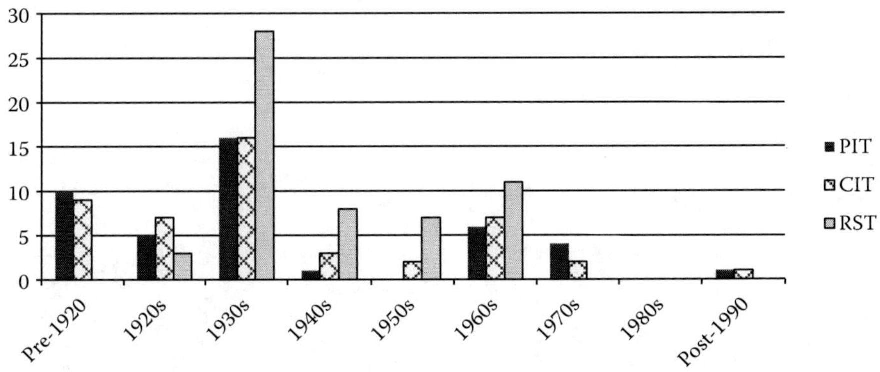

Figure 3.2 Adoptions of broad-based state taxes. PIT, personal income tax; CIT, corporate income tax; RST, retail sales tax.

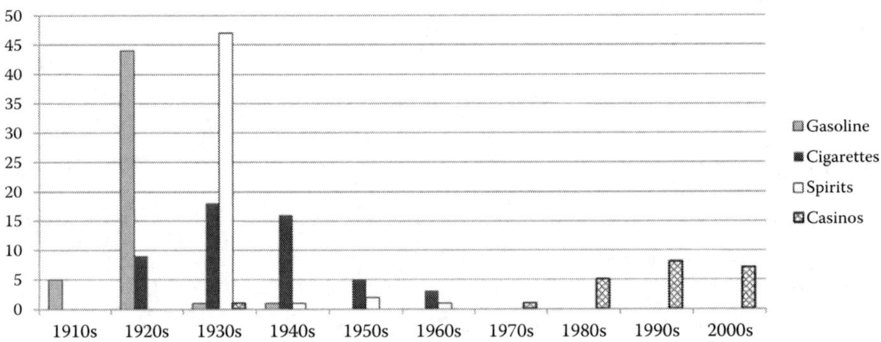

Figure 3.3 Adoptions of selected narrow-based state taxes.

taxes, one driven by income and the other driven by consumption. Other taxes—the corporate net income and narrow excises, along with the property tax—have become less significant sources of state tax revenues.

The Herfindahl indices for local and federal tax systems show considerably greater concentration than the index for state tax systems. If the index is computed for general sales, motor fuel, alcoholic beverage, tobacco products, public utilities, other selective excises, individual income, corporate income, motor vehicle license, and other taxes (the narrowest categorization available for local taxes), the index for local tax systems equals 0.5642 compared with 0.2371 for state taxes for 2010. The index for federal taxes (individual income, corporate income, social insurance payroll, excises, estate and gift, and customs and duties) stood at 0.3743 (and 0.89 if the three income-based taxes are combined) for the same year.

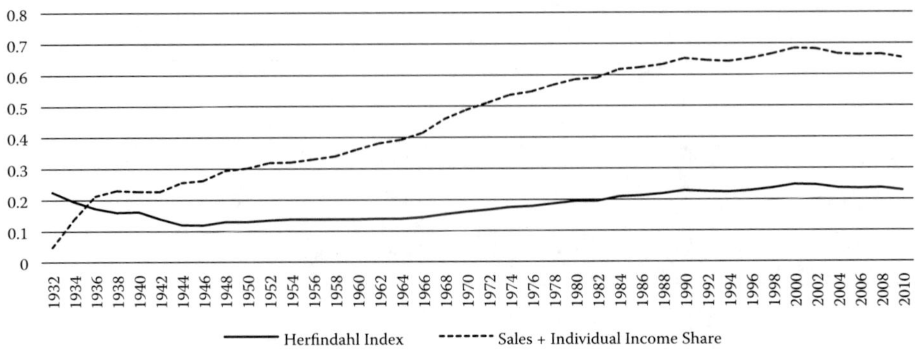

Figure 3.4 State tax system concentration: Herfindahl index and general sales—individual income tax shares, 1932–2010. (From U.S. Bureau of Census, Governments Division, Internal data file archives "State Aggregates.")

This comparison provides clear evidence that state tax systems are considerably more diversified than are the systems for either the federal government or local governments.

Changing Taxes

State tax policies are implemented in a most incremental manner. States adopt a permanent tax code or system of tax laws that remains in place each year unless specifically changed by legislative action.* A change in tax structure occurs when legislation revises or amends the existing tax code. As prior sections have made clear, the state tax systems involving the broad-based, more productive taxes were introduced largely in the 1930s and 1960s, eras in which state economies were substantially different from those in place now. To the extent state tax systems have changed, those changes have been accomplished through changes to the structure of those tax codes. As Wolfson and Hackbart (2004, 114) point out, "the principles of incrementalism dictate that reform efforts, if apparent, will proceed in a markedly cautious fashion."

Table 3.4 portrays the annual change in tax revenues for the major taxes across all states from 1950 through 2010. The data clearly show that tax collections generally change from one year to the next at a rate that would ordinarily be regarded as incremental.† For general sales, individual income, and corporate income taxes,

* Exceptions to this permanence are temporary provisions, like rate increases for a defined period that are adopted with a fixed expiration date. The provisions are not the norm for state tax legislation.

† Anderson and Harbridge (2010), in a recent study of federal budget dynamics, have categorized agency appropriation changes from –10 percent to +10 percent as incremental.

Table 3.4 Annual Percentage Change in Collections by State for Major Taxes, 1950–2010

Range of Change, % Change in Constant 2005 Dollars	*General Sales*	*Individual Income*	*Corporate Income*	*Motor Fuels*	*Alcoholic Beverage*	*Tobacco*
–10% and beyond	2.12%	6.29%	19.67%	3.85%	4.36%	3.46%
–9.99% to –7.5%	1.44%	2.71%	4.74%	3.75%	3.95%	5.63%
–7.49% to –5%	3.37%	3.04%	4.42%	5.46%	8.94%	12.37%
–4.99% to –2.5%	6.41%	5.25%	5.85%	10.37%	14.47%	20.12%
–2.49% to 0	10.58%	7.79%	6.45%	16.60%	20.64%	17.18%
0.01% to 2.5%	17.19%	10.05%	8.24%	21.42%	18.56%	11.51%
2.51% to 5%	21.23%	12.38%	5.45%	17.10%	11.29%	6.29%
5.01% to 7.5%	15.14%	13.84%	6.61%	7.33%	5.29%	4.49%
7.51% to 10%	8.17%	10.38%	4.82%	3.65%	3.58%	2.63%
10.01% to 12.5%	4.09%	7.75%	5.18%	1.77%	1.98%	1.87%
12.51% to 15%	2.20%	5.59%	3.26%	1.67%	1.24%	1.38%
15.01% to 17.5%	1.76%	3.46%	3.54%	1.31%	1.21%	1.66%

Continued

Table 3.4 (*Continued*) Annual Percentage Change in Collections by State for Major Taxes, 1950–2010

Range of Change, % Change in Constant 2005 Dollars	*General Sales*	*Individual Income*	*Corporate Income*	*Motor Fuels*	*Alcoholic Beverage*	*Tobacco*
17.51% to 20%	1.28%	2.42%	3.18%	1.44%	0.80%	1.18%
20.01% to 22.5%	1.00%	1.75%	3.26%	0.70%	0.47%	0.86%
22.51% to 25%	0.72%	1.50%	2.27%	0.60%	0.44%	0.93%
25.01% and beyond	3.29%	5.79%	13.06%	2.98%	2.78%	8.43%
Range –10% to +10%	83.53%	65.44%	46.58%	85.68%	86.73%	80.23%
Range –5% to +5%	55.41%	35.47%	26.00%	65.50%	64.96%	55.10%
Negative	23.92%	25.09%	41.12%	40.03%	52.36%	58.76%

Source: Computed from U.S. Bureau of Census, Governments Division, Alaska and Hawaii from 1958 only.

a high percentage of the state annual changes fall in the –10 percent to +10 percent range, and a considerable share are in the narrower –5 percent to +5 percent range. Big structural change in state tax systems—changes large enough to jolt collections for a particular tax beyond the boundaries of incremental change—are rare. State tax systems thus reflect much of the framework put in place when the taxes were adopted decades ago.

The Rest of the Money

States sell some services to the public, generating money that can be used to support the service being provided, and thus relieving pressure on the general revenue system. In some cases, the sales may even provide surplus proceeds that can support other government operations. States raise current revenue from sources other than taxes to differing degrees. Across states, current charge and miscellaneous general revenue accounts for just below 30 percent of state own-source revenues.* This overall share is relatively large, but it includes a wide variety of revenue producers, none of which individually represents a major component of general state revenues.

A considerable share of miscellaneous revenue comes from earnings on property and investments. For charges, most support a particular government service and collections are not available for the support of general state operations. Collections from charges are useful for covering at least some of the costs of providing the service for which the charge is being applied and are helpful in requiring payment from those directly using the service. They also relieve a cost burden on the general tax system, even if they do not support general government services. Data generally available do not indicate the extent to which proceeds might be available for other uses. Hence, the revenue from charges cannot be interpreted in the same way as tax revenue that can support whatever public functions might be chosen in the budget process. Indeed, sometimes charges are restricted to being no greater than the cost of providing the service, a clear restriction on use of charges as a mechanism for general finance.

Table 3.5 indicates the relative contribution of the larger components of charge and miscellaneous revenue to that total. Few categories represent a sizable contribution on their own. Only charges by institutions of higher education, by hospitals, from highways, and for state lotteries constitute more than 5 percent of the charge and miscellaneous revenue total. Over the 1951–2008 period, hospital and higher education charges as a share of own-source revenue have more than doubled, but the share for toll highways is roughly the same now as it was more than 50 years ago. In light of increased highway traffic, the needs for funding of highway infrastructure,

* Miscellaneous general revenue includes interest earnings, special assessments, revenue from sales of property, and other revenues, a significant element of which constitutes net lottery proceeds. This analysis will include only the lottery revenue.

Table 3.5 State Current Charge and Miscellaneous Revenue, Fiscal 2009

	Total ($K)	*Share of Charge and Miscellaneous Revenue*
Charges and miscellaneous general revenue	84,610,425	
Current charges	61,238,746	56.7%
Education	89,846,450	31.6%
Institutions of higher education	88,603,712	31.1%
School lunch sales (gross)	35,283	0.0%
Hospitals	39,235,615	13.8%
Highways	6,770,119	2.4%
Air transportation (airports)	1,276,602	0.4%
Parking facilities	13,987	0.0%
Sea and inland port facilities	1,079,691	0.4%
Natural resources	2,496,535	0.9%
Parks and recreation	1,516,742	0.5%
Housing and community development	799,389	0.3%
Sewerage	506,688	0.2%
Solid waste management	486,068	0.2%
Other charges	17,210,860	6.0%
Miscellaneous general revenue	123,371,679	43.3%
Net lottery proceeds available	17,671,807	6.2%
Other general revenue	105,699,872	37.1%

Source: U.S. Bureau of Census, Governments Division, *2009 Annual Survey of State Government Finances*, http://www.census.gov.

and problems with motor fuel tax financing created by electric, alternative fuel, and high-mileage vehicles and increased fuel economy standards, the absence of an increased share for toll and other direct user financing represents a missed revenue opportunity for the states.*

Charges from housing, nonhighway transportation, parks, natural resources, and other categories represent much smaller shares of state revenues. Because many of these services have direct beneficiaries, this relatively small contribution of charges to state revenues can be seen as a missed opportunity for efficient and effective government finance. Financing programs that provide benefits primarily to an identifiable beneficiary through the general revenue system, rather than through prices paid by the users, would appear to present an excellent opportunity for revenue reform and for preservation of services in difficult fiscal environments.

As states develop future revenue strategies, the modest current contribution from charges for services that have clear and direct beneficiaries should be an area for increased consideration. If tax structures are challenged, greater application of charges for service would relieve pressure on the tax system, assign responsibility for payment for services to those using them, provide public decision makers better information about what services the public actually wants most, and provide incentives for more efficient utilization of public resources. Charges cannot replace taxes in the financing of public goods, but that does not mean that taxes should replace charges where service beneficiaries are clear and direct.

Conclusion

State revenue systems are more diversified than the systems of either the federal government or local governments. The diversification is primarily the result of balanced use of two major taxes, the general sales tax and the individual income tax. Both entered the state revenue systems many years ago and have undergone only marginal changes since then, generally to expand the scope of preferences, both targeted and general. Given that state economies have undergone significant changes since the major taxes were adopted, virtually every state tax system could profit from a general rethinking to make sure that it fits the needs of the state fiscal system and the nature of the state economy.

A restructuring of state tax systems will face several challenges, beginning with the role of local governments. Many states have substantially constrained the capacity of local governments to finance their operations with a real property tax. This limits the ability of local governments to respond to service requirements, putting states under pressure to provide more transfer assistance to local governments or

* Duncan and Graham (2013) argue that mileage fees provide a robust and potentially politically acceptable alternative to the motor fuel tax for highway finance.

to assume additional service responsibilities. State capability to support traditional state services is pressed by these now-transferred local service demands.

Another challenge facing the states is that economic activity has changed in ways that reduce the potential productivity of traditional revenue sources. These changes include the shift in household consumption from goods to services (a shift away from purchases typically included in state sales tax base), and a shift from tangible to intangible wealth, a change that makes it more difficult to track the tax base. In addition, economic activity has become more mobile. Capital flows with ease across boundaries, and consumption activity through the Internet faces no limits. Tax bases have become more responsive to rate differentials, and tax enforcement has lost the ability to collect tax owed. Rate differentials create extra problems because the range of tax competition has become global.

A third challenge is that corporate net income taxes make only a modest contribution as states balance an interest in revenue production against a fear of discouraging economic activity. The relatively small contribution of businesses to state revenues is compounded by the increasing efforts of businesses to organize as "pass-through" structures not subject to corporate taxation, i.e., S-corporations, limited liability companies, and partnerships. States do not know how or even whether to tax business activity, and that presents a challenge to useful restructuring.

A fourth challenge is that narrow-based taxes play only a modest role in state revenue systems. Those that compensate for some social cost can be sensible even with low revenue contribution, but their rates should be sufficient to cover that cost. Many of the rates are seldom changed. However, other narrow taxes are targets for elimination, given their probable distortions and high collection costs. Every state needs to sort through these taxes to reform each tax that does not appropriately fulfill the primary task of the revenue system, that of generating revenue for state operations. Revenue administrations have better uses of their time than to work for collection of unproductive taxes.

Revenue from sales of state services is modest, coming mostly from institutions of higher education, hospitals, and toll highways, and serving mostly to provide some direct user support. State lotteries are an exception because their services are sold to provide net proceeds that can be used to support other government services, and can thus be considered on the same grounds as the tax system. States need to more aggressively levy user charges both in areas now partly charge financed and in areas not now supported by charges.

The productive parts of state revenue systems were installed typically in the 1960s or before, when the economic structure and social environment were much different than today. State tax systems continue to yield growing revenue, except during recessions, but there have been few dramatic changes in the systems in the last half century. While there have been many state tax reform and restructuring movements over the past decade, their practical impact has been minimal overall. The appropriate tax policy direction in these efforts has usually been clear, but political will to improve has been lacking. Future restructuring of state tax systems will require both.

References

Anderson, S., and Harbridge, L. (2010). Incrementalism in Appropriations: Small Aggregation, Big Changes. *Public Administration Review*, 70(3), 464–474.

Bernthal, J., Gavrila, D., Schumacher, K., Spencer, S., and Sydor, K. (2012, May). Single Sales-Factor Corporate Income Tax Apportionment: Evaluating the Impact in Wisconsin. Workshop in Public Affairs, Robert M. LaFollette School of Public Affairs, University of Wisconsin-Madison. Prepared for the Wisconsin Department of Revenue.

Duncan, D., and Graham, J. (2013). Road User Fees Instead of Fuel Taxes: The Quest for Political Acceptability. *Public Administration Review*, 73(3), 415–426.

Gade, M.N., and Adkins, L.C. (1990). Tax Exporting and State Revenue Structures. *National Tax Journal*, XLIII, 39–52.

Goolsbee, A., and Maydew, E.L. (2000). Coveting Thy Neighbor's Manufacturing: The Dilemma of State Income Apportionment. *Journal of Public Economics*, 75, 125–143.

Holtz-Eakin, D., and Rosen, H. (1990). Federal Deductibility and Local Property Tax Rates. *Journal of Urban Economics*, 27, 269–284.

Metcalf, G. (1993). Tax Exporting, Federal Deductibility, and State Tax Structures. *Journal of Policy Analysis and Management*, 12, 109–126.

Mikesell, J.L., and Zorn, C.K. (1986). State Lotteries as Fiscal Savior or Fiscal Fraud: A Look at the Evidence. *Public Administration Review*, 46(4), 311–320.

Wildasin, D. (2007). Preemption: Federal Statutory Intervention in State Taxation. *National Tax Journal*, 60, 649–662.

Wolfson, G.S., and Hackbart, M.M. (2004). Changes in State Tax Structures: True Comprehensive Reform or Artifacts of Incrementalism. *Journal of Public Budgeting, Accounting, and Financial Management*, 16(1), 114.

Zelenak, L.A. (2010). The Federal Retail Sales Tax That Wasn't: An Actual History and an Alternate History. *Law and Contemporary Problems*, 73, 149–205.

Chapter 4

State Tax Structures: Past Trends, Future Possibilities

David L. Sjoquist
Georgia State University

Contents

Introduction

How state governments were financed at the end of the 20th century bears little resemblance to their financing at the end of the 19th century. In 1900, over 50 percent of state tax revenue came from the property tax, while much of the rest came from taxes imposed on banks and insurance companies. There were no sales taxes, no tobacco taxes, and no motor fuel taxes. While some states taxed income, the tax as we know it today did not exist.* Currently, states get an inconsequential amount of revenue from the property tax, while in 2010, personal and corporate income taxes, sales taxes, motor fuel taxes, and tobacco taxes comprised 95.4 percent of total state tax revenue. What a difference 100 years makes!

How will state taxes change over the rest of the 21st century? Rather than attempting to project that far into the future, this chapter presents how we think state tax structures are likely to change over the next couple of decades. The next section provides a historical context by discussing how the level and composition of state taxes have changed over the past 30 years, as well as the differences across states in their reliance on income and sales taxes. We then examine each major tax, how each has changed in the last 30 years, explanations for these changes, and the role of each expected in the future. The chapter closes with some conclusions about the future of state fiscal resources.

Recent Trends in the Composition of State Tax Revenue

Before discussing the future of state taxation, it is informative to consider changes to the composition and structure of state tax revenue since 1980. In 2010, total state taxes accounted for $702.2 billion, which is down from a historic high of $757.5 billion in 2007.† Over the entire 30-year period, real total state taxes per capita increased by 25.8 percent, or by an annual average rate of increase of 7.7 percent.

Dividing state taxes by total personal income yields an average effective tax rate, that is, the percentage of total income that is paid out in state taxes. Figure 4.1 shows the annual average effective tax rate for the period 1980–2010; total state taxes were, on average, 6.2 percent of total personal income. Over this period, state taxes as a percentage of personal income ranged from a low of 5.7 percent in 2010 to a high of 6.4 percent in 1995, a difference of 0.7 percentage points. Had state taxes been 6.4 percent of personal income in 2010, state tax revenue would have been $86.6 billion larger.

* Some states did impose taxes on certain types of income. Some states imposed taxes on property based on the income they could generate. Seligman (1914) classified these forms of property taxes as taxes on income.

† All tax revenue data were provided to us by the U.S. Bureau of the Census, but are available on the Census Bureau's State Government Tax Revenue Division's website: http://www.census.gov/govs/statetax/.

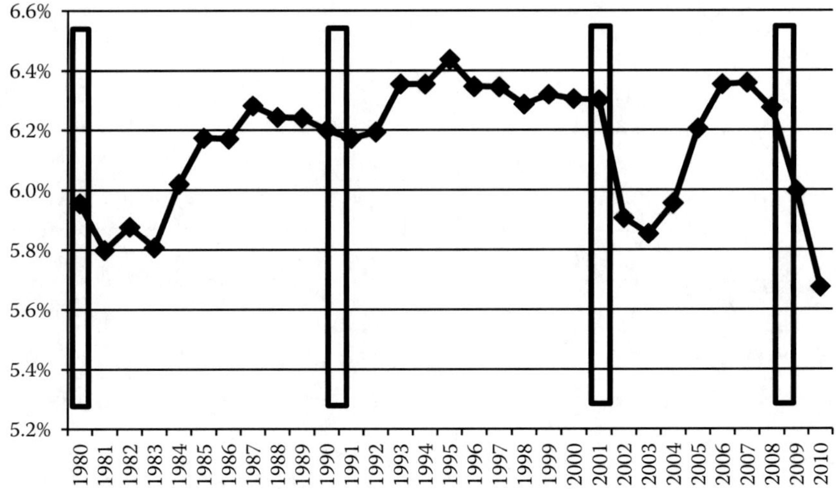

Figure 4.1 State taxes as a percentage of personal income, 1980–2010. Rectangles mark national recessions as determined by the National Bureau of Economic Research, available at http://www.nber.org/cycles/cyclesmain.html (accessed May 4, 2012). (From U.S. Bureau of the Census, State Government Tax Collections, available at http://www.census.gov//govs/statetax/historical_data.html [accessed March 17, 2012]; U.S. Bureau of Economic Analysis, National Income and Product Accounts, Table 2.1, available at http://www.bea.gov [accessed April 15, 2012].)

Figure 4.1 also displays the timing of the four recessions that the United States experienced during the 30-year period. Generally, the effective tax rate decreased during and in the years immediately succeeding each recession. This was followed by a return to effective tax rates that ranged between 6.2 and 6.4 percent, a relatively narrow band. However, state taxes as a percentage of personal income were generally higher in the years prior to the 2001 and 2007–2009 recessions than in those prior to the 1980 and 1991 recessions, suggesting that the average effective tax rate drifted up over this period.

Table 4.1 shows the distribution of total state tax revenue by type for 1980 and 2010, ranked by the tax's share of total revenue in 1980. The table also shows the percentage point change in the relative importance of each tax.* In 1980, the general sales tax was the most important tax revenue source, accounting for 31.5 percent of total state tax revenue. But by 2010, the personal income tax had replaced the sales tax as the most important tax; over the period personal income tax increased from 27.1 to 33.6 percent of total state taxes, a 6.5 percentage point increase, while the sales tax's share remains virtually unchanged. Together, sales

* The list of taxes is based on the classification of revenue sources used by the U.S. Bureau of the Census.

Table 4.1 Tax as a Percent of Total Taxes, 1980 and 2010

	Year		
	1980	*2010*	*Difference*
General sales tax	31.5%	31.9%	0.4%
Individual income tax	27.1%	33.6%	6.5%
Corporate income tax	9.7%	5.2%	–4.5%
Motor fuels tax	7.1%	5.2%	–1.9%
Motor vehicle license	3.6%	3.0%	–0.6%
Severance tax	3.0%	1.6%	–1.5%
Tobacco tax	2.7%	2.4%	–0.3%
Public utility tax	2.5%	2.1%	–0.4%
Insurance premium tax	2.3%	2.2%	0.0%
Property tax	2.1%	2.0%	–0.1%
Alcoholic beverage tax	1.8%	0.8%	–1.0%
Death and gift tax	1.5%	0.6%	–0.9%
Corporation license	1.0%	1.4%	0.4%
Other selective excise tax	1.0%	3.4%	2.4%
Occupation and business license tax, NEC	0.8%	1.8%	1.0%
Document and stock transfer tax	0.7%	0.6%	–0.1%
Parimutuel tax	0.5%	0.0%	–0.5%
Hunt and fish license	0.3%	0.2%	–0.1%
Motor vehicle operation license	0.3%	0.3%	0.1%
Amusement tax	0.2%	0.9%	0.7%
Alcoholic beverage license	0.1%	0.1%	–0.1%
Public utility license	0.1%	0.1%	0.0%
Other license taxes	0.1%	0.1%	0.1%
Amusement license	0.1%	0.1%	0.0%

Table 4.1 (*Continued*) Tax as a Percent of Total Taxes, 1980 and 2010

	Year		
	1980	*2010*	*Difference*
Taxes, NEC	0.0%	0.3%	0.3%
Total	100.0%	100.0%	

Source: U.S. Bureau of the Census, State Government Tax Collections, available at http://www.census.gov//govs/statetax/historical_data.html (accessed March 17, 2012).

Note: NEC, not elsewhere classified.

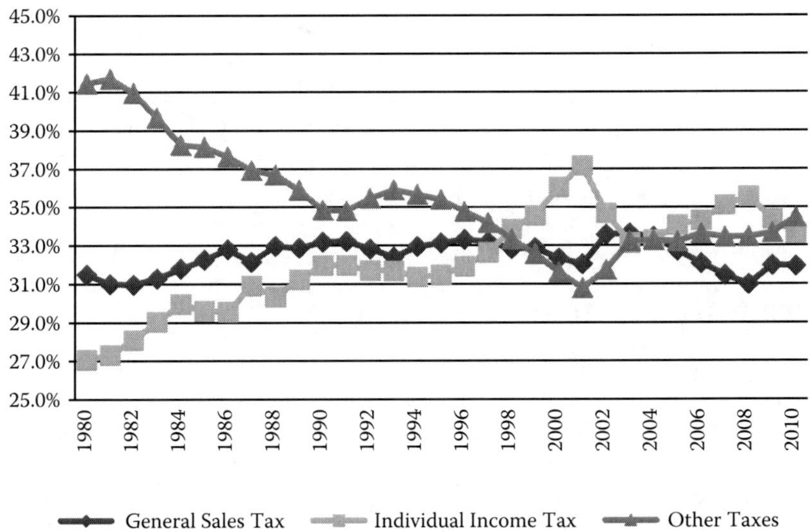

Figure 4.2 Share of total taxes, 1980–2010. (From U.S. Bureau of the Census, State Government Tax Collections, available at http://www.census.gov//govs/statetax/historical_data.html [accessed March 17, 2012].)

and personal income taxes accounted for 58.6 percent of total state tax revenue in 1980, increasing to 65.5 percent by 2010.

Figure 4.2 plots the annual share of total taxes for the sales tax, the personal income tax, and for all other taxes. The sales tax share of total taxes is relatively flat, changing little from year to year. The personal income tax steadily increased from 1980 to 2001, reaching a peak of 37.2 percent of total state taxes in 2001. Its share decreased following the 2001 recession, then increased again until the Great Recession hit in 2007. Given relative increases in sales tax and personal income tax revenue, the relative importance of other taxes naturally fell. Between 1980 and 2001, other taxes fell from 41.4 percent of total tax revenue to 30.8 percent, but by 2010 the share of other taxes increased to 34.5 percent of total tax revenue. This decline is largely the result of the decrease in the relative importance of the corporate income and motor fuel taxes. In 1980, these two taxes accounted for 28.7 percent of other taxes, while in 2010 they accounted for only 15.9 percent. Each of the other taxes that make up this tax category account for a very small percentage of total taxes, that is, generally less than 3 percent.

There are substantial variations across states in their tax revenue composition. Seven states (Alaska, Florida, Nevada, South Dakota, Texas, Washington, and Wyoming) do not impose a personal income tax, and two others (New Hampshire and Tennessee) only tax dividend and interest income. Five states (Alaska, Delaware, Montana, New Hampshire, and Oregon) do not levy a general sales tax. Excluding the 12 states that do not impose either an income or a sales tax, the percentage of state tax revenue in 2010 derived from the sales tax ranges from 12.4 percent (Vermont) to 59.6 percent (Hawaii), while the percentage derived from the personal income tax ranges from 11.5 percent (North Dakota) to 54.4 percent (New York).* The percentage of tax revenue from the total of income and sales taxes ranges from 31.9 percent (Vermont) to 80.4 percent (Georgia).

Future Changes in State Taxes

In this section we turn to a discussion of how state taxes are likely to change in the next couple of decades, considering likely changes of each tax separately. The changes in revenue for all states from a tax, in total and as a percentage of personal income, can be explained by changes in the size of tax bases, changes in tax rates, and changes in the mix of taxes that states choose as revenue sources. The tax base will change due to fluctuations in the economy (for example, changes in consumption levels and patterns will affect sales tax revenue) and to legislative changes (for example, changes in what goods the state taxes as part of the sales tax). To project the future of each state tax, we first describe past changes and their causes. We then consider how these and other forces will likely change the tax going forward. We focus on those taxes that generated at least 2 percent of total tax revenue in 2010, with two exceptions. First, we do not discuss motor vehicle license taxes. While the U.S. Census Bureau classifies these as taxes, they are really charges imposed on owners or operators of motor vehicles for the right to use public highways, including charges for title registration and inspection of vehicles. Second, we ignore the other selective excise taxes category. This is a catchall category of

* Washington has the largest percentage of tax revenue from the sales tax (59.6 percent), and Oregon has the largest percentage from the income tax (66.1 percent).

excise taxes imposed on specific commodities or services, for example, lubrication oil, fuel other than motor fuel, meals, margarine, and cement, that are not separately enumerated by the Census Bureau. Each individual excise tax accounts for a very small amount of revenue, and so we do not explore the changes to these taxes.

Personal Income Tax

Between 1980 and 2001, real personal income tax revenue increased every year, although the rate of growth slowed during the two recessions of the 1980s and 1990s (see Figure 4.1). However, during the past decade real personal income tax revenue declined in 5 of 10 years, dropping precipitously.

There has also been a decrease in the stability of real personal income tax revenue. McGranahan and Mattoon (2012) explored the increase in the sensitivity of personal income tax revenue to economic conditions since 2000. They attribute this increased instability to the nonwage and salary component of taxable income, and in particular, to investment income. This is consistent with the findings of Sjoquist et al. (2011b), who note the large increase in capital gains prior to 2001 and again prior to 2008, followed by their collapse as a result of the tech bust at the end of the 20th century and the housing market collapse in 2008, respectively.

Personal income tax revenue as a share of total personal income increased almost continuously over the last two decades of the 20th century, going from 1.6 percent of personal income in 1980 to 2.3 percent in 2001 (Figure 4.3).

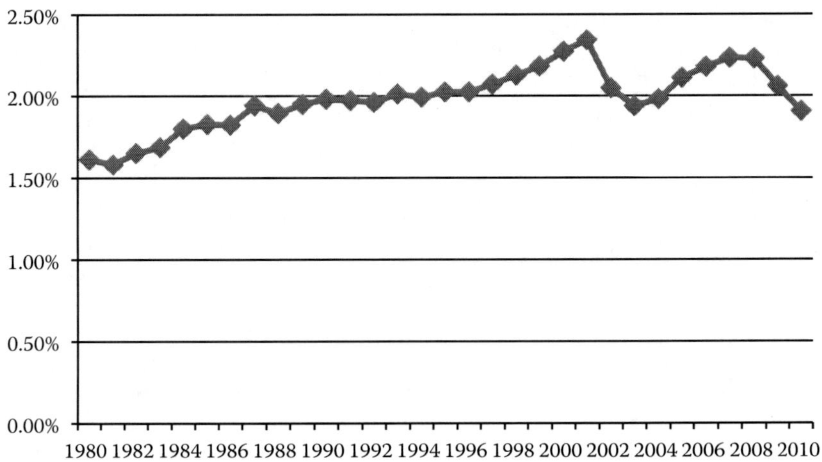

Figure 4.3 Individual income tax as a share of personal income. (From U.S. Bureau of the Census, State Government Tax Collections, available at http://www.census.gov//govs/statetax/historical_data.html [accessed March 17, 2012]; U.S. Bureau of Economic Analysis, National Income and Product Accounts, Table 2.1, available at http://www.bea.gov [accessed April 15, 2012].)

Since 2001, the share dropped significantly during the two recessions (2001 and 2007–2009), increased in the years between, but never regained to the 2001 level. The trend seen in Figure 4.3 is consistent with the findings of the U.S. Government Accountability Office (2010) that between 1977 and 2007, personal income tax revenue grew faster than personal income in all but four states.

In the absence of legislative changes that may affect personal income tax revenue (discussed below), we expect that personal income tax revenue as a share of personal income will increase at a rate similar to that observed during the 1980s and early 1990s. While another investment-related financial bubble is possible, such an event is unlikely over the next decade or two. Thus, the increased fluctuations in personal income tax revenue that were observed in the first decade of this century are not likely to repeat themselves. Whether the annual growth rates in real personal income going forward will also return to the levels seen in the 1980s and early 1990s will depend on the growth in personal income, which depends on increases in economic productivity.

The Congressional Budget Office forecasts that real gross domestic product (GDP) will grow at an annual rate of 3.2 percent over the period 2014 through 2022. The annual rate of increase is expected to be 4.4 percent over the period 2014 to 2016 and 2.6 percent from 2017 to 2022.[*] For the period 1980 to 1995, real GDP increased an average of 2.8 percent per year, with the increases ranging from –0.3 to 7.2 percent.[†] Thus, it appears likely that the increase in real personal income will grow at a rate similar to, if not somewhat greater than, the growth in the 1980 to 1995 period. This suggests that state personal income tax revenue will grow at a rate similar to that seen between 1980 and 2001.

On the other hand, this potential revenue growth ignores possible legislative actions, at both the federal and state levels. Regarding federal legislative changes, we note that all but five of the states with a personal income tax use federal adjusted gross income (AGI) or federal taxable income as their starting point for their individual income tax.[‡] Thus, federal changes to the definition of AGI or taxable income get reflected in state income taxes. Some of the observed changes to state personal income taxes between 1980 and 2010 are therefore due to changes in the federal personal income tax.

---

[*] Congressional Budget Office, "The Budget and Economic Outlook: Fiscal Years 2012 to 2022," January 31, 2012, available at http://www.cbo.gov/publication/42905 (accessed May 17, 2012).

[†] U.S. Bureau of Economic Analysis, "Table 1.1.1: Percent Change from Proceeding Period in Real Gross Domestic Product," available at http://www.bea.gov/iTable/iTable.cfm?ReqID=9&step=1 (accessed May 17, 2012).

[‡] Federation of Tax Administrators, "State Personal Income Taxes: Federal Starting Points (as of January 1, 2012)," 2012, available at http://www.taxadmin.org/fta/rate/stg_pts.pdf (accessed May 7, 2012). For a detailed description of each state's personal income tax, see Olin and Swain (2011).

At the federal level, proposals have been made to substitute a tax on consumption for the personal and corporate income taxes. The "fair tax" is one such proposal to replace the federal income tax with a national sales tax (Boortz and Linder 2005, 2008).* Hall and Rabushka (2007) have also proposed a simple way of taxing consumption, rather than income.† The elimination of the federal personal income tax would have significant effects on state personal income tax. First, it would significantly increase the compliance cost to the taxpayers and increase the administrative cost for each state. Second, it would lead to increasingly divergent personal income tax structures as states adopt changes to their income tax system without the federal income tax serving as a common model. Some have suggested that without a federal income tax, states would likely repeal their own income taxes (Bucks 1995). However, given the magnitude of such change to the federal income tax, its elimination seems unlikely, certainly in the foreseeable future.

Rather than replacement, the federal income tax could undergo major reform, similar to that which occurred in 1986. That is, there have been increasing calls by academics, politicians, and editorial writers for the federal government to eliminate or reduce various exemptions, deductions, and special provisions associated with this tax in order to expand its base.‡ Other reform proposals include reducing federal income tax rates and the number of tax brackets. Such changes at the federal level would result in an increase in taxable income for most states. States would respond by either collecting additional income tax revenue or reducing their tax rates, or some of both. But, the 1986 tax reforms came about because the context for change existed—public mood pressed for change and Congress and the president were able to agree on changes (Birnbaum and Murray 1987). Given the current inability of Congress to agree on much of anything, the probability of major federal tax reform seems very low.

Another major change in personal income tax revenue would occur if states without an income tax were to adopt one, or if states with an income tax were to scrap it. Four states added the personal income tax in the 1960s, and four in the 1970s. Over the period 1980 to 2010, there were only two changes made by states with an income tax. In 1980, Alaska dropped its income tax, and in 1992, Connecticut expanded its limited income tax on dividends and interest income to a full income tax. Two states without a personal income tax (Tennessee and Washington) recently considered adding one, but neither effort was successful. In Tennessee in the past, gubernatorial proposals to adopt a broad-based income tax have generated strong legislative opposition (Bourdeaux 2010). There is currently

* For more information, see the website for Americans for Fair Taxation: http://www.fairtax.org.

† Hall and Rabushka call their tax a flat tax, which is not to be confused with the flat tax proposed by Steve Forbes.

‡ See, for example, Marron (2011), Weisman (2012), and Brooks (2012).

an effort in this state to hold a referendum in 2014 that would insert language into the state constitution that explicitly prohibits a tax on personal income.* In Washington, a referendum to adopt a state personal income tax was held in 2010, and 64 percent voted against it.† In 1999, the Tax Reform 2000 Committee in Wyoming proposed adding an income tax, but it was not adopted (Bourdeaux 2010). In light of these examples, it does not seem likely that any of the 11 states without a broad-based income tax will add one anytime soon.

In fact, there have been proposals in several states to eliminate the income tax. For example, the 2005–2007 Tax Review Commission in Hawaii suggested investigating the elimination of the income tax, while recent tax reform commissions in Oklahoma and Oregon also recommended getting rid of the tax. In Oregon, consideration was to replace the income with a sales tax (Bourdeaux 2010). None of these changes were enacted, however. Hamilton (2012a) reviewed gubernatorial proposals in play in March of this year (2012) and found four states (Idaho, Nebraska, New Jersey, and Ohio) in which the governor had proposed major one-time cuts in the state's personal income tax rates. He also found three states (Kansas, Missouri, and Oklahoma) in which serious consideration was given for phasing out the personal income tax.

The chief concern with all proposals that reduce the reach of or eliminate the personal income tax is lost revenue; replacing revenue generated from a broad-based personal income tax is difficult. Most states without an income tax have a unique situation that would be hard or impossible for other states to duplicate, for example, tourism in Florida, gambling in Nevada, and energy in Alaska, Texas, and Wyoming. States without an income tax generally impose much higher sales taxes, and in general, all of the other taxes are higher (Sjoquist 2010).

Importantly, there is no evidence that eliminating the personal income tax would be seen to be politically popular. There have been periodic national surveys that ask citizens to rank a set of taxes in terms of which is "the worst tax—that is, the least fair." In surveys conducted annually between 1972 and 1989, and then five times since (the last conducted in 2006), that offered choices of the federal income tax, the state income tax, the state sales tax, and the property tax, the state income tax was ranked the least unfair in every one, with only about 10 percent of the respondents listing it as the least fair (Cole and Kincaid 2006). And, in a 2006 Gallup poll, 62 percent of respondents said that the state income tax was very or

* See Ballotnews.org, "Tennessee Income Tax Proposal One Step Away from 2014 Ballot," January 26, 2012, available at http://ballotnews.org/2012/01/26/tennessee-income-tax-proposal-one-step-away-from-2014-ballot/ (accessed May 17, 2012).

† Ballotpedia.org, "Washington Income, Initiative 1098 (2010)," available at http://ballotpedia.org/wiki/index.php/Washington_Income_Tax,_Initiative_1098_%282010%29 (accessed May 17, 2012).

somewhat fair.* We also note that North Dakota recently voted on eliminating the property tax, which is seen as the least liked tax, by a vote of 75 to 25 percent.†

Generally, the state personal income tax has not generated a lot of political heat over time, other than a proposal for a state without the tax to adopt it, or that regarding any very large increase in the tax. For example, Brunori (1998, 199) explains that New Jersey Governor James Florio's loss to Christine Todd Whitman in 1991 and the changes in party control and recall of two state senators in Michigan in the early 1980s were likely due to large increases in these states' income taxes. Nor has there been much significant litigation or widespread demands for reform such as the Proposition 13 movement surrounding property taxes (Brunori 1998, 200).

Hamilton (2012a) points out that the states considering a reduction or elimination of the personal income tax have Republican governors and, in most cases, Republican state legislatures. He asks what the real agenda is for these policies: economic development, which is what the governors generally claim to be the purpose, or to "hobble state fiscal systems and create a condition of ongoing fiscal imbalance" (2012a, 967). Regardless of motivation, we expect that there will be continued efforts on the part of Republican governors, especially, to eliminate or significantly reduce the individual income tax. On the other hand, given the difficulties of replacing revenues lost by eliminating the income tax, we think it is very unlikely that more than a couple of states will abandon their income tax over the next 20 years. Also, given the strong opposition to adopting an income tax in those states currently without one, we doubt that any of those states will add an income tax.

Another way that the personal income can change is through state-specific legislative changes to tax rates, exemptions and deductions, and credits. In the past three decades, many states changed their income tax rates, mostly reducing them. For example, of the 13 states whose top income tax rate in 1980 was 10 percent or higher, 12 reduced their top rate to less than 10 percent.‡ Five other states also reduced their personal income tax rates. Another common change was to the number of tax brackets. In the same period, 18 states reduced the number of tax brackets; for example, New York went from 18 to 8 brackets, and West Virginia went from 24 to 5. In addition, most states increased the income level that defines the top tax bracket. Two states, Colorado and Utah, adopted a flat tax, that is, a one-tax-rate structure, while three states (Nebraska, Rhode Island, and Vermont)

* Survey conducted by Gallup Organization in 2006 or 802 telephone interviews, obtained from the IPoll databank at the Roper Center for Public Opinion Research (accessed May 18, 2012).

† See http://results.sos.nd.gov/resultsSW.aspx?text=BQ&type=SW&map=CTY (accessed June 13, 2012).

‡ The 1980 tax rates were taken from Table 82 of Advisory Commission on Intergovernmental Relations (1980), while the 2012 tax rates were obtained from Federation of Tax Administrators, "State Individual Income Taxes, 2012," available at http://www.taxadmin.org/fta/rate/ind_inc.pdf (accessed May 17, 2012).

shifted from a one-rate system to a multirate system. These changes are consistent with recommendations of state tax commissions to lower tax rates and flatten the rate structure; state tax reform commissions in Georgia, Maine, and Utah, for example, called for flattening their state's income tax rate structures. Also, three of eight states whose personal income tax systems were not linked to the federal income tax system in 1980 became linked by 2012.

If, as suggested above, real income tax revenue begins to again increase at sustained growth rates, we expect to see states reducing tax rates. This is what states indicate in the previous 30 years. And, for the period 1999–2008, Buschman and Sjoquist (2012) report that states cut income taxes, while increasing other taxes.

Buschman (2010) and Cordes and Juffras (2012) provide summaries of recent state personal income tax legislative changes; Buschman considers the period 1999–2010, while Cordes and Juffras consider a longer period. These scholars rely on data collected by the National Conference of State Legislatures. They find that some states (Connecticut, Hawaii, Maryland, New Jersey, New York, and Oregon) have recently added new brackets that apply to taxpayers with very high incomes, although most of these changes are temporary increases and were made largely in response to the fiscal effects of the Great Recession. Oregon added two new tax brackets for tax years 2010 and 2011 on incomes over $250,000.

To the extent that states are concerned that tax rates on high incomes will cause higher-income families to leave or avoid the state, state officials work to keep tax rates competitive. But exactly what effect personal income tax rates have on migration is unclear. There is a common belief among economists that states should not adopt tax systems that are very progressive because of the concern that this provides incentives for higher-income families to migrate. This case is made by Oates (1972) and many others; however, this is not a universally held opinion (Pauly 1973; Goodspeed 1989; Chernick 1997, 2010). In fact, a report from the Institute on Taxation and Economic Policy (2012) suggests that the economic performance of states with high tax rates was better than that of other states. Tannenwald et al. (2011), considering the effect of a 2004 increase in the tax rate on high-income earners in New Jersey, conclude that the rates have had little effect on migration. On the other hand, a report prepared by Arduin, Laffer and Moore Econometrics (2011) for the Oklahoma Council of Public Affairs claims that eliminating the income tax in Oklahoma would result in a substantial increase in economic activity.

There have been some efforts to identify factors that explain differences in tax progressivity across states, though the results are mixed. Chernick (2010) finds that tax exporting through the deductibility of state and local taxes and greater inequality of pretax income distribution increase tax progressivity, while Republican control reduces progressivity. Fletcher and Murray (2008) explore various provisions of state income taxes and attempt to identify factors that explain interstate differences in provisions. They do not find any effect of the provisions of neighboring states, or that higher poverty rates are associated with states that have provisions benefiting low-income populations.

Considering state histories and the aforementioned research, it is hard to determine whether state income tax systems will become more or less progressive. On the one hand, there are efforts to flatten rate structures, which should lead to less progressive tax systems. There is also concern that higher-income families have become more mobile, which should put downward pressure on tax progressivity. However, states have taken steps to both increase the progressivity of the income tax and flatten the tax rate structure. For example, in 1986 Rhode Island became the first state to adopt a state version of the federal earned income tax credit (EITC). Since then, 22 other states have added an EITC; most of these states are in the Midwest and Northeast regions of the nation.* It is possible that other states will add an EITC in the future, particularly when the growth in income tax revenue becomes strong.

There are two trends that are likely to have negative effects on the growth in personal income tax revenue. The first is the growth in fringe benefits, which are not subject to income taxes. Fringe benefits as a share of worker compensation have grown, and an increasing percentage of worker compensation is not taxed. The second trend is the aging of the population. According to the national population projections of the Census Bureau, the percentage of the population 65 years of age and over will increase from 13.0 percent in 2010 to 19.3 percent in 2030, an almost 50 percent increase.† Aging will have two effects on personal income tax revenue. First, income falls as an individual ages, so a larger share of elderly means lower income per capita. Second, states provide special tax provisions for the elderly (Edwards and Wallace 2004), and an increase in the population who qualify for these special provisions will result in slower growth in personal income tax revenue. The Iowa Department of Revenue (2006) predicted that revenue from the state's personal income tax will actually decline as the state's population ages. Conway and Rork (2012) document the increase in state income tax breaks that are targeted to the elderly; for example, between 1964 and 1994 the number of states that allow an exemption for pension income increased from 1 to 23.

The special provisions noted include exemption of certain sources of income, such as social security and other sources of retirement income (Snell 2011). States have expanded these exemptions, and are likely to continue to do so. As the elderly become a larger share of voters, states will likely be pressured to increase exemptions of retirement income.

Regarding the personal income tax, we expect to see some states reduce their reliance on the tax, for tax rates to fall, and tax rate structures to flatten. However, we would be surprised if any state completely eliminated its income tax. Nonetheless, over the next 20 years, we predict that the share of state tax revenue derived from the individual income tax will decline from its 2010 level.

* See Williams et al. (2011) for a discussion of state EITCs.

† U.S. Bureau of the Census, "Table 2: National Population Projections," available at http://www.census.gov/population/www/projections/summarytables.html (accessed May 18, 2012).

Sales and Use Tax

Over the period 1980 to 2010, real sales tax revenue increased at an annual growth rate of 2.8 percent, for a total increase of almost 75 percent. But relative to revenue from the personal income tax, that from sales tax has grown very little; the annual average growth rate over the entire period was slightly less than zero, while over the period 1980 to 2006 it was 0.5 percent per year.

By 1980, all states that currently have a sales tax had adopted it; in 1969, Vermont became the last state to adopt the sales tax. There does not seem to be any sentiment among states with a sales tax to eliminate it, nor does there seem to be discussion of adding a sales tax in those states without such a tax. As noted above, the Oregon tax reform commission did recommend adding a sales tax as a replacement for the state's income tax.

Compared to the personal income tax the sales tax is simple, consisting of setting the rate and determining what will be taxed. The most significant change over the past three decades has been the steady increase in sales tax rates, as shown in Table 4.2. In 1980, 78.3 percent of the states had sales tax rates of less than 5 percent. But by 2012, only 23.9 percent had tax rates that low. Over the 30-year period, the average state sales tax rate increased by 42.5 percent.

Table 4.2 Distribution of Sales Tax Rates

	Year			
	1980	*1990*	*2000*	*2012*
2.0–2.9%	1	0	1	1
3.0–3.9%	17	4	1	0
4.0–4.9%	18	15	12	10
5.0–5.9%	7	15	17	8
6.0–6.9%	2	11	13	21
7.0–7.9%	1	0	2	6
8.0–8.9%	0	1	0	0
Average	3.95%	4.88%	5.17%	5.63%

Source: 1980 and 1990 are from Table 2.3 of Due, J.F., and Mikesell, J.L., *Sales Taxation: State and Local Structure and Administration,* 2nd ed., Washington, DC, Urban Institute Press, 1994; 2000 and 2012 are from the Urban Institute/Brookings Institution Tax Policy Center, available at http://www.taxpolicycenter.org/taxfacts/Content/PDF/state_sales_tax.pdf (accessed April 15, 2012).

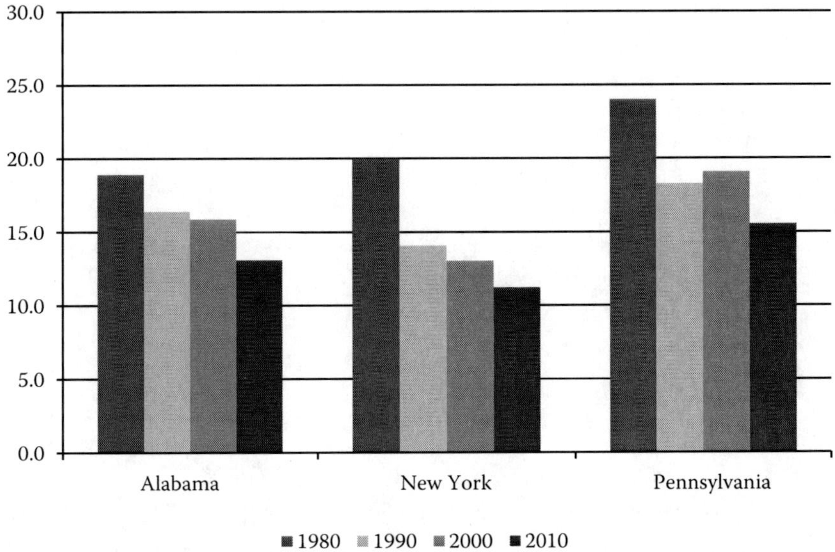

Figure 4.4 Sales tax base per $1,000 of personal income. (Author's calculation based on data from U.S. Bureau of the Census, State Government Tax Collections, available at http://www.census.gov//govs/statetax/historical_data.html [accessed March 17, 2012]; U.S. Bureau of Economic Analysis, National Income and Product Accounts, Table 2.1, available at http://www.bea.gov [accessed April 15, 2012].)

Sales tax revenues have not grown relative to the economy, though sales tax rates increased, suggesting that the tax base has not grown, and probably declined, relative to the growth in personal income. To illustrate that, consider Figure 4.4, which shows sales tax revenue per $1,000 of personal income for the three states that did not change their sales tax rates over the entire period. For the period of interest, there has been a general decline in sales tax revenue as a share of personal income.

There are three main reasons why the sales tax base has not kept up with the growth in personal income. When the sales tax was first adopted, it applied to the purchase and lease of tangible personal property but not to purchases of services. While some states have added selective services to their sales tax base, services are still a relatively small part of the sales tax base. Since 1970, only one state, Iowa, significantly expanded its sales tax base by including a long list of services. But, services have grown significantly as a share of personal consumption; for example, services increased from 52.6 percent of total personal consumption expenditures in 1980 to 63.3 percent in 2011.* Thus, the sales

* Bureau of Economic Analysis, National Income and Product Accounts, "Table 2.3.5U: Personal Consumption Expenditures by Major Type of Product and by Major Function."

tax is being applied to a smaller share of consumer purchases. Mikesell (2012) conducted an extensive analysis of the decline in the state sales tax base relative to personal income; he attributes the absence of services in the tax base as the primary cause of the downward trend.

States differ in the extent to which they include services in their sales tax base. The Federation Tax Administrators (FTA) has conducted periodic surveys of the states regarding the services they tax.* In its last survey, conducted in 2007, the FTA identified 168 individual services that at least one state included in its sales tax base. There is substantial variation in the number of services that states tax. While no state taxes all 168 services, three states tax more than 150 of the identified services. Between the 1990 and 2007 surveys, most states increased the number of services that they tax. In most cases, states added 10 or fewer services over the 17-year period, although five states added more than 20 services each.

Another reason that a sales tax base has not kept up with the growth in personal income is that states have increased their sales tax exemptions. When sales taxes were first adopted, exemptions were generally restricted to goods and materials that were used as inputs in manufacturing process and goods purchased for resale. Over time, states increased the list of exempt goods, and exempted certain sellers or buyers.† States have been most aggressive in adding exemptions for businesses—adding exemptions for consumables used in agriculture, the purchase of industrial and agricultural machinery and equipment, and energy used in production.‡ While these business exemptions have increased, the nonconsumer share of sales taxes is still very significant (Ring 1999). States also added exemptions of consumer goods, with food-for-home consumption being the largest exemption in terms of tax revenue loss. In 1980, 25 states exempted food-for-home consumption, while one other state taxed food at a lower rate. By 2012, 31 states exempted food, while 7 taxed food at a lower rate.§ The exemptions of consumer expenditures are generally adopted to enhance the equity of the sales tax.

Another type of sales tax exemption is the sales tax holiday. New York is usually credited with the adoption of the first sales tax holiday in 1997, which exempted purchases of clothing over a period of eight specified days

---

* A summary of the most recent survey (2007) can be found at http://www.taxadmin.org/fta/pub/services/btn/0708.html#table. A summary of the 1990 survey can be found in Table 6.10 of Graeser and Maury (1992).

† For a discussion of sales tax exemptions, see Chapters 3 and 4 of Due and Mikesell (1994).

‡ There is no known document that reports the year that states adopted exemptions of business purchases.

§ Exemptions for 1980 were taken from Table 77 of Advisory Commission on Intergovernmental Relations (1980), while the 2012 exemptions were obtained from Federation of Tax Administrators, "State Sales Tax Rates and Food & Drug Exemptions," available at http://www.taxadmin.org/fta/rate/sales.pdf (accessed May 8, 2012).

(Hawkins and Mikesell 2001).* Since then, 24 states have held sales tax holidays.† In 2012, only 15 states held sales tax holidays, as many cancelled these holidays for budgetary reasons. States have also begun to exempt certain sales or purchases made by particular nonprofits.

We expect the trend of decreasing sales tax base relative to the economy to continue. It is possible that states will add more services to their sales tax base, but we do not expect any to add services sufficient for the sales tax base to keep up with the growth in income. Nearly every recent state tax reform commission recommends adding services to the tax base, and several have recommended removing the exemption for food-for-home consumption. But in the end, only a few services are added, and all states that exempted food-for-home consumption in 1980 still exempted such goods in 2012. In 1987, Florida expanded its sales and use tax to include a very broad range of services. Hellerstein (1988, 1) explains that this action "triggered an enormous storm of protest," and the state quickly dropped the sales tax on most services. Florida's experience is frequently cited when states consider a significant broadening of the sales tax. Also, Florida tried to impose the tax on services that were produced outside the state but used in state, including advertising in magazines shipped into the state. In 2009, Maine passed legislation as part of a tax reform package that added more than 100 goods and services to its sales tax base, but in 2010, 61 percent of state citizens voted to repeal it.‡

Taxing many services, such as haircuts, is administratively difficult. Many haircutters operate as sole proprietors, so there are a very large number of establishments that have to be registered and for which tax collections have to be monitored. Expenditures on health care are a major component of service consumption, but given the federal government's role in financing health services, any sales tax on health services is severely restricted. Although the pressure to add services to the sales tax base will continue to grow and states are likely to expand their sales tax base to include more services, evidence such as that noted above suggests that states are likely to do so in a piecemeal fashion. And, both because of federal funding of health care and the concern that taxing health care is unfair, health care services that are generally covered by health insurance are unlikely to be added to the sales tax base.

Economists have argued that the retail sales tax should be applied only to purchases by the final consumer and not to goods that are inputs to products consumed (McLure 2000). The principal reason is the issue of tax pyramiding, that is, the sales taxes on

---

* Hawkins and Mikesell (2001) report that Michigan and Ohio had sales tax holidays for new vehicles in 1980.

† The history of sales tax holidays is from Urban Institute/Brookings Institution Tax Policy Center, "States with Sales Tax Holidays, 1997–2008," available at http://www.taxpolicycenter.org/taxfacts/Content/PDF/sales_tax_holiday_hist.pdf (accessed April 25, 2012). Current sales tax holidays are from Federation of Tax Administrators, "2012 State Sales Tax Holidays," available at http://www.taxadmin.org/fta/rate/sales_holiday.html (accessed May 7, 2012).

‡ See http://ballotpedia.org/wiki/index.php/Maine_Tax_Code_People%27s_Veto,_Question_1_%28June_2010%29 (accessed May 22, 2012).

inputs becomes part of the price of the intermediate good or service produced, so that the cumulative sales tax on the final purchase will be larger than the nominal tax rate and will depend on the number of times the intermediate goods are sold. This argument seems to hold sway given the increase in sales tax exemptions of purchases by businesses. In addition, states appear to be using sales tax exemptions to make the state more competitive, for example, exempting certain purchases by film producers. We expect to see states adding additional sales tax exemptions for business purchases.

A third factor influencing state sales tax revenue is online sales. If a vendor does not have a physical presence (nexus) in a state, the state cannot require the vendor to collect sales taxes; this is the result of a federal Supreme Court ruling in the *Quill* case. While the consumer is obligated to pay a use tax, very little use tax is collected (Alm and Melnik 2012).* Bruce et al. (2009) estimated annual national state and local sales tax losses on e-commerce in 2012 to be $11.4 billion, or about 5 percent of sales tax revenue. States have attempted to find ways to force remote vendors to collect the sales tax. Toward that end, several states have passed so-called Amazon laws in which states determine nexus based on a remote vendor's use of in-state affiliates. Not surprisingly, Amazon laws are opposed by firms such as eBay and Amazon, and have resulted in litigation and the cancelation of contracts with in-state affiliates. If the Supreme Court rules in favor of the states, we will see a dent in the $11.4 billion revenue loss, and expect other states to adopt Amazon laws. Within the next decade there will probably be another case like *Quill*.

The other effort to force remote vendors to collect sales taxes is the Streamline Sales Tax Project (SSTP), which is a national effort to make collecting the sales tax by remote vendors simpler, for example, by having states use common definitions of products and the ability to determine what tax rate to apply in order to eliminate the risk of penalties from imposing an incorrect sales tax rate. The hope is that the SSTP will encourage remote vendors to voluntarily collect sales taxes and result in either Congress passing legislation that would require remote vendors to collect the sales tax or the Supreme Court overturning *Quill*.

At least three bills have been introduced in Congress aimed at solving state problems with collecting sales tax revenue from remote sales. For example, the Main Street Fairness Act, S. 1452, has been introduced by U.S. Senator Richard J. Durbin. This legislation would codify the Streamlined Sales and Use Tax Agreement, thereby providing state governments with the authority to collect sales taxes on remote sales. Other legislation has been introduced by Senator Michael B. Enzi (Hamilton 2012b). A concern of Congress regards imposing additional administrative burden on the large number of small vendors who sell online, as these vendors account for a substantial percentage of online sales.

Economists sing the mantra that states should adopt low tax rates applied to a broad tax base, but it is not clear that states are listening. We expect to see

* Every state has a use tax as a companion to the sales tax. The use tax requires that if a purchase is made out of state and it is used in state, the individual or firm is required to pay the use tax.

states continue to add to their sales tax exemptions, particularly for purchases by businesses, and to add services to the sales tax base, though not in great numbers. At the same time, we predict that sales tax rates will continue to increase. It is not clear how high states can raise sales tax rates, but given that voters seem inclined to support increases in sales tax rates in local referenda, states appear to have some wiggle room before voters strongly resist such increases. In summary, we expect sales taxes as a share of state tax revenue to increase in the future.

Corporate Income Taxes

Between 1980 and 2007, corporate income tax revenue in real terms increased from \$39.9 billion to \$57.0 billion, an increase of 43.0 percent. However, by 2010 real corporate income tax revenue had fallen to \$36.8 billion. Relative to the U.S. economy, corporate income tax revenue fell by half over the 1980 to 2010 period, from about \$6.00 per \$1,000 of U.S. personal income to about \$3.00 (Figure 4.5).

Several reasons explain this trend, including the shift in organization form, more aggressive tax planning, reduced tax rates, and increased tax credits (see Fox and Luna 2002; Cornia et al. 2005). First, there has been a change in the legal structure of corporations from C-corporation to S-corporation and LLCs. The federal tax code distinguishes between two types of corporations: C-corporations and S-corporations. S-corporations and limited liability corporations (LLCs)

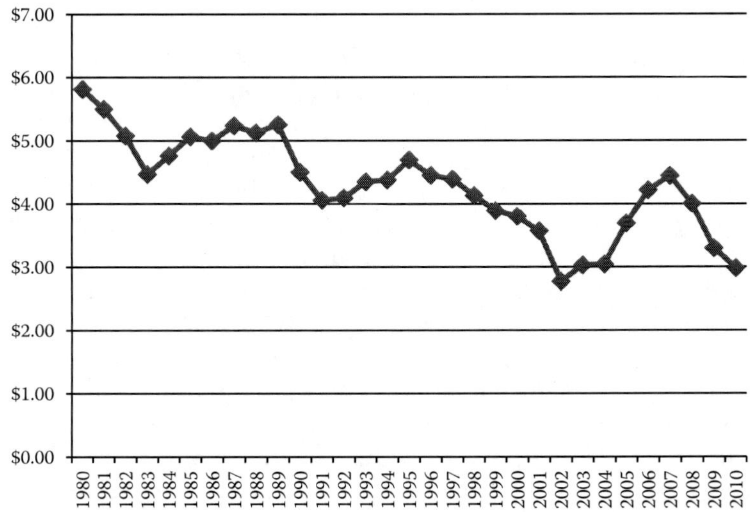

Figure 4.5 Corporate income tax revenue per \$1000 of personal income. (From U.S. Bureau of the Census, State Government Tax Collections, http://www.census.gov/govs/statetax/historical_data.html [accessed March 17, 2012]; U.S. Bureau of Economic Analysis, National Income and Product Accounts, Table 2.1, http://www.bea.gov [accessed April 15, 2012].)

are "pass-through" entities, so that profits are passed through to the owners of the firm and taxed under the personal income tax, not under the corporation income tax. The tax advantage of operating as an S-corporation or LLC has resulted in many smaller corporations converting from a C-corporation to an S-corporation and LLC status.

Second, corporations have engaged more aggressive tax planning that has reduced their taxable profits and state corporation tax receipts (Pomp 1998). There are several ways that multistate corporations can engage in tax planning to reduce their state tax burden. Luna (2004) and Mazerov (2007) examine tax planning devices, but do not provide empirical evidence regarding how extensive the use of tax shelters is or the effects of shelters on corporate tax revenue. One common tax planning device is to reclassify business income to nonbusiness income (the former is apportioned to the several states in which the firm does business, while nonbusiness income is allocated to the state in which the firm is domiciled). A second planning device is to establish a passive investment company (PIC), sometimes referred to as a Delaware holding company, as a wholly owned subsidiary. The parent corporation sells an intangible asset such as a trademark to the PIC, which then leases back to the parent company. The result is to transfer profits to Delaware, which does not tax income from intangibles.

In addition, states have expanded the number and value of tax credits, particularly for economic development purposes. Between 1977 and 1988, the number of states that enacted exemptions for corporate income taxes for economic development purposes increased from 21 to 31 (Pomp 1998). Investment tax credits and job tax credits are now very common (Enrich 1998). A current inventory of economic development tax credits is hard to find, though the expansion of income tax credits aimed at the film and entertainment industry provides some indication of the general expansion of income tax credits. In 1992, Louisiana became the first state to adopt an income tax credit aimed at the film industry. By 2000, four states had incentive programs for the film industry. By 2009, 28 states had a film tax credit, and many states had other incentives aimed at this industry as well, such as sales tax exemptions. An additional 12 states in 2009 offered incentives to the film industry other than an income tax credit (Henchman 2011).

On the other hand, several states have reduced or eliminated film tax credits (Henchman 2011), and several state tax reform commissions have suggested eliminating or reducing economic development tax credits. Michigan completely restructured its economic development tax incentives by replacing the existing tax credit programs with an annual appropriation of funds to be used to provide economic development incentives.

There are 44 states that have a corporate income tax. Of the seven that do not impose a personal income tax, four (Nevada, South Dakota, Washington, and Wyoming) do not impose a corporate income tax either. During the last three decades, three states made significant changes in how they tax businesses. In 1976, Michigan adopted the single business tax (SBT), essentially a form of a value-added tax, replacing several taxes on businesses, including a corporate income tax. In 2008, Michigan replaced the SBT with the Michigan business tax (MBT), which is based on business income and gross receipts net of purchases from other firms. However, effective in 2012, Michigan replaced its MBT with a corporate income tax. While the Texas state constitution prohibits a state income tax, in 2006, Texas adopted a business tax, known as the margin tax, which is meant to mimic a tax on income. For the margin tax, corporations choose one of three tax bases: total revenue minus cost of goods sold, total revenue minus wages and benefits, or 70 percent of total revenue. In 2005, Ohio adopted the commercial activity tax (CAT) as a replacement for its corporate franchise tax. Under the corporate franchise tax, a corporation would pay the higher of a net worth tax or a corporate income tax. The CAT is a tax on gross receipts rather than on net income.

Of the 45 states with a corporate income tax, 32 have a flat rate tax. For the 13 states with multiple brackets, the top marginal tax rate applies to income of less than $250,000, except for New Mexico, whose top rate applies to income of $1 million or more. Thus, the top rate applies to all but small corporations. Top marginal tax rates in 2012 range from 4 percent (Kansas) to 12 percent (Iowa), with 26 states having a top rate of between 5 and 8 percent.[*] Since 1980, 17 states increased and 17 states reduced their corporate income tax rates. Generally, states with lower than average marginal tax rates in 1980 raised their rates, while many states with higher than average tax rates in 1980 lowered their rates. The result is that the variation in tax rates fell over this period.

A major feature of state corporate income taxes is the apportionment of the net income of multistate firms to the states. After states adopted corporate income taxes, there were substantial efforts made to get states to use what is called the equally weighted three-factor formula, the three factors being the firm's share of its property, sales, and payroll located in the state.[†] By 1981, 35 states used the equally weighted three-factor formula in all cases, while 4 states double-weighted the sales factor, 1 weighted the sales factor at 70 percent, 1 used only two factors, 1 used only the sales factor, and 4 used a mix of formulas (Comptroller General of the United States 1982). However, by 2012, several states had moved away from the traditional three-factor formula and only 10 still used the equally weighted three-factor formula.[‡] Other states increased the weight on the sales factor, so that in 2012, 15 states double-weighted the sales factor, 6 weighted the sales factor more than double, and 10 used only the sales factor.

[*] Taken from Federation of Tax Administrators, "Range of State Corporate Income Tax Rates," available at http://www.taxadmin.org/fta/rate/corp_inc.pdf (accessed April 30, 2012).

[†] See Hildreth et al. (2005) for a discussion of the history of the efforts to adopt a common apportionment formula.

[‡] Based on Federation of Tax Administrators, "State Apportionment of Corporate Income," available at http://www.taxadmin.org/fta/rate/apport.pdf (accessed May 8, 2012).

Tax reform commissions in several states have proposed reducing or eliminating their corporate income tax. For example, tax reform commissions in California, Hawaii, Oregon, and Utah proposed eliminating their corporate income tax, and in the case of the first three, the proposal was to replace the corporate income tax with a tax on receipts or value added. On the other hand, tax reform commissions in Washington and Wyoming proposed adding a corporate income tax.

The relative importance of the corporate income tax is likely to continue its decline. Interstate competition for jobs and the increased geographic mobility of capital will lead states to reduce their tax on mobile capital, mainly by reducing corporate income tax rates. Still, we expect some states will actually eliminate their corporate income tax and replace their business income taxes with gross receipts tax, following the model of Ohio. While there have been suggestions that states replace their corporate income tax with a value-added tax, such a change would likely be seen as extreme, even though New Hampshire has adopted a value-added tax (Kenyon 1996).

Tax credits will continue to play an important role in the corporate income tax (and the taxation of business, in general), but we expect states will rein in some of the credits by tailoring them to provide incentives that have a significant effect at the margin. Also, we predict that states will continue to increase the weight on the sales factor in their apportionment formulas.

Fuel Taxes

Fuel taxes are generally earmarked for transportation, and usually are restricted to expenditures on roads and bridges. State motor fuel tax revenue, combined with transportation grants financed by the federal motor fuel tax revenue (generated by an 18.4 cents per gallon federal tax), is the principal source of revenue for transportation. Some states, such as New York and Florida, have local fuel taxes, but they amount to only about 3.6 percent of total state plus local fuel taxes.

All 48 states adopted fuel taxes by 1930.* Over the past 32 years, all but four have increased their tax rate on gasoline; Florida reduced its state fuel tax, shifting the tax to a local option. In 2012, state gasoline tax rates ranged from 4 cents per gallon in Florida to 38.9 cents per gallon in North Carolina; the gasoline tax rate for 39 states ranges between 15 and 30 cents per gallon. In 1980, the average tax on gasoline was 8.7 cents per gallon, while in 2012 the average tax rate was 22.2 cents per gallon.† However, adjusting for inflation, the real tax rate declined over the period. In 1980 dollars, the current (2012) average gasoline

* Hawaii adopted a fuel tax in 1932, and Alaska adopted it in 1946.

† Tax rates in 1980 are from Table 98 of Advisory Commission on Intergovernmental Relations (1980), while the 2012 rates are from Federation of Tax Administrators, "State Motor Fuel Tax Rates," available at http://www.taxadmin.org/fta/rate/mf.pdf (accessed May 7, 2012). The tax rates do not include special fees per gallon or the state sales tax.

tax rate is 8.06 cents per gallon. The real value of state fuel tax revenue has been decreasing. In the first decade of this century, fuel tax revenue in real terms decreased 15.9 percent, while in real per capita terms it decreased 23.4 percent.

The decrease in real fuel tax revenue per capita is due to the reluctance of states to increase fuel tax rates fast enough to accommodate inflation, and to improved fuel efficiency. At the same time, vehicle miles traveled per person has increased. But the net result is that transportation funding has not kept up with the need to expand and maintain the transportation network. The decline in the real value of the gasoline tax per mile driven provides a strong incentive to increase the fuel tax rate.

Related to this is the substantial backlog of transportation infrastructure needs. A recent report from the Miller Center of Public Affairs (2010) estimates that an additional $134 to $262 billion must be spent each year through 2035 on roads, rail, and air transportation. The American Society of Civil Engineers lists a price tag of $1.7 trillion for investments by 2020 for roads, bridges, and water/sewage systems, while the Urban Institute put the cost at $2 trillion (Halsey 2012). Once the economy recovers from the Great Recession, the public is likely to place pressure on state governments to address the infrastructure backlog. Because many of these needs are in urban areas, it will be politically difficult for state governments to raise fuel taxes statewide, only to spend the bulk of the revenue in metropolitan areas. Because of this, states are likely to look for alternative revenue sources to support transportation-related expenditures.

Increasing fuel tax rates is politically unpopular. Most public opinion surveys find that only a minority of respondents support increases in the gasoline tax. Consider public mood regarding the national gasoline tax. A recent (December 2011) nationwide poll of 1,200 adults conducted by Reason-Rupe found that 56 percent of the respondents strongly opposed such an increase and 21 percent somewhat opposed an increase.* Similar results were obtained in an Associated Press/CNBC national survey, which found that 52 percent of respondents strongly opposed raising the tax on gasoline by 15 cents per gallon for the purpose of building and repairing roads and highways.† However, the responses do differ depending on the context of the question. For example, when asked about increasing the federal gasoline tax if it would reduce U.S. dependence on foreign oil, 64 percent favored the increase in a 2007 poll, although a 2009 poll found that only 41 percent responded favorably.‡

---

* Reason–Rupe Public Opinion Survey, Winter 2011, available at http://reason.org/files/reason_rupe_transportation_poll.pdf (accessed May 15, 2012).

† Survey conducted by GfK Roper Public Affairs & Corporate Communications, November 2010, based on 1,000 telephone interviews, obtained from the IPoll databank at the Roper Center for Public Opinion Research (accessed May 15, 2012).

‡ Surveys conducted by CBS News/*New York Times*, based on more than 1,000 telephone interviews, and obtained from the IPoll databank at the Roper Center for Public Opinion Research (accessed May 15, 2012).

Similar results are found in statewide surveys. In a 2012 poll, 62.1 percent of Iowans opposed an increase in the state gasoline tax of 8 cents per gallon.* A survey conducted in Georgia in 2011 found that 66 percent of the respondents opposed a 10 cents per gallon increase in the gasoline tax (Sjoquist et al. 2011a). Dill and Weinstein (2006) note that since 2000, surveys conducted in the San Francisco Bay Area, Connecticut, South Carolina, New Jersey, and Washington State found that less than 40 percent of the respondents supported an increase in gas taxes. Based on these public opinion results, the likelihood of significant increases in state fuel tax rates is low. Furthermore, opposition to increasing the fuel tax is probably strongest in periods of increasing gasoline prices.

Because of the increasing fuel efficiency and the rise of alternative fuel vehicles, there is concern that fuel tax revenue is not keeping pace with vehicle miles traveled, that is, with the demands placed on the transportation system. Thus, many students of transportation financing have suggested going to a tax based on vehicle miles traveled, or VMT tax. There is no example of a fully operational VMT tax, although there have been two successful demonstration programs in the United States—one in the Portland, Oregon, area and one in the Puget Sound (Seattle) area.† Technology exists to implement a VMT tax; however, because citizens are generally unfamiliar with a VMT tax, and given concerns about confidentially, there is currently little public support for the idea.

Another option for preventing inflation from eroding fuel tax revenue is to index the fuel tax to inflation.‡ Rather than requiring state citizens to vote for an increase in the fuel tax, some states allow the fuel tax to increase with inflation, including Florida, Kentucky, and North Carolina.§ Florida ties its tax rate to increases in the consumer price index; Kentucky and North Carolina tie their fuel tax rate to the wholesale price of gasoline. Other states have indexed their fuel tax in the past, only to rescind it, including Michigan, Wisconsin, and Ohio. Others (Washington, Texas, and Nevada) considered indexing their fuel tax, but opted not to. Georgia's recent Special Council on Tax Reform and Fairness for Georgians recommended it, but the idea was rejected by the state legislature. Given past experience, it is unlikely that we will see states indexing their fuel taxes.

As noted above, the federal gasoline tax is 18.4 cents per gallon, while the average state fuel tax rate is 22.2 cents per gallon. There have been suggestions to significantly reduce or eliminate the federal role in financing transportation. If that were to happen, states would be under tremendous pressure to raise their fuel taxes.

---

* *Sioux City Journal*, February 13, 2012, available at http://siouxcityjournal.com/news/local/poll-iowans-oppose-gas-tax-increase/article_6923f8c0-368e-5240-9f2e-2d8766a79b88.html (accessed May 15, 2012).

† For a discussion of the Portland, Oregon, VMT tax experiment see Rufolo and Kimpel (2008).

‡ For a discussion of indexing fuel taxes see Sundeen and Reed (2006) and Ang-Olson et al. (1999).

§ GasBuddy.com/Tax.Info.aspx (accessed May 14, 2012) provides a description of the fuel taxes in each state.

However, the public generally supports maintaining the federal fuel tax, even if they oppose increasing the tax rate.* Thus, while the federal fuel tax is not likely to increase, it is unlikely that the fuel tax will decrease in the near future. We expect that the pressure to expand and maintain transportation systems, combined with the likelihood that the federal government transportation funding will be stagnant, will likely lead to increases in state fuel tax revenue per capita in real terms over the next two decades. We do not expect states to adopt a VMT tax or index fuel tax rates to inflation.

Tobacco Taxes

While states have not raised their gasoline tax rates to match inflation, they have substantially increased tax rates on tobacco products. The average tax on a pack of cigarettes was 12.8 cents in 1980, increasing to about $1.50 in 2012.† In real terms, this amounts to more than a threefold increase in the tax rate. State taxes on cigarettes range from 17.0 cents per pack (Missouri) to $4.35 per pack (New York). Thirty states impose a tax of more than $1.00 per pack, and five have tax rates of over $3.00 per pack.‡

However, real per capita tobacco taxes increased by 10.2 percent between 1980 and 2010, implying a significant decrease in tobacco consumption. Between 1980 and 2002, real per capita tobacco taxes fell, so the increase in real per capita revenue occurred during the last eight years of the period. This later period saw substantial increases in tobacco tax rates; between 2000 and 2012, 47 states increased their cigarette tax, with many states increasing rates multiple times.§

The opposition to increasing tobacco taxes comes from two primary sources, users and convenience stores, particularly those located on state borders. But users now account for a relatively small share of the public; in 2010, 23 percent of individuals 12 years of age and over smoked, down from 26 percent in 2002 (Substance Abuse and Mental Health Services Administration 2011). Antitobacco campaigns, partly funded by revenue from the Tobacco Master Settlement Agreement, are likely to further decrease the use of tobacco. In light of this and given that there is room for

* In a 2011 NBC News/*Wall Street Journal* survey, 47 percent of the respondents wanted their members of Congress to vote in favor of reauthorizing the fuel tax. When those who opposed the reauthorization were told what the tax revenue was used for, 43 percent of them changed their response to positive. A poll of 1,000 telephone interviews conducted by Hart and McInturff Research Companies, obtained from the IPoll databank at the Roper Center for Public Opinion Research (accessed May 15, 2012).

† Tax rates in 1980 are from Table 99 of Advisory Commission on Intergovernmental Relations (1980), while the 2012 rates are from Federation of Tax Administrators, "State Excise Tax Rates on Cigarettes," available at http://www.taxadmin.org/fta/rate/cigarette.pdf (accessed May 7, 2012).

‡ These are 2012 tax rates as reported by the Federation of Tax Administrators, available at http://www.taxadmin.org/fta/rate/cigarette.pdf (accessed May 17, 2012).

§ Data from Federation of Tax Administrators, available at http://www.taxadmin.org/fta/rate/cig_inc02.html (accessed May 17, 2012).

most states to increase their cigarette tax rates and still be competitive, we expect states to continue to increase these tax rates. One caveat is that any increases will reflect rates in neighboring states so as not to drive customers out of state.

Public Utility Taxes

The Census Bureau defines public utility taxes as those imposed on the gross receipts, gross earnings, or units of service sold of public passenger and freight transportation companies, telephone, telegraph, and light and power companies, and other public utility companies. Meriwether et al. (1989) provide a summary of utility taxes in selective states (and details of the public utility tax in Texas), Adams and Heidelmark (1984) summarize the taxes on railroads and other transportation companies, and Howe and Reeb (1999) discuss utility taxes on electrical utilities.* While the structure and components of these taxes differ substantially across states, generally public utility taxes are imposed on the gross receipts of public utilities at a fixed tax rate, and are imposed in lieu of income taxes. However, not all states impose these taxes or apply a common tax rate to all firms subject to the tax. These taxes were adopted a long time ago; for example, Texas's tax dates back to 1905 (Meriwether et al. 1989).

Public utility tax revenue as a share of personal income declined between 1980 and 2002 by 30 percent, but has held steady since. The major issue with public utility taxes is the changing nature of competition in these industries. These taxes were levied when utilities were regulated monopolies, but many of them now face significant competition.† Cornia and Walters (1997) cite a study conducted by Deloitte and Touche (1996) for the National Council on Competition and the Electric Industry that finds that taxes (this is total taxes, not just state taxes on gross receipts) on gas, electric, and telecommunication utilities are usually double the rate imposed on other industries. To the extent that new competitors are not subject to public utility taxes, the utilities are put at a competitive disadvantage. This leads to our expectation that states will slowly reduce their public utility tax rates, and thus revenue growth from this source will be slower in the future.

Insurance Premium Tax

The insurance premium tax is a gross receipts tax levied as a fixed percentage of the value of the premiums written in the state. But insurance premium taxes have two very unique characteristics. First, states can discriminate against out-of-state commerce by imposing higher tax rates on out-of-state carriers. A state can, but typically does not, impose a higher foreign tax rate compared to its domestic tax rate. Second, states impose retaliatory taxes that penalize companies domiciled in

---

* McHugh (1996) provides a description of the public utility tax in Ohio.

† McHugh (1996) provides a discussion of the nature of the new competition public utilities now face.

high-tax states but operating in other states. The result is that a company pays the higher premium tax in either the state in which the insurance policy is written or the state in which the company is domiciled.

Insurance premium tax revenue as a percentage of personal income has remained relatively constant over the period 1980–2010. Available evidence suggests that states have not significantly changed their insurance premium tax rates (Grace et al. 2014).

There is nothing to suggest that states are going to dramatically change their insurance premium tax. For example, a recent Georgia tax reform commission proposed reducing Georgia's very high premium tax rate, but the state legislature declined to consider it. However, as with the corporate income tax, competition for jobs may lead states to marginally lower their insurance premium tax rates, and perhaps even replace the tax with an income tax. This pressure to reduce insurance premium taxes may also be driven by the estimate that the premium tax is almost twice what a life insurance company would pay if it were subject to the state corporate income tax (Neubig et al. 2002).

Property, Severance, and Death and Gifts (Inheritance) Taxes

The property tax is considered a local government tax, with state government property tax revenue now accounting for only about 3 percent of total property tax revenue, which is down from 4.2 percent in 1980. There are 14 state governments that report not having a property tax. Real per capita state property taxes increased about 20 percent between 1980 and 2009, while local property taxes (real per capita) increased almost 60 percent.*

The property tax structure is largely determined by the state government, although in many states local governments have some control over the structure of the property tax as it applies in their jurisdiction. The state government defines what property will be taxed (including decisions regarding full and partial exemptions) and how (for example, fair market value, current use value, limitations on assessment increases, etc.). While these decisions do affect the state property tax revenue, they are not considered here.

The only state decision of concern examined in this chapter is the state property tax rate. Given state property tax revenue relative to local property tax revenue, the implication is that state property tax rates are very low relative to local property tax rates, and that the state rates have not changed much. Perhaps more importantly, state governments have a significant set of revenue alternatives at their disposal compared with local governments. Coupled with the fact that there exists strong and continued voter resistance to property tax increases, we expect states will not increase their property tax rates. As the growth in other state revenues returns to healthier levels, some states are likely to reduce or even eliminate the state property tax, a move that Georgia is currently phasing in.

---

* The most recent Census Bureau data on local government revenue is for the year 2009.

Severance tax revenue is likely to increase given the discovery of new energy sources in states like North Dakota and Ohio and the increases in the price of oil and other natural resources. The simple correlation coefficient between severance tax revenue and the consumer price index for energy over the period 1980 to 2010 is 0.88, suggesting that the price of natural resources is the principal driver of changes in severance tax revenue. Severance tax rates do not seem to change much, and with increasing nominal severance tax revenue from increases in the prices of natural resources, it is hard to imagine states increasing their severance tax rates.

Prior to the federal tax reforms of 2001, all states levied a tax on estates, and all but seven coupled their inheritance tax with the federal estate tax. Under this arrangement, the federal government allowed a credit, up to some maximum, for state inheritance taxes paid.* Typically, states set their inheritance tax level at the value of the credit. In 2001, the federal government phased in a repeal of that credit. Only 15 states that had been coupled with the federal estate tax decoupled; that is, they no longer set the tax at the value of the credit, and so continued to collect inheritance taxes. The other states that were coupled with the federal system lost all of their inheritance tax revenue. As a result, state inheritance tax revenue fell in the past decade, declining each year from $8 billion in 2000 to less than $4 billion in 2010.

The federal government seems unlikely to reinstate the credit provision, and it also seems unlikely that other states will take action to decouple from the federal system. Finally, at the federal level, the magnitude of estate that is exempt from the estate tax has increased, and is likely to continue to increase. To the extent that the states adopt the federal exemption level, inheritance tax revenue will fall for these states. We predict that state inheritance tax revenue will continue its slow decline.

Conclusions

With the exception of the state corporate income tax, we do not expect major changes in the specific taxes that states employ. While there are proposals to eliminate certain taxes, we predict that aside from in a couple of states, it will be extremely difficult, if not impossible, to generate the political support among voters to enact major changes to state tax structures. We expect that individual income tax rates will go down and that sale and excise tax rates (on tobacco and fuel, for example) will increase. With the increased mobility of businesses and individuals, there will be pressure for states to keep tax rates similar to those of other states, especially neighboring states. Overall, we expect a reduction in state tax rate differences. We anticipate that in 2040, an equivalent to Table 4.1 will look similar to what it looked like in 2010. The share of some taxes will be smaller—in particular, shares of the individual income tax, the corporate income tax, the inheritance

* For a discussion of state inheritance taxes, see McNichol (2012) and McNichol et al. (2003).

tax, and the property tax, with the share for the corporate income tax being substantially smaller. On the other hand, the shares for the sales tax and excise taxes will increase. Finally, we expect that states will likely turn to greater use of fees and charges for revenue and to heavier reliance on minor tax revenue sources as other sources shrink in importance.

Certainly, state tax revenue suffered during the Great Recession, and as the economy has recovered, state tax revenues have been growing again. While we expect that the state tax structure will change over the next 20 years, in the absence of efforts to actually shrink the size of state government or greatly expand the scope of state government, we expect that over the long run states will be able to generate the revenue necessary to fund public services. While state government revenue as a share of state income has fluctuated over time, over the 1980 to 2010 period, the trend has been remarkably flat; in fact, a trend line for the data in Figure 4.1 is actually slightly positive.

References

Adams, S., and Heidelmark, W. (1984). State and Local Taxation of Railroads and Other Transportation Companies: A Survey of Statutory Treatment. *Transportation Journal*, 23, 50–61.

Advisory Commission on Intergovernmental Relations. (1980). *Significant Features of Fiscal Federalism 1979–1980 Edition*, M-123. Washington, DC.

Alm, J., and Melnik, M.I. (2012). Does Online Cross-Border Shopping Affect State Use Tax Liabilities? *State Tax Notes*, 63, 1013–1017.

Ang-Olson, J., Wachs, M., and Taylor, B.D. (1999). *Variable-Rate State Gasoline Taxes*, working papers. Institute of Transportation Studies, UC Berkeley. Available at http://scholarship.org/uc/item/1kf5d54p.

Arduin, Laffer and Moore Econometrics. (2011). *Eliminating the State Income Tax in Oklahoma: An Economic Assessment.* Report prepared for the Oklahoma Council of Public Affairs.

Birnbaum, J.H., and Murray, A.S. (1987). *Showdown at Gucci Gulch: Lawmakers, Lobbyists, and the Unlikely Triumph of Tax Reform*. New York: Random House.

Boortz, N., and Linder, J. (2005). *The FairTax Book*. New York: HarperCollins.

Boortz, N., and Linder, J. (2008). *Fair Tax: The Truth: Answering the Critics*. New York: HarperCollins.

Bourdeaux, C. (2010). *A Review of State Tax Reform Efforts*, Technical Report 216. Fiscal Research Center, Andrew Young School of Policy Studies, Georgia State University.

Brooks, D. (2012). America Is Europe. *New York Times*, February 24, *p.* A27.

Bruce, D., Fox, W.F., and Luna, L. (2009). *State and Local Government Sales Tax Revenue Losses from Electronic Commerce*. University of Tennessee. Available at http://cber.bus.utk.edu/ecomm/ecom0409.pdf.

Brunori, D. (1998). State Personal Income Taxation in the Twenty-First Century. In *The Future of State Taxation*, ed. D. Brunori. Washington, DC: The Urban Institute Press.

Bucks, D.R. (1995). Federal Tax Restructuring: Perils and Possibilities for States. *State Tax Notes*, 9, 415.

Buschman, R. (2010). *A Review of State Revenue Actions, 1999–2010*. FRC Report 217. Atlanta, GA: Fiscal Research Center, Georgia State University.

Buschman, R., and Sjoquist, D.L. (2012). Recent State Legislative Tax Changes in the Face of Economic Recession. *State Tax Notes*, 63, 623–630.

Chernick, H. (1997). Tax Progressivity and State Economic Performance. *Economic Development Quarterly*, 11, 249–267.

Chernick, H. (2010). Redistribution at the State and Local Level: Consequences for Economic Growth. *Public Finance Review*, 38, 409–449.

Cole, R.L., and Kincaid, J. (2006). Public Opinion on U.S. Federal and Intergovernmental Issues in 2006: Continuity and Change. *Publius: The Journal of Federalism*, 36, 443–459.

Comptroller General of the United States. (1982, July 1). *Report to the Chairman, House Committee on Ways and Means, Key Issues Affecting State Taxation of Multijurisdictional Corporate Income Need Resolving*. Washington, DC: U.S. General Accounting Office.

Conway, K.S., and Rork, J.C. (2012). No Country for Old Men (or Women)—Do State Tax Policies Drive Away the Elderly? *National Tax Journal*, 65, 313–356.

Cordes, J.J., and Juffras, J.N. (2012). State Personal Income Taxes. In *The Oxford Handbook of State and Local Government Finance*, ed. R.D. Ebel and J.E. Peterson. New York: Oxford University Press.

Cornia, G.C., Edmiston, K.D., Sjoquist, D.L., and Wallace, S. (2005). The Disappearing State Corporate Income Tax. *National Tax Journal*, 68, 115–138.

Cornia, G.C., and Walters, L.C. (1997). The Implications of Utility and Telecommunication Deregulation on Local Finance. *State and Local Government Review*, 29, 172–187.

Deloitte and Touche. (1996). *Federal, State and Local Tax Implications of Electric Utility Industry Restructuring*. An analysis for the National Council on Competition and the Electric Industry.

Dill, J., and Weinstein, A. (2006). How to Pay for Transportation? A Survey of Public Preferences. In First International Conference on Transport Infrastructure Funding. Available at http://dspace.ucalgary.ca/bitstream/1880/44364/1/TransportPaper-Dill_Weinstein.pdf.

Due, J.F., and Mikesell, J.L. (1994). *Sales Taxation: State and Local Structure and Administration*, 2nd ed. Washington, DC: Urban Institute Press.

Edwards, B., and Wallace, S. (2004). State Income Tax Treatment of the Elderly. *Public Budgeting and Finance*, 24(2), 1–20.

Enrich, P.D. (1998). The Rise—and Perhaps the Fall—of Business Tax Incentives. In *The Future of State Taxation*, ed. D. Brunori. Washington, DC: The Urban Institute Press.

Fletcher, J.M., and Murray, M.N. (2008). What Factors Influence the Structure of the State Income Tax? *Public Finance Review*, 36, 475–496.

Fox, W.F., and Luna, L. (2002). State Corporate Tax Revenue Trends: Causes and Possible Solutions. *National Tax Journal*, 55, 491–508.

Goodspeed, T.J. (1989). A Reexamination of the User of Ability to Pay Taxes by Local Governments. *Journal of Public Economics*, 38, 319–342.

Grace, M.F., Sjoquist, D.L., and Wheeler, L. (2014). The Effect of Insurance Premium Taxes on Interstate Differences in the Size of the Property-Casualty Insurance Industry. *National Tax Journal*, 67(1), 151–181.

Graeser, L., and Maury, A. (1992). Sales Tax on Services: State Trends. In *Sales Taxation: Critical Issues in Policy and Administration*, ed. W.F. Fox. Westport, CT: Praeger.

Hall, R.E., and Rabushka, A. (2007). *The Flat Tax*, updated ed. Palo Alto, CA: Stanford University Press.

Halsey III, A. (2012). Infrastructure Projects Need Public Support, Transportation Experts Say. *Washington Post*, April 23. Available at http://www.washingtonpost.com/local/trafficandcommuting/experts-want-to-build-public-support-for-infrastructure-projects/2012/04/23/gIQAvmMXcT_story.html.

Hamilton, B. (2012a). Adios, Income Tax. *State Tax Notes*, 63, 963–967.

Hamilton, B. (2012b). Reason to Believe: An Interview with Streamlined President Russ Brubaker. *State Tax Notes*, 64, 251–255.

Hawkins, R.R., and Mikesell, J.L. (2001). Six Reasons to Hate Your Sales Tax Holiday. *State Tax Notes*, 20, 801–804.

Hellerstein, W. (1988). Florida's Sales Tax on Services. *National Tax Journal*, 41(1), 1–18.

Henchman, J. (2011). *More States Abandon Film Tax Incentives as Programs' Ineffectiveness Becomes More Apparent*. Fiscal Fact 272, The Tax Foundation.

Hildreth, W.B., Murray, M.N., and Sjoquist, D.L. (2005). Interstate Tax Uniformity and the Multistate Tax Commission. *National Tax Journal*, 58, 575–589.

Howe, E.T., and Reeb, D.J. (1999). State and Local Electric Utility Taxes: Evolutionary Taxation of Deregulating Monopoly. *American Journal of Economics and Sociology*, 58(1), 115–128.

Institute on Taxation and Economic Policy. (2012). *"High Rate" Income Tax States Are Outperforming No-Tax States: Don't Be Fooled by Junk Economics*. Washington, DC.

Iowa Department of Revenue. (2006). *Issue Paper: State Tax Policy Implications of an Aging Population*, technical report. Available at http://www.iowa.gov/tax/taxlaw/IssuePaper1-AgingPopulation.pdf.

Kenyon, D.A. (1996). A New State VAT? Lessons from New Hampshire. *National Tax Journal*, 49, 381–399.

Luna, L. (2004). Corporate Tax Avoidance Strategies and States' Efforts to Prevent Abuses. *Journal of Multistate Taxation and Incentives*, 14(2), 6–17, 46–48.

Marron, D.B. (2011, February 2). Cutting Tax Preferences Is Key to Tax Reform and Deficit Reduction. Testimony before the Senate Committee on the Budget, Urban-Brookings Tax Policy Center. Available at http://taxpolicycenter.org/UploadedPDF/1001492-Marron-Cutting-Tax-Preferences.pdf.

Mazerov, M. (2007). *State Corporate Tax Shelters and the Need for "Combined Reporting."* Center for Budget and Policy Priorities. Available at http://www.cbpp.org/cms/index.cfm?fa=view&id=777.

McGranahan, L., and Mattoon, R.H. (2012, June). *State Tax Revenue over the Business Cycle: Patterns and Policy Responses*, Chicago Fed Letter 299. Chicago: Federal Reserve Bank of Chicago.

McHugh, R. (1996). The Gross Receipts Tax. In *Taxation and Economic Development: A Blueprint for Tax Reform in Ohio*, ed. R. Bahl. Columbus, OH: Battelle Press.

McLure, C. (2000). Rethinking State and Local Reliance on the Retail Sales Tax: Should We Fix the Sales Tax or Discard It? *Brigham Young University Law Review*, 2000(1), 77–137.

McNichol, E. (2012). *State Taxes on Inherited Wealth Remain Common: 22 States Levy an Estate or Inheritance Tax*, technical report. Center on Budget and Policy Priories.

McNichol, E.C., Lav, I.J., and Llobrera, J. (2003). *States Can Retain Their Estate Taxes Even as the Federal Estate Tax Is Phased Out*, technical report. Center on Budget and Policy Priorities.

Meriwether, H., Kelly, C., and Curry, R. (1989). Texas Utility Taxes: Revenue and Regulation. In *Rethinking Texas Taxes: Final Report of the Select Committee on Tax Equity: Analysis of Tax System*, ed. B.C. Hamilton, vol. 2, pp. 275–285. Austin, Texas: Select Committee on Tax Equity.

Mikesell, J.L. (2012). The Disappearing Retail Sales Tax. *State Tax Notes*, 63, 777–791.

Miller Center of Public Affairs. (2010). Well Within Reach: America's New Transportation Agenda. Presented at David R. Goode National Transportation Policy Conference.

Neubig, T.S., Jaggi, G., and Messina, K. (2002). Excessive Taxation of Life Insurance Companies in the 50 States. *State Tax Notes*, 25, 513–524.

Oates, W.E. (1972). *Fiscal Federalism*. New York: Harcourt Brace Jovanovich.

Olin, R., and Swain, S. (2011). *Individual Income Tax Provisions in the States*, Informational Paper 4. Wisconsin Legislative Fiscal Bureau. Available at http://legis.wisconsin.gov/lfb/publications/Informational-Papers/Documents/2011/4_individual%20income%20tax%20provisions%20in%20the%20states.pdf.

Pauly, M.V. (1973). Income Distribution of a Local Public Good. *Journal of Public Economics*, 2(1), 35–58.

Pomp, R. (1998). The Future of the State Corporate Income Tax: Reflections (and Confessions) of a Tax Lawyer. In *The Future of State Taxation*, ed. D. Brunori. Washington, DC: Urban Institute Press.

Ring Jr., R.J. (1999). Consumers' Share and Producers' Share of the General Sales Tax. *National Tax Journal*, 52(1), 79–90.

Rufolo, A.M., and Kimpel, T.J. (2008). Responses to Oregon's Experiment in Road Pricing. *Transportation Research Record: Journal of the Transportation Research Board*, 2079, 1–7.

Seligman, E.R.A. (1914). *The Income Tax: A Study of the History, Theory, and Practice of Income Taxation at Home and Abroad*, 2nd ed. New York: The Macmillan Co.

Sjoquist, D.L. (2010). A Comparison of the Fiscal Structure of States with and without an Income Tax. In *State and Local Fiscal Policy "Out of the Box,"* ed. S. Wallace. Northampton, MA: Edward Elgar, pp. 67–97.

Sjoquist, D.L., Ellen, P.S., Laury, S., Almada, L., and Stoycheva, R. (2011a). *Implications of Alternate Revenue Sources for Transportation Planning*, Final Report GDOT Research Project 10-15.

Sjoquist, D.L., Stephenson, A., and Wallace, S. (2011b). The Changing Effect of Capital Gains on State Budgets. *Public Budgeting and Finance*, 31(4), 31–50.

Snell, R. (2011). *State Personal Income Taxes on Pensions and Retirement Income: Tax Year 2010*, technical report. National Conference of State Legislatures.

Substance Abuse and Mental Health Services Administration. (2011). *Results from the 2010 National Survey on Drug Use and Health: Summary of National Findings*, NSDUH Series H-41, HHS Publication (SMA) 11-4658. Rockville, MD. Available at http://www.samhsa.gov/data/NSDUH/2k10NSDUH/2k10Results.htm#Ch4.

Sundeen, M., and Reed, J.B. (2006). *Surface Transportation Funding: Options for States*, technical report. National Conference of State Legislatures.

Tannenwald, R., Shure, J., and Johnson, N. (2011). *Tax Flight Is a Myth: Higher States Taxes Bring More Revenue, Not More Migration*, technical report. Center on Budget and Policy Priorities.

U.S. Government Accountability Office. (2010). *State and Local Governments: Fiscal Pressures Could Have Implications for Future Delivery of Intergovernmental Programs*, GAO-1-899. Washington, DC.

Weisman, J. (2012). Ryan's Rise from Follower to G.O.P. Trailblazer. *New York Times*, April 28, p. 1.

Williams, E., Johnson, N., and Shure, J. (2011). *State Earned Income Tax Credits: 2010 Legislative Update*, technical report. Center on Budget and Policy Priorities.

Chapter 5

State Competition for Debt Resources

Dwight V. Denison
University of Kentucky

Robert A. Greer
University of Georgia

Contents

Introduction

It is commonly understood that the operating budgets of state and local governments are under strict requirements to be balanced. Debt may be used by state and local governments to expand the resources available to finance new construction of buildings and other tangible assets. However, debt is not a source of revenue; debt is a financial obligation that commits future taxes and fees in order to make the financial resources available in the present. The amount that a government can borrow is restricted by the jurisdiction's capacity to repay the liability, which depends upon the property and income wealth of the citizens that reside in the jurisdiction. Property values, sales transactions, and aggregate income are the three major tax bases utilized by state and local governments. These tax bases have a limited capacity to support debt. Very often these tax bases are shared among multiple jurisdictions such as cities, school districts, counties, and special districts. As a result, these overlapping jurisdictions must compete with each other for the available debt capacity. When one jurisdiction issues debt, it reduces the amount available for other jurisdictions to borrow. In this chapter, we discuss the dynamics of intrastate competition for debt. The next section highlights some of the characteristics of the municipal bond market. Then, we examine debt capacity and affordability in the context of intrastate competition.

Markets for State and Local Debt

State and local governments issue municipal bonds to finance infrastructure used for a wide range of purposes, including education, public utilities, judicial services, hospitals, and transportation. While state and local governments may borrow money from a bank in terms of the note, loan, or mortgage, the majority of the debt held by state and local government is in the form of tax-exempt bonds. Qualifying municipal bonds are exempt from the investor's taxable income, and therefore offer lower interest rates. Of the $434.2 billion of debt issued by state and local governments in 2010, about 13 percent was issued by states, 20 percent was issued by cities and counties, and the remaining 67 percent was issued by special districts and authorities.[*] The volume of outstanding state and local debt exceeded $2.8 trillion in 2010.[†]

Municipal bonds are issued as general obligation debt or revenue-backed debt. General obligation (GO) bonds are backed by the full faith and credit of the issuing government, which means the general tax revenues of the government

[*] Board of Governors of the Federal Reserve System, statistical supplement to the Federal Reserve Bulletin, monthly, May 6, 2013. Based on percentage calculations of lines 4–6. Available at http://www.federalreserve.gov/econresdata/releases/govsecure/current.htm.

[†] Board of Governors of the Federal Reserve System, statistical supplement to the Federal Reserve Bulletin, monthly, May 6, 2013.

are obligated to pay the bonds. Revenue-backed debt, or nonguaranteed debt, is supported from dedicated fees or other earmarked sources of revenue. GO bonds are most subject to intrajurisdictional competition, because the backing for these bonds comes from a shared tax. Still, the bond market generally considers revenue bonds to be a moral obligation of the issuing jurisdiction; that is, shortfalls in the pledged revenues may be fulfilled through general revenue sources. This moral obligation contributes indirectly to the competition for debt among overlapping jurisdictions. Leased-backed bonds represent a type of revenue bond, but they are different in that the pledged revenues are future appropriations through the general fund or other tax revenues. For this reason, leased-backed bonds induce more intrajurisdictional competition than a typical revenue bond. Even the fees pledged for a generic revenue bond may be influenced by the actions of overlapping jurisdictions because such jurisdictions share a common population and income base.

Constraints on Debt Financing

There are various constraints that are placed on state and local government debt that dictate the amount and characteristics of debt that can be issued. States can institute constitutional debt limits that restrict the amount that can be issued by these governments. One estimate by the National Association of State Treasurers (2001) finds that 27 states have some combination of constitutional or statutory limitations on general obligation debt. In contrast, only four states restrict revenue or nonguaranteed debt. Hackbart et al. (2004) identify 14 states as having "umbrella policies," which encompass both GO and nonguaranteed debt. States can also impose taxation and expenditure limits on local governments, which then indirectly limits the amount of GO debt those local governments can issue.

Governments can also have indirect or informal debt limitations. The informal debt limitation is not established through law, but is determined by the amount of debt a jurisdiction may issue without altering its credit rating. Thus, informal debt limits are determined by credit quality of the jurisdiction and the bond markets. These market-driven constraints are referred to as the debt affordability or debt capacity of a government. Debt affordability and capacity are related, but distinct, terms. *Debt affordability* is defined as the amount of debt that any one government can financially support. *Debt capacity* is more specifically defined as the level of debt or debt service relative to current revenues that an issuing entity could support without creating undue budgetary constraints that might impair the issuer's ability to repay outstanding bonds or make timely debt service payments (Denison and Hackbart 2006). Another practical approach to limiting and managing debt levels is the use of "rules of thumb" that might include setting ceilings on debt service payments as a percentage of state government expenditures, total debt per capita, or other level of debt or debt service ratios.

While it is generally agreed upon that debt affordability and debt capacity are important factors in debt management, there is little consensus on how to measure affordability. There is no clear standard for making judgments about the specific amount of debt that is affordable for a jurisdiction. To this end, there have been some attempts to provide a more concrete structure for the analysis of debt affordability. Brecher et al. (2003) identify several steps to measure affordability of state debt. They start by identifying the amount of long-term debt and then adjust that figure to include unfunded pension liabilities. Then they recommend identifying resources available to repay debt, including taxes, fees, and intergovernmental transfers. By comparing the ratio of adjusted debt to total resources, governments can identify a range within which most jurisdictions fall. They recommend that governments participating in debt markets regularly monitor their ratio and range.

The last step may be the most challenging because it calls for predicting possible economic downturns, and their impact. Hildreth and Miller (2002) argue that debt affordability depends on factors of economic concentration in revenue sources and *inter*jurisdictional coordination. They posit that resource bases are at risk of being drawn upon by multiple jurisdictions. According to their framework, the ability to repay debt burdens with balanced revenue resources is significantly different than the ability to repay with concentrated revenue sources when overlapping jurisdictions are competing with each other. In the case of a concentrated tax base and competing jurisdictions, whoever issues first will get the best deal.

Empirically there has been little research to test theories of debt affordability or capacity. Martell's 2007 study is an exception that examines the effect of jurisdictional overlap, specifically the effect of special districts, on county debt affordability. The study investigates Jefferson County, Colorado, and finds that the number of overlapping jurisdictions is negatively related to various levels of debt. This would suggest that the number of overlapping jurisdictions may not be a concern for local governments in regard to debt affordability. Martell (2007) did find that the type of overlapping jurisdictions did matter, and that metropolitan districts yielded much greater debt burdens relative to municipal governments.

The bond referendum is a common restriction on general obligation bond issues requiring new bond issues to receive voter approval. A bond referendum may have the same effect as a debt limit if citizens vote down bond issues that exceed the public's notion of acceptable debt levels.

Government jurisdictions face restrictions in the amount of debt that can be issued as a result of formal (legal) debt policies, informal administrative rules, and fiscal constraints of debt affordability. These constraints can lead to competition among departments within a single government, between different government entities, and throughout various levels of government. These departments and governments compete over the ability to issue debt, the amount they can issue, and the interest rates they receive on that debt. Bond referendum laws and debt limits, both formal and informal, restrict the amount of debt that can be issued and create a scarcity in debt financing. This scarcity results in a competition for debt resources.

The Nature of Debt Competition

There are four ways debt competition can manifest itself within state governments. State governments can compete with each other to issue debt, which is called interstate debt competition. State agencies within a single state government can compete with each other in interagency debt competition. A state government can compete with local governments within the state, or various levels of local governments can compete with each other in intrastate vertical debt competition. Finally, local governments of the same or similar type can compete with each other in intrastate horizontal debt competition.

Interstate Debt Competition

Interstate competition is the competition among state governments issuing debt. State governments generally issue large amounts of tax-exempt debt, and so when they enter the market the supply of tax-exempt debt increases significantly. This is especially true for large governments such as California, Texas, and New York. When state governments issue a large amount of high-quality tax-exempt bonds, then the market gets flooded with bonds available for sale. This increase in debt supply results in a decrease in the price of the bonds, which is observed through higher bond interest costs. Figure 5.1 shows the total amount of debt outstanding for the three most populous states: California, Texas, and New York. Combined, these three states make up roughly 30 percent of total state debt outstanding.

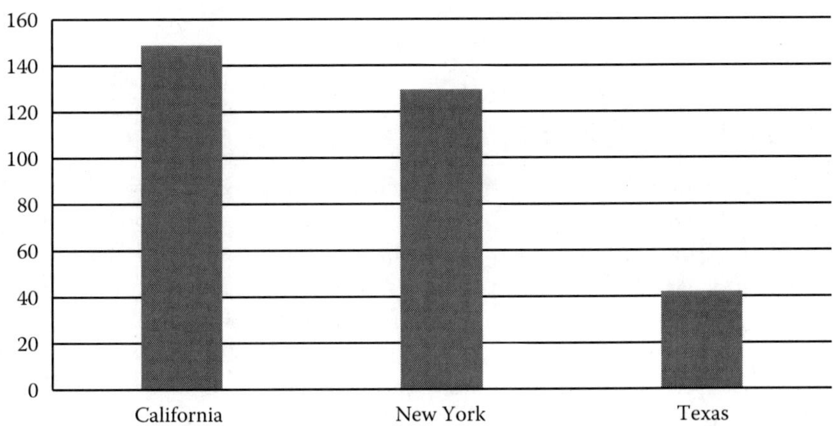

Figure 5.1 Debt outstanding for the three most populous states (in billions). (From U.S. Census Bureau, State and Local Government Finances, http://www.census.gov/govs/local [accessed May 8, 2013].)

Interagency Debt Competition

The second type of debt competition is between departments or agencies within a single state government. In states with balanced budget requirements and binding limits on the amount of state debt that can be issued, policy makers are forced to choose among several types of budgetary trade-offs.

One trade-off is among a variety of agencies that may have different infrastructure needs. Both state tax revenues and new debt resources can be used to acquire capital assets in a given year. However, taxes are generated each year, while debt issued is a liability that carries over into future fiscal periods. Therefore, debt needs to be managed on two dimensions in regard to debt capacity and competition. The first dimension is the accumulated debt balances issued for various purposes in the past, and the second dimension is the annual amount of debt that is newly issued for various purposes. Debt limit policies and financial constraints will restrain the amount of debt a state and its composite agencies may issue, thereby forcing competition for available bond capacity. The debt issuance allocation process can produce winners and losers among those agencies competing for available credit.

Denison et al. (2009) report that trade-offs for debt resources occur between the highway debt and other state debt in those states with formal umbrella debt policies. In states without umbrella debt limits there is not intrastate competition among the highway debt and all other state debt. Instead, the relationship is complementary in that increases in all other debt lead to dramatic increases in highway debt. It appears that the intensity of the intrastate competition for debt resources depends on the amount of debt "slack" available to the state, and whether binding debt limits are on both general obligation and revenue bonds. The states that decreased their overall debt show the most evidence of intrastate competition for the remaining debt resources (Denison et al. 2009).

Intrastate Vertical Debt Competition

The third type of debt competition is vertical competition between state and affiliated local governments. This type of debt is the most complicated, given that jurisdictions overlap. Overlapping jurisdictions describes two governments that are providing services to and levying taxes on a shared geographic area. This is relevant for debt management because as one government issues general obligation debt, it obligates future tax revenues. If the issuing government shares the tax base in part or entirely with another government, then the second government to issue debt may face a higher default risk and interest costs. This creates a debt competition scenario where governments compete on timing and issue size of their debt in the pursuit of the most favorable municipal interest costs.

Vertical debt competition can occur among various levels of state and local governments. One key factor in vertical debt competition is whether the state's

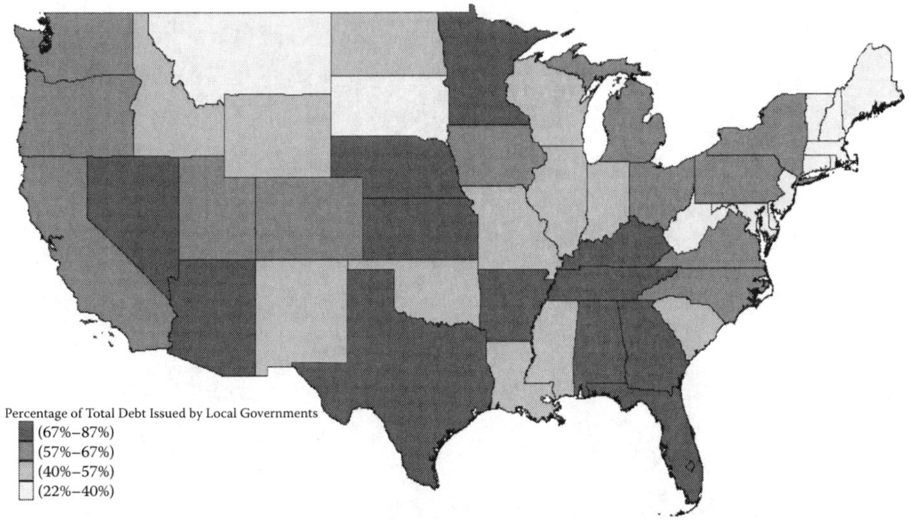

Figure 5.2 Local proportion of aggregate state and local debt. (Authors' calculations using data from U.S. Census Bureau, State and Local Government Finance, http://www.census.gov/govs/local [accessed May 8, 2013].)

debt issuance process is centralized or decentralized. Some states issue the majority of total debt at the state level and pass funds through to local governments, while other states issue relatively little at the state level and allow their local governments to issue debt as needed. The map in Figure 5.2 shows a breakdown by state of the percentage of total state and local debt issued by local governments in 2009. In 2009, Rhode Island had the lowest percentage of debt issued by its local governments at around 22 percent. Tennessee had the highest with 87 percent. In general, the map shows that southern states tend to have higher proportions of government debt issued at the local level than northeastern states.

Vertical debt competition can also manifest between different levels of local governments. As an example of vertical debt competition among local governments, Figure 5.3 is a map of Denton County, Texas, a north-central Texas county that is about 45 minutes north of the Dallas–Fort Worth metro area. Figure 5.2 is outlined by the Denton Country border visualized with a thick grey border. Census places (towns, cities, etc.) are the shaded areas outlined by the thin black border. The shading is only for visualization purposes. Independent school district borders are outlined with a thick grey border and not shaded. In Texas, school districts and counties do not have coterminous boundaries. This map illustrates the complexity of overlapping government jurisdictions that typically can be seen across the United States.

Table 5.1 is a list from a recent Denton County bond issue with all of the overlapping jurisdictions and their tax rates for the county. In total, Denton County has 34 overlapping cities, 17 overlapping school districts, and 17 overlapping special

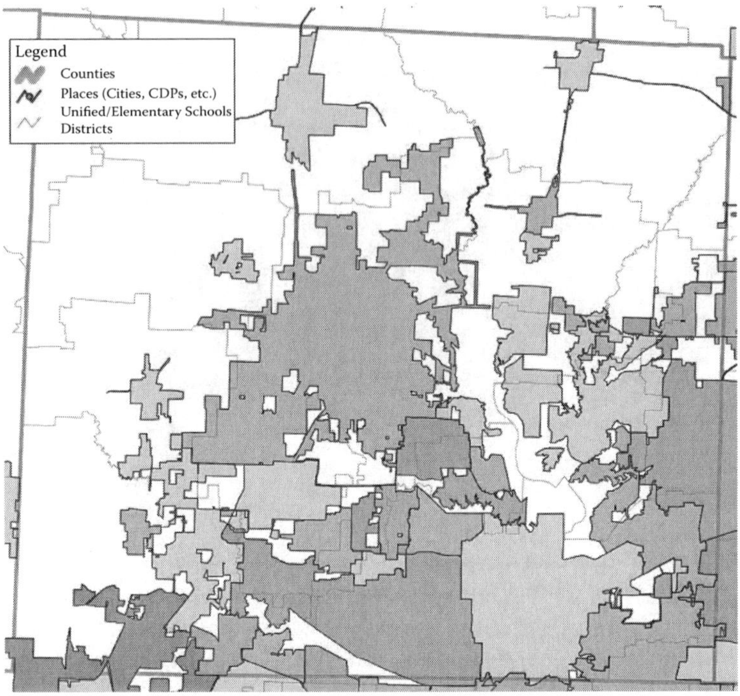

Figure 5.3 Denton County, Texas, and overlapping jurisdictions. (From U.S. Census Bureau, On The Map, http://onthemap.ces.census.gov [accessed May 8, 2013].)

districts for a total of $4.4 billion in direct and overlapping debt principal. Thus, if one city issues $10 million worth of general obligation debt and an overlapping school district issues another $10 million worth of tax-supported debt, then should Denton County attempt to issue debt, the county tax base would already be leveraged for $20 million in tax-supported bonds. Buyers in the municipal bond market will expect higher interest returns as compensation for the higher financial risk, given the leveraged tax base. Of course, higher interest returns to the bond buyers means higher interest costs for the bond issuer.

The 2010 bond offering statement for Denton County in Table 5.1 shows that in total there are 68 local government entities that share a portion of the tax base. In the aggregate, these overlapping local governments have about $4.4 billion worth of outstanding debt. In contrast, the county has about $513 million worth of its own outstanding debt. All told, Denton County has $6,907 per capita in direct and overlapping outstanding debt. This total amount is not transparent, and in fact, citizens may be unaware of their total debt burden. Denton County is not a unique government in the number of overlapping school districts and special districts. Such "stacking" of local governments with debt issuing authority likely results in nontransparent total debt burdens across the country.

Table 5.1 Denton County Official Bond Statement

Taxing Entity	*As of*	*2009 Tax Rate*	*Net Debt Principal Outstanding*	*Percent Overlapping Denton County*	*Amount Overlapping Denton County*
Cities					
Carrollton	2/28/2010	0.6178	165,285,000	49.69%	82,130,117
Frisco	1/9/2009	0.465	274,045,194	35.63%	97,642,303
Lewisville	9/30/2009	0.4402	106,190,000	99.22%	105,361,718
Flower Mound	9/30/2009	0.4497	124,900,000	100.00%	124,900,000
Denton	9/30/2009	0.6665	141,580,000	100.00%	141,580,000
Other cities					326,594,781
School Districts					
Little Elm ISD	9/30/2009	1.54	136,313,148	100.00%	136,313,148
Northwest ISD	9/30/2009	1.355	512,158,638	43.40%	222,276,849
Frisco ISD	9/30/2009	1.39	1,144,315,745	26.71%	305,646,736
Denton ISD	9/30/2009	1.49	626,713,437	100.00%	626,713,437
Lewisville ISD	11/30/2009	1.4087	994,835,121	100.00%	994,835,121
Other school districts					429,009,522

Continued

Table 5.1 (*Continued*) Denton County Official Bond Statement

Taxing Entity	*As of*	*2009 Tax Rate*	*Net Debt Principal Outstanding*	*Percent Overlapping Denton County*	*Amount Overlapping Denton County*
Special Districts					
Denton FWSD 1E	9/30/2009	0.9	25,000,000	100.00%	25,000,000
Denton FWSD 1D	9/30/2009	0.9	27,975,000	100.00%	27,975,000
Denton Co. FWSD 9	9/30/2009	1	28,125,000	100.00%	28,125,000
Denton Co. FWSD 10	9/30/2009	1	33,590,000	100.00%	33,590,000
Denton FWSD 6	9/30/2009	1	60,574,983	100.00%	60,574,983
Other special districts					115,187,780
Total gross overlapping principal					3,883,456,495
Denton County		0.2498	513,080,733	100%	513,080,733
Total direct and overlapping principal					4,396,537,228
Ratio of direct and overlapping debt principal to 2009 net taxable value					8.24%
Total direct and overlapping debt principal per capita					6,907

Source: Denton County Bond Counsel, Preliminary Office Statement, CUSIP Prefix 248775, June 1, 2010.

Note: ISD, Independent School District; FWSD, Fresh Water Supply District.

There are several different approaches for analyzing overlapping debt issues. One approach is to consider the magnitude of the competition by counting the number of overlapping jurisdictions in a defined area. For example, a county with two subsumed cities has two jurisdictions that are sources of competition. Denton County has 68 units of competition, the total of its cities and school and special districts. A second approach is to count the number of securities that have been issued among the aggregate jurisdictions. In the prior example, if one of the cities had issued two different bond series, then the county may have been more concerned with the fact that there were three bond issues rather than issues by two governments. The third approach, and perhaps most meaningful, is concerned with the total amount of debt that has been issued by all overlapping governments—this method is less interested in the number of governments or bond issues.

Overlapping debt and jurisdictional relationships can be more clearly seen if we compare the ratio of debt to personal income and interest costs paid as a percentage of total expenditures. In Figure 5.4, this relationship shows that on average as the level of debt increases, interest costs increase. This relationship is also important for overlapping jurisdictions because an overlapping government can increase the level of debt per personal income, and thus increase another government's interest costs. For example, in the Denton County example, if the City of Denton issues additional debt, the county's debt per personal income ratio will increase and the county's interest costs will increase as well.

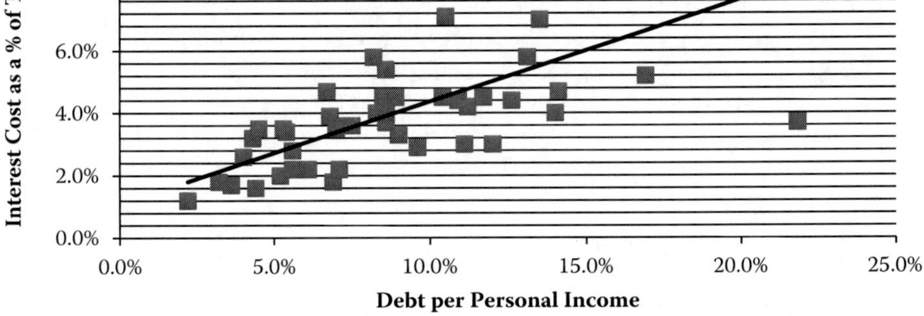

Figure 5.4 Relationship between level of debt and interest costs. (Authors' calculations using data from Annual Survey of State Government Finances 2011, http://www.census.gov/govs/state [accessed September 30, 2012].)

Figure 5.4 plots the relationship of the ratio of debt per personal income (PI) to interest costs as a percentage of total expenditures (TE) for all 50 American state governments. As shown, there is a positive relationship ($R^2 = 0.56$), indicating that debt per personal income explains 56 percent of the variance in interest costs as a percentage of total expenditures. If we look at several other specific examples from these data, we note that California presents a debt-to-PI ratio of 8.6 percent and interest as a percentage of TE of 5.4 percent. New York indicates a debt-to-PI ratio of 13.5 percent and interest as a percentage of TE of 8.0 percent. An outlier is Alaska, with a debt-to-PI ratio of 21.8 and interest as a percentage of TE of just 3.7 percent. On average, a ratio of debt to PI of 10.0 percent results in an interest cost as a percentage of TE of 4.3 percent. Increasing the debt ratio to 15.0 percent increases the interest cost percentage to 6.0 percent.

Horizontal Debt Competition

The fourth type of debt competition is horizontal competition across local governments. This competition is similar to the state-to-state competition, though in this case involves two or more local governments of the same or similar type competing to issue municipal securities. This competition can occur between local governments that share a border or between local governments that are similar in their socioeconomic makeup. For example, cities may compete for debt if they share common risk factors resulting from attributes such as similar population and industry composition.

Conceptualizing horizontal competition can take advantage of the well-known tax competition literature. Tax competition among local governments has its roots in Tiebout (1956), who hypothesized that residents would sort themselves into different local governments based on their preferences for public goods and services and the associated tax costs accorded to them. Since residents are mobile, and jurisdictions compete for those residents, competition results in a type of sorting of citizens into municipalities that offer a mix of goods and services to match citizen preferences. The result will be tax structures that represent those preferences, and those tax structures then dictate the debt capacity and affordability of the local government. Thus, debt competition is inherently tied to tax competition among local governments.

Consequences of Intrastate Debt Competition

Excessive intrastate competition among state and local governments may produce several adverse effects. One outcome is that excessive competition may result in a shortage of debt capacity available to the other jurisdictions desiring to issue debt. As previously discussed, the jurisdiction that issues bonds first will have the advantage in terms of reduced credit risk and interest costs. The incentive for jurisdictions that issue bonds first will be to maximize the size of the bond issues in order to lock in debt at lower interest rates. Without coordination, competing jurisdictions may find that the available debt capacity gets used to support very parochial interests without consideration of the holistic priorities of the area.

Intrastate debt competition influences interest rates primarily from the supply perspective. The supply of bonds in the markets is influenced by both horizontal and vertical competition, and the increase in bond supply will put downward pressure on bond prices and drive up interest rates.

Also, fragmented financial reporting of debt obligations of overlapping jurisdictions may reduce the public transparency of the overall debt burden. Referring back to Table 5.1, note that Denton County has just over $513 million in outstanding direct debt. Since Denton County has a population of around 636,000, the direct debt per capita is $806 per person. However, debt per capita for the county dramatically underestimates the real debt burden to residents since the total direct and overlapping debt is $6,907 per capita. Lack of transparency may lead to excessive debt (and tax) burdens. Acknowledging this problem, the Governmental Accounting Standards Board (GASB) issued Statement 44, which requires the statistical section of a government's comprehensive annual financial report to include information about direct and overlapping debt related to governmental activities. In addition, GASB Statement 44 requires 10 years of debt ratios expressed as two ratios: (1) total outstanding debt to personal income and (2) total debt per capita (Gauthier 2004). On the other hand, under generally accepted accounting principles (GAAP) it is not mandatory to disclose the statistical section of the financial report, though presentation of these data by state and local governments is encouraged by GASB.

Management Strategies for Intrastate Debt Competition

One method for managing the externalities associated with intrastate debt competition is to centralize debt management services. Generally, centralized debt management occurs at the state level through a dedicated agency that monitors debt issued by the state and its local governments and ensures that debt policies are followed. Centralized debt management requires jurisdictions and public authority boards to submit their debt request to a central office. Each request for debt finance essentially competes against the others based on economic and political merits. Centralized management may increase the competition among the various requests, but helps ensure that available debt capacity is used for the greatest needs or priorities across the state.

An example of this centralized debt management is the Local Government Commission in North Carolina. The Local Government Commission is a division of the Office of the State Treasurer established in 1931 in response to the

Great Depression as a way to control the debt issued by cities and counties in North Carolina. The commission reviews and authorizes local government requests for bond issues and generally issues the bonds on behalf of the local government. Furthermore, the commission provides oversight of financial audits and monitors the fiscal health of the local government in North Carolina.*

Bond banks are another strategy for managing intrastate debt competition. A bond bank periodically issues bonds that are then loaned back to subjurisdictions based on formal requests. Indiana established a bond bank through statute in 1984. The Indiana bond bank operates as a financing conduit and purchases bonds and notes from local communities throughout the state. These local bonds and notes are bundled and issued to the bond markets as a debt obligation of Indiana. The local jurisdictions benefit from savings achieved by sharing the fixed costs of bond issuance and other economies of scale.†

A final management strategy for coping with intrastate debt is through administrative coordination and memoranda of understanding. Debt coordination agreements establish priorities for debt use and provide procedures for mitigating negative competition. The Government Financial Officers Association (GFOA) recommends that state and local governments adopt comprehensive written debt management policies that reflect local, state, and federal laws and regulations. Such written debt policies can easily incorporate guidelines to reduce negative consequences of intrastate debt competition.‡

In circumstances where there is more intense intrastate debt competition, then like the prisoner's dilemma in economic theory, each jurisdiction will be motivated to act in its own self-interest, producing a suboptimal outcome for the region.§ The only way to optimize the total benefit to society is for the competing jurisdictions to coordinate and cooperate according to overarching priorities. These overarching priorities may be established through a benevolent dictator, that is, centralized state agency, or through negotiation among the various jurisdictions to establish the objectives through compacts or agreements.

---

* "About the Local Government Commission," available at http://www.nctreasurer.com/slg/Pages/Local-Government-Commission.aspx (accessed May 13, 2013).

† "Indiana Bond Bank-General Information," available at http://www.in.gov/tos/bond/2411.htm (accessed May 5, 2013).

‡ See "Government Financial Officers Association Best Practices: Debt Management Policy," available at http://www.gfoa.org/index.php?option=com_content&task=view&id=1573 (accessed May 5, 2013).

§ The prisoner's dilemma has two partners in crime being questioned in separate rooms. If one prisoner confesses and the other does not, then the confessor gets a 6-month prison term but the other gets 10 years. If both confess, then both get a three-year sentence. If neither confesses, then they each get two years. In the absence of communication, both prisoners will generally confess, producing an outcome less desirable than if both did not confess. (See Nicholson 1992, 625.)

The sluggish economy and meager tax collections since the end of the Great Recession have pressured state and local governments to issue more debt in recent years. As the aggregate debt burden of these overlapping jurisdictions increases, the competition for debt intensifies among overlapping jurisdictions. It is important for public managers and policy makers to better understand the nature of intrastate competition and the repercussions of acute competition on interest costs and access to the bond market. Strategies to mitigate the negative effects of debt competition should be considered and implemented. The magnitude of state and local debt is not likely to diminish quickly, so intrastate debt competition will remain relevant even after the economy recovers and tax revenues begin to grow.

References

Brecher, C., Richwerger, K., and Van Wagner, M. (2003). An Approach to Measuring the Affordability of State Debt. *Public Budgeting and Finance*, 23(4), 65–85.

Denison, D.V., and Hackbart, M. (2006). State Debt Capacity and Debt Limits: Theory and Practice. In *Public Financial Management*, ed. H. Frank. New York: Marcel-Dekker, pp. 315–336.

Denison, D.V., Hackbart, M.M., and Moody, M.J. (2009). Intrastate Competition for Debt Resources. *Public Finance Review*, 37(3), 269–288.

Gauthier, S.J. (2004). Major Changes to CAFR Statistical Section: GASB Statement No. 44 Will Significantly Modify the Statistical Section of the Comprehensive Financial Report, with the Aim of Providing a Broader Focus, Improving Comparability, and Encompassing Accrual-Based Data. Free Library. Available at http://www.thefreelibrary.com/MajorchangestoCAFRstatisticalsection:GASBstatementno.44will...-a0121134021.

Hackbart, M., Sapp, S.P., and Hur, Y. (2004). *Debt Capacity and Debt Limits: A State Road Fund Perspective*, technical report. Kentucky Transportation Center, College of Engineering, University of Kentucky.

Hildreth, W.B., and Miller, G.J. (2002). Debt and the Local Economy: Problems in Benchmarking Local Government Debt Affordability. *Public Budgeting and Finance*, 22(4), 99–113.

Martell, C.R. (2007). Debt Burdens of Overlapping Jurisdictions. *Municipal Finance Journal*, 28(2), 1–23.

National Association of State Treasurers. (2001). *State Treasury Activities and Functions*. Lexington, KY.

Nicholson, W. (1992). *Microeconomic Theory*, 5th ed. New York: Dryden Press.

Tiebout, C.M. (1956). A Pure Theory of Local Expenditures. *Journal of Political Economy*, 64(5), 416–424.

Chapter 6

State Debt Management Challenges

Merl Hackbart and Dwight V. Denison

University of Kentucky

Contents

Introduction

The increased use of debt financing at all levels of government and the consequent accumulation of outstanding indebtedness has raised questions about the ability of governments to effectively manage their debt levels and debt-related processes. While public concerns have principally focused on debt levels, state and local government debt management concerns have emerged regarding other debt policy issues, such as the appropriate role of debt financing, the purpose for which bonds are issued, bond structures, credit enhancements, bond issuing strategies and processes, as well as debt policy issues and concerns. Also, while the federal government's debt accumulation has received the majority of public attention, the increase in state and local debt outstanding has also been noted by citizens, public officials, the rating agencies, and the media (Bahl and Duncombe 1993).

In contrast to the federal government's history of using bond issuance to finance budget deficits, state and local governments have traditionally relied on debt financing for capital and infrastructure investment. Consequently, in their efforts to meet the demand for new infrastructure and the growing need to maintain the existing facilities, state and local governments' debt outstanding has increased in recent decades, although not at the rate experienced by the federal government. Still, concerns have arisen whether state and local governments have established and followed debt management policies that will assure the sustainability of debt levels and provide access to capital markets in an efficient manner and at the least cost.

Therefore, in addition to concerns about debt levels, state and local governments and issuing authorities face a multiplicity of debt policy issues. They have to establish policies about the role of debt financing in their capital budgeting process, the types of capital expenditures that should be financed by bond issues, the types of bonds to be issued, and how to structure the bonds and the debt service pledges so that credit ratings are preserved while complying with self-imposed debt limits. Meanwhile, new debt management and debt policy issues continue to emerge. For example, some states are issuing bonds to finance the unfunded liabilities of pension plans (Peng 2013, 311), and in rare situations, states have followed the federal government's lead in using debt financing to fund current services budgets. Such emerging debt issues expand the set of debt management challenges of state and local governments.

This chapter reviews the debt positions of the U.S. federal, state, and local governments and then considers the debt management challenges faced by states. In doing so, it suggests grouping state debt management issues into three areas: debt policy issues, debt stock and flow issues, and processes of debt issuance. Given that the main goal of state debt management is to monitor and manage the stock of debt obligations so as to insure financial sustainability and provide investment capital at the least possible cost, several debt management policies and decisions play a role in meeting that goal. While the management of the stock of debt is a major public concern, active debt management also includes other initiatives, such as (1) identifying capital and infrastructure needs and priorities, (2) actively monitoring the debt stock to identify opportunities to reduce the cost of carrying the stock, and (3) insuring that new issues are structured in a manner that reflects changes in market conditions and permits the acquisition of new capital at the lowest possible capital cost subject to risk tolerances and debt limits.

Use of Debt Financing

As noted, the use of debt financing differs by level of government. Bonds issued by the federal government are principally used to finance current services and raise funds for fiscal policy or economic stimulus initiatives. Meanwhile, bonds issued by state and local governments are primarily used to finance infrastructure and capital projects. Also, in contrast to the federal government, state and local governments maintain both operating and capital budgets. The state and local capital budgeting process involves assessing needs for capital investments such as highways, schools, and buildings, as well as other facilities needed to provide public services and support economic development. The capital budgeting process also involves the setting of priorities and identifying funding sources. Although funding of the capital budget may involve current revenue and intergovernmental funds (particularly for transportation funding from the Federal Highway Trust Fund), increasingly, capital budgets authorize the sale of bonds to finance capital or infrastructure facilities.

State and local government operating budgets fund current expenditures such as employee salaries, payment for services, and interest payments on debt. Current revenues, such as taxes, fees, user charges, and intergovernmental aid, finance these expenditures. Since the receipt of some state and local revenue sources may not match spending demands, state and local governments may also issue short-term debt, such as revenue and tax anticipation notes, to finance current spending. Those notes are then liquidated within the same fiscal year when revenues are received. Other debt issuance may involve the refinancing of existing bonds to take advantage of declining interest rates, and issuing tax-exempt bonds for private purpose investments such as industrial and commercial development, housing, and student loans.

The ability of state and local governments to issue bonds to subsidize and support economic development and other private purpose projects was capped by the Tax Reform Act of 1986 (Temple 1993; Lemov 1989). In that legislation, state ability to issue private purpose bonds was limited to a state per capita debt issuance allocation, which reduced the federal tax expenditure associated with tax-exempt municipal bonds (Hildreth and Zorn 2005). However, since 1986, Congress has periodically raised the state caps on private purpose bond issuance in response to natural disasters or special emergencies such as the authorization of Liberty bonds, which increased New York State's normal allotment of private purpose bonds to provide tax-exempt funds to encourage companies in the area around Ground Zero in Manhattan. Similarly, the 2008 Heartland Disaster Tax Relief Act provided assistance to 10 midwestern states hit by flooding and other weather-related disasters.

Debt Stock Overview

The focus on government debt is primarily due to the significant increase in federal debt accumulation in the last decade. As shown in Figure 6.1, by 2011, federal debt outstanding was approaching $16 trillion, with more than $12 trillion of that debt

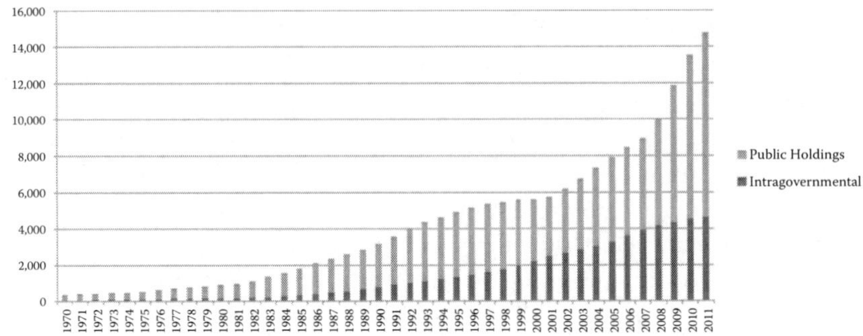

Figure 6.1 Federal debt outstanding: 1970–2011, in billions of dollars. (From U.S. Office of Management and Budget, Historical Tables, 1970–2011.)

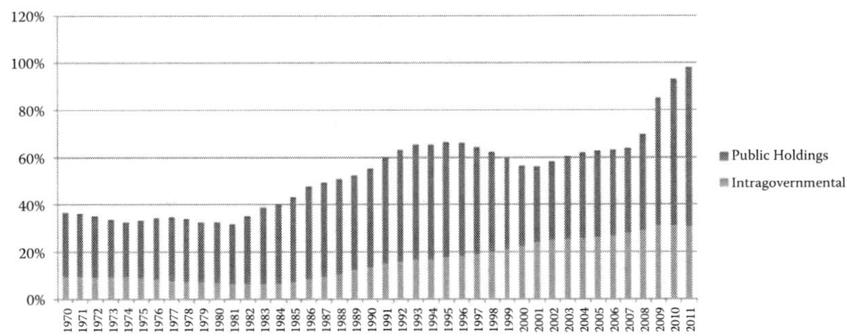

Figure 6.2 Federal debt outstanding as a percentage of GDP: 1970–2011. (From U.S. Office of Management and Budget, Historical Tables, 1970–2011; U.S. Bureau of Economic Analysis, 1970–2011.)

being held outside of the federal government and approximately $4 trillion being held internally (via intragovernmental borrowing). The growing concern about the nation's outstanding debt is also based on the fact that the accumulated federal debt was about equal to the nation's gross domestic product (GDP). This was the first time that the debt-to-GDP ratio was that high since federal debt exceeded the nation's GDP during World War II. As shown in Figure 6.2, for the period 1970 to 2011, the debt outstanding as a percentage of GDP had been in the range of 40 to 60 percent until 2009, when the ratio of debt to GDP grew rapidly and approached 100 percent in 2011.

Thus, it is understandable that citizens and public officials have expressed increasing concern about the level of outstanding debt or the federal government's debt stock. While opinions vary regarding the appropriate or acceptable ratio of outstanding debt to GDP, the fact that the ratio historically varied between 40 and 60 percent might indicate an acceptable debt stock-to-GDP ratio goal.

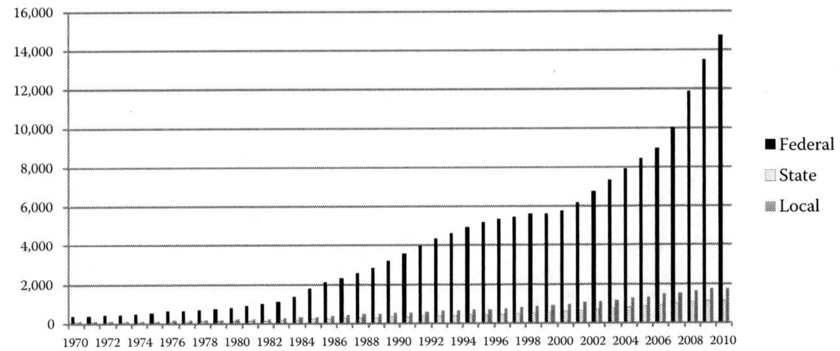

Figure 6.3 Federal, state, and local debt outstanding: 1970–2011, in billions of dollars. (From U.S. Census Bureau, State and Local Government Finances Survey, various years.)

As indicated in Figure 6.3, debt outstanding for all levels of government has grown almost continuously since 1970. The exception was a brief period in the late 1990s when federal debt levels stabilized due to the fact that the federal government balanced its budget and did not have to issue additional bonds to finance a budget deficit, as had been the case for the rest of the period. Figure 6.3 also compares the debt accumulation by the federal and state and local governments. For the period 1970 to 2011, federal debt, in nominal terms, has grown an average 9.1 percent per year, while state and local debt has grown from $882 billion in 1971 to $2.86 trillion (Table 6.1), for an average of 5.6 percent per year for the period. While state and local debt has experienced a modest, but continuous growth rate over the period, the federal government's debt growth rate accelerated in the recent decade, averaging 9.25 percent per year between 2001 and 2011. More concerning is the fact that the per year increase in federal debt was 19 percent in 2009 and 14 percent in 2010.

The more modest growth of state and local indebtedness reflects the debt issuance constraints of these governments based on constitutional, statutory, and administrative policy, coupled with the obligation that states and local governments must balance their budgets. In addition, state and local governments rarely issue bonds to finance current services or to implement economic growth-stimulating fiscal policies.

It is also noted (see Table 6.1) that although state debt has increased since 1971, state and local debt as a percent of GDP has remained relatively stable over the same period, ranging from 14 to 19 percent. The ratio of state and local debt to GDP increased by approximately 4 percentage points since 2000 due to a significant increase in new issues over this period. That increase was probably in response to historically low interest rates and an increased use of borrowing to finance capital projects due to the severe budget constraints that limited current revenue financing of needed infrastructure.

Table 6.1 State and Local Government Debt Overview

Year	*Real Total Debt (in 2011 billion dollars)*[a]	*Debt as a Percentage of GDP*	*State Share of Debt*	*Local Share of Debt*
2011	$2,863	19.0%	38.7%	61.3%
2006	$2,406	16.5%	39.5%	60.5%
2001	$1,970	15.1%	37.1%	62.9%
1996	$1,680	14.9%	38.7%	61.3%
1991	$1,510	15.3%	37.7%	62.3%
1986	$1,351	14.8%	37.6%	62.4%
1981	$901	11.6%	37.1%	62.9%
1976	$948	13.2%	35.1%	64.9%
1971	$882	14.1%	30.1%	69.6%

Source: U.S. Census Bureau, State and Local Government Finances Survey, various years; U.S. Bureau of Economic Analysis, National Income Accounts, various years.

[a] Calculated using the consumer price index (CPI) deflator, U.S. Bureau of Labor Statistics.

It is interesting that in fiscal year 2008, state and local debt outstanding as a percentage of own-source revenue was 131.2 percent, with state debt being 94 percent of own-source revenue and local government debt reported to be 176.4 percent of own-source revenue (U.S. Census Bureau 2010). It is also observed that there has been an increase in the share of total state and local debt issuance attributable to states over the period 1971 to 2011 (Table 6.1). This adjustment increased the states' issuance share from 30.1 percent in 1971 to 38.7 percent in 2011.

Investors in the State and Local Government Debt Stock

In addition to formal and informal debt constraints, state and local government debt issuance is influenced by the economy and financial markets. The relative safety of state and local government bonds and the federal income tax exclusion of interest payments on state and local bonds together create strong demand for state and local government bonds among risk-averse investors. Figure 6.4 illustrates the distribution of holders of state and local debt outstanding for select years 1980 through 2010. Individuals and mutual funds were the primary holders of state and local government debt in 2010, holding nearly 77 percent of outstanding debt. The mix of investors in 1980 is significantly different. At that time households and mutual funds comprised less than 35 percent of investors in state and local

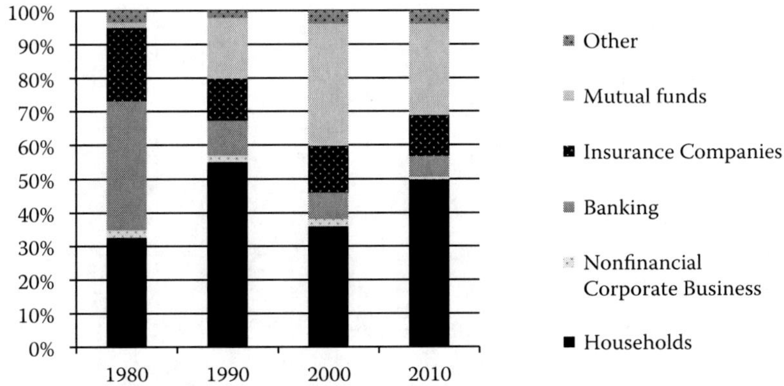

Figure 6.4 Holders of state and local government debt outstanding, 1980–2010. (From Federal Reserve Board, Flow of Funds Accounts, Table L.211.)

government debt. Banks and insurance companies held about 60 percent of state and local debt outstanding. The Tax Reform Act of 1986 altered the incentives for banks and insurance companies to hold municipal securities, and therefore their share decreased substantially to 40 percent in 1990. By 2010, this proportion had decreased to 18 percent. The decline in holdings by banks and insurance companies was offset by increased holdings by households and mutual funds.

Debt Flow Issues and Opportunities

State and local governments issue two types of bonds: general obligation (GO) bonds and revenue bonds. GO bonds or guaranteed bonds are secured by the pledge of the government's full faith, credit, and taxing power as security. The issuing government may use revenue raised from any tax or fees to repay the debt. Revenue or nonguaranteed bonds pledge revenues only from the revenue generated from the operation of the project being financed or a category of facilities, or from other nontax sources (e.g., tolls roads and bridges, dormitory fees). Investors generally perceive revenue bonds as investments carrying higher risk, and thus require higher interest rates from issuing governments.

Table 6.2 demonstrates the level of U.S. municipal bond issuance and the distribution of various characteristics of bonds issued from 1996 to 2011. Except for the significant decline in municipal bonds issued in 2011, there has been a positive trend in the level of issuance over this period. The distribution between GO and revenue bonds issued by state and local governments has been quite stable since 1996. Over the last 15 years, revenue bonds have consistently accounted for about two-thirds of new state and local bonds issued. On average, over 80 percent of municipal bonds issued over this period carry a fixed-rate coupon. Until recently,

Table 6.2 Municipal Bond Issuance and Percent of Distribution by Issuance Characteristics, 1996–2011

	Total Amount Issued (in billions of dollars)	*Bond Type*		*Coupon/Rate Type*			*Bid Type*			*New Capital/Refunding*	
Year		*General Obligation*	*Revenue*	*Fixed*	*Variable*	*Other*	*Competitive*	*Negotiated*	*Private Placement*	*New Capital*	*Refunding*
1996	$185.2	35%	65%	86%	12%	3%	25%	73%	2%	67%	33%
1997	$220.7	33%	67%	83%	14%	4%	22%	75%	3%	62%	38%
1998	$286.8	33%	67%	87%	10%	3%	23%	75%	2%	56%	44%
1999	$227.5	31%	69%	82%	13%	5%	23%	73%	4%	69%	31%
2000	$200.9	33%	67%	73%	20%	7%	24%	73%	3%	82%	18%
2001	$287.7	35%	65%	79%	15%	5%	22%	77%	1%	69%	31%
2002	$357.5	35%	65%	77%	15%	8%	20%	79%	1%	66%	34%
2003	$382.7	37%	63%	75%	13%	11%	20%	79%	1%	69%	31%
2004	$359.7	36%	64%	73%	15%	13%	19%	80%	1%	64%	36%
2005	$408.2	35%	65%	75%	16%	9%	19%	81%	0%	54%	46%
2006	$386.8	30%	70%	75%	15%	10%	18%	81%	1%	66%	34%
2007	$424.5	31%	69%	75%	15%	11%	17%	82%	1%	64%	36%
2008	$386.4	29%	71%	67%	32%	1%	14%	85%	1%	53%	47%
2009	$406.8	38%	62%	88%	10%	1%	14%	85%	1%	64%	36%
2010	$430.3	34%	66%	91%	7%	3%	17%	82%	1%	65%	35%
2011	$285.2	37%	63%	87%	8%	5%	20%	77%	3%	51%	49%

Source: Securities Industry and Financial Markets Association, *U.S. Municipal Issuance*, 1996–2011, Thomson Reuters.

there has been a decline in the number of issues using a competitive bid process, with more issues coming to the market under negotiated contracts.

GO and revenue bonds require different approaches to debt management. GO bonds are backed by the wealth of the government. Government wealth is measured through the size of the tax base often on a per capita basis. The metrics used to assess GO debt capacity usually consists of ratios of outstanding general obligation debt divided by one of the three primary tax bases: assessed property value, aggregate personal income, and state GDP (Hackbart and Ramsey 1993; Hildreth et al. 2002). The metrics used to assess revenue debt capacity focus specifically on the pledged revenue source relative to the debt outstanding. In other words, GO debt capacity focuses on whether the jurisdiction has potential to increase taxes to support an increase in debt levels (a stock perspective). By contrast, revenue debt capacity focuses on whether the pledged revenues (income flow) will be sufficient to meet required debt service payments (flow perspective) (Brecher et al. 2003).

The total annual aggregate dollars of state and local debt issued is plotted in Figure 6.5 as a ratio to the aggregate total expenditures. Here, total expenditures are used as a proxy for total revenues since these jurisdictions are required to balance their operating budget. The ratio average is 0.15, which means, on average, state and local governments combined issue 15 cents in debt for every $1 in annual expenditures. The ratio values ranged between 0.11 and 0.17 for the 15-year period. While the calculated ratios include both GO and revenue debt in the numerator and total

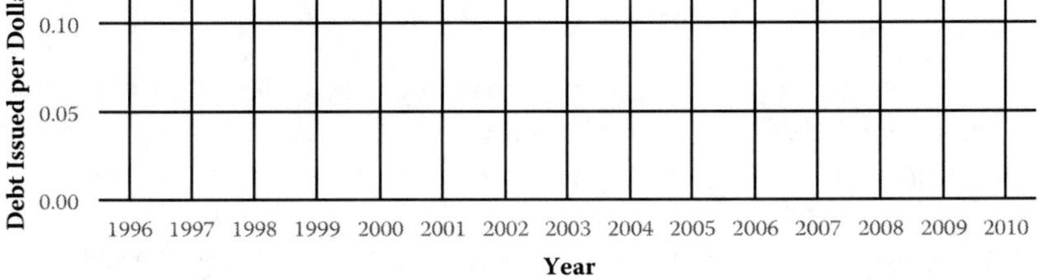

Figure 6.5 Ratio of annual aggregate dollars of state and local debt issued to total expenditures. (Authors' calculated ratio using debt data from Securities Industry and Financial Markets Association, Municipal Bond Issuance, available at http://www.sifma.org/research/statistics.aspx [accessed August 2013]; Expenditures from State and Local Finance Data Query System, Tax Policy Center, Urban Institute and Brookings Institution; Debt from Securities Industry and Financial Markets Association, U.S. Municipal Issuance, 1996–2012, Thomson Reuters.)

expenditures in the denominator, the range suggests that states and other jurisdictions are managing the flow of debt issued each year. Ideally, this ratio would compare the revenue debt to the aggregate pledged revenue, but this level of detail is not available in aggregate.

Debt Management Challenge: A State Perspective

Given the growth in state debt and the complexity of state debt issuing processes, including debt issuance purposes, debt structures, and the like, the management of the state's debt is a major financial management challenge. Included in this challenge is defining the role of debt financing in a state's overall capital investment plan, insuring that debt service commitments on existing bonds are met, and that the debt flow issues such as refinancing opportunities are pursued. Estimates of future debt capacity must be effectively provided so that such capacity can be considered in the capital planning activities of the government. Also, changes in federal laws and state statutes must be monitored for their potential impact on debt management policies and processes.

The state debt management challenge has increased in importance and complexity in recent decades due to multiple factors, including changes in the types of bonds issued, the purposes for which debt is issued, periodic changes of federal laws regarding eligibility for tax-exempt status, and the number of authorities issuing bonds for the states (Clingermayer and Wood 1995; Ellis and Schansberg 1999; Kiewiet and Szakaly 1996). In meeting state debt management challenges, it is useful to categorize debt management issues into debt policy management, debt stock and flow management, and debt issuance management. Figure 6.6 provides a schematic overview of the interaction of the four major elements of a state's debt management activities (Trautman 1995; Hackbart and Leigland 1990).

State Debt Management: The Debt Policy Role

As indicated in Figure 6.6, debt policy management provides the overall guidance for the other debt management areas. Among the critical guidelines are the state's policy regarding the use of debt financing in its capital budgeting process, information about state debt limits (Denison et al. 2006) and restrictions, guidance regarding the estimation of debt affordability as well as policy guidance regarding the need for referendum for certain issues (i.e., a GO issue), and the procedures for establishing debt issuance authorities (Ramsey and Hackbart 1996; Simonson et al. 2001). A state's debt policy is a comprehensive statement regarding the purposes for which debt may be issued, the types of bonds that can be issued, the role and responsibilities of special authorities, as well as methods of determining debt capacity. It also provides guidance for the debt issuance process, including when competitive or negotiated bonds sales may be used. The major debt policy management functions are shown in Figure 6.7.

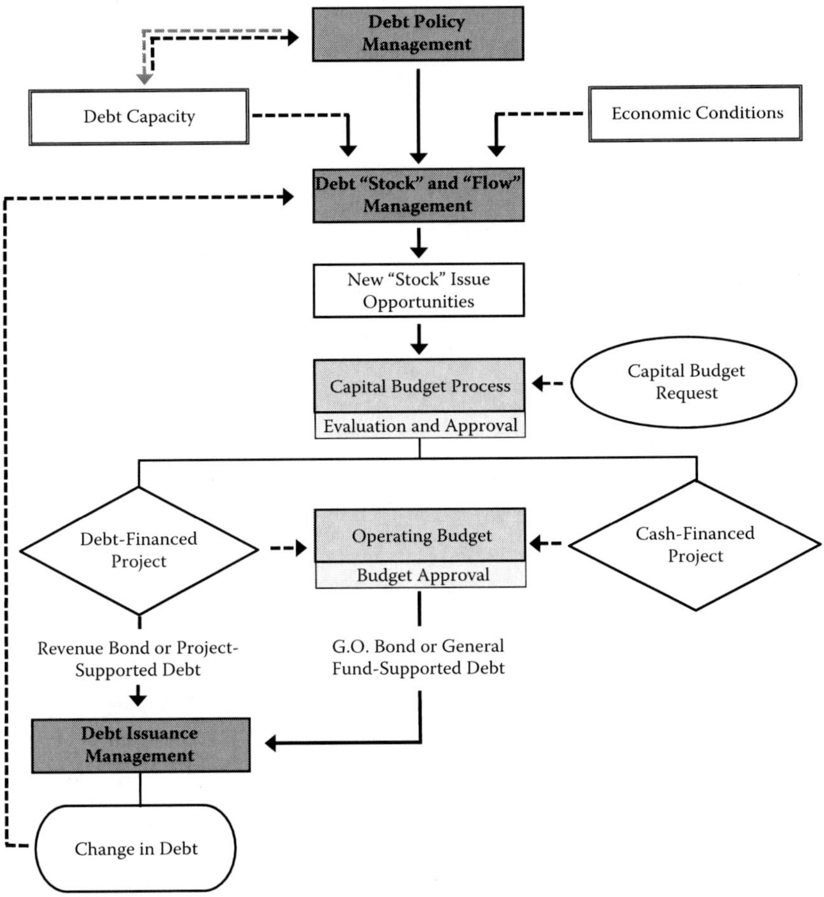

Figure 6.6 Overview of debt management issues.

State Debt Management: The Stock and Flow Management Role

The management of debt stocks and flows involves different processes and assessments that are interrelated. Debt stock management involves monitoring the existing state indebtedness by bond types (GO or revenue), indebtedness by state issuing authority, bond maturity schedules, as well as debt service obligations of the outstanding debt portfolio. By contrast, debt flow management focuses on insuring that refinancing opportunities are taken advantage of, the estimation of future debt capacity is carried out with reference to prevailing and anticipated economic and financial market conditions, and the future reductions in the debt stock due to future stock reduction as maturity dates are met. In estimating debt capacity, states often benchmark their debt levels to comparable states and may consider

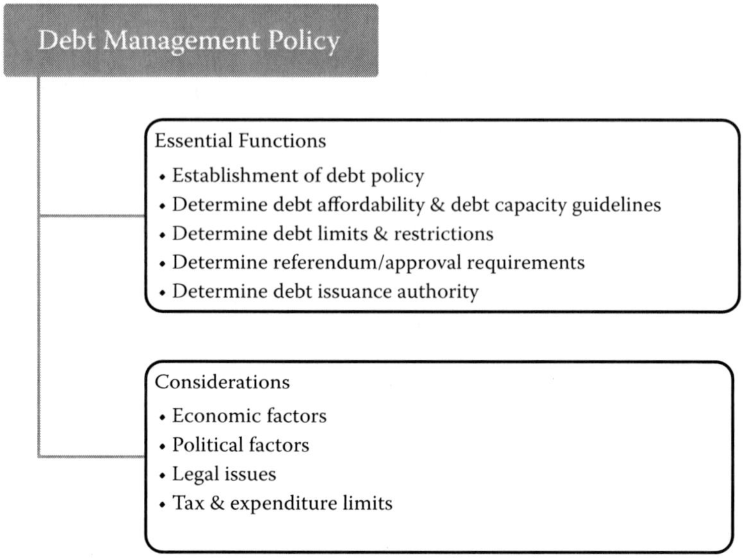

Figure 6.7 Debt management policy functions and considerations.

comparisons such as debt outstanding as a percentage of state per capita income, debt outstanding as percent of own-source revenue (e.g., taxes and fees, excluding federal transfers), and similar metrics (Bahl and Duncombe 1993).

Recent reports from the Congressional Research Service use other metrics that account for unfunded pension liabilities and assess the proportion of debt service costs to general fund expenditures.[*] The difference between estimated future debt capacity and the current debt stock provides an estimate of the "slack" debt capacity, which could be used to finance new capital needs (Marlowe et al. 2009). Such information flows into the capital budgeting process. The capital budgeting process considers capital requests, as well as options for financing those requests. Included in the funding options are direct appropriation cash funding from a state's general fund, which is typically limited to small capital projects, and the issuance of bonds, which has become the predominant funding source. When bond or debt financing is considered, capital project budget decisions focus on both the availability of debt capacity and viable debt service source, but capital budget decisions also involve assessments of the debt issuing entities' financial ability to absorb the ongoing operating and maintenance costs associated with the proposed capital project. Figure 6.8 presents essential functions and considerations related to debt stock and flow management.

[*] The Congressional Research Service reports state-by-state ratios that examine the combined total of debt outstanding and unfunded pension liabilities as a percentage of state GDP.

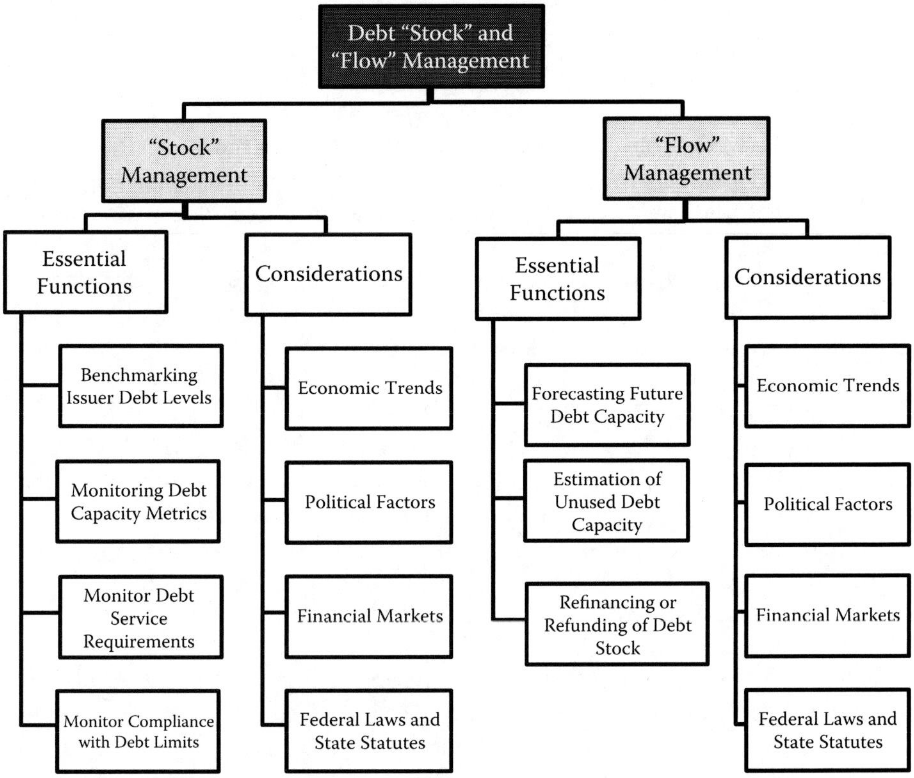

Figure 6.8 Debt stock and flow management.

State Debt Management: Bond Issuance

Debt issuance management involves a series of bond sizing, bond structuring, and financial-, legal-, and market-related decisions regarding new issues authorized for sale (Denison 2013). The sizing of an issue involves not only the cost of the proposed capital project, but also the underwriter discount and bond issuing fees and expenses. The issuer must decide whether to issue GO bonds backed by taxes or revenue bonds backed by earmarked revenues and fees. The issuer must also decide how the bond will be sold: through competitive bidding, negotiation, or private placement. While the goal of a state bond sale is to acquire capital at the lowest cost of capital, the optimal sale method to achieve that goal may depend on the complexity of the transaction, market conditions, and whether the issuer has been active in the bond market previously. While, generally, it is expected that a competitively bid sale (which is frequently required for GO bonds) may achieve a lower coupon, a negotiated sale may be preferred if markets are unstable, if the bond is new, or if the bond is backed by a new revenue source. The negotiated sales method allows the utilization of a greater scope of services from the underwriter.

Bond structuring involves several issues and decisions, including the maturity of the bond, whether the bond will be issued as a serial or term bond, and whether the bond will include capitalized debt service that may be required for a revenue bond if the debt service cash flow will not be available until the project is completed. Other features include call or put options, sinking fund provisions, and issue date. A bond call option allows the issuer the right to redeem the bonds prior to maturity. A put option permits the bondholder to redeem a bond prior to the maturity date. A sinking fund provision requires the issuer to set aside funds at regular intervals in order to pay the large principal payments due at maturity.

The bond issuance management process also involves consideration of current market conditions. In some cases, states may do interim financing with notes while delaying the longer-term bond issue because of unique market conditions. Other bond structure issues include whether it is in the interest of the issuer to issue variable rate bonds, or discount or premium bonds. Such decisions are based on the nature of the project, the special nature of the issuing entity (the state or an authority of the state), and other conditions such as establishing a debt service reserve to enhance the credit rating.

A key component of bond issuance management is the bond rating and the decision to provide credit enhancement. Bond ratings are the primary feature influencing interest costs. The credit rating is ultimately tied to a specific bond issue at the time of sale and varies with the financial health of the issuer. Over time, the pledged revenue sources, adequate reserve funds, and sinking fund provisions may all affect the credit rating of that bond issue. Some states have turned to credit enhancements such as bond insurance and letters of credit (LOCs) to provide added protection for investors in municipal securities so as to enhance the credit rating and bond marketability.

When a bond is issued through a competitive bid, the preliminary characteristics are critical, as they become the basis on which the underwriters submit a bid. For this reason, issuers often engage a financial adviser to assist in determining the preliminary bond logistics (Robbins and Simonsen 2007). When a bond is issued through negotiated sales, on the other hand, the preliminary bond logistics are the result of conversations between the underwriter and the issuer or issuer's financial adviser.

Once the bond contract has been vetted and the bond rating and credit enhancements have been considered, the process nears completion. The bond characteristics are finalized, the preliminary official statement is published, and the bonds are ready to be sold to the underwriter through either a competitive bid or negotiated sale, and then marketed to investors. The newly issued bonds then become part of the issuers' inventory or stock of bonds outstanding. Figure 6.9 distinguishes bond issue preparation and sale components.

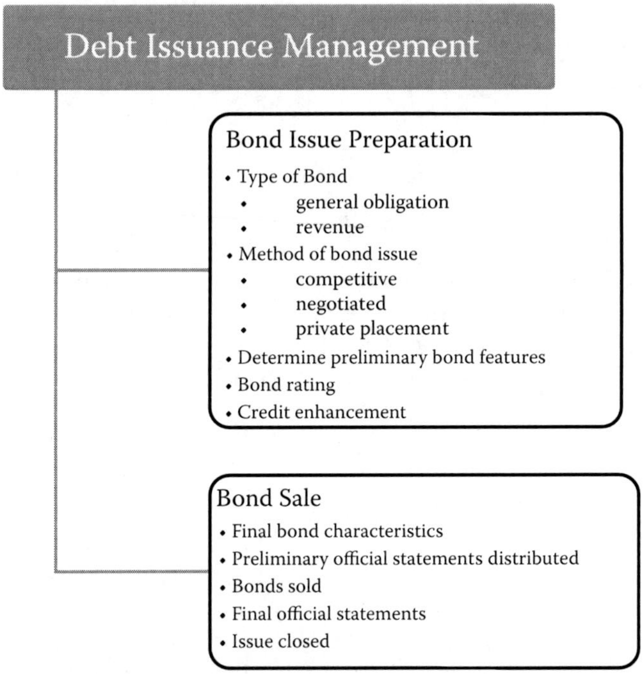

Figure 6.9 Debt issuance management.

Conclusions

Public debt has grown for all levels of government in the United States over recent decades. While the growth of state and local debt has been relatively steady, the rate of growth of federal debt has increased rather dramatically in the past decade following a cut in federal taxes, a slowdown of the economy, and major military involvement in Iraq and Afghanistan. The impact of this rapid growth of federal debt is that total federal debt outstanding now approaches the nation's GDP—a ratio not realized since World War II. The ratio of debt to GDP, which is now above 100 percent, compares to a ratio of about 40 to 60 percent, which has been traditionally maintained over the past several decades. By contrast, the ratio of combined state and local debt to GDP is approximately 18 percent, reflecting an increase in the ratio in the past decade (from 14 percent), as states have responded to the low cost of capital by increasing use of tax-exempt funding to meet new infrastructure and capital maintenance needs and to manage the budgetary impacts of the nation's economic slowdown.

This chapter has presented an overview of U.S. federal, state, and local debt accumulation trends in recent decades. The analysis focuses on debt accumulation growth as well as trends regarding who is providing the capital to finance growing public debt levels. The critical steps involved in the management of a state's debt stock and debt flow issues have been reviewed. A state's comprehensive debt management strategy includes the establishment of a debt management policy to guide the overall debt management process as well as to manage the debt issuance process.

As suggested, meeting a state's debt management challenges requires a broad-based approach that considers the overall debt level and stock of debt as well as the various debt flow processes. Such processes include managing the liquidation of maturing bonds, adding new bond issues to the debt stock, providing estimates of a state's debt capacity and affordability, determining compliance with debt limits, and identifying opportunities for reducing debt carrying costs by refinancing bonds and related activities. Such debt flow management processes are critical in defining slack debt capacity, which will be available as a financing tool in the state's capital budgeting process.

References

Bahl, R., and Duncombe, W. (1993). State and Local Debt Burdens in the 1980s: A Study in Contrast. *Public Administration Review*, 53(1), 31–40.

Brecher, C., Richwerger, K., and Van Wagner, M. (2003). An Approach to Measuring the Affordability of State Debt. *Public Budgeting and Finance*, 23(4), 65–85.

Clingermayer, J.C., and Wood, B.D. (1995). Disentangling Patterns of State Debt Financing. *American Political Science Review*, 89(1), 108–120.

Denison, D. (2013). Debt Management. In *Debt Management Policies in Local Government Finance*. Washington, DC: ICMA Press, pp. 279–295.

Denison, D., Hackbart, M., and Moody, M. (2006). State Debt Limits: How Many Are Enough? *Public Budgeting and Finance*, 26(4), 22–39.

Ellis, M.A., and Schansberg, D.E. (1999). The Determinants of State Government Debt Financing. *Public Finance Review*, 2(6), 571–587.

Hackbart, M., and Leigland, J. (1990). State Debt Management Policy: A National Survey. *Public Budgeting and Finance*, 10(1), 37–54.

Hackbart, M., and Ramsey, J. (1993). Debt Management and Debt Capacity. In *The Handbook of Municipal Bonds*, ed. R. Lamb, J. Leigland, and S. Rappaport. New York: Institute of Public Finance, pp. 316–359.

Hildreth, W.B., Bentley, W., and Miller, G.J. (2002). Debt and the Local Economy: Problems in Benchmarking Local Government Debt Affordability. *Public Budgeting and Finance*, 22(4), 99–113.

Hildreth, W.B., and Zorn, C.K. (2005). The Evolution of State and Local Municipal Debt Markets over the Past Half Century. *Public Budgeting and Finance*, 25(4s), 122–153.

Kiewiet, D.R., and Szakaly, K. (1996). Constitutional Limitations on Borrowing: An Analysis of State Bonded Indebtedness. *Journal of Law, Economics, and Organization*, 12(1), 62–97.

Lemov, P. (1989). The Municipal Bond Market after Reform. In *Capital Projects: New Strategies for Planning, Management and Finance*, ed. J. Matzer Jr. Washington, DC: International City Management Association, pp. 135–147.

Marlowe, J., Rivenbark, W., and Vogt, J. (2009). *Capital Budgeting and Finance*, 2nd ed. Washington, DC: ICMA Press.

Peng, J. (2013). Cash, Investments, and Pensions. In *Management Policies in Local Government Finance*, 6th ed. Washington, DC: ICMA Press, pp. 297–317.

Ramsey, J., and Hackbart, M. (1996). State and Local Debt Management. In *Handbook of Debt Management*, ed. G.J. Miller. New York: Marcel Dekker, pp. 255–276.

Robbins, M.D., and Simonsen, B. (2007). Competition and Selection in Municipal Bond Sales: Evidence from Missouri. *Public Budgeting & Finance*, 27(2), 88–103.

Securities Industry and Financial Markets Association. U.S. Municipal Issuance. Available at http://www.sifma.org/research/.

Simonson, B., Robbins, M.D., and Kittredge, B. (2001). Do Debt Policies Make a Difference in Finance Officers' Perceptions of the Importance of Debt Management Factors? *Public Budgeting and Finance*, 21(1), 87–102.

Temple, J. (1993). Limitations on State and Local Government Borrowing for Private Purposes. *National Tax Journal*, 46(1), 41–52.

Trautman, R.R. (1995). The Impact of State Debt Management on Debt Activity. *Public Budgeting and Finance*, 15(2), 33–51.

U.S. Bureau of Labor Statistics. Consumer Price Index, various years Available at http://www.bls.gov/cpi/home.htm.

U.S. Census Bureau. (2010, July). *State and Local Government Finances, FY2009*. Available at http://www2.census.gov/govs/local/09_summary_report.pdf.

U.S. Census Bureau. *State and Local Government Finances Survey*, various years. Available at http://www.census.gov/govs/estimate.

U.S. Department of Commerce, Bureau of Economic Analysis. National Economic Accounts Data, various years. Available at http://www.bea.gov.

Chapter 7

State Pension Plans in Crisis

Cynthia S. Searcy and William R. Darnell
Georgia State University

Contents

Introduction

States making decisions about how to reduce expenditures in response to decreased revenues during an economic crisis face short-term and long-term trade-offs. States can reduce spending for education, corrections, parks, and other current services, or they can forego long-term investments for infrastructure and employees' future benefits. Unlike a reduction in education spending that leads to fewer teachers in the classroom today, a state delaying contributions to its pension plan(s) faces long-term implications almost exclusively. Creating the political will to address future problems is especially challenging when governments face acute short-term deficits during an economic crisis.

The aftermath of the Great Recession for public pensions, however, has been an exception to this challenge. At no other point in U.S. history has the topic of public pensions been as widely publicized and debated. Reasons for the attention are the size of the problem—estimated at $757 billion—and its seeming uncontrollability (Pew Center on the States 2012). This chapter describes the performance of state pension plans from 2001 to 2010 and how the current economic crisis lays bare the poor decisions of state policy makers over this period. It identifies five states that have the biggest problems and reports their liabilities and what steps they are taking to reduce them (if any). Although it is difficult to predict the health of pension funds in the future, this chapter evaluates general fund revenue trends to see what resources are available to these states to address their pension liabilities given the competing demands of current services. Further, this chapter seeks to explain the circumstances that have produced today's pension crisis so that policy makers may avoid them in the future.

What Is a Pension?

A pension is an income stream promised to an employee when he or she retires. Pensions are benefits that employees accrue as they work; however, unlike wages or health insurance, employees do not receive the benefit until the future. The amount an employee can expect to receive as a benefit when he or she retires depends on the type of pension plan used by his or her employer. A *defined benefit plan* promises to pay an employee a defined proportion of the employee's salary at retirement for every remaining year of his or her life, with some adjustment for the cost of living. A *defined contribution plan* promises to give the employee a set percentage of his or her salary each pay period to be invested for use during retirement. How much the employee earns in retirement each year depends on how much money accrues in his or her retirement account as he or she works. The primary difference in the two plans is the certainty of the benefit—defined benefit plans are designed to assure an employee a fixed benefit when he or she retires until death; defined contribution plans fix a contribution to an employee's retirement savings, but the amount of benefit and length of time receiving them depends on the performance of his or her savings during his or her working life.

State governments as employers or administers of local government pension plans decide what type of plans to create for their own employees as well as those of local governments. States with defined contribution plans make current payments to employees' retirement accounts, with the size of these payments tied to the shares of employees' salaries that states are contractually obligated to make each pay period. States can change the share of the salary contributed at any time when it is politically feasible to amend the benefits contract. Thus, all of the pressure on state coffers lies in the current period.

States with defined benefit plans, however, make current payments to a pension fund that vary based on an estimated amount that the state should make today to pay the benefits that workers are accruing for payment to them in the future. These payments go to a fund that should grow over time to afford the payments that workers are promised after they retire. The bulk of a state's costs for a defined benefit plan, therefore, rests in the current period if all estimated contributions are made according to the plan to pay accrued benefits of its employees. Too often during economic downturns, however, states chose to defer these payments to a future period when state funds are less constrained.

Of the 50 states, all have defined benefit plans for some or all state employees, 13 have defined contribution plans, and three have hybrid plans that combine both types (Center for Retirement Research 2010; Government Accountability Office 2012). The problems for state pension plans after the Great Recession affect exclusively ones with defined benefit plans and the liabilities these plans have accrued for the benefits promised to future retirees.

How Pensions Benefits Are Calculated and Funded

When a state develops a pension plan for its employees, assumptions are made by actuaries to determine what the future liabilities (promises to pay) will be and how much revenue needs to be set aside in order to pay for these liabilities (to "make good" on the promises). Questions considered by actuaries include the following:

- How many employees are in the plan?
- What is each employee's annual wage?
- What percentage of an employee's wage is promised, per year of employment, as a future pension benefit?
- How much is the employee's wage expected to increase over his or her employment period?
- How many years will it be until each employee retires?
- What is the life expectancy for each employee, or how long will promised benefits need to be paid?

- Will the employee choose to receive his or her full retirement benefit, or will he opt to receive a lesser amount in return for the option to have his or her beneficiary receive a benefit after the employee is deceased?
- Will the benefit increase through cost-of-living adjustments?
- What discount rate will be used to turn the future value of all promised benefits into a present value?

The previous questions help pension fund actuaries determine the current value of a pension fund's promised future benefits. Current value of a fund is known as the pension benefit obligation (PBO). Once the PBO is estimated, state legislatures must decide if and how to pay for the liability. In order for the state to be able to properly fund its pension plan, actuaries determine an appropriate annual required contribution (ARC) for government to make each year. Theoretically, if a state funds its ARC each year, over the long run, it will be able to pay future benefits to its employees.

Conceptually the ARC is composed of two parts. First, if there is a shortfall between the present value of the PBO and the present value of plan assets, an amount must be contributed each year in order to close this gap; this is done by amortizing the shortfall. Second, assuming a certain rate of return on invested pension contributions, an amount must be calculated to fund the benefits of workers that are accruing contemporaneously.

One of the most important factors in estimating a state's ARC is the long-term rate of return that it expects to earn on the contributions made to the fund each year by employers and employees. The long-term rate of return is determined by the performance of the plan's investments. If an actuary estimates a state's ARC assuming a higher long-term rate of return than the assets actually realize in a given period, the ARC payments up to that point will be insufficient to meet the PBO. As described shortly, proper determination and payment of full ARCs, along with new accounting rules by the Government Accounting Standards Board (GASB) that affect the rates states use to determine their PBO, have affected the financial health of state pension plans.

Current Problems with State Pension Plans

On July 10, 2013, the *Wall Street Journal* ran the headline "No Pension Reform, No Pay," reporting on the decision by the governor of Illinois to withhold the pay of state legislators until they agreed on a means of funding the state's PBO (Levy 2013). The severity of this tactic speaks to challenges facing many state plans, including the lack of fiscal discipline that state legislatures have exhibited in funding their ARCs, the pension "sweeteners" that legislatures have enacted in preceding decades to increase the benefits promised to employees, the decreased value of pension fund assets in a slow economy, and the lack of political will required to change pension benefits or better fund pension plans when the liability for inaction does not surface for decades in the future.

As of 2010, state pension plans across the country had funded between 99.8 percent (Wisconsin) and 45.4 percent (Illinois) of their PBOs. In this same year, 35 states had less than the recommended 80 percent funded ratio (Barkley 2012). As mentioned earlier, when a plan is underfunded, the state's ARC includes payments on the portion of the PBO that is unfunded, in addition to making annual contributions to cover the future benefits earned by employees that year. Current pension accounting standards require this unfunded gap to be amortized over a period of no longer than 30 years. This amortized amount adds to a state's ARC compared to a plan with no shortfall.

Further complicating the process of closing the unfunded gap is that losses on plan assets are typically smoothed. This means that a loss in market value of pension fund assets is not immediately marked against the plan's assets; the loss is smoothed over a period of years so as not to "shock" the system by creating an instantly larger unfunded gap compared to previous years. The result of smoothing is that for several years following a market loss (an economic downturn) the unfunded liability steadily grows, which in turn means the ARC steadily increases. This smoothing rule was instituted as a measure to alleviate the budgetary constraints a state would face with a volatile ARC, but the end result is that the decision to pay the higher ARC is pushed to the future.*

For states with large unfunded pension liabilities, a lack of fiscal discipline is the primary cause of their crises today. Fiscal discipline involves both paying the plan's full ARC and resisting the urge to enhance benefits in good economic times when state coffers are flush. Failing to make full ARC payments can be a decision driven by revenue shortfalls, or sometimes state legislation requires its contribution to be a defined percentage of employee payroll, which may not generate enough resources to cover its ARC in a given year. States may also fail to pay their ARCs fully when the legislature decides to fund other priorities. Although the exact reasons for a lack of fiscal discipline are difficult to know in every case, 29 states did not fully fund their ARCs in 2010 (Center for Retirement Research 2010).

Lack of fiscal discipline and losses in the value of pension fund assets in the aftermath of the Great Recession are two reasons for the large unfunded liabilities for most state pension plans. As pension assets invested in equities decreased during the financial crisis, states' PBOs increased. Further, some states discounted their PBO at a rate of nearly 8 percent over this period, which has the effect of producing a lower present value of the PBO. This estimation method makes the unfunded liability/asset gap smaller (if not overfunded), though incorrect.

Most economists argue that a state's risk-free rate, the municipal bond rate (which happens to be smaller than most expected rates of return), is the correct rate to use since the PBO is essentially a balance sheet liability. Using a municipal bond rate to discount the PBO produces a higher present value of liabilities.

* Smoothing has the opposite effect when economies recover. The increased value of plan assets is not realized in the PBO until several years after recovery.

By using larger discount rates, states handicap themselves in the long run; the smaller unfunded liability gap results in a smaller ARC, which, when corrected at revaluation, actually expands the *true* unfunded liability gap.

To mitigate the errors that some states make in valuing their PBO and subsequent ARC payments, GASB passed Statements 67 and 68 that affect reporting pension liabilities. These statements take effect for most state plans in fiscal year 2015. GASB argues that its new rules "should substantially improve the transparency, consistency, and comparability of the pension information reported by state and local governments and pension plans" (Government Accounting Standards Board 2012). The new rules affect a state's PBO by requiring use of a blended discount rate, replacement of smoothing with valuing plan assets at market rates for immediate recognition of liabilities, and use of a cost method called age-entry normal to estimate obligations for current employees' benefits that values expected growth in salaries. As explained below, each of these changes is expected to make pension funds appear worse off in the aftermath of the Great Recession.

GASB Statements 67 and 68

The changes in pension plan reporting for state and local governments required by GASB are intended to standardize how plans calculate their PBOs and provide greater transparency to the public, credit rating agencies, and municipal bond market about the liabilities states have to pay in the form of retirement benefits to employees. The two changes that will have the most immediate effect if the economy continues to lag is the requirement that plan assets are valued at current market rates and the use of a blended rate to estimate the growth in assets that will pay for future benefits.

The effect of the first change is easy to understand. When most pension plan assets are invested in bonds and equities, poor performance of these instruments will lower their value. Unless a plan's benefits become less generous or fewer retirees are eligible for benefits as the value of assets decreases, a state's PBO will increase. Declines in the stock market after the 2008 economic crisis are responsible for declines in the funded ratios of state pension plans even with smoothing practices in place. As of 2011, funded ratios for state plans on average are 73.1 percent, a 10.3 percentage point decline from the year before the crisis that started in 2007 (Center for Retirement Research 2011; Barkley 2012).

The blended discount rate requirement of the new GASB rules has less certain effects, although it is expected to decrease funded ratios further since most plans currently are underfunded. The new blended rate permits states to use their expected long-term rate of return on plan assets when estimating their PBOs for liabilities for the portion that is funded by plan assets; the unfunded portion of the plan liabilities should be discounted using a "riskless" rate, or the rate that a state or local government pays to borrow money in the municipal market. Since most state plans estimated their PBOs using a long-term rate of return that is higher than the riskless rate, liabilities are expected to grow using the new blended rate. The Center for

Retirement Research estimates that the new blended rate will reduce funded ratios of pension plans to 62.1 percent under pessimistic expectations, but possibly as high as 75.6 percent if optimistic circumstances are realized in the year 2015 (Munnell 2013).

Finally, the age-entry normal cost method for estimating pension liabilities requires states to account for workers' benefits earned through future service and salary increases in creating its contribution to funding future benefits. The present value of estimates of these costs is then set to a level payment, with equal amounts paid each year to the liability. This method smooths costs to the plan for the benefits of its active workforce, but also frontloads payments that would be larger in the future if calculated using alternative methods like the projected unit credit approach. Frontloading the expense of future benefits, of course, can lower a pension plan's funded ratio and creates a larger gap for states to fill along with GASB's other new requirements. This change, however, is not expected to have as serious consequences for states as the others since 78 percent currently use the age-entry normal cost method exclusively and another 10 percent use age-entry normal for at least some state plans (Center for Retirement Research 2010).

Although GASB claims that Statements 67 and 68 will improve transparency and comparability across state and local government pension plans, critics argue that the new rules will have the opposite effect. Prior GASB statements provided guidance about how to calculate and report ARC payments. The new rules give plans the option to report annual contributions set by statute or one that is calculated by an actuary, with less guidance on the parameters actuaries must use. Although states that use the actuarial estimated contribution method must report their assumptions and methods, choices will vary across states and compromise comparability. For states using statutory contributions, they will not have to report how the rate was developed, and this could tempt states to set their rates lower than required to fully fund their pension plans (Munnell 2012).

Although these are valid critiques, it remains unclear how states will respond to GASB rule changes until fiscal year 2015. It is certain that the major changes for reporting will increase PBOs for all states as they continue to recover from the Great Recession. When funding gaps show up on a state's balance sheet, it will put pressure on them to increase their annual pension contributions or take action toward pension reform. Increased contributions further squeeze resources for current services when revenues are stagnant. Responses for plans in several states indicating the worst financial health are discussed next and illustrate the difficulties these governments face in funding their liabilities going forward.

State Pension Plan Performance 2001–2010

Determining the performance of state pension plans depends on how one measures unfunded liabilities. The value of the unfunded actuarial accrued liability (UAAL) of a pension plan reports the magnitude of the liability but does not account for the size of the state or number of beneficiaries. For example, in 2010, California's UAAL was almost $111 billion, but the funded ratio of its plans was 78.2 percent; Idaho had a funded ratio of 78.4 percent, but its UAAL was only $2.7 billion (Barkley 2012). It would be misleading to state that California's pension plans are in greater peril than Idaho's plans simply because the UAAL is larger.

Analyzing several different measures of liability provides an opportunity to determine which states had the least healthy performance over the last decade and which ones offer lessons for policy makers about mistakes to avoid in the future. This section reports five measures of pension liability that pose a burden on a state's budget, the plan itself, and taxpayers. These measures identify the five least healthy state plans by counting the number of times their liabilities place them among the lowest performers on five measures over the decade. This ranking provides a summary of states with plans in habitual distress relative to those of their peers.

Data and Methods

To analyze the potential peril state pension plans face, it is important to think about the challenges states might face in fulfilling their pension obligations. How much has been promised to beneficiaries versus how much is available to pay for these promises? How much must the state contribute every year to actuarially fund these promises, and how much of the state's general fund revenues will this payment consume? What kind of tax base is available to tap in order to properly fund these liabilities?

To evaluate the performance of state pension plans, we compute five relative measures of pension plan health using data from the Center for Retirement Research Public Plans Database and MorningStar®: the average funded ratio of a state's pension plans, UAAL per capita, percentage of ARC made each year, ARC payment as a percentage of general fund revenues, and annual deductions to pay for benefits as a percentage of plan assets. Once the measures were calculated, we ranked each state from lowest to highest performance in each category for each year between 2001 and 2010. States with plans that land them most frequently among the lowest five of the measures in 2010 and over time are presented in Table 7.1. These states are Illinois, Rhode Island, Oklahoma, West Virginia, and Connecticut. Illinois ranks lowest in four of the five measures compared to three of the five measures for the remaining four states in 2010. Over time, Illinois ranks in the lowest five on 32 year-measures (out of 50). Comparatively, Rhode Island is a distant second with 23, and the remaining states range from 19 to 17 occurrences.

Funded Ratio

Probably the most telling measure of state pension health is the funded ratio. No other measure shows how far behind a plan is from fully funding its PBO—the smaller the funded ratio, the larger the problem. Also, the smaller the funded ratio,

Table 7.1 Summary of States Rankings per Category

Number of Categories a State Was among Worst 5 (2001–2010) (5 is max. no.)		*Number of Times a State Was among the Worst 5 in Any Category (2001–2010) (50 is max. no.)*	
Illinois	4	Illinois	32
Rhode Island	3	Rhode Island	23
Oklahoma	3	Oklahoma	19
West Virginia	3	West Virginia	19
Connecticut	3	Connecticut	17

Table 7.2 Funded Ratio

	Value 2010	*Average 2008–2010*	*Percentage Point Change 2008–2010*	*Average 2001–2010*	*Percentage Point Change 2001–2010*
Illinois	45.6%	50.3%	–8.9%	56.2%	–17.9%
Rhode Island	48.4%	56.1%	–13.1%	60.8%	–29.2%
Oklahoma	53.8%	55.7%	–4.1%	58.4%	–8.5%
West Virginia	57.0%	56.6%	–5.3%	50.7%	12.0%
Connecticut	53.4%	57.5%	–8.2%	58.5%	–9.7%

Source: Center for Retirement Research, Public Plans Database, authors' own calculations.

the higher the ARC payment will grow each year to "catch up" on prior underpayments. Table 7.2 reports the funded ratios for the five least healthy states as identified in Table 7.1. Funded ratios in 2010 among these five states ranged from 45.6 percent (Illinois) to 57.0 percent (West Virginia), well below the traditionally accepted ratio of 80.0 percent. All five states realized declines in their funded ratios since the 2008 economic crisis, ranging from 4.1 percentage points for Oklahoma to 13.1 percentage points for Rhode Island. Only West Virginia made improvements in its funded ratio over the decade (a 12.0 percentage point increase).

UAAL per Capita

The UAAL per capita is a measure that represents how much each resident would have to pay to fully fund his or her state's unfunded pension liabilities. Table 7.3 reports the UAAL per capita as well as the 2008–2010 and 2001–2010 percentage

Table 7.3 UAAL per Capita

	Value 2010	*Percentage Change 2008–2010*	Percentage Change *2001–2010*
Illinois	5,795	38.4%	197.7%
Rhode Island	6,492	62.4%	293.9%
Oklahoma	3,649	16.5%	88.5%
West Virginia	3,298	24.6%	29.3%
Connecticut	5,811	30.5%	346.6%

Source: Center for Retirement Research, Public Plans Database, authors' own calculations.

changes for the five least healthy states identified in Table 7.1. A 2012 report by a pension analyst at MorningStar, an investment firm, identifies $3,000 per capita as the threshold for determining troubled states (Barkley 2012). According to this rule of thumb, all five of the states in Table 7.3 are carrying unfunded pension liabilities that represent unusual burdens on their residents. Rhode Island ($6,492) has the highest UAAL per capita among these states, and West Virginia has the lowest ($3,298). Since the Great Recession, Rhode Island also has experienced the highest growth on this measure (62.4 percent); however, Connecticut's UAAL per capita grew the most over the decade.

ARC Payment Percentage

The actuarial required contribution (ARC) is the sum that states must contribute annually to plans in order to properly fund them. While most states fully pay their annual ARCs, some states experiencing fiscal stress fail to make their full ARCs. Partially paying the ARC will eventually lead to an underfunded plan, so it is in a state's best interest to keep up with these contributions. Table 7.4 shows the ARC payment percentage results for the five states in this analysis. Examining this measure helps explain why these states have large UAAL per capita. First, it is interesting to note that Rhode Island fully paid its ARC in the most recent year and every year of the decade, yet among the state plans examined here, it has the highest UAAL per capita. This result indicates that its ARC is not enough to make up for historical underfunding and a population that is small relative to plan liability. West Virginia and Connecticut have similar circumstances, although recent contributions have not fully met their ARCs. Illinois and Oklahoma have not fully paid their ARCs recently or over the decade, with Illinois averaging just 68.3 percent of its ARC between 2001 and 2010. Both states made higher contributions to their ARCs in 2010 compared to their average for the decade, although Oklahoma's most recent payment lagged its contribution from 2008.

Table 7.4 ARC Payment Percentage

	Value 2010	*Average 2008–2010*	*Percentage Point Change 2008–2010*	*Average 2001–2010*	*Percentage Point Change 2001–2010*
Illinois	86.7%	71.8%	28.9%	68.3%	5.9%
Rhode Island	100.0%	100.0%	0.0%	100.0%	0.0%
Oklahoma	77.8%	82.2%	–7.8%	72.4%	3.9%
West Virginia	90.6%	97.4%	–15.5%	132.6%	–14.7%
Connecticut	87.9%	148.4%	–173.6%[a]	110.9%	–9.4%

Source: Center for Retirement Research, Public Plans Database, authors' own calculations.

[a] In 2008, Connecticut paid 261 percent of its ARC.

Table 7.5 ARC as a Percentage of General Fund Revenues

	Value 2010	*Average 2008–2010*	*Percentage Point Change 2008–2010*	*Average 2001–2010*	*Percentage Point Change 2001–2010*
Illinois	8.7%	7.6%	1.9%	6.4%	4.4%
Rhode Island	4.5%	4.9%	–0.8%	3.7%	1.8%
Oklahoma	5.8%	5.6%	0.5%	5.7%	0.7%
West Virginia	5.5%	4.9%	1.2%	4.6%	1.3%
Connecticut	6.6%	6.2%	0.9%	5.0%	2.9%

Source: Center for Retirement Research, Public Plans Database, authors' own calculations.

ARC Payment as a Percentage of General Fund Revenues

By comparing a state's ARC payment with its general fund revenues, we can grasp the constraint that a pension plan could place on its own-source revenues. The larger the portion of general revenues consumed by ARC payments, the less likely a full ARC payment will be made in the future. Table 7.5 reports the ARC as a percentage of general fund revenues for the five least healthy states. Illinois' ARC consumes the highest proportion of its own-source revenues (8.7 percent) among the five states, and this share has grown the most over the past decade

(4.4 percentage points). Interestingly, although Rhode Island has the largest UAAL per capita among the five states, its ARC as a percent of general fund revenues is the lowest. Again, this raises concerns that its ARC is not high enough to fully fund its pension liabilities. The remaining three states paid between 5.5 percent (West Virginia) and 6.6 percent (Connecticut) of their general fund revenues as ARC in 2010. These proportions are roughly equivalent to what a state spends, on average, for correction services each year.

Annual Deductions as a Percentage of Plan Assets

The final measure of this analysis borrows from a loose rule of thumb from retirement planning. It calculates annual deductions from a plan for benefit payments as a percentage of plan assets. When inflation and expected asset returns are considered, and if deductions can be kept below 4 percent of assets, the likelihood of plan sustainability increases. Alternatively, when deductions as a percentage of assets are high, the likelihood of plan sustainability decreases. Table 7.6 presents this measure for the five states considered here. All five states have been making deductions to their plans to pay benefits that exceed the 4 percent estimate for sustainability. In 2010, Rhode Island and Connecticut drew down similar funds for benefits at over 11 percent of plan assets, while other state deductions ranged between 8.8 percent (Oklahoma) and 9.7 percent (West Virginia). All states saw this percentage grow after the 2008 economic crisis, largely reflecting the loss in assets over this period. Only West Virginia and Connecticut paid out less in deductions as a percentage of assets in 2010 than in the prior decade, perhaps reflecting their shift in pension plan assets to less risky investments.

Table 7.6 Annual Deductions as a Percentage of Plan Assets

	Value 2010	*Average 2008–2010*	*Percentage Point Change 2008–2010*	*Average 2001–2010*	*Percentage Point Change 2001–2010*
Illinois	8.9%	8.2%	1.3%	6.9%	3.4%
Rhode Island	11.9%	10.8%	2.3%	9.2%	5.7%
Oklahoma	8.8%	8.6%	0.7%	8.4%	0.6%
West Virginia	9.7%	9.7%	1.1%	10.4%	–1.1%
Connecticut	11.4%	8.2%	6.3%	10.5%	–5.9%

Source: Center for Retirement Research, Public Plans Database, authors' own calculations.

The Future for State Pension Plans

Given the poor performance of the state pension plans examined here, one may ask what the future holds for their beneficiaries and the taxpayers that will have to absorb the liabilities. From the discussion of the current problem with pension plans above, we know that the immediate future for these plans and other state pension funds will not improve as long as plan assets perform poorly in a weak economy. Further, GASB's new reporting rules will make state PBOs increase when smoothing the value of assets gives way to the use of the new blended rate of return for valuation purposes. Unless states can afford to raise their annual contributions to their pension funds substantially over the next few years, funded ratios will stay below 80 percent, certainly for all five states examined in this chapter, and unfortunately, for many others as well. Prospects that states will increase their annual contributions to pensions are weak barring a dedication of a new funding stream to pension payments. Figure 7.1 illustrates the compound growth of state general fund revenues over the past decade relative to their UAAL growth over the decade. At no point has the compounded growth of general fund revenues matched the compounded growth of state UAALs. Today, with unemployment still above 8.0 percent in Illinois (9.2 percent), Rhode Island (8.9 percent), and Connecticut (8.2 percent), it is doubtful legislatures will find the political will to identify a significant new source of revenue for pension liabilities or to cut funds from other services and functions to apply to these liabilities (Bureau of Labor Statistics 2013).

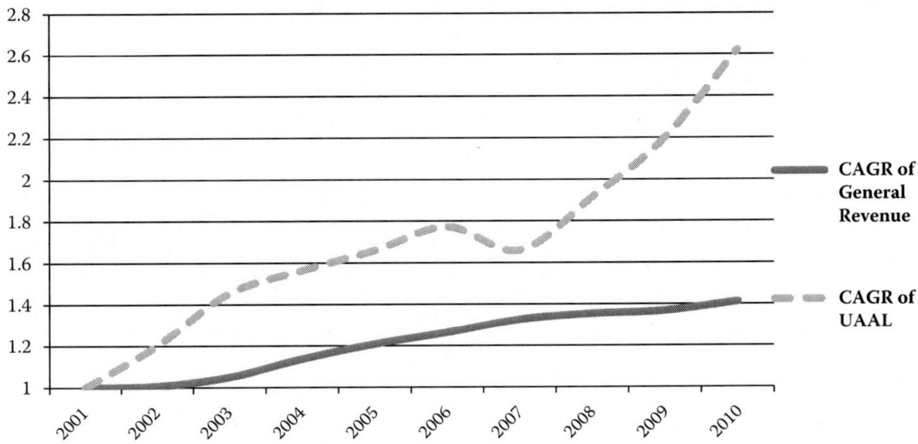

Figure 7.1 CAGR for general revenue and UAAL of five study states. The average annual growth rate of each state's general revenue and UAAL growth (year over year) was calculated, and then annual growth rates were combined to create a compound annual growth rate (CAGR), and these rates were plotted with 2001 as the base year. (Data from U.S. Census [state government general revenue]; Center for Retirement Research, Public Plans Database.)

Table 7.7 Changes Made to State-Sponsored Pension Plans, January 2008–July 2011

	Adjusted Benefit Formula		*Raised Age or Increased Service Requirements*		*Reduced or Eliminated Postretirement Increases*	
	Future	*Some Current*	*Future*	*Some Current*	*Future*	*Some Current*
Rhode Island	x	x	x	x	x	x
Illinois	x		x		x	
West Virginia	x		x			
Oklahoma			x			
Connecticut						

Source: Government Accountability Office, State and Local Pension Plans.

Many states have attempted to reduce their pension liabilities by changing the benefits promised to employees. A report by the Government Accountability Office (GAO) that updates analyses conducted by the National Conference of State Legislatures (NCSL) indicates that most states have reformed their pension plans since the Great Recession. Nearly half adjusted benefit formulas (24) and increased employee contributions (25), while 29 raised the retirement age or increased service requirements. Table 7.7 shows the reforms made to pension plans by the states in this analysis. Rhode Island has enacted the most changes for both current and future beneficiaries, including adjusting benefit formulas, raising the retirement age or service requirements to qualify for benefits, and reducing postretirement benefit increases. Illinois has made similar changes for future beneficiaries only. Connecticut had made no changes to its pension plans by July 2011. None of the five states had chosen to increase employee contributions to pay a higher share for their future benefits (Government Accountability Office 2012).

Since most reforms between 2008 and 2011 among the five states affect the benefits of future employees only (new hires), the effects of the reforms are not expected to impact UAALs positively, at least in the short term. Table 7.8 summarizes how many reforms were made by each state in this study and the relative growth of UAALs and funded ratios of their plans between 2008 and 2011. Rhode Island was able to reduce its UAAL by 8.3 percent and increase its funded ratio by 2.2 percent between 2008 and 2011; of the five states, it made the most changes to its pension plan (see Table 7.7). Just making one change between 2008 and 2011, Oklahoma was able to reduce its UAAL by 8.9 percent and increase its funded ratio by 4.9 percentage points. Interestingly, these positive changes in performance occurred despite the state not making its full ARC contribution over this period. Illinois' reforms

Table 7.8 State-Sponsored Pension Plan Reforms and Changes to UAAL and Funded Ratio

State	*No. of Reforms*	*UAAL ($ billions)*		*Percentage Change*	*Funded Ratio*		*Percentage Change*
		2008	*2011*		*2008*	*2011*	
Rhode Island	6	4.9	4.5	–8.3%	56.4%	58.6%	2.2%
Illinois	3	42.2	82.9	96.6%	62.6%	43.4%	–19.2%
West Virginia	2	5.3	6.3	18.3%	54.7%	57.9%	3.2%
Oklahoma	1	10.5	9.6	–8.7%	62.1%	67.0%	4.9%
Connecticut	0	14.9	20.9	40.3%	56.5%	53.4%	–3.1%

Source: Center for Retirement Research, Public Plans Database; Government Accountability Office, State and Local Pension Plans (analysis of annual NCSL reports); author's own calculations.

from 2008 to 2011 had no impact on its pension performance over this period, with its UAAL nearly doubling and its funded ratio dropping 19.2 percentage points.

Conclusion

The Great Recession elevated the distress of state pension plans to new heights of public attention. A confluence of poor market performance, generous pension benefit increases in prior decades, and underinvestment in required contributions to pay these liabilities produced record-high unfunded liabilities for many states. While the pension crisis has spurred many legislatures to modify benefits for state employees to address these liabilities, the sustainability of state pension plans depends on a commitment to fiscal discipline going forward. In the short term, as GASB rules 67 and 68 go into effect, states will face liabilities that will keep reform on the minds of policy makers; however, when asset markets recover and state liabilities decrease, the hope is that states can learn from past mistakes and resist committing themselves to benefits that compromise financial health in the next recession.

References

Barkley, R. (2012). The State of State Pension Plans: A Deep Dive into Shortfalls and Surpluses. *MorningStar*, November 28. Available at http://corporate.morningstar.com/us/documents/reports/statepensions.pdf (accessed June 20, 2013).

Bureau of Labor Statistics. (2013). Local Area Unemployment Statistics: Unemployment Rates for States. Available at http://www.bls.gov/web/laus/laumstrk.htm (accessed July 31, 2013).

Center for Retirement Research. (2010). Public Plans Database. State and Local Defined Contribution Plans Data Set. Available at http://pubplans.bc.edu/pls/apex/f?p=1988:22:1597890094337::NO:RP:: (accessed June 20, 2013).

Center for Retirement Research. (2011). Public Plans Database. State and Local Defined Benefit Plans Data Set. Available at http://pubplans.bc.edu/pls/apex/f?p=1988:20:1597890094337::NO:RP:: (accessed June 20, 2013).

Government Accountability Office. (2012). State and Local Government Pension Plans: Economic Downturn Spurs Efforts to Address Costs and Sustainability. Available at http://www.gao.gov/products/GAO-12-322 (accessed July 20, 2013).

Government Accounting Standards Board. (2012). *Pension Fact Sheets*. Available at http://www.gasb.org/cs/ContentServer?site=GASB&c=Page&pagename=GASB%2FPage%2FGASBSectionPage&cid=1176160426013 (accessed July 30, 2013).

Levy, C. (2013). No Pension Reform, No Pay. *Wall Street Journal*, July 10. Available at http://online.wsj.com/article/SB10001424127887323740804578597683905687760.html (accessed July 29, 2013).

Munnell, A.H. (2012). *State and Local Pensions: What Now?* Washington, DC: Brookings Institute Press.

Munnell, A.H. (2013). The Funding of State and Local Pensions: 2012–2016. Center for Retirement Research. Available at http://crr.bc.edu/wp-content/uploads/2013/07/slp_32.pdf (accessed July 26, 2013).

Pew Center on the States. (2012). The Widening Gap Update. Available at http://www.pewtrusts.org/uploadedFiles/wwwpewtrustsorg/Reports/Retirement_security/Widening%20Gap%20Brief%20Update_webREV.pdf (accessed July 26, 2013).

Chapter 8

The Future of State Spending

Carolyn Bourdeaux
Georgia State University

Contents

Introduction

The economic shock in 2009 and 2010 caused one of the largest declines in state revenues (on average) since the Great Depression (Boyd and Dadayan 2010) and opened up a national conversation on the future of state finances. Some of the major groups commenting on the state fiscal outlook included the State Budget Crisis Task Force convened by Comptroller of New York State Richard Ravich and former Federal Reserve Chairman Paul Volker, the Pew Center on the States, and the Center on Budget and Policy Priorities, as well as ongoing reports and discussion from the National Association of State Budget Officers (NASBO) and the National Conference of State Legislatures (NCSL). Key themes related to future problems in state expenditure portfolios included (1) the increasing pressures associated with Medicaid spending (Maciag 2013; National Association of State Budget Officers 2012; State Budget Crisis Task Force 2012; Vestal 2012), (2) the ever-growing problem of unfunded and underfunded state pensions coupled with the unsustainability of promised postemployment benefits (Maciag 2013; Pew Center on the States 2010, 2011; State Budget Crisis Task Force 2012), and (3) the effect on states of declining federal stimulus monies and other federal funding cuts (Johnson and Leachman 2013; State Budget Crisis Task Force 2012).

Other concerns included the ability of states to recover to prerecession funding levels across a host of service areas (Johnson and Leachman 2013), and the related impact of the recession on local government fiscal health (State Budget Crisis Task Force 2012). While these reports raise important concerns, many validated by this analysis, this chapter examines these identified pressures in the overall context of state expenditure portfolios and policy aspirations with a focus on four major "business lines" that dominate state spending: K–12 education, higher education, Medicaid, and highways. The Great Recession interrupted an ongoing conversation at the state level about improving K–12 education, increasing access to higher education, and reinvesting in national infrastructure. At the same time, the nation is about to make a major investment in health care reform and significantly expand the shape and scope of Medicaid. This analysis examines these national concerns by looking at the changes in these service areas for the average state in the country. The analysis examines intergovernmental contributions to service areas and trends from 2000 to 2008, the impact of the Great Recession, and then develops a plausible scenario for future funding. An important question considered here is: *Do current investment trends equal state and national ambitions?* Findings indicate that states made substantial investments during the early part of the 21st century, particularly in K–12 education, but the Great Recession reset state financing back to levels of the early 2000s. Given this, and coupled with the problems in Medicaid, increasing pension and long-term liabilities, and future disinvestment at the federal level, most states do not appear positioned to make investments that reflect their aspirations for the 21st century.

The Current Structure of State Spending

Although American states have a variety of important regulatory and judicial roles, their expenditure portfolios are dominated by a few policy areas (see Table 8.1). These core areas are Medicaid, K–12 education, higher education, transportation, and corrections, together comprising 65 percent of total expenditures and 71 percent of state general fund expenditures in 2011. This analysis focuses on the first four areas as well as pensions and other postemployment benefits (OPEBs). Corrections, though important, is a smaller policy area, similar in magnitude to transportation. However, transportation dominates state capital spending and, as such, is a good proxy for the extent to which states are making the infrastructure investments generally viewed as important to the long-term fiscal health of a jurisdiction.

Table 8.1 shows that these business lines have been relatively stable over the past 20 years, with most categories shifting no more than a percentage point or two as a share of the overall state spending portfolio between 1992 and 2008. The one exception is Medicaid, which has been growing as a share of state expenditures both in total (from 18 to 24 percent of share) and as a share of state general funds (from 14 to 17 percent of share). This may understate the state general fund share in 2011 since federal stimulus funds received through the American Recovery

Table 8.1 Major Expenditure Categories for State Government

	Total State Expenditures by Business Line 1992, 2002, 2008, 2011[a]				*Total State General Fund Expenditures by Business Line 1992, 2002, 2008, 2011*[a]			
	1992	*2002*	*2008*	*2011*	*1992*	*2002*	*2008*	*2011*
Medicaid	18%	21%	21%	24%	13%	16%	16%	17%
K–12 education	21%	22%	22%	20%	35%	35%	35%	35%
Higher education	10%	11%	10%	10%	13%	13%	11%	11%
Transportation[b]	9%	8%	8%	7%	1%	1%	1%	0%
Corrections	3%	4%	4%	3%	6%	7%	7%	8%
All other	38%	35%	36%	35%	33%	28%	30%	29%

[a] Based on NASBO State Expenditure Reports, 1991–1993, 2001–2003, 2007–2009, 2010–2012.

[b] Transportation gas tax revenues are not counted as state general funds by many states but are "other state funds," and so their true magnitude is not reflected in the state general fund expenditures.

and Reinvestment Act (ARRA) of 2009 were used to support the Medicaid program in that year.

Data and Methodology

This chapter examines how average state spending on core services has changed since 2000, and then considers what has driven any shifts in spending.* Key areas of focus include intergovernmental shifts in funding, shifts in cost per recipient in a particular program, as well as enrollment shifts. Then, given underlying drivers of change, what does this suggest about the future of state expenditure patterns, and do these expenditures support current national goals? Because the focus of this chapter is on *state* behaviors (and not outcomes for a recipient population), the average state is the nonweighted average across all states. In other words, average spending per person in Texas is treated the same as average spending per person in Delaware. The focus here is on the behavior of each state and its expenditure choices in allocating funds, rather than how much we are spending per person as a nation.

Expenditure patterns of the states were significantly affected by the Great Recession and states' subsequent receipt of federal funding through the ARRA. Data for this research span 2010 through 2012, depending on the policy area, which means that the expenditure patterns capture the depths of the recession, but not necessarily state choices during the recovery. As a result, this analysis generally looks at trends from 2000 to 2008 for an assessment of underlying state investments and priorities, and then at the impact of the recession in resetting the base for many state services.†

* This chapter draws on a variety of data sources to examine underlying trends in state budgets across four major policy areas: K–12 education, higher education, Medicaid, and highways. In most cases, because recipient revenue data are better than state expenditure data, the analysis uses revenue data as a substitute for state expenditures. For instance, for K–12 education, the analysis uses U.S. Census F-33 Financial Survey data from school districts. This data record state-financed revenues remitted to school districts, which should be equivalent to state expenditures in this area. Although there may be differences in fiscal year or variances in timing, this analysis is simply looking at broad aggregated statewide trends over time, so any lack of precision is unlikely to significantly affect results.

† To the extent possible, projections are built off of existing projections from credible sources, such as the Congressional Budget Office or the National Center for Education Statistics. However, in some cases these are adjusted based on recent data reflecting state choices coming out of recession. For instance, some recent assessments of 2012–2013 spending patterns suggest that state spending has not fully replaced the lost federal stimulus funds and is now growing off of a lower base (Oliff et al. 2012; Smith et al. 2012). Where available, this information is built into the analysis. Projections are meant to reflect a plausible scenario rather than a prediction of the future. The analysis provides an assessment of whether states are on a trajectory to meet stated state and national policy aspirations and examines potential pressures that some areas may place on the rest of the budget.

K–12 Education

K–12 education funding in most states is a shared state–local responsibility with a modest federal contribution thrown in for good measure. The bulk of state funding takes the form of some type of formula-driven grant-in-aid to local school districts. This service area dominates the state-funded portion of state budgets, making up 35 percent of total expenditures, and has been a major area of investment for states in the last 10 years.

For the past decade, education policy has been dominated by the issues surrounding the federal No Child Left Behind (NCLB) Act of 2002. This legislation expanded the scope of federal influence over education, requiring that states adopt a host of new school testing and accountability provisions. The legislation also authorized a substantial increase in federal funding for education. Although the federal share increased by 43 percent between 2000 and 2008, these funds only accounted for around 60 percent of the authorized increase, and there was national debate as to whether the federal government was honoring its commitment to fully fund the legislation.* Based on the calculations in Table 8.2, the federal increase was equivalent to around $300 per student between 2000 and 2008 for the average state (in 2010 dollars).

While the federal percentage change looks large, the federal increase is dwarfed by the overall magnitude of the state and local increase. Over the same time period, states, on average, increased funding by over $1,100 per student, an annual real rate of growth of 2.6 percent; local governments matched this dollar increase. Further, unlike the growth in federal funds, the state investment trend does not begin with the NCLB Act. That is, states' rate of growth actually slowed relative to the late 1990s, when state real per FTE funding grew by an average of 5 percent a year (between 1996 and 2000). Since the mid-1990s, states have been making a substantial real investment in education that is reflected in per student numbers as well as aggregate funding levels. Between 2000 and 2008, the vast majority made double-digit real per FTE investments in K–12 education.

The impact of the Great Recession is visible in the 2010 numbers with local funding flatlining on a per student basis, state funding dropping, and federal funding actually making up slightly more than the difference. The federal funding includes the ARRA funds.

Outlook for K–12 Education

The funds provided from NCLB ended in 2007 and reauthorization legislation has failed to pass Congress. The original act was supposed to ensure that all students met student achievement standards by 2014; however, there is little evidence that

* Reflecting concern about fully funding the bill, the National Education Association (2007) argued that in 2007, $23.6 billion was provided for NCLB, although $39.4 billion was authorized.

Table 8.2 Real K–12 per Pupil Revenues to School Districts for the Average State[a]

	Trend between 2000 and 2008					*Impact of the Recession*			*Trend in 2020*		
Fund Source	*2000*	*Share of Total*	*2008*	*Share of Total*	*Percent Change from 2000*	*2010*	*Share of Total*	*Percent Change from 2008*	*2020*	*Share of Total*	*Percent Change from 2008*
Local	$4,135	41%	$5,239	42%	27%	$5,232	41%	0%	$6,028	44%	15%
State	$5,119	51%	$6,288	50%	23%	$5,893	46%	–6%	$6,589	48%	5%
Federal	$728	7%	$1,043	8%	43%	$1,593	13%	53%	$984	7%	–6%
Total	$9,982		$12,570		26%	$12,719		1%	$13,601		8%
Enrollment (millions)	46		48		4%	48		0%	51		6%
Total state revenues to local school districts (billions)	$233		$287		23%	$258		–10%	$338		18%

[a] In 2010 $.

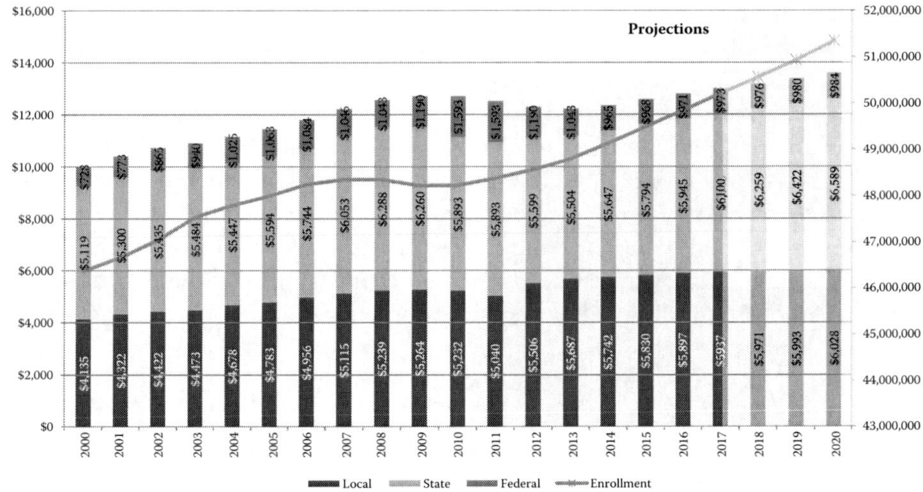

Figure 8.1 Real per FTE revenues and projected revenues for K–12 education for the average state and total enrollment (2010 $).

most states reached close to the mark. For example, a 2007 assessment of the funding increases required to meet NCLB standards in Missouri and Kansas by 2011 ranged between 46 and 10 percent, respectively, over 2007 amounts for the average district. The relatively small 10 percent increase in Kansas reflects the state setting a low threshold for student achievement (Duncombe et al. 2006).

The projections or plausible scenario are shown in Table 8.2 and Figure 8.1. The trends are built off of National Center for Education Statistics (NCES) expenditure and enrollment projections adjusted based on more recent surveys reflecting the impact of the Great Recession on state and local spending. Layoffs in the local education sector suggest that as federal stimulus funding has vanished, states and localities have not been able to fill the gap (Oliff et al. 2012). This could permanently lower the base for education spending going forward. This projection assumes that should funding stabilize in 2014, state commitment will resume the 2000–2008 investment pattern, which may be aggressive given the likely pressures from Medicaid, pensions, and other retirement obligations. Additionally, the scenario accounts for the impact of federal retrenchment on funding for education given proposed education cuts as part of the more recent federal American Taxpayer Relief Act (ATRA) of 2013. The ATRA would reduce federal education funding by 7.3 percent reduction in 2014, declining to 5.5 percent by 2021 (Kogan 2012).

In this scenario, the results show that the average state might reach an 8 percent per student increase over 2008 by 2020, close to the NCLB "low bar" suggested in the research on Kansas referenced earlier. Federal education funding appears slated to drop to a level that predates the NCLB legislation.

Perhaps in tacit recognition of overly ambitious goals of the NCLB as well as the fiscally strapped circumstances of governments at all levels, policy makers appear to be scaling back the original NCLB criteria. The Obama administration has been changing the program through waivers, allowing states increased flexibility to revise their accountability standards in return for setting up programs that better track and evaluate student progress and reward teachers for student improvement. While the education community may bemoan the slowing investment in education, it is worth noting that this policy area has realized substantial public investment. Even if the 2012 and 2013 projected declines in government spending are correct, the 2013 per student spending still represents a more than 20 percent increase from 2000 for the average state.

Medicaid

An often expressed concern is the pressure that Medicaid is putting on state budgets. In fact, while total state spending on K–12 education has grown by 23 percent between 2000 and 2008, the average state's commitment to Medicaid spending grew by 37 percent in real dollars for the same period.* Unlike education, this growth has not been driven by higher spending per enrollee, which grew by only 3 percent from 2000 to 2008—just slightly above the rate of inflation as measured by the gross domestic product (GDP) price deflator. States have been able to control costs over the past decade in large part by limiting provider payment rates, expanding managed care, limiting the use and pricing of prescription drugs, and expanding community-based long-term care programs (Holahan and Yemane 2013).

Instead, growth of Medicaid has been driven by increasing enrollments, which are closely tied to rising poverty rates and the aging population in the nation (Garfield et al. 2012; Holahan and Yemane 2013). Findings here show a 37 percent increase in enrollment between 2000 and 2008 and a 21 percent increase from 2008 to 2011. Real per enrollee spending has declined in part as a result of this dramatic increase in enrollment.

In 2009 through 2011, states benefitted from federal stimulus funds increasing the federal share of the Medicaid match. These funds allowed states to drop

* This estimate is derived from National Association of State Budget Officers (NASBO) reported numbers from each state. State fund expenditures reported were checked against their Federal Medical Assistance Percentages (FMAP) rates for 2000 and 2008 and showed a correlation of 0.76 and 0.67 for each of the years, respectively. There are reasons that the shares may not match, including differences in administrative spending, which is matched at a 0.50 rate, as well as differences in states' individual programs and effort. But, there is no way to validate the accuracy of state reporting.

their own contributions to the program in nominal dollars by 1 percent in fiscal 2009 and another 10 percent in fiscal 2010.* In 2012, states faced the "cliff" from vanishing federal funds, and thus increased their share by 20 percent. However, this sudden demand for more funds precipitated "intense state efforts to mitigate the increase in state spending" (Smith et al. 2012, 6). Early reports from 2012 and budgeted 2013 suggest that the growth in overall Medicaid spending has slowed to one of the lowest growth rates in Medicaid history (Smith et al. 2012).

Outlook for Medicaid

Given national health care reform, major changes are on the horizon for state health spending, and the future is perhaps more uncertain than in many other policy areas. The Patient Protection and Affordable Care Act (ACA) of 2010 allows expansion of Medicaid up to 138 percent poverty for all adults, with the federal government paying for the entire expansion from 2014 to 2016, and then tapering off to 90 percent from 2020 and onward. While this expansion was originally conceptualized as a mandatory part of health care reform, in June 2012, the U.S. Supreme Court ruled that states could not be required to expand Medicaid as a condition of their receipt of federal funds for the current Medicaid program. As a result, there is substantial variation in the projections for Medicaid growth, in part because of uncertainty about how and when states will adopt the Medicaid expansion. There is also potential for states to use state health insurance exchanges, which are almost entirely federally funded, as an alternative to Medicaid for the population between 100 and 138 percent of poverty. To give some sense of the differential in estimates, in June 2012, the Centers for Medicaid and Medicare Systems (CMS) projected that the program will expand from 56 million enrollees in 2013 to 76 million in 2014, and then to 84 million by 2020 (Centers for Medicare and Medicaid Services 2012). In February 2013, the Congressional Budget Office (CBO) estimated that the program will expand from 54 million average annual enrollees in 2013 to 57 million in 2014 and 66 million by 2020 (Congressional Budget Office 2013b).

Expenditure projections based on the CMS estimates suggest that expenditure growth will continue to be largely driven by growth in the number of enrollees; meanwhile, the CBO estimate projects upward pressure on costs. A case can be made in either direction: The new Medicaid program will enroll a healthier population, which should be less expensive than current enrollees. However, a sudden influx into the medical system of millions of new people may

* Based on numbers reported by the NASBO for FY2008, FY2009, and FY2010. The number includes state general fund and other state fund spending combined.

put pressure on supply and drive up prices. A third factor is that states may try to contain costs.*

Even assuming conservative estimates, enrollment would grow by 56 percent and total state funding would grow by 73 percent, from \$136 billion to \$236 billion in constant dollars (this includes the federal increased matching rate for the new population covered). If states were able to keep real per enrollee costs constant at 2011 levels, the increase would then be to \$198 billion in constant dollars, a 45 percent increase. Assuming the most minimal expansion scenario, state Medicaid spending will grow almost twice that of K–12 education over 2008.

There are also other uncertainties related to Medicaid spending. While state direct Medicaid costs will increase due to the ACA, state costs will likely be offset by savings in other parts of the budget—such as those in public health, mental health, and corrections (Ollove 2013), as well as increased revenues from hospital provider payments or insurance premium taxes (Angeles 2012). The health care expansion has the potential to entirely reshape state expenditures in these areas. For example, it may largely end the need for clinical services provided through state public and mental systems (or allow them to be almost entirely reimbursed through private health insurance or Medicaid), and thus lead to savings of hundreds of millions of dollars, depending on how state current services are structured.

In addition to the ACA, the increase in state Medicaid expenditures is also influenced by the aging population. While more enrollees going forward are low-income children, Medicaid spending is by far dominated by that for the aged and disabled (Smith et al. 2012). Given anticipated demographic shifts, much of the remaining state-level growth is attributable to pressure from the more expensive portion of the Medicaid population.

Higher Education

Of the four major expenditure areas in state portfolios, higher education is the one that has borne a significant portion of the cutbacks from the Great Recession. The recession appears to have accelerated an underlying trend of slowing state

* Because CBO is more current and conservative, the scenario reflected in Table 8.3 and Figure 8.2 largely reflects the CBO growth estimates for enrollment. The expenditure estimates use CMS growth rates but are built off a base of state-reported expenditures from the National Association of State Budget Officers adjusted for a Kaiser Family Foundation state survey of reported expenditure growth through 2013. These estimates produce a 2020 projection that is almost exactly the same as the implied CBO total expenditure estimate. CBO estimates total federal outlays only, so total expenditures have to be estimated off of these numbers based on the national average federal matching rate.

Table 8.3 Real per Enrollee Medicaid Expenditures for the Average State[a]

	Trend between 2000 and 2008					*Impact of Recession*			*Trend in 2020*		
Fund Source	*2000*	*Share of Total*	*2008*	*Share of Total*	*Percent Change from 2000*	*2011*	*Share of Total*	*Percent Change from 2008*	*2020*	*Share of Total*	*Percent Change from 2008*
Federal funds	$4,623	58%	$4,708	58%	2%	$5,209	65%	11%	$6,276	64%	33%
State funds	$3,291	42%	$3,431	42%	4%	$2,750	35%	–20%	$3,593	36%	5%
Total	$7,913		$8,140		3%	$7,959		–2%	$9,869		21%
Total enrollees (millions)	32		44		37%	53		21%	68		56%
Total state expenditures (billions)	$99		$136		37%	$143		5%	$236		73%

[a] In 2011 $.

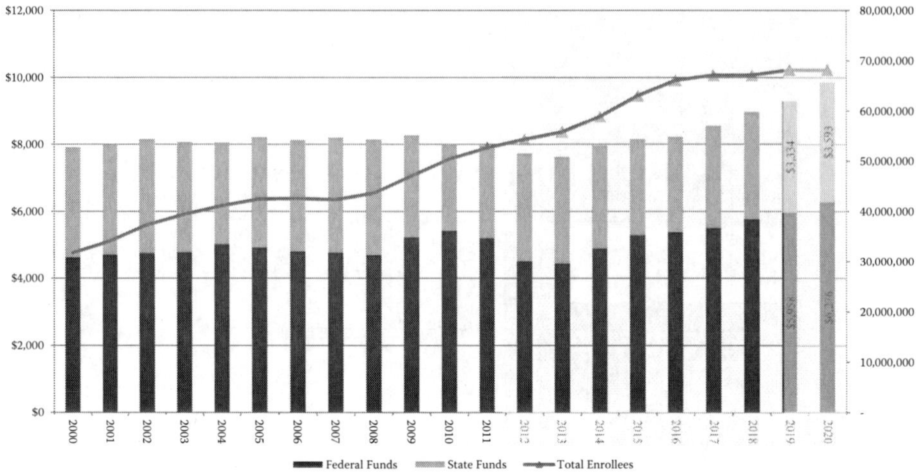

Figure 8.2 Real Medicaid expenditures and projected expenditures per enrollee for the average state (2011 $) and enrollment.

investment in higher education.* The combination of slowing state investment, enrollment growth, and to a smaller degree, the costs of education services provided by public colleges and universities, has created pressures on tuition that run counter to avowed national goals for higher education. As shown in Table 8.4, total real state spending on higher education declined by 14 percent in real dollars between 2008 and 2012. Per student funding declined 23 percent over this period, on top of a 2 percent decline during the "good years" from 2000 to 2008. State spending does include federal budget stabilization funds during 2010, 2011, and 2012, but even this supplement was insufficient to keep spending at prior levels.

Meanwhile, enrollments have been growing at a rapid clip, with a 22 percent increase from 2000 to 2008, even before the countercyclical uptick realized during the Great Recession. The price tag (tuition and fees plus state and local appropriations) for higher education did go up 9 percent per student early in the decade, but this growth has been almost entirely reversed during the recession. The 2012 total per FTE price of education at public universities in the average state grew only 2 percent over 2000. Thus, contrary to conventional wisdom (Thurm 2012), public university and college tuition and fees are rising not so much because the average price of higher education per student is growing, but because each student causes state funding to be spread over a larger and larger share of students, and the difference in per student revenue is made up with tuition increases.

* Some states do have local governments provide some funding for higher education. Overall, around 12 percent of total state and local funding is provided by local governments. For the purposes of this analysis, the two are combined.

Table 8.4 Higher Education Real per FTE Revenues for the Average State[a]

	Trend between 2000 and 2008					*Impact of the Recession*			*Trend to 2020*		
Fund Source	*2000*	*Share of Total*	*2008*	*Share of Total*	*Percent Change from 2000*	*2012*	*Share of Total*	*Percent Change from 2008*	*2020*	*Share of Total*	*Percent Change from 2008*
State/local appropriations	$7,747	67%	$7,561	60%	–2%	$5,835	49%	–23%	$5,733	47%	–24%
Tuition and fees	$3,813	33%	$5,036	40%	32%	$5,975	51%	19%	$6,388	53%	27%
Total	$11,560		$12,598		9%	$11,810		–6%	$12,121		–4%
Total enrollment (millions)	8.6		10.5		22%	11.5		10%	14.2		36%
Total state/local spending (billions)	$66.26		$77.80		17%	$66.82		–14%	$80.37		3%

[a] In 2011 $.

Meanwhile, state funding is actually declining in real terms, thereby accelerating this effect. In 2012, tuition grew 19 percent over 2008 and 57 percent over 2000.

Outlook on Higher Education

In the area of higher education, the direction of state fiscal policy runs counter to national policy and to many states' own assertions about the desirability of increasing access to a college education (Kelderman 2013). President Obama has called for this country to raise the college graduate rate from the current 40 to 60 percent of young adults by 2020 (deNies 2010, Obama 2013). This shift would increase the number of college graduates by 8 million per year. In 2010, around 79.4 percent of students were educated in public institutions of higher education (Dunbar et al. 2011). If public universities and colleges continue to maintain the same share of students, a 20 percent increase in graduates would mean states would educate around 6 million more students annually by 2020. This would require a $33 billion increase in state annual investment, assuming states keep their per student contributions constant from 2012 onward. Given the current priorities of states, this is not likely to happen. Assuming states keep their spending growth rate at the 2000 to 2008 levels and the real per student price tag grows by 0.1 percent annually, this increase in enrollment would lead to a 47 percent increase in tuition.

A more likely scenario is presented in Figure 8.3. In this projection, state and local total funding is assumed to grow at the 2000 to 2008 annual rate of

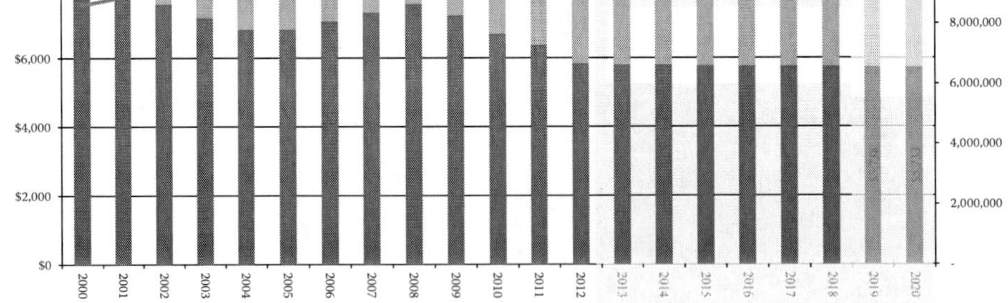

Figure 8.3 Real per FTE higher education revenues and projected revenues for the average state and total enrollment.

around 2 percent a year. This growth rate may inflate potential state investment in higher education, given pressures from Medicaid and public pensions. This analysis assumes that the total price tag per student for a public university education continues to grow at the current rate of around 0.1 percent per year for the average state (almost constant with GDP). Student enrollment growth continues at an average rate of 3 percent per year. Even with this slower enrollment growth, by 2020 state real appropriations per student will have declined by 24 percent from 2008. This projection suggests that state funding for higher education will not recover from the recession and tuition will rise by 27 percent over 2008 (or 7 percent over 2012).

Much like national aspirations regarding K–12 education, those regarding higher education appear to have outpaced the will to fund such aspirations, at least in light of current service delivery and financing models. Because affordability is strongly linked to higher education attendance and completion (Titus 2006), growth in tuition is likely to depress future enrollment below the projections described here.

One issue that states may end up considering is that the current funding model for higher education is not particularly socially efficient. Most states provide a fixed-level appropriation to their university systems, which has the effect of broadly subsidizing higher education, regardless of student ability to pay. One possibility for stretching higher education dollars would be to shift state funding away from a "block grant" to a voucher or scholarship model tied to student ability to pay. New technology may also fundamentally reshape higher education, including the recent popularity of massive open online courses (MOOCs). MOOCs offer higher education to a wider audience for a lower price. There are several ways that MOOCs may change higher education: State institutions may forego hiring faculty and provide selected courses as MOOCs, and students would receive course credit for completing these courses. Universities might also create entire academic programs online using MOOCs, opening up these courses to more students and generating a significant new revenue stream without the brick-and-mortar overhead.

Highways and Transportation

A convergence of several trends is putting pressure on transportation revenues, which, combined with an increased need for basic maintenance, presents real challenges for state transportation spending. These pressures will limit state and federal ability to make any ambitious infrastructure investments in the future. Currently, state transportation spending is dominated by expenditures on highways. On average, states spend 62 percent of total transportation dollars on highway and bridge maintenance and expansion; around 20 percent is spent on transit and 2 percent on bicycle/pedestrian projects. The remainder is used for highway safety projects, administration, and planning (Tri-State Transportation Campaign 2012).

Table 8.5 and Figure 8.4 show the trends in state and federal funding for highways per lane mile and in aggregate for states. The analysis breaks out bond funding since this is a significant form of infrastructure finance. Centerline or lane miles grew by a modest 3 percent, reflecting the built-out nature of the national highway system. The general fiscal trend from 2000 to 2008 suggests that transportation was an area of modest public investment relative to the economy. Real per lane mile spending increased by 7 percent, and real state funding, in aggregate, increased by 19 percent. Unlike the other spending areas examined here, transportation funding is lumpy, but smoothing with a three-year rolling average yields similar trends. The impact of the recession on state revenues, and in particular on motor fuel revenues, is visible in 2010, where real state spending per lane mile and in aggregate declined, even as federal funding ramped up significantly. However, even in 2010, total transportation spending increased by 5 percent over 2008.

Outlook for Highways and Transportation

"Warnings that the United States is underinvesting in infrastructure, including transportation, have been sounded for decades despite continuous growth in overall funding" (Bipartisan Policy Center and Eno Center for Transportation 2012, 12). While the numbers for the average state suggest a consistent and steady level of investment, ongoing concerns include that national transportation investments are not well prioritized and the future for federal transportation funding is not particularly rosy. A key example of poor prioritization is exhibited by examining the nations' bridges. In his 2013 State of the Union address, President Obama raised the issue of deteriorating bridges across the country, noting that around 70,000 of them (~11 percent) in the United States were structurally deficient.* The price tag for fixing the current backlog of bridge repairs is $71 billion (Shoup et al. 2011).

Issues related to prioritizing transportation investment dovetail with those surrounding the potential decline in federal and state funding. The federal Highway Trust Fund is largely supported by an 18.4 cent gas tax, which has begun to decline as a revenue source, as both vehicle miles traveled peaked in 2007 and fuel efficiency has grown. Because the gas tax is not indexed to inflation, funding growth relies on increased driving. Since 2008, these trust fund revenues have been supplemented with transfers from regular appropriations. The CBO projects that the trust fund will again face a shortfall starting in 2015. The revenues plus fund balance in the fund will be sufficient to support around

* This number is based on a report by T4 America, an advocacy coalition for transportation funding and reform (Shoup et al. 2011).

Table 8.5 Real per Lane Mile Highway Revenues for the Average State[a]

	Trend between 2000 and 2008					*Effect of Recession*			*Trend in 2020*		
Fund Source	*2000*	*Share of Total*	*2008*	*Share of Total*	*Percent Change*	*2010*	*Share of Total*	*Percent Change 2008*	*2020*	*Share of Total*	*Percent Change 2008*
State	$10,636	70%	$11,163	68%	5%	$11,160	65%	–0.02%	$12,136	74%	9%
Federal	$4,558	30%	$5,143	32%	13%	$5,905	35%	14.82%	$4,245	26%	–17%
Total	$15,194		$16,306		7%	$17,066		4.66%	$16,381		0%
Bonds	$2,478		$2,309		–7%	$3,881		68.13%	$3,607		56%
Total lane miles (millions)	8.22		8.48		3%	8.54		0.65%	8.87		5%
Real total state revenues for transportation (no bonds) (billions)	$75		$89		19%	$86		–3.04%	$107		20%

[a] In 2010 $.

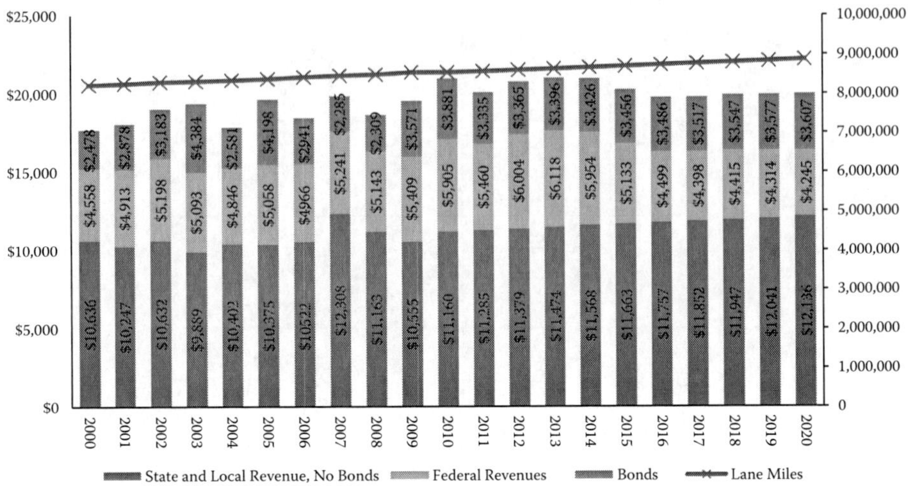

Figure 8.4 Real per lane mile highway revenues and projected revenues for the average state (in 2010 $).

$44 billion in federal outlays in 2015 and $40 billion in 2016, after which funding flatlines in nominal dollars (Congressional Budget Office 2013a). This represents an 18 percent decline over 2012 outlays, including $42 billion for highways and $7 billion for transit. Current pressures on the U.S. budget heighten the possibility that the federal government will no longer shore up the trust fund with appropriations. A decline in federal share will have a disproportionate impact on transit projects and will more heavily affect rural areas across the country (Bipartisan Policy Center and Eno Center for Transportation 2012).

Further pressures on transportation funding will stem from new fuel economy standards that will go into effect in 2017 and require 49.6 miles per gallon for the average vehicle—a significant shift from the 2016 standard of 34.1 miles per gallon. CBO estimates in 2012 indicate that the impact on federal gas tax revenues through 2022 will be less than 1 percent. But, by 2040, the new fuel standard will have reduced these revenues by 21 percent (Congressional Budget Office 2012).

The same trends are expected to affect state revenues for highways (Transportation Revenue Forecast Council 2012); however, state highway funds are more diversified than federal funds. In 2010, of the $86 billion in state revenues for highways, only $30 billion was from motor fuel taxes. The remainder is covered by a mix of state appropriations as well as tolls or motor vehicle or motor carrier taxes and other miscellaneous revenues.

The analysis in Table 8.5 is based on a simple linear regression forecast for each state from the 2000 to 2010 state revenues per lane mile. This strategy produced a compound growth rate for the average state of 0.7 percent in real state revenues per lane mile for the period from 2011 through 2020, slightly less than the 0.9 percent annual growth rate of the prior decade. The analysis predicts a 1.7 percent annual growth in aggregate state revenues across all states, and this growth rate seems in alignment with available analyses from selected states. For instance, Washington State projects around 1.6 percent annual growth in transportation revenues between 2012 and 2021 (Transportation Revenue Forecast Council 2012). Arizona projects approximately 3.4 percent annual growth in highway user fee revenues in nominal dollars, or 1.4 percent real growth between 2013 and 2020 (Financial Management Services 2012).

The 2020 scenario therefore reflects almost stagnant transportation spending per lane mile—federal revenues decline in response to federal retrenchment and state revenues grow just enough to make up the difference. According to this projection, state revenues must grow in aggregate by 20 percent over 2008 to shore up lost federal funding and keep up with modest growth in lane miles. Unless a substantial reprioritization occurs, it is unlikely that this funding trajectory alone will be sufficient for major interstate investment in new transportation initiatives, such as the national high-speed rail network advocated by the Obama administration.

Pensions and Long-Term Liabilities

The funded status of state pensions has slipped significantly in the last decade and is cause for concern. This shift has coincided with an effort by the Governmental Accounting Standards Board (GASB) to change the standards for reporting pension valuation, requiring states to report the funded status of long-term liabilities such as retiree health benefits. Analysts expect all states to feel some impact from these growing liabilities, although the impact may vary widely by state.

Analysts at the Center for Retirement Research have estimated the impact of pension obligations on state and local budgets, given their funded status in 2009. Assuming that liabilities are discounted at 8 percent, and states increase their contributions incrementally to pay their full annual required contributions (ARCs) by 2013 and amortize their liabilities over a 30-year period, pension contributions for the average state will grow from 3.8 percent of state and local budgets in 2009 to 5 percent in 2014, and then remain at this level until the state's unfunded liability has been paid down in 2043. As explained in Chapter 7, there is substantial variation across the states; Illinois, for example, has underfunded its pensions for years and its contributions need to increase from 3.5 percent of state and local expenditures in 2008 to 8.7 percent (Munnell et al. 2010). The center's analysis does not account for the loss of valuation from the 2008 recession, so its estimates may be on the low end of future costs to states.

GASB has since issued a ruling making a variety of changes in calculating state retirement liabilities, the most significant being that states recalculate and report their liabilities based on a blended rate of return. The ruling is in response to the charge that pension liabilities are mandatory obligations of states, and as such, the valuation rate of these liabilities should be equivalent to the return on near certain or "riskless" assets. Currently, many states discount their liabilities assuming an 8 percent rate of return. The GASB proposed change would allow states to value liabilities that are fully funded at a rate of return equivalent to that on their current mix of assets, and the unfunded liabilities must be valued at the riskless rate of return. This shift would have the effect of changing the funded status of average state and local pension funds in 2010 from 76 percent funded to 57 percent (Munnell et al. 2012).*

The 2009 Center on Retirement Research report also estimated the impact on budgets if states had to fully fund their pensions and discounted liabilities at 5 percent (the riskless rate of return). In this case, states would have pension obligations closer to 9.1 percent of expenditures starting in 2014. Also, states that have underfunded their pensions would face an even larger impact—Illinois would face expenditures equivalent to 13 percent of total state and local spending (Munnell et al. 2010).

To give some context to the impact of these changes, one can estimate the impact on state budgets using the Center on Retirement Research's ratios. The Pew Center, considering current state accounting practices, reports that state-only ARCs were $58 billion in 2010 and the unfunded liability was $16 billion. Making a rough adjustment for state funds shows that around $35 billion in required contribution was paid out of state funds.† Using the center's ratios and accounting for the new GASB rules regarding amortizing existing unfunded liabilities, state spending would have to increase to roughly $70 billion in 2020 to meet current pension obligations—a $35 billion increase. For comparison, if the $35 billion were invested in higher education, states might reach the 2020 goal of graduating 60 percent of young adults from college. Notably, this increase does not include states' OPEBs—comprised largely of retiree health insurance. However, OPEBs are typically a moral obligation rather than a contractual one, and states could choose not to provide such benefits. Pension benefits are more typically prescribed in a state constitution, in law, or interpreted as a contract.

State OPEBs are significantly underfunded, but even with this underfunding the magnitude is much smaller than that of state pensions. While states have an estimated $3 trillion pension liability, the OPEB liability was closer to $659 billion

* The Center on Retirement Research maintains a database of 126 state and local plans and regularly estimates the impact of different policy changes from this sample.

† State-funded pensions cover employees who are federally funded as well as state funded, and so the numbers need to be adjusted to only examine the impact of state-funded employees since these funds are directly competing with other state priorities.

in 2010 (Pew Center on the States 2011). While the future of OPEB liabilities is hard to predict, it would require $33 billion more a year (roughly $20 billion in state funds) for states to fully fund their current liabilities associated with these benefits.

Conclusion

The first decade of the 21st century might be characterized as one of ambitions not achieved. State investments in K–12 education, higher education, and transportation were essentially wiped out by the Great Recession. The change from 2000 to 2010 in state real per capita spending in Table 8.6 shows that state per capita spending has been reset almost back to 2000 levels. The 2010 decline in total state funding was, in part, shored up by federal stimulus funds, but there is no indication that states have been or will be able to fully replace these funds now that they are gone. The net impact is that states will not come close to achieving No Child Left Behind goals; efforts to move more young adults into higher education are growing, but not at the rate hoped for, and the country is grappling with deteriorating infrastructure. Given the current federal fiscal outlook, shoring up state spending in these areas is not likely to be top priority among federal budget makers either.

The challenge for states going forward is likely to be a rear guard action: how to retain the gains made in human and physical capital investment in the last century in the face of an aging population and increased fiscal demands from health care and pensions. Tables 8.6 and 8.7 suggest that these pressures may be significant, although not crushing. The 2020 scenario, while rough, indicates that even assuming state funding for education, higher education, and transportation grows at the 2000 to 2008 rates from 2014 on, health care and pensions will require significant investment to meet demands. Between 2010 and 2020, Medicaid will likely dwarf investments in all other areas, requiring an estimated $120 billion increase in state funds.* Pensions will require around $35 billion if fully funded over this period, greater than any other growth area outside K–12 education. State services of the future will be more heavily weighted toward Medicaid and pensions compared to higher education and highways.

Because this analysis looks at expenditures, there is an underlying assumption that state revenues will continue to grow along the 2000 to 2008 trajectory. However, there are real concerns that state tax structures are failing to keep pace with changes in technology, globalization, and new business practices. If so, the situation described here will be exacerbated, placing even greater pressure on nonmandatory parts of state budgets.

---

* Part of this increase is due to the loss of federal stimulus funds and the need for states to backfill into Medicaid.

Table 8.6 Total Real per Capita State Spending[a]

Service Area	*2000*	*2008*	*Percent from 2000*	*2010*	*Percent from 2000*	*2020*	*Percent from 2000*
K–12 education	$827	$945	14%	$853	3%	$1,018	23%
Higher education	$235	$257	9%	$243	3%	$240	2%
Medicaid	$352	$448	27%	$378	7%	$707	101%
Transportation	$266	$293	10%	$286	7%	$320	20%
Total	$1,681	$1,942	16%	$1,760	5%	$2,285	36%
Pension payments[b]	$74	$115	57%	$113	54%	$211	186%
Unfunded liability	$0	$14		$32		$0	

[a] In 2011 $.

[b] Pension payments are measured as total state spending and so encompass federal funds as well as other state fund sources outside state general funds.

Table 8.7 Total Real Spending by State Government (billions)

Service Area	*2000*	*Share*	*2008*	*Change from 2000*	*2010*	*Change from 2000*	*Change from 2008*	*2020*	*Share*	*Change from 2000*	*Change from 2008*	*Change from 2010*
K–12 education	$233	49%	$287	$54	$263	$30	–$24	$340	45%	$107	$53	$77
Higher education	$66	14%	$78	$12	$75	$9	–$3	$80	10%	$14	$2	$5
Medicaid	$99	21%	$136	$37	$116	$17	–$20	$236	31%	$137	$100	$120
Highways	$75	16%	$89	$14	$88	$13	–$1	$107	14%	$32	$18	$19
Total	$473		$590		$542			$763				
Pension payments[b]	$21		$35	$14	$35	$14	$0	$70		$50	$35	$35
Unfunded liability	$0		$4		$10			$0				

[a] These numbers vary slightly from those reported in the other tables: All numbers are in 2011 dollars, and the middle years are 2008 and 2010, whereas the previous tables used the final year to establish real dollars and reported the last year of data available, which ranged from 2010 to 2012.

[b] Pension payments are from Pew Center on the States (2010, 2011) and then adjusted for inflation to reflect state expenditures financed by state funds (or 60 percent) as opposed to state expenditures financed by federal funds.

Appendix 8.A Data Sources and Methodology

Data Name	*Data Source*	*Calculation/Notes*
Gross domestic product price deflator	U.S. Department of Commerce, Bureau of Economic Analysis, National Income Product Accounts, Table 1.1.4: Price Indices for Gross Domestic Product (line 1), last revised February 28, 2013 (accessed March 1, 2013). Where needed, GDP projections from Moody's Analytics developed in November 2012 were used.	
Education	The data for education enrollment and revenues are based on U.S. Census, F-33 Financial Survey, available at http://www.census.gov/govs/school/ (accessed February 21, 2013); U.S. Census Bureau (2012).	These data differ from others collected by the National Center for Education Statistics (NCES), which may cause slight variation in totals and per student amounts. State schools as well as charter schools are not included in the dataset used in this analysis but are included in the other datasets. The dataset chosen for this analysis included FY2010 expenditure data, while the other datasets are not as current. The enrollment numbers differ from other datasets collected by NCES. The difference between this and other NCES datasets is small (a difference of around 1 million students, 2.5 percent). The other datasets are used for NCES projections and so must be harmonized for the 2011–2020 projections.

Appendix 8.A (*Continued*) Data Sources and Methodology

Data Name	*Data Source*	*Calculation/Notes*
Education projections—enrollment	National Center for Education Statistics, Projections of Education Statistics to 2021 (updated January 2012), Table 6, available at http://nces.ed.gov/programs/projections/projections2021/tables.asp.	Note that the underlying enrollment numbers that NCES used for projections do not precisely match the census ones. Thus, the projection for this analysis was created by taking the growth trend from the NCES projections and applying them to the enrollment dataset used in this analysis. The enrollment dataset used in this analysis matches the expenditure data.
Education projections—expenditure growth	National Center for Education Statistics, Projections of Education Statistics to 2021 (updated February 2012), Table 18, available at http://nces.ed.gov/programs/projections/projections2021/tables.asp; Bureau of Labor Statistics, Series CES9093161101, Employment Hours and Earnings from the Current Employment Survey (local government, education, all employees)	The analysis assumes that federal funding follows a trajectory much like that outlined in the ATRA (Kogan 2013), with cuts of around 7.3 percent starting in 2014 and gradually being reduced to 5.7 percent by 2020. The 2011–2013 numbers are projected based on an assumption that ARRA funds are phased out and inflation-adjusted federal funding per student returns to 2008 levels. State funding is projected based on a Center on Budget and Policy Priorities survey that reports that state funding declined by 5 percent for the median state in 2012, and then by 1.7 percent in 2013. After this point, the analysis assumes that states will return to their pre-2008 investment in education of around 2.6 percent annually, which may be an ambitious assumption. Local funding then makes up the difference. The analysis uses NCES projected real per FTE expenditure growth to project real per FTE revenue growth (assuming revenues must equal expenditures)

Continued

Appendix 8.A (*Continued*) Data Sources and Methodology

Data Name	*Data Source*	*Calculation/Notes*
	(accessed March 4, 2013). (Note that 2012 estimated employment was preliminary as of the writing of this book.)	from 2014 to 2020; 2011–2013 is projected based on employment changes nationally in the education sector (employment data are from BLS). The numbers were then checked to see if they matched projections/observed trends in a Center on Budget and Policy Priorities report (Oliff et al. 2012).
Higher education	State Higher Education Executive Officers Association (2012)	The data for higher education are based on State Higher Education Executive Officers Association (SHEEO) data; however, the numbers are adjusted differently from SHEEO, which adjusts each state based on cost of living and cost of educating its current student mix. SHEEO also adjusts based on a higher education inflation index. Because this analysis focuses on aggregate state spending behavior across different service types rather than comparing higher education investment between states, the analysis takes out these adjustments and uses GDP as a common deflator across service areas.
Real annual higher educational appropria-tions	State Higher Education Executive Officers Association (2012)	Educational appropriations include state and local support for public higher education. Amount includes federal budget stabilization funds through the American Reinvestment and Recovery Act (ARRA) of 2009 but subtracts funding for special purpose research, hospitals, and medical education, as well as appropriations to nonpublic institutions. These funds include state scholarship funding for students attending public institutions as well as direct appropriations. These funds include local appropriations; local support makes up \$9 billion out of the total \$74 billion in support for higher education (12 percent). These data are derived from an annual survey of state higher education conducted by SHEEO (2011, 29).

Appendix 8.A (*Continued*) Data Sources and Methodology

Data Name	*Data Source*	*Calculation/Notes*
Real annual net tuition revenue	State Higher Education Executive Officers Association (2012)	Net tuition is calculated by taking total tuition and fees less state support and financial aid. Medical student tuition is subtracted out; debt financed with tuition is included (SHEEO 2011, 31).
Total higher education revenues	State Higher Education Executive Officers Association (2011)	Total education revenues are used to calculate the projections for future state appropriations and net tuition. This total deducts tuition currently being used for capital or debt service spending from the projection. Tuition for capital and debt service is included in the 2000–2011 numbers, so the analysis essentially is conservative in assuming that states will save by not using tuition for these purposes. Either way, the effect is small (less than 1 percent of total tuition revenues go to this purpose).
Enrollment	State Higher Education Executive Officers Association (2012)	Enrollment captures full-time equivalent students based on student credit hours. This variable excludes medical students (SHEEO 2011, 27).
Medicaid expenditures	National Association of State Budget Officers, State Expenditure Reports 1999–2001 through 2010–2012, available at http://www.nasbo.org/publications-data/state-expenditure-report/state-expenditure-report-fiscal-2010-2012-data; Cuckler et al. (2011).	This report is a survey of all 50 states and captures state and federal spending on Medicaid. Alaska is omitted because of nonresponse. During this period Alaska's total expenditures on Medicaid were less than 0.25 percent of national spending, so its omission is not likely to affect overall conclusions. Connecticut and Massachusetts reported all funds as state funds in some years, and so federal funds were broken out based on that year's FMAP rate. A concern is whether NASBO numbers accurately reflect Medicaid expenditures in states where Medicaid is largely administered at the local level. However, the NASBO numbers do match Medicaid

Continued

Appendix 8.A (*Continued*) Data Sources and Methodology

Data Name	*Data Source*	*Calculation/Notes*
		expenditures reported by the Centers for Medicaid and Medicare Services (CMS) between 2000 and 2009, with an average annual variance of 1.73 percent. While using the CMS survey would be preferable, it ends with 2009, so this analysis relies on NASBO numbers. Finally, caution should be exercised when comparing the state per FTE and federal per FTE amounts. While the aggregate numbers match well to CMS, it is not clear how accurately states accounted for the federal versus state funding on an individual basis. Cross-checks of federal-to-total ratios reported in the NASBO survey compared to the state FMAP rates showed correlations that vary from 0.76 in 2000 to 0.54 in 2011. While FMAP rates are not a perfect measure since states may have varying FMAP rates for different parts of their Medicaid programs, the bulk of the Medicaid program falls under the regular state FMAP rate, and so the federal-to-total expenditures should be close to the state's FMAP rate.
Medicaid enrollment	Kaiser Commission on Medicaid and the Uninsured (2012)	Medicaid enrollments are counts for June of each year and are collected and reported by the Kaiser Foundation.
Medicaid enrollment projections	Centers for Medicare and Medicaid Services (2012), Smith et al. (2012)	Enrollment projections use preexisting projections from the Congressional Budget Office (CBO) and the percentage growth to calculate growth off of the Kaiser Family Foundation–reported Medicaid enrollment numbers. As discussed in the analysis, CBO's numbers differ substantially from those of the Centers on Medicaid and Medicare Services (CMS), with CBO assuming a much larger use of the

Appendix 8.A (*Continued*) Data Sources and Methodology

Data Name	*Data Source*	*Calculation/Notes*
		exchanges and employer health coverage, and thus a much lower take-up of Medicaid. The enrollment numbers have been adjusted by recent reports from the Kaiser Foundation on actual enrollment in 2012 and 2013.
Medicaid expenditure projections	Centers for Medicare and Medicaid Services (2012), Smith et al. (2012)	Medicaid expenditure projections and expenditure projections per enrollee were developed by using the NASBO base numbers and then projecting growth in expenditures similar to CMS expenditure projections. CMS projections are developed on a calendar basis and so are converted to match most state fiscal years by taking half of each year's projections and averaging to reach a "fiscal year." This has the effect of spreading the growth impact of the ACA over two fiscal years, as most states will experience part of the increase in FY14 and then a second increase in FY15 as the increase in enrollment and related expenditures is annualized. The expenditure projections almost exactly mirror the CBO projections for federal outlays (between –1 and 4 percent difference across years). The one exception is that the analysis modifies 2012 and 2013 expenditure growth based on reports from the Kaiser Foundation on actual expenditures reported by the states for these years. The total expenditures are not the same as the expenditures per enrollee for the average state. The average state spending is approximately $944 less per enrollee than spending per enrollee on a national basis because the impact of large high-spending states such as New York

Continued

Appendix 8.A (*Continued*) Data Sources and Methodology

Data Name	*Data Source*	*Calculation/Notes*
		are reduced by averaging expenditures across the states. To match the growth back to the average state, it is assumed that expenditure per enrollee for the average state will grow at the same rate as average spending per enrollee nationally. This may overstate expenditure growth since states such as New York may grow more aggressively, although recent efforts by the state to reduce Medicaid expenditures suggest that this will not actually be the case. This growth amount is used to generate total expenditures per enrollee. Next, the analysis calculates the federal versus the state share. The federal government will cover 100 percent of newly eligible enrollees for 2014 through 2016, and then phase down to 90 percent in 2020. The base federal match for the average state from 2012 to 2020 (which differs from the actual FMAP because of the averaging effect across states) is based on the observation that the average federal match is around 0.3 to 0.4 percent below the average FMAP, and so is set at 0.560. The actual national average FMAP rate, for instance, for 2012 is 0.572 once weighted by state enrollment. Note that the enhanced FMAP for enrollees under the ACA does not vary by state, so it is safe to assume that it is fixed, rather than needing to calculate an alternative federal match for the average state. These numbers were used to calculate a new ratio of federal coverage: New federal match = (% New enrollees × Enhanced FMAP) + (% Eligible under prior Medicaid × Estimated average regular FMAP)

Appendix 8.A (*Continued*) Data Sources and Methodology

Data Name	*Data Source*	*Calculation/Notes*
		This federal matching rate was then used to calculate state versus federal share per enrollee. To calculate federal versus state share for total expenditures, the actual average FMAP rates were used for 2012 and 2013 and then assumed to continue at a similar rate through 2020.
Highway lane miles	Office of Highway Policy Information Highway Statistics Series, Table HM-60 for 2000–2011, 2011 posted December 2012, available at http://www.fhwa.dot.gov/policyinformation/statistics.cfm (accessed March 1, 2013).	Lane miles measuring center lane miles for rural and urban roads in each state. The numbers are an estimate made by the Federal Highway Administration based on an annual survey of state Departments of Transportation each year.
Highway revenues; Highway lane mile projections	Office of Highway Policy Information Highway Statistics Series, Table SF-1 for 2000–2011, 2010 posted December 2011, available at http://www.fhwa.dot.gov/policyinformation/statistics.cfm (accessed November 2012).	This form captures revenues remitted to states to finance state roads each year and includes motor fuel taxes, motor vehicle and motor carrier taxes, roll and crossing tolls, appropriations from general funds, other state imposts, miscellaneous revenues, bond proceeds, federal funds, as well as funds remitted from local government to the state to finance state road projects. These amounts are not expenditures on roads in a particular year but reflect revenue received by the Department of Transportation and other state transportation entities, and so from the perspective of state *budget* would be equivalent to the state outlays that year.

Continued

Appendix 8.A (*Continued*) Data Sources and Methodology

Data Name	*Data Source*	*Calculation/Notes*
		Lane miles that have a relatively smooth upward trajectory were forecast using an annual compound rate of growth for 2000–2010 and then projected through 2020 based on the assumption that lane miles would continue to grow at a similar rate. In general, growth has been very slow, and so the growth rate is less than 1 percent a year.
Highway revenues	Congressional Budget Office (2013a)	The analysis uses CBO projections of available revenues in the federal Highway Trust Fund to project federal expenditures since the analysis looks at the impact of the Highway Trust Fund running out of money and being required to rely on existing revenue streams. The state revenues are projected using a basic linear forecast function in Excel for each state and forecasting based on 2000–2010 trends the 2011–2020 numbers. This essentially is equivalent to a straight-line forecast. Since revenues are "lumpy," this strategy was chosen over using an average annual compound growth rate; however, the results are quite similar to using such a growth rate. This projection was checked against state forecasts that were readily available, and generally, this simple forecast was close to those projected by the states. The general finding is that state transportation revenues are slated for relatively slow but steady growth of between 1 and 2 percent in real dollars for the next decade. This is noted in the analysis.

Appendix 8.A (*Continued*) Data Sources and Methodology

Data Name	*Data Source*	*Calculation/Notes*
Pension payments	Pew Center on the States (2010, 2011)	The Pew Center reports that state-only annual required contributions were $58 billion in 2010. When divided by NASBO-reported total state expenditures, this amount of funding is equivalent to 3.6 percent, compared to the 3.8 percent reported by the Center on Retirement Research. The center is using the U.S. Census state and local expenditures, so it is not surprising that the numbers vary slightly. Assuming the ratio of 3.8 in 2009/9.1 in 2020 can be translated to the NASBO and PEW numbers, with an adjustment for difference in magnitude and slight adjustment in year (so 3.6 in 2010 to 8.62 in 2020), this would suggest that state spending would have to increase to roughly $139 billion in 2020 to meet current obligations as well as to amortize existing unfunded liability. This amount needs to be adjusted to see the impact on state funds specifically, which make up only about 60 percent of total state expenditures.

References

Angeles, J. (2012). *How Health Reform's Medicaid Expansion Will Impact State Budgets: Federal Government Will Pick Up Nearly All Costs, Even as Expansion Provides Coverage to Millions of Low-Income Uninsured Americans*, technical report. Center on Budget and Policy Priorities.

Bipartisan Policy Center and Eno Center for Transportation. (2012). *The Consequences of Reduced Federal Transportation Investment*, technical report.

Boyd, D., and Dadayan, L. (2010). *Revenue Declines Less Severe, but State's Fiscal Crisis Is Far from Over*, technical report. Nelson A. Rockefeller Institute of Government.

Centers for Medicare and Medicaid Services. (2012). *National Health Expenditure Projections 2011–2021*, technical report. Office of the Actuary.

Congressional Budget Office. (2012). *How Would Proposed Fuel Economy Standards Affect the Highway Trust Fund*, technical report.

Congressional Budget Office. (2013a). *Projections of Highway Trust Fund Accounts under CBO's February 2013 Baseline*, technical report.

Congressional Budget Office. (2013b). *Spending and Enrollment Detail for CBO's February 2013 Baseline: Medicaid*, technical report.

Cuckler, G., Martin, A., Whittle, L., Heffler, S., Sisko, A., Lassman, D., and Benson, J. (2011). Health Spending by State of Residence 1991–2009. *Medicare and Medicaid Research Review*, 1(4).

deNies, Y. (2010). President Obama Outlines Goal to Improve College Graduation Rates in U.S. ABC News. Available at http://abcnews.go.com/WN/president-barack-obama-outlines-college-education-goal-university/story?id = 11359759.

Dunbar, A., et al. 2011. *Signature Report: National Postsecondary Enrollment Trends before, during, and after the Great Recession*, technical report. National Student Clearinghouse Research Center.

Duncombe, W., Lukemeyer, A., and Yinger, J. (2006). The No Child Left Behind Act: Have Federal Funds Been Left Behind? Center for Policy Research: Education Finance and Accountability Program at Syracuse University.

Financial Management Services. (2012). *Arizona Highway User Revenue Fund, Forecasting Process and Results FY2013–2022*, technical report.

Garfield, R., Clemans-Cope, L., Lawton, E., and Holahan, J. (2012). *Enrollment-Driven Expenditure Growth: Medicaid Spending during the Economic Downturn FY2007–2010*, technical report. Henry J. Kaiser Family Foundation.

Holahan, J., and Yemane, A. (2013). Enrollment Is Driving Medicaid Costs—but Two Targets Can Yield Savings. *Health Affairs*, 32, 1453–1465.

Johnson, N., and Leachman, M. (2013). Four Big Threats to State Finances Could Undermine Future US Prosperity, technical report. Center on Budget and Policy Priorities.

Kaiser Commission on Medicaid and the Uninsured. (2012). Medicaid Enrollment: June 2011 Data Snapshot. In *Medicaid Facts*. Henry J. Kaiser Family Foundation.

Kelderman, E. (2013). College Education Is Expected to Remain a High Priority for States. *Chronicle of Higher Education*. Available at http://chronicle.com/article/College-Education-Is-Expected/136427/.

Kogan, R. (2012). *Two Sequestrations: How the Pending Automatic Budget Cuts Would Work*, technical report. Center on Budget and Policy Priorities.

Kogan, R. (2013). *The Pending Automatic Budget Cuts: How the Two "Sequestrations" Would Work*, technical report. Center on Budget and Policy Priorities.

Maciag, M. (2013). State of the State Addresses: What Are Governors' Priorities? *Governing*, March 11. Available at http://www.governing.com/blogs/by-the-numbers/gov-state-of-the-state-speeches-summary.html.

Munnell, A., Aubry, J.-P., Hurwitz, J., and Quinby, L. (2012). *How Would GASB Proposals Affect State and Local Pension Reporting?*, technical report. Center for Retirement Research at Boston College.

Munnell, A., Aubry, J.-P., and Quinby, L. (2010). *The Impact of Public Pensions on State and Local Budgets*, technical report. Center for Retirement Research at Boston College.

National Association of State Budget Officers. (2012). *State Expenditure Report: Examining Fiscal 2010–2012 State Spending*, technical report.

National Education Association. (2007). *House Appropriations Subcommittee Mark, FY2008*. Washington, DC.

Obama, B. (2013). Higher Education. *Education: Knowledge and Skills for the Jobs of the Future.*

Oliff, P., Mai, C., and Leachman, M. (2012). *New School Year Brings More Cuts in State Funding for Schools*, technical report. Center on Budget and Policy Priorities.

Ollove, M. (2013). Easiest Path to Mental Health Funding May Be Medicaid Expansion. Stateline.org. Available at http://www.pewstates.org/projects/stateline/headlines/easiest-path-to-mental-health-funding-may-be-medicaid-expansion-85899443812.

Pew Center on the States. (2010). *The Trillion Dollar Gap: Underfunded State Retirement Systems and the Roads to Reform*, technical report. Pew Charitable Trusts.

Pew Center on the States. (2011). *The Widening Gap: The Great Recession's Impact on State Pension and Retiree Health Care Costs*, technical report. Pew Charitable Trusts.

Shoup, L., Donohue, N., and Lang, M. (2011). *The State of Our Nation's Bridges*, technical report. Transportation for America.

Smith, V., Gifford, K., Ellis, E., Rudowitz, R., and Snyder, L. (2012). *Medicaid Today: Preparing for Tomorrow: A Look at State Medicaid Program Spending, Enrollment and Policy Trends*, technical report. Henry J. Kaiser Family Foundation.

State Budget Crisis Task Force. (2012). *Report of the State Budget Crisis Taskforce*, technical report.

State Higher Education Executive Officers Association. (2011). State Higher Education Finance FY2011. Boulder, CO.

State Higher Education Executive Officers Association. (2012). State Higher Education Finance FY2011, All SHEF Data Table. Boulder, CO.

Thurm, S. (2012). Who Can Still Afford State U? *Wall Street Journal*. Available at online.wsj.com/article/SB10001424127887323501404578163290734542674.html

Titus, M. (2006). No College Student Left Behind: The Influence of Financial Aspects of a State's Higher Education Policy on College Completion. *Review of Higher Education*, 29, 293–317.

Transportation Revenue Forecast Council. (2012). *September 2012 Transportation Economic and Revenue Forecasts, Volume 1 Summary*, technical report.

Tri-State Transportation Campaign. (2012). *Tracking State Transportation Dollars*, technical report.

U.S. Census Bureau. (2012). *Public Expenditure Finances: 2010 (G.D.E.F.a.S.S. Branch, Trans.)*, vol. G10-ASPEF. Washington, DC.

Vestal, C. (2012). Medicaid: A Year of Excruciating Decisions. Stateline.org. Available at http://www.pewstates.org/projects/stateline/headlines/medicaid-a-year-of-excruciating-decisions-85899376388.

Chapter 9

State Education Expenditures

Sean P. Corcoran, Sarah A. Cordes, and Amy Ellen Schwartz

New York University

Contents

Introduction

In 2012, states spent almost 20 percent of their budgets on elementary and secondary education, and another 10 percent on postsecondary education. Expenditures on education from own-source revenues surpassed even those for Medicaid as a share of state budgets (National Association of State Budget Officers 2012). The current level of state expenditure on education reflects not only growth in enrollment and the cost of education, but also a substantially increased role of states in K–12 education over the past century. In 1920, for example, 83 percent of revenues for K–12 education were raised at the local level. Almost 90 years later, the local share had dropped to 41 percent, while state revenues accounted for nearly half of all such expenditures. States are also the primary revenue source for public two- and four-year institutions of higher education, accounting for over one-fifth of all revenues to both types of institutions. While the share of higher education revenue attributable to state governments has fallen over time due to the growth of auxiliary services such as university hospitals, the absolute levels of revenue have grown dramatically, from \$10 billion in 1960 to \$72 billion in 2010.* Beyond direct aid to K–12 and postsecondary institutions, states also indirectly affect education spending through policies that shape local taxes and spending, such as the setting of maximum or minimum required tax rates, or mandates in service provision. Additionally, state governments are largely responsible for managing the pension and health care plans of their retired educators, so that changes in the cost of postemployment health care directly impact state budgets.

In this chapter, we provide an overview of state spending on elementary, secondary, and postsecondary education. In addition to describing the structure of K–12 and higher education finance, we highlight evolving issues that are likely to affect state education budgets in the coming years. Although we limit our discussion to these two main categories of education spending, it is important to point out that states' investment in human capital extends beyond these activities, from early childhood education to adult education and training. These investments also compete for scarce state tax dollars. In the first section below, we focus on elementary and secondary education, with a description of K–12 expenditures, the changing role of states in K–12 school finance, and the long-run implications of this shift. The next section turns to higher education, with a discussion of the complex nature of higher education finance and trends in higher education that affect state budgets. We conclude with a discussion of issues to watch in state education finance.

* In real (2010) dollars.

K–12 Education Finance

Direct State Aid and the Rising State Share of K–12 Education Expenditures

In the United States, public elementary and secondary education spending decisions are made primarily at the local level, by school districts, counties, and municipalities. That said, states play a large role in financing these decisions. In 2007–2008—the last fiscal year before the Great Recession—close to half of all revenues for K–12 education (48.3 percent) were raised at the state level and distributed to districts as intergovernmental aid; a slightly smaller share of revenues (41.4 percent) was raised locally, largely from property taxes; and the remainder (8.2 percent) was financed by grants from the federal government.*

School finance historically was a local responsibility. In the early part of the 20th century, local governments provided an average of 80 percent or more of all revenues for public schools.† As shown in Figure 9.1, the role of states in financing

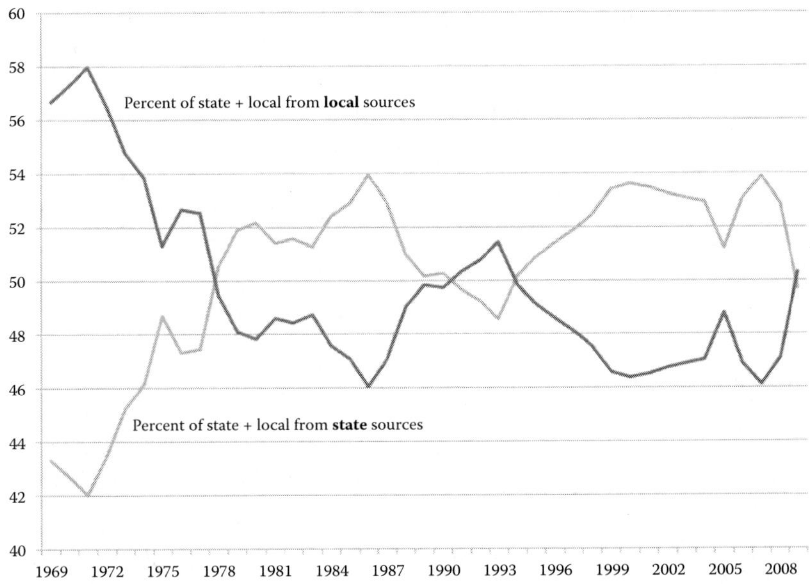

Figure 9.1 Percent of state and local revenues from local and state sources, 1969–2009. (From Snyder, T.D., and Dillow, S.A., *Digest of Education Statistics 2011*, NCES 2012-001, National Center for Education Statistics, Institute of Education Sciences, U.S. Department of Education, Washington, DC, 2012.)

* Authors' calculations using data from the *Digest of Education Statistics 2011* (Snyder and Dillow, 2012).

† Ibid.

K–12 education increased markedly beginning in the 1970s, reflecting, in part, court-ordered and legislative reforms to school funding formulas that increased state aid to local districts (Murray et al. 1998; Corcoran and Evans 2008; Yinger 2004). The trend of rising state revenue shares was apparent, however, even before California's landmark *Serrano v. Priest* ruling (1976), which declared California's school funding system unconstitutional and sparked finance reforms nationwide. The growing role of the states, then, reflected not only concerns about school finance equity and adequacy, but also rising incomes and a response to an increasing return to schooling.

Nationally, the share of combined local and state revenues coming from state sources rose 9.5 percentage points since 1969. As is clear from Figure 9.2, the overall increase in the states' share of K–12 revenue masks considerable differences across states.[*,†] Over this period, 14 states increased their share by 20 points or more, and of these states, 9 increased their state share 25 points or more (including Vermont, Oregon, California, Montana, Idaho, Kansas, New Hampshire, South Dakota, and Iowa). Much of the observed increase may well have been driven by litigation. Of the nine states with a 25-point or greater increase in the state share, five implemented court-ordered school finance reform during this period (Vermont, California, Montana, Kansas, and New Hampshire), while two others (Idaho and Oregon) survived court challenges, but nonetheless made substantial changes to their school finance systems.[‡]

That said, not all states saw increasing shares over this 40-year period, and in fact, 11 states *reduced* their state revenue share. During this time, only three of these states saw their school funding formula overturned (Connecticut, Texas, and New York).[§]

Legislative and court-mandated school finance reforms were intended to improve the *equity* or *adequacy* of K–12 spending. The early wave of reforms focused on equity, to ameliorate highly unequal patterns of spending resulting from a reliance

---

[*] Federal revenues are not included in this calculation, so shares in Figure 9.1 represent the proportion of nonfederal revenues coming from state, instead of local, sources. We use 2007–2008 as an endpoint to limit the influence of the recession that first affected the 2008–2009 fiscal year.

[†] Hawaii, which consists of one statewide school district, and the District of Columbia are excluded.

[‡] See appendix Table A19.1 in Corcoran and Evans (2008) for a list of significant court rulings.

[§] Seven of these 14 states survived challenges in court. The litigation in Connecticut and Texas followed somewhat different paths than that in other states. In Connecticut, a 1977 court overturn in *Horton v. Meskill* resulted in modest changes to the state's aid formula. When the state revisited the issue in the 1996 adequacy case *Sheff v. O'Neill*, the state Supreme Court found the state's funding system to be inadequate, but only as a consequence of racial segregation. Its remedy required additional funding for magnet schools and interdistrict transfer programs, but no major changes to its finance formula. Similarly, Texas's funding system was found to be unconstitutional in a series of cases spanning 1989 to 1995 (*Edgewood v. Kirby*). After implementing a new funding formula, high-property-wealth districts sued the state and won, claiming the new formula amounted to a statewide property tax, which is unconstitutional in Texas (*West Orange Cove v. Nelson*).

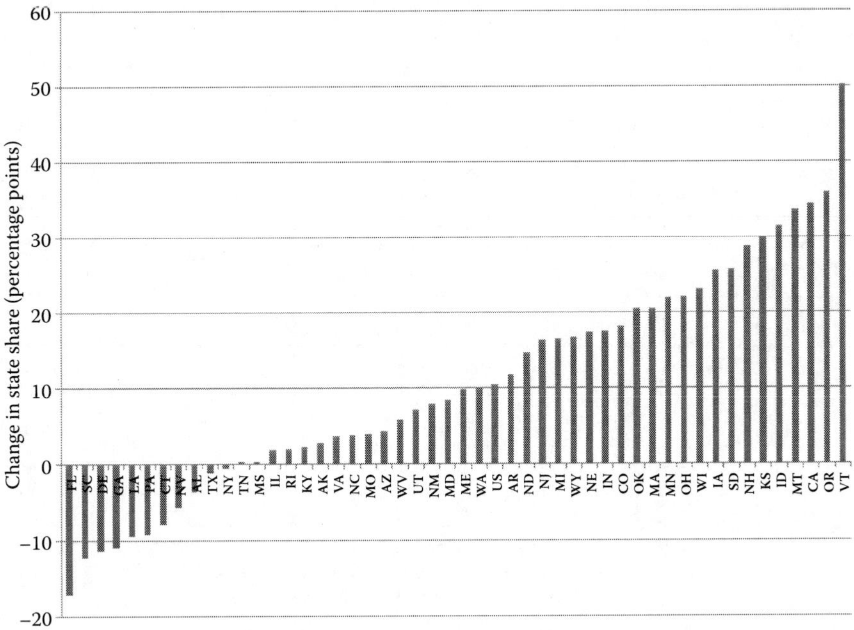

Figure 9.2 Change in state share of combined state and local revenues, 1969–1970 to 2007–2008. Excludes Hawaii and the District of Columbia. State shares are calculated as the percent of combined local and state revenues from state sources. (From Snyder, T.D., and Dillow, S.A., *Digest of Education Statistics 2011*, NCES 2012-001, National Center for Education Statistics, Institute of Education Sciences, U.S. Department of Education, Washington, DC, 2012.)

on local property taxation for public schools. These reforms sought to reduce the association between local property wealth and spending per student. The later wave of reforms focused to a greater extent on adequacy—that is, providing all districts with sufficient (i.e., adequate) resources for students to meet a defined educational goal such as proficiency in basic subjects or a high school diploma.* Under both approaches the state revenue share rose as states introduced foundation aid programs guaranteeing a minimum level of education spending per student, and grant formulas with matching rates that varied with local property wealth or income (Corcoran and Evans 2008; Hoxby 2001; Yinger 2004).

A substantial research literature examining the effects of school finance reform documents large impacts on both the level and distribution of K–12 expenditure

* Kentucky's *Rose v. Council for a Better Education* (1989) exemplified this approach (Flanagan and Murray 2004). The equity/adequacy distinction is a bit of a false dichotomy, as many school finance cases included elements of both (Briffault 2007). It is a common distinction made in the literature, however, and suits our purposes here.

Table 9.1 Inequality in per Pupil Current Expenditures on K–12 Education, 1972–2008

Year	*Gini Coefficient (× 100)*	*Theil Index*	*Theil Index (within state)*	*Theil Index (between state)*
1972	16.2	43.1	14.0	29.2
1982	13.7	30.7	13.8	16.9
1992	14.9	37.6	12.2	25.4
2000	12.3	27.1	8.2	18.9
2002	12.9	29.7	8.8	20.9
2004	13.8	34.0	9.6	24.4
2006	14.4	38.3	10.3	28.0
2008	15.0	41.5	10.9	30.6

Note: 1972–2004 are from Corcoran and Evans (2008); 2006 and 2008 are authors' calculations using data from the U.S. Bureau of Census.

(e.g., Murray et al. 1998; Corcoran and Evans 2008; Springer et al. 2009). Corcoran and Evans (2008), for example, report that between 1972 and 2002, spending per pupil rose by 9.2 percent more in states where a court overturn occurred than in those without a court order. This increase, moreover, appears to have been entirely funded by increases in state aid. At the same time, within-state inequality in spending per pupil fell 15 to 19 percent more in states with a court-ordered finance reform than in those without such reform.

As shown in Table 9.1, a variety of measures indicate that spending inequality declined between 1972 and 2008.* From 1972 to 2002 there was an overall decline in spending inequality, as states implemented reforms that reduced both within- and between-state inequities. However, in the years that followed—a period spanning the end of one recession and the beginning of another—inequality in per pupil spending began to rise. According to the Theil index, that is, a common measure of inequality, spending inequality between states was higher in 2008–2009 than at any time in the prior 36 years. We revisit this trend later in the context of education spending during the Great Recession.

To this point we have largely ignored federal contributions to school expenditures, because until very recently, revenues from federal sources only constituted a small share of K–12 spending. Prior to 1965, when President Lyndon Johnson signed the Elementary and Secondary Education Act (ESEA) into law, the federal

* Berne and Stiefel (1984) describe the properties of these measures and their application to school funding equity.

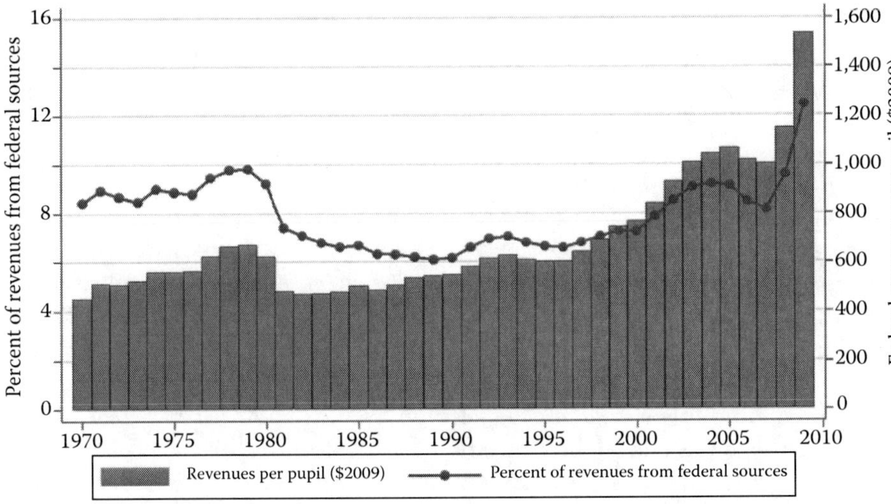

Figure 9.3 Elementary and secondary education revenues from federal sources, 1970–2009. (Authors' calculations using Snyder, T.D., and Dillow, S.A., *Digest of Education Statistics 2011*, NCES 2012-001, National Center for Education Statistics, Institute of Education Sciences, U.S. Department of Education, Washington, DC, 2012; U.S. Census Bureau, *Public Education Finances: 2012*, G10-ASPEF, U.S. Government Printing Office, Washington, DC, 2012.)

share of K–12 revenues had never been higher than 4.4 percent.* Since then, the federal share has fluctuated from a low of 6.1 percent (1989–1990) to a high of 9.8 percent (1978–1979 and 1979–1980), at least until the recent recession, when the share rose above 12 percent (Figure 9.3).† The long-run growth can be attributed to a multitude of factors, including federal accountability measures (No Child Left Behind (NCLB)), expansion of Title I aid to cover immigrant and limited English-proficient students, and a booming special education population.

The majority of federal dollars for K–12 education originates from the Department of Education (DOE), with another large share provided by the Department of Agriculture (DOA) (primarily for the school lunch program) and the remainder coming from various other federal departments and agencies. Funds for disadvantaged students are the largest form of aid provided by the DOE, accounting for 40 percent of its K–12 grants, while special education accounts for nearly one-third of its aid (32.5 percent). Other funding streams from the DOE include school improvement programs such as NCLB, class size reduction, and charter schools (17.4 percent); vocational and adult education

* Snyder and Dillow (2012).

† Ibid.

programs (4.5 percent); impact aid programs, which provide funds for children who live on federal property with no suitable local school district (3.3 percent); English language acquisition (1.9 percent); and Indian education (0.3 percent) (Snyder and Dillow 2012).

Beginning in 2009, the federal government has played an unprecedented, albeit temporary, role in helping states fill revenue gaps brought about by the Great Recession. During that time, federal aid to K–12 education jumped to record levels, with per pupil grants rising 53 percent in real terms between 2007–2008 and 2009–2010.* Anticipating a decline in state tax revenues, the federal government passed the American Recovery and Reinvestment Act (ARRA) in February 2009, a $787 billion economic stimulus package with a combination of tax benefits and spending increases, including $91 billion for education.† Of this, $48.6 billion was a one-time allocation to the State Fiscal Stabilization Fund (SFSF), general aid to the states for K–12 and higher education for the 2008–2009, 2009–2010, and 2010–2011 fiscal years.‡ Another $23.5 billion was allocated to states as categorical funding for compensatory and special education, and $5 billion was reserved for Race to the Top, a competitive grant program run by the DOE.§ ARRA was followed by another round of federal aid through the Education Jobs Fund, a $10 billion supplement to help states retain, hire, or rehire public school employees in 2010–2011.¶ The greater reliance on federal funds in recent years is important from a state perspective because it means that state and local school district budgets are more vulnerable to changes in the federal budget.

The Indirect Role of State and Federal Policy on K–12 Education Finance

State and federal policies affect K–12 education finance in ways that extend beyond direct revenue provision. These include regulations governing testing and accountability, the treatment of students with special needs (e.g., students with disabilities or limited English proficiency), and constraints on local revenue raising capacity (e.g., tax limitations). While additional funds may be provided to offset the cost of compliance (i.e., Title I, Individuals with Disabilities Education Act (IDEA), Parts B and C formula grants, Title III grants for limited English-proficient and immigrant students), in other cases *unfunded mandates*

* Snyder and Dillow (2012) and U.S. Census Bureau (2012).

† Available at http://www.recovery.gov/Transparency/fundingoverview/Pages/fundingbreakdown.aspx (accessed October 30, 2012).

‡ U.S. Department of Education, available at http://www2.ed.gov/policy/gen/leg/recovery/factsheet/stabilization-fund.html (accessed October 30, 2012).

§ Ibid.

¶ Education Jobs Fund, available at http://www.educationjobsfund.gov/Pages/home.aspx (accessed October 30, 2012).

require states or local governments to provide or expand services without additional revenues to compensate for increased costs.

Perhaps the most well-known example of the indirect role of the federal government in state and local education in recent years is the 2001 reauthorization of the ESEA (now NCLB), which tied receipt of federal Title I funds to the adoption of new accountability measures, including yearly standardized testing in grades 3 through 8 and high school, and public reporting on student progress. This historic law not only increased state and local costs related to test administration, data collection, and reporting, but also made future federal funding contingent on compliance with the accountability rules (Gordon 2008; Chingos 2012). Federal funding per student increased markedly with the implementation of NCLB, rising 31 percent in real terms between 2000 and 2003 (see Figure 9.3). Many have questioned, however, whether this increased funding (amounting to $240 per student, on average) was sufficient to cover the additional costs of meeting NCLB's requirements (e.g., Imazeki and Reschovsky 2006; Duncombe et al. 2008; Mathis 2005).

As with NCLB, the IDEA of 1997, a reauthorization of Education of the Handicapped Act (EHA) of 1975, represents an unfunded mandate to states in the provision of services to students with disabilities. IDEA and its predecessors increased services to students currently served by the public schools and expanded access to students not previously served by the public system. Prior to 1975, more than 1.75 million disabled students were entirely excluded from the public school system, and another 3 million in the public schools did not receive services appropriate to their needs (Katsiyannis et al. 2001). Specifically, IDEA has been interpreted to mean that disabled students are conferred with "an enforceable substantive right to public education ... and conditions federal financial assistance upon states' compliance with substantive and procedural goals of the act" (*Honig v. Doe* 1988). The federal government provides formula aid to states and local education agencies complying with the law; this aid was never meant to provide for the full cost of special education. Congress intended for IDEA funding to cover 40 percent of states' cost in special education services, but in practice it supports only 8 to 10 percent of states' total special education expenditures (Katsiyannis et al. 2001). Furthermore, funds from the federal government may not supplant state spending, but rather must be used to increase expenditures on special education. Therefore, almost by construction, state compliance with IDEA requires increased state expenditures on special education.

Another indirect role of state governments in K–12 finance is the setting of policies governing the taxing and spending decisions of local governments, and the deductibility of property taxes. States may set minima for local tax rates as a condition for receiving state aid, limit the growth or level of property taxes, or implement any of a wide range of policies that constrain or enhance districts' ability to raise revenue (Baker and Corcoran 2012). For example, some states constrain revenue raising capacity by either prohibiting local supplementation or imposing tax limitations (such as California's Proposition 13). Others, however, adopt policies that have the potential to enhance revenue raising capacity, for instance, through guaranteed tax base formulas, which lower the price of additional spending at the local level.

The federal and state governments indirectly support spending on schools by allowing tax deductions for educational expenditures and local property tax payments (which in turn support K–12 education).* By reducing the tax price of local spending financed through the property tax, deductions for property tax payments could create incentives for either increasing or decreasing reliance on property taxes, with the magnitude and direction of the change depending on federal income tax rates. Evidence suggests, however, that deductions of state and local property taxes increase property tax rates, and may lead to small increases in local revenues from the property tax (Holtz-Eakin and Rosen 1990). Estimates regarding the effect of federal deductions for education expenditures show that these deductions tend to benefit wealthier districts by decreasing the price of state and local spending. Including deductibility in calculations of federal support to education more than doubles the federal contribution to schools, and due to the regressivity of these deductions, this federal funding tends to disproportionately benefit high-income districts (Loeb and Socias 2004). Therefore, the evidence suggests that elimination or reduction of these implicit subsidies could result in decreased state and local spending on education.

Finally, teacher pension and health care costs are emerging issues that will play a more prominent role in state budget discussions in the coming years. This topic is discussed further at the end of this chapter.

Implications of Centralized K–12 Financing: Lessons from the Great Recession

The long-run shift in education financing away from local school districts and toward state governments raises several important issues for the future of K–12 expenditures, issues that became more apparent during the recent recession. First, education budgets now rely much more heavily on revenues from state sources, typically income and sales taxes, which are more volatile and vulnerable to economic downturns than local property taxes (Dadayan 2012). Historically, school districts took advantage of the relative stability of the property tax base in recessions, offsetting losses in state aid by increasing property tax rates. The Great Recession, however, has been unique because of the concurrent decline in housing values and, in turn, tax revenues (Dye and Reschovsky 2008).† As assessed values typically lag

* The federal government also provides tax credits for education, but these primarily focus on higher education and are discussed later in the chapter.

† Between the first quarter of 2007 and the first quarter of 2012, U.S. housing prices declined by 16.7 percent. Several states, including Nevada, Arizona, Florida, and California, have experienced declines of 30 percent or more (Dadayan 2012).

behind market prices, it remains to be seen how much districts can continue to rely on property taxes as a stabilizing source of revenues in the coming years. Notably, revenues from the property tax declined for the first time only in the fourth quarter of 2010, which coincided with the expiration of federal relief (Dadayan 2012).

Second, equity in school funding across districts and within states is driven heavily by the distribution of state aid, upon which low-income and low-property wealth districts are the most reliant. State budget crises that reduce aid may therefore have the largest impacts on neediest districts. Ultimately, the overall impact on equity in spending will depend upon how states distribute cuts across all districts and how district own-source revenues respond. Indeed, an emerging consequence of the fiscal crisis has been a gradual shift in tax burdens back to local governments, a reversal of long-run trends. As shown previously in Figure 9.1, the local share of combined local and state revenues has increased each year since 2007–2008 (the year preceding the Great Recession). The latest school funding report from the U.S. Census Bureau, covering the 2009–2010 fiscal year, reported that the local share of K–12 revenues (44 percent) exceeded the state share (43.4 percent) for the first time in 16 years, with state revenues per student dropping 6.5 percent, the largest drop in more than 35 years (U.S. Census Bureau 2012).

Finally, equity in school spending *across states* will also depend heavily on state budgets. With greater reliance on state funding sources, education systems will tend to rise and fall with the fortunes of their state government. With some states substantially more affected by the Great Recession than others, this link has important implications for between-state equity. As seen previously in Table 9.1, inequality in K–12 spending per pupil rose in recent years, and in the most recent year of data was at its highest point since 1972 (see also Armour-Garb et al. 2009).

The federal ARRA and Education Jobs Fund described earlier provided considerable, but temporary, relief to state budgets, but these funds were not always sufficient to guarantee spending at prerecession levels. In 2011–2012, after the stimulus funding expired, 37 states spent less on general aid to local districts than they did in the previous year. In the following year, 35 states spent less on state education aid than they did in 2007–2008, the year prior to the recession (Oliff and Leachman 2011; Oliff et al. 2012).

Whether and how the recent fiscal crisis has impacted the quality of K–12 education, or whether the recession differentially affected low- and high-wealth districts, remains an unanswered question, but will be important issues for researchers and policy makers to consider in the coming years.

Higher Education Finance

While much attention is typically paid to the role of states in financing K–12 education, state governments also play an important role in financing education in public postsecondary institutions. Nearly one out of every three state education dollars is spent on higher education. The rising demand for postsecondary schooling—attributable to the rising return to higher education and (in recent years) reduced labor market opportunities for young adults—has fueled competition for increasingly scarce state resources.

Between 2000 and 2010, enrollment in public four-year institutions increased by almost 1.9 million, while enrollment in public two-year institutions increased by 1.5 million. This increase is substantial when contrasted with the relatively stable enrollment during the 1990s. Notably, the biggest increase in enrollment occurred between 2008 and 2009, coinciding with the start of the Great Recession. Enrollment in two-year institutions is also far above what it was in earlier decades. The growing demand for postsecondary education has real implications for state budgets, as states provide 22.6 percent of revenues for public four-year institutions and 30 percent of revenues for public two-year institutions. Put simply, rising enrollment will ultimately require more spending to maintain the same level and quality of services. Although higher education institutions benefit from a broader revenue base than K–12 schools, some additional spending will necessarily come from state support. In the sections that follow, we provide an overview of revenue sources for postsecondary education, trends in higher education finance, and issues to watch in higher education.

Sources of Revenue for Higher Education

Higher education finance is considerably more complex than K–12 funding. While K–12 education is financed primarily through local taxation and direct aid from state and federal government, higher education is financed through a combination of federal, state, local, and private monies. Public financing of higher education occurs directly, through funding to institutions, and indirectly, through funding to individuals. Each source is described below.

State Funding

State appropriations are the largest source of revenue for public postsecondary institutions, accounting for 22.6 percent of total revenues at four-year and 30 percent of revenues at two-year institutions. This aggregate figure masks a great deal of variation across states, however, with some state governments (such as Wyoming) providing nearly all revenues to public institutions and other state governments (such as Colorado) providing only a small share of revenues (Figure 9.4).

Over time, the role of the states in providing direct funding for institutions has grown. Figure 9.5 shows the growth in state appropriations for operating expenses of higher education since 1960–1961 (in thousands of current dollars).*

* These appropriations do not include income received by higher education institutions from nontax sources or reappropriations by state legislatures. The appropriations contained in these figures include funds not only for instruction, but also research, adult education programs, hospitals, etc.

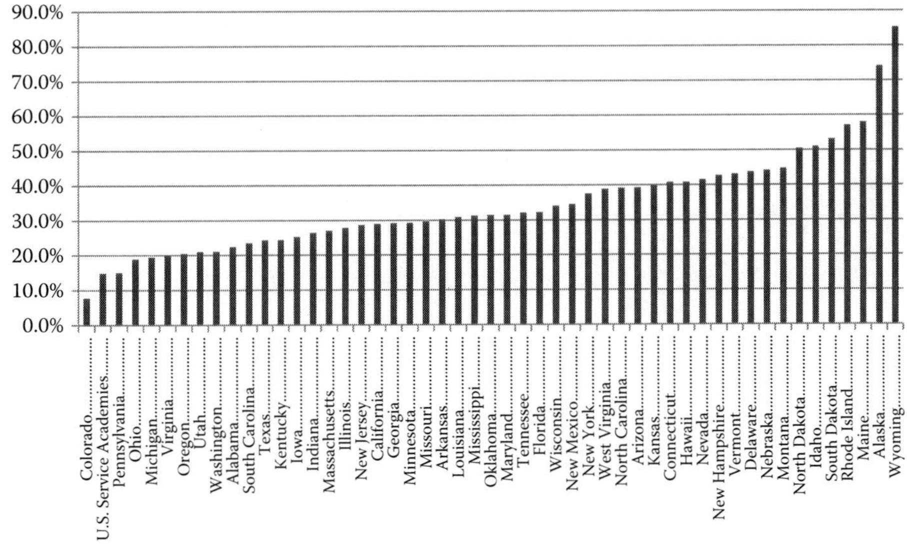

Figure 9.4 State and local revenues as a share of total revenues by state, all public higher education institutions, 2009–2010. (From Snyder, T.D., and Dillow, S.A., *Digest of Education Statistics 2011,* NCES 2012-001, National Center for Education Statistics, Institute of Education Sciences, U.S. Department of Education, Washington, DC, 2012.)

There appear to be three distinct periods characterizing state appropriations for higher education. From FY 1960–1961 to 1977–1978, state appropriations for higher education grew at an increasing rate. Then from 1979–1980 to 2007–2008, state appropriations continued to rise, but at a variable pace. Finally, beginning in FY 2008–2009 there was a sharp decline in state appropriations to higher education coinciding with the Great Recession. This drop was particularly steep in FY 2011–2012, when appropriations dropped by about 10 percent, as federal stimulus funds expired. The role of ARRA funds in maintaining state support for higher education is shown in detail in Figure 9.6. In 2009–2010, $4.5 billion of state funding for higher education was financed with federal ARRA dollars. Federal support decreased to $2.8 billion by 2010–2011 and to only $46.7 million by 2011–2012. Therefore, while the overall level of state-generated funding decreased rather dramatically from 2008–2009 to 2009–2010, the real impact of the Great Recession was not experienced until 2011–2012, when federal stimulus money ran out (Center for the Study of Education Policy 2012).

In addition to direct appropriations, state funding for higher education also flows indirectly through grants, scholarships, and loans to individuals. In 2010–2011, approximately $9 billion in state grants was awarded to students nationwide (Baum and Payea 2012). States vary in their eligibility criteria

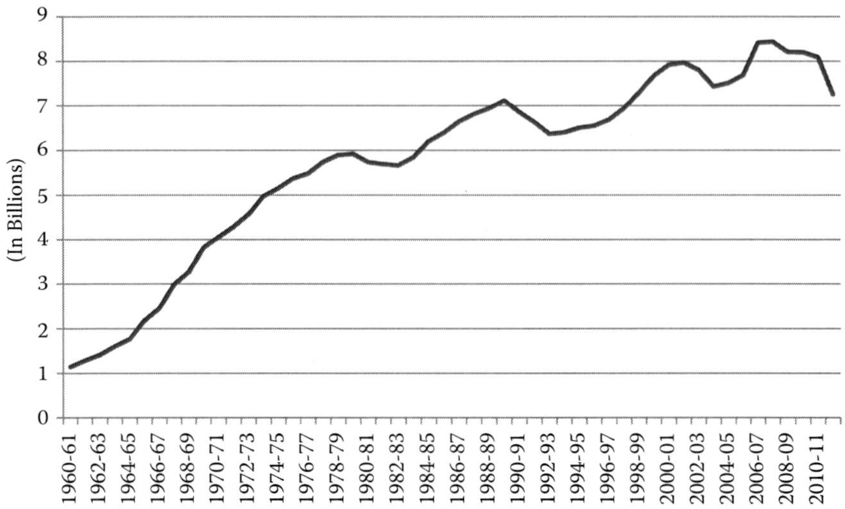

Figure 9.5 Total state appropriations for higher education, FY 1960–1961 to 2011–2012. (From Center for the Study of Education Policy, An Annual Compilation of Data on State Fiscal Support for Higher Education, Grapevine, 2012, available at http://grapevine.illinoisstate.edu/.)

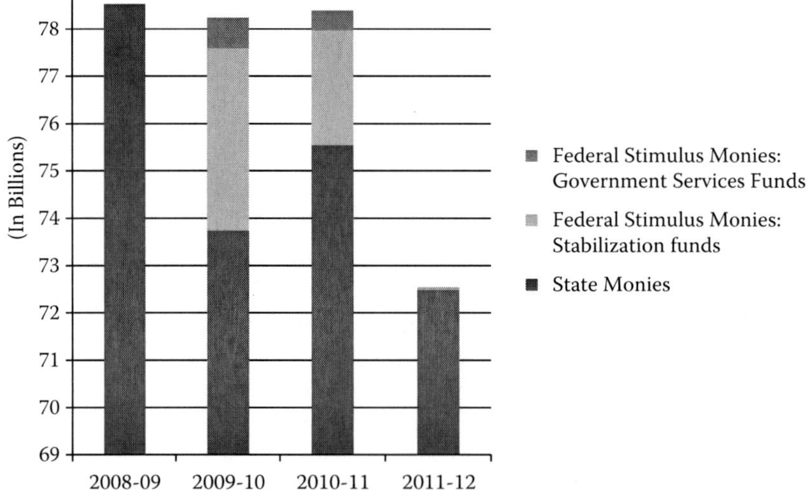

Figure 9.6 Total state appropriations by source, FY 2008–2009 to 2011–2012. (From Center for the Study of Education Policy, An Annual Compilation of Data on State Fiscal Support for Higher Education, Grapevine, 2012, available at http:// grapevine.illinoisstate.edu/.)

for grants, but many tie the awards to financial need. In 31 states, for example, over 80 percent of state grant aid is awarded based on need. This is not true for all states, however, and grant aid is increasingly distributed without regard to need, focusing instead on student merit (The College Board 2011). For instance, in five states, less than 20 percent of grant aid is awarded based on need, and at the extreme, all aid in Georgia is awarded based on academic merit (Baum and Payea 2012).*

Federal Funding

The federal government also provides substantial support to public postsecondary institutions. Federal funding is the fifth largest revenue source for public four-year institutions, where it accounts for 15.8 percent of all revenues, and the second largest source for two-year institutions, where it accounts for nearly one-quarter of revenues (22.8 percent). Like state support for higher education, federal aid flows both directly through aid to institutions and indirectly through aid to individuals.

In the category of direct aid, the federal government provides support to institutions of higher education through grants and contracts for training, research, and public service activities. In 2009–2010, federal direct aid to public postsecondary institutions totaled \$31.3 billion, with \$28 billion going to four-year colleges and universities, \$3.3 billion to two-year colleges, and \$45 million to other institutions (Delta Cost Project 2011).†

Indirect federal aid to individuals, which plays a much larger role in financing higher education than direct support, comes in three forms: grants and work study programs, student loans, and personal tax credits. By far the largest grant program is the Pell Grant, awarded to undergraduate students with financial need.

---

* State merit-based grants yield mixed evidence on enrollment. A number of studies find large enrollment effects of the Georgia HOPE scholarship, estimating around a 3 percent increase in enrollment for every \$1,000 (Dynarski 2002a; Cornwell et al. 2001). Similarly, California's Cal-Grant program was estimated to increase enrollment by 4 to 6 percentage points (Kane 2003). The Adams Scholarship in Massachusetts, however, was found to have no significant impacts on enrollment among recipients (Cohodes and Goodman 2012). Further evidence that merit aid does not increase enrollment is provided in a broader survey of merit-based aid programs in 15 different states (Fitzpatrick and Jones 2012).

There is more consistent evidence that state grants influence the choice of institution. Georgia's HOPE scholarship was found to increase the likelihood that students attended a college costing \$1,000 or more (in 2001 dollars) (Long 2004b). Additionally, while the Adams scholarship did not increase overall enrollment, it increased the likelihood that recipients would attend one of the eligible public universities within Massachusetts (Cohodes and Goodman 2012). Therefore, while state-funded merit-based aid programs appear to change the types of institutions students are likely to attend, these programs do not appear to increase the overall demand for these institutions in a way that would require additional state funding.

† This amount is reported net of Pell Grants, which are discussed in the following paragraph as a form of indirect aid.

Expenditures on Pell Grants nearly doubled between 2008–2009 and 2010–2011, from $18.1 to $34.8 billion (Baum and Payea 2012).* Federally subsidized student loans constitute another significant source of indirect federal support of higher education, the costs of which include the cost of administering loans and subsidizing student interest ($40 billion), tax expenditures for the income tax exemption for loan interest payments ($1.1 billion), and the cost of student defaults (an estimated $38.4 billion net of recoveries).†,‡

Finally, federal tax credits provide additional support to individuals enrolled in school (and their parents). The most widely used of these credits are the American opportunity tax credit (AOTC) and the lifetime learning credit. In fiscal year 2011, federal expenditures on these two tax credits totaled $7.1 billion and $1.9 billion (Joint Committee on Taxation 2012). Other favorable tax treatments for education include the deductibility of scholarship or fellowship income, parental exemptions for students ages 19 to 23, education savings accounts such as 529 plans and Coverdell education savings accounts, and tax-exempt employer tuition and education assistance (Internal Revenue Service 2012).§

As federal support accounts for an average of 15 to 23 percent of revenues to public postsecondary institutions, these institutions are quite sensitive to changes in the federal budget. If the worsening economy leads to declining revenues from federal sources, this may mean that states will need to increase funding to public institutions in order to maintain the same services without increasing costs to students.

* Evidence suggests that Pell Grant receipt may actually have little impact on enrollment among the traditional college-aged populations, with the exception of small increases at public two-year institutions (Hansen 1983; Kane 1994). To the extent that costs at public two-year institutions exceed tuition, Pell Grants will have at most small impacts on state financing of higher education. Among older students (ages 22–35), there is some evidence that Pell Grant eligibility increased the probability of college attendance by a little more than 1 percent (Seftor and Turner 2002).

† See http://cbo.gov/sites/default/files/cbofiles/attachments/43054_StudentLoanPellGrantPrograms.pdf.

‡ Evidence regarding the impact of federal loans on college enrollment is extremely limited, but what does exist suggests that loan access increases college attendance and may shift attendance toward four-year institutions (Reyes 1995; Dynarski 2002b). When there is a dollar-for-dollar trade-off between loans and grants, however, the probability of attending college falls (Savoca 1991). Therefore, the impact of loan availability on demand for higher education appears to depend at least in part on the mixture of loans and grants being offered.

§ Tax credits appear to have little impact on rates of college enrollment—eligibility for the credit does not increase the likelihood of enrolling in any college, the likelihood of enrolling in a four-year college, or the likelihood of enrolling full-time. This may be due to both low take-up rates and the fact that the main beneficiaries of these tax credits are not likely to be marginal students (Long 2004a). It should be noted, however, that this study is based on the HOPE tax credit, which was not refundable. Therefore, the impacts of tax credits on college going may differ somewhat with the AOTC, as low-income individuals are more likely to benefit from a refundable tax credit than they would from a nonrefundable one.

Private Support

Tuition and fees paid on behalf of students attending higher education institutions are the second largest revenue source for four-year colleges and universities, where they account for 19 percent of revenues, and the fourth largest at two-year institutions, where they account for 16 percent of revenues.* Other sources of private support include endowment income, gifts, and sales. Gifts and income from endowments and investments account for 19 percent of revenue at four-year colleges and universities, but only 9 percent at two-year institutions. Sales from auxiliary services such as university bookstores and hospitals contribute a large share of revenues (18 percent) to four-year institutions. Taken together, private sources of funding from tuition to auxiliary services are critical to the operation of public postsecondary institutions, and particularly four-year institutions.†

Trends in Higher Education Finance

As described above, a distinguishing feature of higher education is that a sizable portion of its public and private financing occurs indirectly, through loans and grant aid to students, which offsets the cost of tuition, fees, and other expenses. Consequently, higher education budgets, to a large extent, reflect enrollment.

Enrollment among all degree-granting institutions has risen over the last century (Snyder and Dillow 2012). In 1970, less than 6 percent of the nation's population aged 18–44 was enrolled in a public four-year college or university. By 2010, the number of students enrolled in public four-year institutions nearly doubled to over 8 million students, representing slightly more than 7 percent of the adult population and an overall increase in enrollment of almost 4 million. Enrollment in two-year institutions grew even more dramatically, as the percentage of the adult population in these institutions doubled over the same period from 3 to 6 percent.‡ As shown in Figures 9.7 and 9.8, this upward trend in enrollment is continuing and visible in all types of postsecondary institutions, with the exception of private two-year institutions where enrollment remains relatively flat or has declined slightly. Rising enrollment will require ever-greater revenues from states or other sources, if the same level of quality is to be maintained.

---

* Note that within these percentages some institutions include revenue from individual grants, including Pell Grants (which are treated as a pass-through at some private institutions) and student loans.

† Note that revenue sources are reported in mutually exclusive categories. For example, tuition and fees exclude revenues from student loans.

‡ Based on authors' calculations from the *Digest of Education Statistics* and intercensal population estimates.

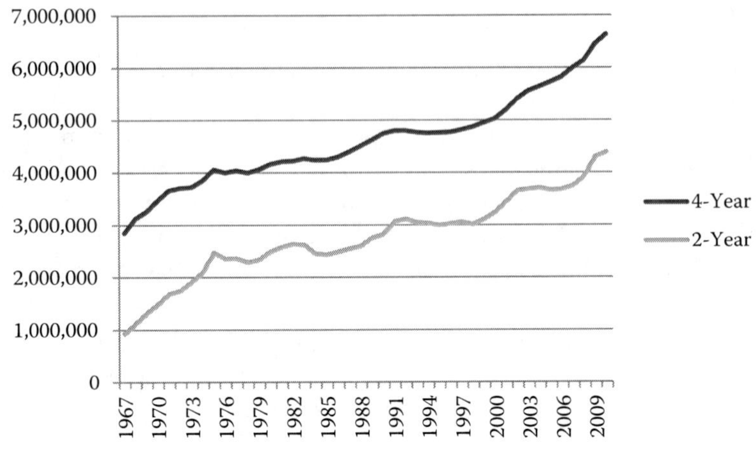

Figure 9.7 Total state enrollment in public higher education institutions, 1967–2010. (Authors' calculations based on Snyder, T.D., and Dillow, S.A., *Digest of Education Statistics 2011*, NCES 2012-001, National Center for Education Statistics, Institute of Education Sciences, U.S. Department of Education, Washington, DC, 2012; U.S. Census Bureau, 2012.)

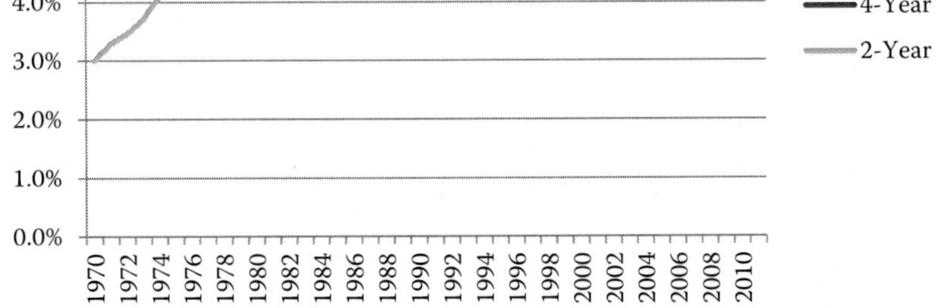

Figure 9.8 Percent of 18- to 44-year olds enrolled in public state higher education institutions, 1970–2011. (Authors' calculations based on Snyder, T.D., and Dillow, S.A., *Digest of Education Statistics 2011*, NCES 2012-001, National Center for Education Statistics, Institute of Education Sciences, U.S. Department of Education, Washington, DC, 2012; intercensal estimates from U.S. Census Bureau, 2012.)

Issues to Watch in State Education Finance

So far, this chapter has focused on the composition and growth of K–12 and postsecondary education funding. We now turn to emerging issues in education and their implications for state budgets and support for public education. These issues include market-based reforms to K–12 schooling, special education, competition within the education sector for state funding, increasing college costs, and the funding of pension and health care obligations to retiring educators.

Privatization of Elementary and Secondary Education: Choice and Vouchers

The changing market of K–12 education is evident in the growth of charter schools and publicly funded vouchers subsidizing enrollment at private schools. Charter schools are public schools of choice, funded with public dollars but privately operated by nonprofit or for-profit organizations. Under most state charter laws, states are responsible for providing the same per pupil aid to charter schools as they do to the charter's parent district. In some cases, there are also provisions for state aid to charter schools for capital projects. To the extent total enrollment is unchanged, a shift in enrollment from traditional public schools to charter schools will have little or no effect on state aid to local districts; local districts lose aid, but the total state allocation remains the same. However, if charter schools induce an increase in total enrollment by attracting students from the private sector, then pressures on state budgets will increase.

There is little research to date on the fiscal impacts of charter schools on state budgets. While enrollment growth in charter schools is strong, it remains a very small share of overall public school enrollment. According to the National Center for Education Statistics, charter enrollment increased from less than 1 percent of all public school enrollments in 2000–2001 to approximately 2.2 percent of students in 2009–2010.

Another key factor of changing education markets is the slow but steady growth of publicly funded voucher programs. As of December 2012, voucher programs serving general education students operated in seven states and the District of Columbia. Of these, three states also offered vouchers to special needs students attending nonpublic schools, with an additional five states offering vouchers exclusively to special needs students. Rather than directly financing student enrollment at private K–12 institutions, some states indirectly finance private education through tax expenditures. Eleven states now have tuition tax credit programs that allow corporations or individuals to allocate a portion of the taxes they owe to the state to private nonprofit organizations that issue scholarships to K–12 students (National Conference of State Legislatures 2012). At least at this time, the potential for voucher programs to alter the face of state education financing is limited. This is due in part to the relatively small number of states utilizing such programs and in part to the scope of these programs.

Rising Enrollments and Changing Institutional Structures in Postsecondary Education

The market structure of postsecondary education is also evolving. The role of the for-profit sector is continuing to increase, although this will likely have small impacts on state education finance, as these institutions are primarily financed through tuition, fees, and federal aid. What is likely to have a larger impact on state education finance is the growing interest in and support for increasing enrollment in higher education. President Obama, for example, has called for an additional 5 million graduates from community colleges by 2020. The push is not limited to community college, however, as "college for all" initiatives gain traction nationwide. In 2012, educational attainment reached a record high with 57 percent of 25- to 29-year-olds completing at least some college and 31 percent completing a bachelor's degree or higher (Fry and Parker 2012). In 2009, 73 percent of American adults agreed that a college education was necessary to get ahead in life, compared to only 49 percent in 1978 (Fry and Parker 2012). The growing demand for postsecondary education will have real implications for state governments, which provide one-quarter to one-third of revenue for public institutions that educate the vast majority of students enrolled in two- and four-year institutions.

At the same time, the line between K–12 and postsecondary education is becoming increasingly blurred as partnerships to improve college going and completion flourish. A growing number of states, for example, are developing P–16 systems that coordinate the educational process from preschool through postsecondary education. Such systems will require states to coordinate education funding across all levels of education, a departure from the current structure where postsecondary funding decisions are often made in isolation from K–12.

Special Education

Special education is one area of K–12 finance that deserves particular attention going forward. In 2009–2010, 13.1 percent of public school students were served under IDEA, a notable 37.5 percent increase since 1990–1991 (Snyder and Dillow 2012). Under IDEA, all states are required to provide a "free and appropriate public education" for students with disabilities, so that growth in the special education population translates directly into increased expenditure on special education services. It is estimated that 40 percent of all new spending in education between 1996 and 2005 went to special education, and that special education accounted for 15.4 percent of overall per pupil spending in 2005 (Rothstein and Alonso 2010). Recent data on state aid for special education are not available, but in 1998–1999,

47 percent of special education revenues were supplied by the state (Parrish 2001). As special education enrollments continue to grow, expenditures on these students will account for an increasingly large share of state budgets, which in the face of budget constraints may leave less available for general education.

Competition for Funds within the Education Sector

In addition to increased competition for funding between the education sector and other social programs, there is likely to be increased competition within the education sector. With continued budget shortages from the Great Recession, K–12 and higher education are competing for increasing dollars from shrinking budgets. Other areas within education, including early childhood education and after school programs, are also vying for support. Such programs have grown dramatically over the past 20 years: while in 1990, 10 percent of 3- to 5-years-olds were enrolled in public pre-K programs, by 2011 this more than doubled to 22 percent (Snyder and Dillow 2012). Higher education may be particularly vulnerable, as it tends to be the largest discretionary item in state budgets, while a minimum level of K–12 funding is often protected by student funding formulas, court orders, and constitutional guarantees.

Costs of College and Financial Aid

Over the past decade, the posted tuition and fees at public four-year institutions have more than doubled, from $3,810 (average) in 1992–1993 to $8,660 (average) in 2012–2013. The net, or out-of-pocket, cost of college faced by students after accounting for grants and tax benefits, however, has risen by only 50 percent over the same period, from $1,920 to $2,910. The slower growth in net college tuition reflects the extent to which these grants and tax benefits subsidize individuals. While some of the increase in the "sticker price" of college may reflect increasing costs of providing services or decreased reliance on direct financial contributions from federal and state governments, there is concern that at least some of this increase is due to the "capture" of financial aid awards into tuition prices—more specifically that colleges increase tuition in response to increases in federal or state aid, so that the net-of-aid cost to students changes at a rate less than the increase in aid.

How big is this problem? Among public institutions, there appear to be small responses to increases in federal aid. Netz (1999) finds tuition increases among institutions that offer only need-based aid, while others find that tuition responses are generally stronger among private versus public institutions (Acosta 2001; Singell and Stone 2003). In response to federal tax credits, Long (2004a) finds that public two-year institutions with many credit-eligible students experienced faster tuition growth than others, while private institutions did not appear to respond to tax credits by increasing tuition.

Research on state grant aid provides fairly consistent support for the hypothesis, showing evidence of institutional responsiveness to aid increases. Examining the effects of Georgia's HOPE scholarship on tuition prices, Long (2004c) finds that most four-year colleges in the state experienced a net increase in prices after the introduction of the HOPE scholarship, with a net increase of as much as 30 cents for each dollar of aid. There is, however, some evidence that institutions may have asymmetric responses to need- versus merit-based aid. Using national data from IPEDS, Curs and Dar (2010) find that both public and private institutions lower their listed tuition and fees in response to increases in merit-based aid, while they raise net price and lower institutional aid in response to increases in state-funded need-based awards. Understanding the extent to which changes in individual aid are recaptured in the form of higher sticker prices at higher education institutions may have important implications for how financial aid is distributed in the future.

Sustainability of Pension and Retiree Health Care Obligations

Another enduring issue in state education finance relates to the financial sustainability of pensions and retiree health care plans for teachers. Many reports have questioned whether states are setting aside sufficient resources to meet their future obligations to retiring teachers, and noted how a failure to do so sets the stage for future budget pressure. Most public school teachers participate in statewide *defined benefit* plans in which annual pension payments are tied to salaries and years of service (Hansen 2010). In contrast to *defined contribution* plans common in the private sector, defined benefit plans require the plan sponsor to ensure full funding of all future payments. This implies that states bear all of the risk related to funding rates, investment returns, longevity, and so forth (Hansen 2010). Additionally, pension recipients are often entitled to cost-of-living adjustments (COLAs), which must be planned for, and unlike in the private sector, frequently receive postemployment health care benefits as well.

States vary substantially in the extent to which liabilities generated by obligations to retirees are funded by employee and state contributions, and recent studies find revenue shortfalls increased during the Great Recession. For example, a report from the Pew Center on the States (2012) documented a $1.38 trillion gap between states' assets and their liabilities for employees' retirement and health care benefits. (These liabilities are for all public workers, including teachers.) In 2010, 34 out of 50 states were below the 80 percent ratio of assets to liabilities, a traditional benchmark necessary for financial sustainability. This was an increase from 22 states only two years before, just prior to the Great Recession. Chapter 6 indicates several states with funding ratios well below the 80 percent benchmark. The extent of unfunded liabilities appears even worse when applying a more conservative expected rate of return on investments, as many have argued state pension sponsors should do (Hansen 2010; Pew Center on the States 2012). If state pension funds are insufficient to cover obligations when workers retire, these governments face three options: raising taxes, cutting spending, or defaulting on obligations to retired employees, including teachers. Even if states do not default, pension liabilities could lead to massive deficits, and ultimately a restructuring of pension plans. Although no state has yet defaulted on pensions, the concern is real, as several municipalities, including Pritchard, Alabama, Cedar Falls, Rhode Island, and most notably Detroit, Michigan, have faced bankruptcy and ultimately defaulted on pension payments to retirees.*

Numerous reforms have been proposed to improve the fiscal health of teacher pension and retiree health plans. These include offering defined contribution or hybrid *cash balance–defined benefit* plans to newly hired teachers, as states such as Indiana, Florida, Oregon, and Washington have done (Goldhaber et al. 2012). These new plans have also received support for their appeal to younger, mobile teachers who tend to be disadvantaged by "backloaded," nonportable defined benefit plans (Hansen 2010). The long-run balance in the funding of pension and health care obligations, however, will likely require serious adjustments to benefits, employee contributions, or both, along with limitations on COLAs and formulas that distort retirement behavior (Hansen 2010; Pew Center on the States 2012; Costrell and Podgursky 2008). For states with severely underfunded liabilities, these adjustments will surely be more severe.

The last decades of the 20th century witnessed real changes in the state role in education finance: rising state share of education expenditures, reductions in spending inequality, responses to federal mandates, rising federal role in both providing aid and establishing mandates, and increasing demand for higher and early childhood education and early childhood. It is difficult to know whether these changes will persist. Shrinking budgets will put pressure on all areas of spending, which means that there are hard choices to be made by state governments moving forward.

References

Acosta, R.J. (2001). *How Do Colleges Respond to Changes in Federal Student Aid?*, Working Paper 808. Department of Economics, University of California, Los Angeles.

Armour-Garb, A., Dadayan, L., and Gais, T. (2009). *Spending Is Up, and So Are Interstate Disparities in States' K–12 Revenues.* Albany, NY: Nelson A. Rockefeller Institute of Government.

Baker, B.D., and Corcoran, S.P. (2012). *The Stealth Inequities of School Funding: How State and Local School Finance Systems Perpetuate Inequitable Student Spending.* Washington, DC: Center for American Progress.

Baum, S., and Payea, K. (2012). *Trends in Student Aid.* The College Board. Accessed at http://trends.collegeboard.org/sites/default/files/student-aid-2012-full-report.pdf

* It should be noted, however, that unlike some localities in the United States, state governments do not have the legal option of bankruptcy because they are considered sovereign entities. States confronted with the problem of unfunded pension liabilities therefore face a more limited set of options, including spending cuts, revenue increases, default, or restructuring.

Berne, R., and Stiefel, L. (1984). *The Measurement of Equity in School Finance: Conceptual, Methodological, and Empirical Dimensions*. Baltimore, MD: Johns Hopkins University Press.

Briffault, R. (2007). Adding Adequacy to Equity: The Evolving Legal Theory of School Finance Reform. In *School Money Trials: The Legal Pursuit of Educational Adequacy*, ed. M.R. West and P.E. Peterson. Washington, DC: Brookings Institution Press, pp. 25–54.

Center for the Study of Education Policy. (2012). An Annual Compilation of Data on State Fiscal Support for Higher Education. Grapevine. Available at http://grapevine.illinoisstate.edu/.

Chingos, M.M. (2012). *Strength in Numbers: State Spending on K–12 Assessment Systems*, technical report. Brown Center on Education Policy at Brookings.

Cohodes, S., and Goodman, J. (2012). *First Degree Earns: The Impact of College Quality on College Completion Rates*, HKS Faculty Research Working Paper RWP12-033.

Congressional Budget Office. (2012). *Fair-Value Estimates of the Cost of Federal Credit Programs in 2013*, technical report.

Corcoran, S.P., and Evans, W.N. (2008). Equity, Adequacy, and the Evolving State Role in Education Finance. In *Handbook of Research in Education Finance and Policy*, ed. H.F. Ladd and E. Fiske. New York: Routledge.

Cornwell, C., and Mustard, D. B. (2001). *The Distributional Impacts of Lottery-Funded Aid: Evidence from Georgia's HOPE Scholarship*. Unpublished manuscript. Athens, GA: University of Georgia.

Costrell, R.M., and Podgursky, M. (2008). Peaks, Cliffs, and Valleys: The Peculiar Incentives of Teacher Pensions. *Education Next*, 8(1), 22–28.

Curs, B.R., and Dar, L. (2010). Do Institutions Respond Asymmetrically to Changes in State Need- and Merit-Based Aid? Presented at the 2010 Association for the Study of Higher Education Annual Meeting, Indianapolis, IN.

Dadayan, L. (2012). *The Impact of the Great Recession on Local Property Taxes*, technical report, Nelson A. Rockefeller Institute of Government.

Delta Cost Project Database. (2011). Retrieved from http://www.deltacostproject.org/delta-cost-data

Duncombe, W., Lukemeyer, A., and Yinger, J. (2008). The No Child Left Behind Act: Have Federal Funds Been Left Behind? *Public Finance Review*, 36(4), 381–407.

Dye, R.F., and Reschovsky, A. (2008). Property Tax Responses to State Aid Cuts in the Recent Fiscal Crisis. *Public Budgeting and Finance*, 28(2), 87–111.

Dynarski, S. (2002a). *Loans, Liquidity, and Schooling Decisions*. Kennedy School of Government Working Paper.

Dynarski, S. (2002b). The Behavioral and Distributional Implications of Aid for College. *American Economic Review*, 92(2), 279–285.

Fitzpatrick, M. D., and Jones, D. (2012). *Higher Education, Merit-Based Scholarships, and Post-Baccalaureate Migration* (no. w18530). National Bureau of Economic Research.

Flanagan, A.E., and Murray, S.E. (2004). A Decade of Reform: The Impact of School Reform in Kentucky. In *Helping Children Left Behind: State Aid and the Pursuit of Educational Equity*, ed. J. Yinger. Cambridge, MA: MIT Press.

Fry, R., and Parker, K. (2012). *Record Shares of Young Adults Have Finished Both High School and College*, technical report. Pew Research Center.

Goldhaber, D., Grout, C., Pennucci, A., and Bignell, W. (2012). *Teacher Pension Choice: Surveying the Landscape in Washington State*, technical report. CALDER Center. Available at http://www.caldercenter.org/publications/upload/wp-81.pdf.

Gordon, N. (2008). The Changing Federal Role in Education Finance and Governance. In *Handbook of Research in Education Finance and Policy*, ed. H.F. Ladd and E. Fiske. New York: Routledge.

Hansen, J.S. (2010). An Introduction to Teacher Retirement Benefits. *Education Finance and Policy*, 5(4), 402–437.

Hansen, W. L. (1983). Impact of Student Financial Aid on Access. In *The Crisis in Higher Education*, ed. Joseph Froomkin. New York: Academy of Political Science, pp. 84–96.

Holtz-Eakin, D., and Rosen, H. (1990). Federal Deductibility and Local Property Tax Rates. *Journal of Urban Economics*, 27, 269–284.

Hoxby, C.M. (2001). All School Finance Equalizations Are Not Created Equal. *Quarterly Journal of Economics*, 116, 1189–1231.

Imazeki, J., and Reschovsky, A. (2006). Does No Child Left Behind Place a Fiscal Burden on States? Evidence from Texas. *Education Finance and Policy*, 1(2), 217–246.

Internal Revenue Service. (2012). Tax Benefits for Education: Information Center, technical report. Available at http://www.irs.gov/uac/Tax-Benefits-for-Education:-Information-Center.

Joint Committee on Taxation. (2012). *Estimates of Federal Tax Expenditures for Fiscal Years 2011–2015* (JCS–1-12). Washington, DC: U.S. Government Printing Office.

Kane, T. J. (1994). College Attendance by Blacks since 1970: The Role of College Cost, Family Background and the Returns to Education. *Journal of Political Economy*, 102(5), 878–911.

Kane, T. J. (2003). *A Quasi-Experimental Estimate of the Impact of Financial Aid on College-Going* (no. w9703). National Bureau of Economic Research.

Katsiyannis, A., Yell, M.L., and Bradley, R. (2001). Reflections on the 25th Anniversary of the Individuals with Disabilities Education Act. *Remedial and Special Education*, 22(6), 324–334.

Loeb, S., and Socias, M. (2004). Federal Contributions to High-Income School Districts: The Use of Tax Deductions for Funding K–12 Education. *Economics of Education Review*, 23, 85–94.

Long, B.T. (2004a). The Impact of Federal Tax Credits for Higher Education Expenses. In *College Choices: The Economics of Where to Go, When to Go, and How to Pay for It*, ed. C.M. Hoxby. Chicago: University of Chicago Press, pp. 101–168.

Long, B.T. (2004b). Does the Format of a Financial Aid Program Matter? The Effect of State In-Kind Tuition Subsidies. *Review of Economics and Statistics*, 86(3), 767–782.

Long, B.T. (2004c). How Do Financial Aid Policies Affect Colleges? The Institutional Impact of the Georgia HOPE Scholarship. *Journal of Human Resources*, 39(4), 1045–1066.

Mathis, W.J. (2005). The Cost of Implementing the Federal No Child Left Behind Act: Different Assumptions, Different Answers. *Peabody Journal of Education*, 80(2), 90–119.

Murray, S.E., Evans, W.N., and Schwab, R.M. (1998). Education Finance Reform and the Distribution of Education Resources. *American Economic Review*, 88, 789–812.

National Association of State Budget Officers. (2012). *State Expenditure Report: Examining Fiscal 2010–2012 State Spending*. Washington, DC.

Netz, J. S. (1999). *Non-Profits and Price-Fixing: The Case of the Ivy League*. Unpublished manuscript, Purdue University.

Oliff, P., and Leachman, M. (2011). *New School Year Brings Steep Cuts in State Funding for Schools*, technical report. Center on Budget and Policy Priorities.

Oliff, P., Mai, C., and Leachman, M. (2012). *New School Year Brings More Cuts in State Funding for Schools*, technical report. Center of Budget and Policy Priorities.

Parrish, T.B. (2001). Who's Paying the Rising Cost of Special Education? *Journal of Special Education Leadership*, 14(1), 4–12.

Pew Center on the States. (2012). *The Widening Gap: Update*, technical report. Available at http://www.pewstates.org/uploadedFiles/PCS_Assets/2012/Pew_Pensions_Update.pdf.

Reyes, S. L. (1995). *Educational Opportunities and Outcomes: The Role of the Guaranteed Student Loan*. Unpublished manuscript, Harvard University.

Rothstein, R., and Alonso, J.D. (2010). *Where Has All the Money Gone?*, technical report. Economic Policy Institute.

Savoca, E. (1991). The Effect of Changes in Composition of Financial Aid on College Enrollments. *Eastern Economic Journal*, 17(1), 109–121.

Seftor, N.S., and Turner, S.E. (2002). Back to School: Federal Student Aid Policy and Adult College Enrollment. *Journal of Human Resources*, 37(2), 336–352.

Singell, L.D., and Stone, J.A. (2003). *For Whom the Pell Tolls: Market Power, Tuition Discrimination, and the Bennett Hypothesis*, University of Oregon Working Paper 2003-12.

Snyder, T.D., and Dillow, S.A. (2012). *Digest of Education Statistics 2011*, NCES 2012-001. Washington, DC: National Center for Education Statistics, Institute of Education Sciences, U.S. Department of Education.

Springer, M.G., Liu, K., and Guthrie, J.W. (2009). The Impact of School Finance Litigation on Resource Distribution: A Comparison of Court-Mandated Equity and Adequacy Reforms. *Education Economics*, 17(4), 421–444.

U.S. Census Bureau. (2012). *Public Education Finances: 2012*, G10-ASPEF. Washington, DC: U.S. Government Printing Office.

Yinger, J. (2004). *Helping Children Left Behind: State Aid and the Pursuit of Educational Equity*. Cambridge, MA: MIT Press.

Chapter 10

State Health Care Expenditures

Shanna Rose

Claremont Mckenna College

Contents

Introduction

Health care spending accounts for approximately one-quarter of total state expenditures and represents the fastest-growing component of state spending as well as the greatest long-run fiscal challenge facing state governments (U.S. Government Accountability Office 2008). States, on average, now spend more on health care than on K–12 education, higher education, corrections, transportation, or any other program. Within state health care expenditures, the single largest component is health care for low-income persons provided through two programs: Medicaid and the Children's Health Insurance Program (CHIP). Together, these two programs account for more than three-quarters of total state health care expenditures. The remainder is comprised of spending on public hospitals and health clinics, health-related inspection and regulation, and a variety of smaller programs related to public health.* Medicare, the program that guarantees access to health insurance for persons aged 65 and older and younger people with disabilities, is financed by the federal government and thus does not impact state budgets.

This chapter examines factors that have contributed to the growth of state health care expenditures in recent decades with a focus on Medicaid and CHIP. It also analyzes the likely implications of the federal Patient Protection and Affordable Care Act (ACA) of 2010, which extends eligibility for these programs starting in 2014.

Medicaid and the Children's Health Insurance Program (CHIP)

Medicaid is the primary source of health insurance coverage for low-income people in the United States. Created by the Social Security Amendments of 1965 as an entitlement program to provide medical coverage for low-income families and others who meet specific eligibility requirements, it has been called a giant, a colossus, and the workhorse of the U.S. health system (Myers 1970; Thompson and DiIulio 1998; Weil 2003). In 2012, Medicaid enrolled nearly 73 million people, or more than one in five Americans. CHIP, established in 1997, covered an additional 8 million children (MACPAC 2013).

Medicaid is funded by the states and the federal government. In 2011, Medicaid's total cost was $432.4 billion, of which $275.1 billion (64 percent) was paid by the federal government and $157.3 billion (36 percent) by the states. The federal share is determined by the Medicaid matching rate, known as the Federal Medical Assistance Percentage (FMAP), and varies inversely with state per capita income.† The minimum FMAP is 50 percent; the maximum is 83 percent.

State participation in Medicaid is voluntary, but all 50 states participate. Each state administers its own Medicaid program within broad federal rules that require coverage of certain basic services. These services include inpatient and outpatient hospital services; physician, midwife, and nurse practitioner services; laboratory and x-ray services; and perhaps most importantly, long-term nursing facility and home health care, neither of which is covered by Medicare or private insurance. States have the option of covering other services, such as prescription drugs, dental care, and eyeglasses, and a majority of states voluntarily do so.

Federal Medicaid law limits eligibility to low-income individuals in specific categorically eligible groups: children, pregnant women, adults with dependent children, people with severe disabilities, and the elderly (the ACA extends eligibility to additional groups, as discussed below). Federal law requires participating states to

* Author's estimate based on data from U.S. Census Bureau, State Government Finances; does not include spending on health insurance for public employees.

† The FMAP formula is $1 - 0.45 \times$ (State per capita income/U.S. per capita income).[2]

cover these groups up to federal income thresholds. For example, states must cover pregnant women and children under six years of age up to 133 percent of the federal poverty level and older children up to 100 percent of the federal poverty level. States have the option of extending eligibility beyond the federal thresholds, and many have done so, particularly for children. States also have the option of covering the "medically needy" (categorically eligible individuals with incomes above Medicaid thresholds and high medical expenses), and many states offer such coverage.

Approximately two-thirds of Medicaid spending is attributable to acute care and one-third to long-term care. Although low-income elderly and disabled individuals together account for about one-quarter of Medicaid enrollees, they account for two-thirds of the program spending due to their more intensive use of both acute and long-term care services (see Figures 10.1 and 10.2).

Considerable interstate variation exists in Medicaid spending per enrollee. This variation arises largely as a result of differences in coverage of optional services and populations—particularly long-term care and the medically needy—as well as other factors, such as differences in provider reimbursement rates. For example, New York spends nearly $9,000 per enrollee, while Georgia spends less than $4,000 per enrollee (Table 10.1). Thus, while Medicaid's progressive matching formula is designed to promote interstate equity by encouraging low-income states to spend more, these incentives have not been successful in leveling the field (Holahan 2007).

Medicaid spending has grown rapidly since the program's inception due to a combination of enrollment growth and increased spending per enrollee. Over the past two decades, total Medicaid spending has grown at an average annual rate of about 7 percent, significantly outpacing inflation and economic growth (Henry J. Kaiser Family Foundation 2012). Medicaid's growth imposes an enormous burden on state budgets, crowding out other important policy priorities, such as education

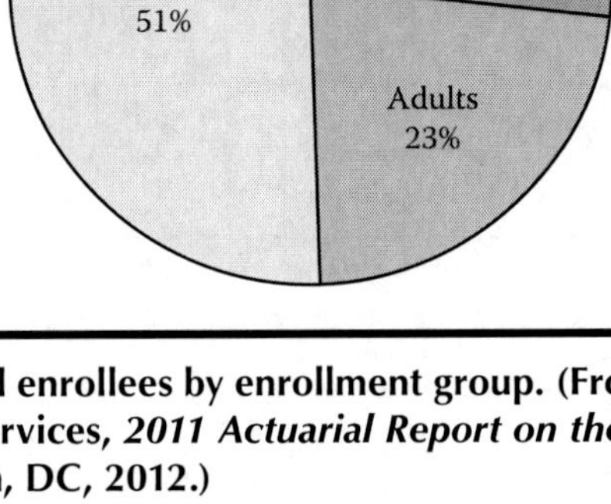

Figure 10.1 Medicaid enrollees by enrollment group. (From U.S. Department of Health and Human Services, *2011 Actuarial Report on the Financial Outlook for Medicaid*, Washington, DC, 2012.)

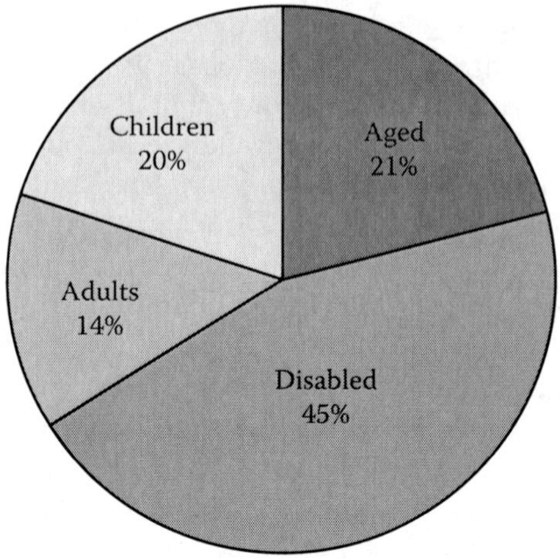

Figure 10.2 Medicaid expenditures by enrollment group. (From U.S. Department of Health and Human Services, *2011 Actuarial Report on the Financial Outlook for Medicaid*, Washington, DC, 2012.)

Table 10.1 Medicaid Payments per Enrollee by Eligibility Group

	Total	*Aged*	*Disabled*	*Adults*	*Children*
National average	$5,527	$13,149	$15,840	$2,900	$2,305
Most Populous 10 States					
California	$3,527	$10,528	$16,269	$1,073	$1,567
Florida	4,168	7,917	10,883	2,569	1,627
Georgia	3,979	8,183	8,999	4,424	1,811
Illinois	4,722	10,105	15,921	3,157	2,271
Michigan	4,965	15,139	12,642	3,625	1,926
New York	8,960	22,494	29,881	4,277	2,505
North Carolina	6,098	10,664	16,050	4,059	2,796
Ohio	6,116	18,900	16,501	3,315	1,838
Pennsylvania	7,397	21,268	12,883	3,692	2,748
Texas	4,884	8,808	13,953	3,063	2,753

Source: Henry J. Kaiser Family Foundation. Data are for 2009. http://kff.org/medicaid/state-indicator/medicaid-payments-per-enrollee.

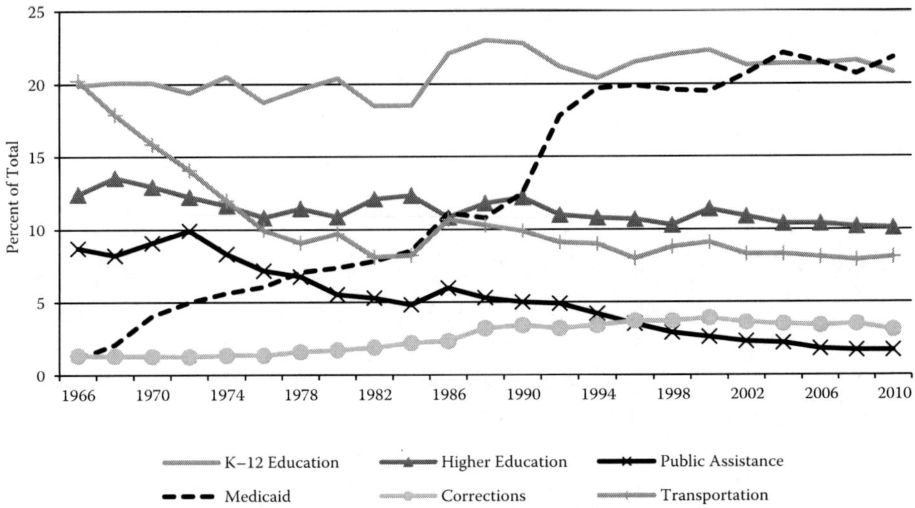

Figure 10.3 State spending by function as a percent of total state spending, 1966–2010. (From U.S. Census Bureau, *Government Finance Statistics*; National Association of State Budget Officers, *State Expenditure Report* [various years].)

and infrastructure (Kane et al. 2005; Marton and Wildasin 2007). Indeed, Medicaid recently surpassed K–12 education as the single largest category of state spending (Figure 10.3). For decades, state governors have complained to federal lawmakers that Medicaid is "breaking our back" and "out of control" (Turque et al. 1993; Pear 2003).

At the same time, Medicaid has contributed to substantial improvements in the health and well-being of low-income Americans. It has significantly improved health outcomes by virtually every measure, including infant mortality, maternal mortality, disease incidence, and life expectancy (Engel 2006). One recent study reported that the expansion of Medicaid eligibility is associated with significant improvements in self-reported health status (Sommers et al. 2012). In a recent randomized experiment, Medicaid beneficiaries reported substantial increases in health, happiness, and financial well-being after enrolling in the program (Finkelstein et al. 2011).

CHIP covers low-income uninsured children with family incomes slightly too high to qualify for Medicaid (typically up to 200 percent of the federal poverty level). Like Medicaid, it is jointly financed by the federal and state governments. CHIP's total cost in 2012 was $12.2 billion, of which approximately 70 percent was federal and 30 percent state spending. The program is financed with matching grants at rates that are typically about 15 percentage points higher than Medicaid rates. For example, a state that receives a 50 percent Medicaid match receives a 65 percent CHIP match. However, unlike Medicaid's open-ended matching grants, CHIP's matching grants are capped, so that federal funds only match state spending up to the state's allotment. States can choose from three program designs: Medicaid expansion (7 states), a separate CHIP program (17 states), or a hybrid approach (26 states). If a state chooses a separate CHIP program, federal law requires it to provide "benchmark" coverage similar to that offered by private insurers. Since CHIP is relatively small and its growth relatively slow, the remainder of this chapter will focus primarily on Medicaid.

Growth of Medicaid Spending

Many factors have contributed to the growth of Medicaid spending. They include federal mandates, financial incentives created by open-ended matching grants, pressure from health care providers and beneficiaries, the aging of the population, and expensive new medical technologies.

Federal mandates requiring the states to expand Medicaid eligibility fueled the program's growth in the 1980s and early 1990s (Johnston 1997). During this period, Congress repeatedly relaxed federal eligibility standards to bring millions of additional Americans into the program. Congressional amendments contributed to a dramatic increase in enrollment, extending coverage to over half a million pregnant women, more than 4 million children, and more than 4 million elderly and disabled individuals (Rosenbaum 1993).

Open-ended matching grants are inherently expansionary because they give states an incentive to shift spending toward the targeted program at the expense of other programs. For instance, a state can spend a dollar on education and get a dollar's worth of benefits, or it can spend a dollar on Medicaid and get $2 to $4 worth of benefits, depending on the federal matching rate. In the language of economics, a matching grant has both an income effect and a substitution effect. It increases the state's total income, leading to increased spending on all programs (the income effect), and also lowers the targeted program's relative price, leading the state to reallocate spending from other programs to the targeted program (the substitution effect). By contrast, if Medicaid was instead funded with a block grant—a lump sum that does not vary with state spending—there would only be an income effect, likely resulting in relatively less spending.

Empirically estimating the sensitivity of state Medicaid spending to federal matching grants is difficult since the low-income states that receive higher matching rates have fewer resources and often weaker preferences for generous eligibility and benefit policies than do higher-income states. Researchers have thus produced a wide range of estimates depending on the methodology used, but most studies conclude that state Medicaid spending is quite sensitive to the federal matching rate (see, for example, Kousser 2002; Kronebusch 2004).*

* This does not mean that low-income states with higher matching rates spend more than high-income states with lower matching rates; rather, it indicates that controlling for income and other factors, the matching rate has a statistically significant positive impact on spending.

Open-ended matching grants are also an "invitation to fiscal entrepreneurship by the states" (Thompson and Fossett 2008, 161) because the size of the federal grant depends on state action. Over the years, the states have found many innovative ways to take advantage of Medicaid's open-ended financing mechanism to bring additional federal money into state coffers. For instance, many states have relabeled existing state-funded health programs as Medicaid expenditures to qualify for the federal match—a technique known as Medicaid supplantation (Merriman 2006). State officials have also used "creative financing mechanisms" to secure additional federal funding without spending any additional state funds (see, for example, Baicker and Staiger 2005). These mechanisms include provider taxes and donations, intergovernmental transfers, and supplemental federal payments to hospitals that serve a "disproportionate share" of low-income patients. States have also applied for waivers to federal laws and regulations to secure additional federal aid to cover populations and services that Medicaid ordinarily would not cover (Thompson and Burke 2007).

Another factor that has contributed to Medicaid's expansion is political pressure from health care providers, including physicians, hospitals, nursing homes, public health clinics, community health centers, and other institutions that are reimbursed for their services by Medicaid (see, for example, Barrilleaux and Miller 1988). Medicaid is a critical source of financial support to health care providers—particularly nursing homes and the safety net institutions that provide care to low-income people—giving providers an enormous financial stake in the program. Although provider lobbying efforts typically focus primarily on securing higher reimbursement rates for existing Medicaid patients, they have also pushed for the expansion of covered services and, to a lesser extent, eligibility throughout the program's history (Grogan 1994; Kronebusch 1997). Despite Medicaid's low reimbursement rates relative to those of Medicare and private insurance, providers typically support the expansion of eligibility because the program covers low-income populations that would otherwise have difficulty paying for care (Sparer 2009). In addition, because Medicare and most private insurers do not cover long-term care, the nursing home lobby is particularly forceful in advocating Medicaid eligibility expansions (Grogan 1994). Managed care organizations, which currently provide care to two-thirds of Medicaid enrollees, also support expanding Medicaid's scope.

Medicaid beneficiaries, their relatives, and advocacy groups representing them have also pushed for the expansion of coverage. The poor are not particularly influential in the policy process due to their limited resources and low political participation rates, but as Medicaid eligibility has expanded to include new populations, it has increasingly become a program for not only the poor, but also the middle class—particularly when it comes to long-term care (see Vladeck 2003). Largely as a result, Medicaid is nearly as popular as the universal Medicare program. Twenty percent of Americans report having received Medicaid benefits, and 31 percent report having a friend or family member who has received Medicaid benefits, such as a parent in a nursing home. Many cite these personal connections as an important reason for their support (Henry J. Kaiser Family Foundation 2011). Moreover, advocacy groups such as the Children's Defense Fund and the American Pediatric Association have also pressured national and state policy makers to expand Medicaid coverage (see Palfrey 2006).

Two other factors that have contributed to rising health care spending across the board (Medicaid, Medicare, and private insurance) include the aging of the population (which has fueled the demand for long-term care) and expensive new medical technologies. Since Medicare and private health insurance provide only limited coverage of long-term care, Medicaid has become the nation's single largest provider of such coverage. Whereas Medicaid accounts for 16 percent of total U.S. health expenditures, it accounts for 32 percent of total nursing home expenditures and 36 percent of total home health care expenditures (U.S. Department of Health and Human Services 2012). And advances in medical technology in recent decades have made it possible to treat previously untreatable conditions and improve health outcomes—but often at an additional cost.

Patient Protection and Affordable Care Act of 2010

The Patient Protection and Affordable Care Act (ACA) of 2010 required states to base Medicaid eligibility solely on income—eliminating categorical eligibility criteria—and to expand eligibility to most individuals under the age of 65 up to 133 percent of the federal poverty level by 2014. The ACA thus expanded Medicaid eligibility to another 17 million people. Following an intense lobbying effort by the state governors, Congress agreed to pay significantly more than its usual share of the cost: 100 percent federal funding for the newly eligible in 2014–2016, phasing down the federal share to 90 percent in 2020 and subsequent years. The ACA also raised the CHIP matching rate by 23 percentage points, bringing the average federal matching rate for CHIP to 93 percent.

Despite the increased federal share, many cash-strapped governors were displeased about being forced to spend more in the future, while others objected on ideological grounds. Following the ACA's passage, 26 Republican-led states filed a lawsuit seeking to overturn the new law. The lawsuit challenged its encroachment on state sovereignty, claiming that it was unduly coercive to require states to either expand coverage or forego *all* federal Medicaid funds. Legal scholars cast doubt on the argument's merits, noting that the funds are essentially a gift to the states for which the federal government is free to set the terms, as it does for numerous other federal-state programs, and which states are free to decline (Jacobs and Skocpol 2010). Nonetheless, the U.S. Supreme Court struck down the Medicaid provision as a "gun to the head of the states," suggesting that the states have grown so dependent on federal Medicaid funds that doing without these funds is simply not a viable option.

The Supreme Court decision makes the ACA's Medicaid expansion voluntary rather than mandatory for states. It remains to be seen how many state governments will comply when the provision goes into effect in 2014. The Congressional Budget Office (CBO) estimates that the possibility of state nonparticipation following the Supreme Court verdict will cut the increase in Medicaid enrollment from 17 million to 11 million, but acknowledges that this estimate is highly uncertain due to the difficulty of predicting what individual states will do (Congressional Budget Office 2012a). As of 2013, 26 governors of both parties have declared that they will support expanded coverage, while 13 governors, all Republicans, have announced that they will not expand coverage (Advisory Board Company 2013). Politically charged statements notwithstanding, there are reasons to believe that a majority of states will expand eligibility eventually. However, there are also reasons to believe that many states will do so more slowly than prescribed by the ACA, and that some will not expand coverage at all.

States face powerful financial incentives to expand Medicaid eligibility. Indeed, experience suggests that Medicaid's open-ended matching grants entice states to voluntarily cover more people and services than required by federal law. For example, most states have already extended coverage beyond federal minimum standards for pregnant women and children, and many have done so for other populations as well. Moreover, all states cover at least some services that are not required under federal law, such as eye exams and dental care. In fact, 60 percent of Medicaid spending goes to optional coverage—much of it for long-term care of the elderly and disabled—and only 40 percent to mandatory services (Sommers et al. 2005). The ACA provides even stronger expansionary incentives than existing Medicaid law, as the federal government will pay for upwards of 90 percent of the cost of the newly eligible compared to the traditional 57 percent federal share, as noted earlier (Congressional Budget Office 2012b).

In addition to paying for most costs associated with the expansion of Medicaid eligibility, the ACA's Medicaid provision offers participating states other financial benefits as well. It will virtually eliminate uncompensated care costs incurred by safety net providers like public hospitals that treat the uninsured (at least for U.S. citizens). It is also expected that the increased federal funds will translate into jobs and income at a time when many states are still struggling to recover from the Great Recession (Rosenbaum and Westmoreland 2012).

In states where lawmakers are threatening to opt out of the Medicaid expansion, powerful stakeholders such as private hospitals (for which the Medicaid expansion will reduce uncompensated and charity care costs) and managed care organizations (which see a growing Medicaid population as a profit opportunity) are already mounting lobbying campaigns to convince them to reconsider. They will likely be joined by other stakeholders, including consumer and patient advocates, civil rights organizations, religious organizations, and local governments that bear much of the cost of uncompensated care (Rosenbaum and Westmoreland 2012).

States, however, also face a number of disincentives to expand Medicaid eligibility. States that elect to extend coverage will, after three years, bear a share of the cost at a time when Medicaid already accounts for nearly one-quarter of total state spending, straining state budgets and crowding out other policy priorities. Although the increase in state Medicaid spending will be small both as a share of the total and relative to the baseline—rising by less than 3 percent compared to what states would have spent in the absence of the ACA—the additional cost is nonetheless a potential obstacle (Congressional Budget Office 2012b). Alan Weil, executive director of the National Academy for State Health Policy, compares the ACA's Medicaid provisions to a $200 pair of shoes on sale for $20. "If you like the $200 pair of shoes, it's a great deal because you only have to pay $20. [But] if you look in your wallet and you have a $10 and a couple of ones and some change and you're not sure you can come up with the $20, it doesn't really matter what a good deal it is" (Rovner 2010).

A second disincentive is that some state leaders believe that expanding Medicaid eligibility and streamlining the enrollment process will exacerbate the so-called woodwork effect, whereby the ACA encourages individuals who are eligible for Medicaid under current law, but not enrolled, to sign up for coverage. Since previously eligible enrollees will not qualify for the higher federal matching rates, the woodwork effect could result in substantial additional costs for participating states (Congressional Budget Office 2012a).

A third disincentive is the possibility that the federal government, which faces its own budgetary pressures, will eventually reduce matching rates and force states to either pick up the slack or bear the political and logistical costs of reversing the eligibility expansion (Congressional Budget Office 2012a). Indeed, only one year after signing the Affordable Care Act into law, President Obama briefly considered reducing federal aid to the states for health care programs. Instead of paying each state several different rates ranging from 50 to 100 percent for previously and newly eligible enrollees under Medicaid and CHIP, the president proposed to pay each state a single "blended" rate reflecting a weighted average of the varying rates, minus some factor designed to generate $65 billion in federal savings. Although he immediately retracted the proposal under pressure from state leaders, federal policy makers could resurrect the idea in the future.

Finally, there are reasons to believe that low-income southern states will be particularly slow to expand Medicaid eligibility. Although these states, with their large numbers of poor uninsured residents, stand to benefit the most from the ACA, their low Medicaid eligibility thresholds will increase the cost of conformity with the new 133 percent federal standard. Moreover, these states have fewer resources of their own, more conservative political cultures, and thus weaker preferences for Medicaid spending than do higher-income states.

In summary, decisions regarding the expansion of Medicaid eligibility by state governments will likely vary widely. Many state leaders have already indicated that they will expand coverage to all residents below 133 percent of the federal poverty level by 2014. Some will likely implement the expansion more slowly than originally prescribed by the ACA. A few states, particularly low-income, conservative southern states, may forgo the expansion altogether despite considerable political and financial pressure to participate.

Conclusion

Health care expenditures consume an enormous and rapidly growing portion of state government budgets and are increasingly crowding out other state policy priorities. Although the federal-state Medicaid program provides vital services to vulnerable Americans and is a critical source of financial support for America's health care safety net providers, the "Pac-Man of state budgets" is on a fiscally unsustainable trajectory, growing considerably more rapidly than economic growth and inflation (Weissert 1992).

Medicaid spending has grown for a variety of reasons, including federal mandates; financial incentives built in to the program's federal-state cost sharing mechanism; political pressure from health care providers, beneficiaries, and advocacy groups; adoption of expensive new medical technologies; and the aging of the nation's population. By creating strong financial incentives and interest group pressure to expand coverage further, the Affordable Care Act will spur additional spending growth starting in 2014.

Concern about Medicaid's fiscally unsustainable trajectory has led numerous scholars and policy makers to propose reforms that would fundamentally restructure the program, and particularly its financing mechanism, in future years. The two most widely discussed reform models—block grants and federalization—reflect the premise that efforts to constrain public health spending in federations are most effective when financial responsibility and policy control are not shared by different levels of government (as under the current Medicaid program) but rather lodged at a single level of government (Banting and Corbett 2002). Block grants, which are often advocated by conservatives, would shift greater responsibility and control to the states by capping federal contributions in exchange for broader state discretion over eligibility and covered services (see Howard 2012). By contrast, a federal takeover of Medicaid—and the preferred reform model of progressives—would shift greater responsibility and control to the federal government (see Anrig 2010).

Despite being seriously considered by national policy makers on numerous occasions throughout Medicaid's history, both reform models have repeatedly failed to overcome political resistance. Since a block grant would restrict federal funding for health care and thus reduce coverage, left-leaning policy makers, many state officials, and the powerful hospital and nursing home lobbies tend to vehemently oppose it. Meanwhile, many conservative policy makers oppose federalization either out of concern about the cost to the federal government or because they fear that it would open the door for a liberal national government to merge Medicaid with Medicare, and perhaps even pave the way for a single-payer universal health care system. In a political system characterized by multiple veto points, with power shared among branches and levels of government, reformers have thus far been unable to overcome such resistance (Rose 2013).

In summary, state health care expenditures are likely to continue to grow rapidly, but there also remains some uncertainty over their future trajectory. In the short term, it remains to be seen whether, and when, the states will expand Medicaid eligibility under the ACA. In the longer term, as health care poses an increasingly unsustainable burden on state budgets, national and state policy makers may finally overcome political obstacles to reform and restructure the program in ways that fundamentally alter the course of health care spending.

References

Advisory Board Company. (2013, June 14). Where Each State Stands on ACA's Medicaid Expansion. Available at http://www.advisory.com/Daily-Briefing/2012/11/09/MedicaidMap.

Anrig, G. (2010). Federalism and Its Discontents. *Democracy: A Journal of Ideas*, 15(Winter). Available at http://www.democracyjournal.org/15/6729.php.

Baicker, K., and Staiger, D. (2005). Fiscal Shenanigans, Targeted Federal Health Care Funds, and Patient Mortality. *Quarterly Journal of Economics*, 120(1), 345–386.

Banting, K., and Corbett, S. (2002). *Health Policy and Federalism: A Comparative Perspective on Multi-Level Governance.* Montreal: Queens University.

Barrilleaux, C.J., and Miller, M.E. (1988). The Political Economy of State Medicaid Policy. *American Political Science Review*, 82(4), 1089–1107.

Congressional Budget Office. (2012a, July). *Estimates for the Insurance Coverage Provisions of the Affordable Care Act Updated for the Recent Supreme Court Decision*, technical report. Available at http://www.cbo.gov/sites/default/files/cbofiles/attachments/43472-07-24-2012-CoverageEstimates.pdf.

Congressional Budget Office. (2012b, March). *Updated Estimates for the Insurance Coverage Provisions of the Affordable Care Act*, technical report. Available at http://www.cbo.gov/sites/default/files/cbofiles/attachments/03-13-Coverage%20Estimates.pdf.

Engel, J. (2006). *Poor People's Medicine: Medicaid and American Charity Care Since 1965.* Durham, NC: Duke University Press.

Finkelstein, A., Taubman, S., Wright, B., Bernstein, M., Gruber, J., Newhouse, J.P., Allen, H., and Baicker, K. (2011). *The Oregon Health Insurance Experiment: Evidence from the First Year*, Working Paper 17190. Oregon Health Study Group, National Bureau of Economic Research.

Grogan, C.M. (1994). Political-Economic Factors Influencing State Medicaid Policy. *Political Research Quarterly*, 47(3), 589–622. See also "Correction Note," 49(3), 673–675.

Henry J. Kaiser Family Foundation. (2011). *Kaiser Health Tracking Poll*, technical report. Available at http://www.kff.org/kaiserpolls/8190.cfm.

Henry J. Kaiser Family Foundation. (2012). *Medicaid Today: Preparing for Tomorrow*, technical report. Available at http://kff.org/medicaid/report/medicaid-today-preparing-for-tomorrow-a-look-at-state-medicaid-program-spending-enrollment-and-policy-trends-results-from-a-50-state-medicaid-budget-survey-for-state-fiscal-years-2012-and-2013/.

Holahan, J. (2007). State Variation in Medicaid Spending: Hard to Justify. *Health Affairs*, 26(6), w667–w669.

Howard, P. (2012). How Block Grants Can Make Medicaid Work: Improving Health, Decreasing Costs. *Issues 2012*, 24(September).

Jacobs, L.R., and Skocpol, T. (2010). *Health Care Reform and American Politics: What Everyone Needs to Know*. New York: Oxford University Press.

Johnston, J.M. (1997). The Medicaid Mandates of the 1980s: An Intergovernmental Perspective. *Public Budgeting and Finance*, 17(1), 3–34.

Kane, T.J., Orszag, P.R., Apostolov, E., Inman, R.P., and Reschovsky, A. (2005). Higher Education Appropriations and Public Universities: Role of Medicaid and the Business Cycle. *Brookings-Wharton Papers on Urban Affairs*, pp. 99–146.

Kousser, T. (2002). The Politics of Discretionary Medicaid Spending, 1980–1993. *Journal of Health Politics, Policy and Law*, 27(4), 639–671.

Kronebusch, K. (1997). Medicaid and the Politics of Groups: Recipients, Providers, and Policymaking. *Journal of Health Politics, Policy, and Law*, 22(3), 839–878.

Kronebusch, K. (2004). Matching Rates and Mandates: Federalism and Children's Medicaid Enrollment. *Policy Studies Journal*, 32(3), 317–339.

Marton, J., and Wildasin, D.E. (2007). Medicaid Expenditures and State Budgets: Past, Present, and Future. *National Tax Journal*, LX(2), 279–304.

Medicaid and CHIP Payment and Access Commission (MACPAC). (2013). *Report to the Congress on Medicaid and CHIP: March 2013*. Washington, DC.

Merriman, D.F. (2006). A Theoretical Analysis of Medicaid Supplantation. *Public Finance Review*, 34, 33–59.

Myers, R.J. (1970). *Medicare*, Homewood, IL: Richard D. Irwin.

Palfrey, J.S. (2006). *Child Health in America: Making a Difference through Advocacy*. Baltimore: Johns Hopkins University Press.

Pear, R. (2003). Governors Resist Bush Plan to Slow Costs of Medicaid. *New York Times*, May 25, p. 1.

Rose, S. (2013). *Financing Medicaid: Federalism and the Growth of America's Health Care Safety Net*. Ann Arbor: University of Michigan Press.

Rosenbaum, S. (1993). Medicaid Expansions and Access to Health Care. In *Medicaid Financing Crisis: Balancing Responsibilities, Priorities, and Dollars*, ed. D. Rowland, J. Feder, and A. Salganicoff. Washington, DC: American Association for the Advancement of Science Press, pp. 45–82.

Rosenbaum, S., and Westmoreland, T.M. (2012). The Supreme Court's Surprising Decision on the Medicaid Expansion: How Will the Federal Government and States Proceed? *Health Affairs*, 31(8), 1663–1672.

Rovner, J. (2010, May 26). Medicaid Pain Might Be Less than Governors Claim. Shots: NPR's Health Blog. Available at http://www.npr.org/blogs/health/2010/05/26/127168826/medicaid-pain-might-be-less-than-governors-claim.

Sommers, A., Ghosh, A., and Rousseau, D. (2005). *Medicaid Enrollment and Spending by 'Mandatory' and 'Optional' Eligibility and Benefit Categories*, technical report, Henry J. Kaiser Family Foundation. Available at http://www.kff.org/medicaid/upload/Medicaid-Enrollment-and-Spending-by-Mandatory-and-Optional-Eligibility-and-Benefit-Categories-Report.pdf.

Sommers, B.D., Baicker, K., and Epstein, A.M. (2012). Mortality and Access to Care among Adults after State Medicaid Expansions. *New England Journal of Medicine*, special article, July 25 (10.1056/NEJMsa1202099).

Sparer, M.S. (2009). Medicaid and the U.S. Path to National Health Insurance. *New England Journal of Medicine*, 360(4), 323–325.

Thompson, F.J., and Burke, C. (2007). Executive Federalism and Medicaid Demonstration Waivers: Implications for Policy and Democratic Process. *Journal of Health Politics, Policy and Law*, 32(6), 971–1004.

Thompson, F.J., and DiIulio, J. (1998). *Medicaid and Devolution: A View from the States.* Washington, DC: Brookings Institution Press.

Thompson, F.J., and Fossett, J.W. (2008). Federalism. In *Health Politics and Policy,* ed. J.A. Morone, T.J. Litman, and L.S. Robins. New York: Delmar.

Turque, B., Murr, A., Rosenberg, D., Katel, P., and Hager, M. (1993). Experimental States. *Newsweek*, May 17, p. 38.

U.S. Department of Health and Human Services. (2012). *2011 Actuarial Report on the Financial Outlook for Medicaid.* Washington, DC.

U.S. Government Accountability Office. (2008). *State and Local Governments: Growing Fiscal Challenges Will Emerge during the Next 10 Years.* Washington, DC.

Vladeck, B.C. (2003). Where the Action Really Is: Medicaid and the Disabled. *Health Affairs*, 22(1), 90–100.

Weil, A.R. (2003). There's Something about Medicaid. *Health Affairs*, 22(1), 13–30.

Weissert, C. (1992). Medicaid in the 1990s: Trends, Innovations and the Future of the 'PAC-Man' of State Budgets. *Publius: The Journal of Federalism*, 22(3), 93–109.

Chapter 11

Future Issues in State Transportation Finance

John R. Bartle and Can Chen
University of Nebraska, Omaha

Contents

Introduction

Transportation is critically important for any nation; it connects businesses, communities, and people, and is necessary to build and support a strong economy. The development of a continental transportation system in the United States facilitated the growth of the economy into a world power. Major technological innovations in transportation in this country in the last 100 years not only undergirded the development of the nation, but are central to most state government economies. In fact, federal innovations required states to help finance turnpikes, canals, roads, airports, and transit lines. The future of transportation in this nation remains challenging, as technology, economic patterns, consumer preferences, and fiscal capacities continue to change. States will be tested to keep up with these changes, and to make policy that facilitates a healthy environment and vibrant economy.

This chapter examines the intergovernmental fiscal structure of public transportation systems in the United States. We identify the factors that will affect the future of state transportation funding: demographic and economic trends, technological innovations, fiscal volatility, and social changes in travel behaviors. We then discuss the looming crisis in transportation finance for states and suggest possible policy solutions to these problems, such as technology, planning, and innovative financing.

Financing Transportation: Federal, State, and Local Roles

Financial responsibility for transportation varies by mode, and the division of responsibility for transportation services and infrastructure among levels of government in the United States has been negotiated over time. State and local governments predominantly own, operate, and maintain most highway and transit infrastructure, and these governments provide approximately 75 percent of the public funding for the systems (Dilger 2012, 3). The federal government accounts for the other 25 percent of funding, primarily in the form of grants. The federal government provides about half of the funding for air and water transportation, the other half coming from states and localities (Fisher 2007, 550–551). Railroads are predominantly privately owned and operated, although historically, railroads have received large federal land grants. Compared with other modes of transportation, all governments combined provide a very small share of funding for railroads.

Federal Transportation Funding

In the past, the federal government played a limited role in funding transportation in America, given concerns about constitutionality and states' rights. To the extent that the federal government became involved in transportation, it was by congressional appropriation to improve river and harbor systems and through land grants to railroads to encourage westward settlement (O'Neil and Ebdon 2003, 5). The Federal Highway Aid Act of 1916 marked significant federal involvement in transportation. This legislation provided a 50 percent federal matching formula to plan, build, and maintain highways under the direction of state highway departments. "It sets several key precedents for how the federal government would finance and regulate highway expansion, including the use of matching grants, state control and restrictions on the use of tolls on federally financed highways" (Hou and Duncombe 2011, 26). The 1956 Highway Revenue Act "expanded and solidified the federal government's role in shaping the nation's transportation system" (Dilger 2012, 12). The newly created Highway Transportation Fund (HTF) received earmarked funds from highway user charges, including excise taxes on gasoline, diesel, and tires and a weight tax for heavy trucks. Also, the federal matching share was increased from 50 to 90 percent for interstate upgrades and to 80 percent for nonhighway projects. Federal influence in financing transportation across the nation grew with the passage of the Urban Mass Transportation Act in 1964. In 1966, the U.S. Department of Transportation (USDOT) was created, and in 1970, the Airport and Airway Revenue Act established the Airport and Airway Trust Fund. Similar to the HTF, this fund draws from charges, aviation user fees, and fuel taxes.

In 1989, with the passage of the Intermodal Surface Transportation Efficiency Act (ISTEA), the federal government began a shift from building interstate highways to maintaining and repairing the 161,000-mile system. ISTEA created the Surface Transportation Program (STP) to provide more flexibility for states and localities in the use of federal highway funds for nonhighway purposes, such as public transportation. In 1998, the Transportation Equity Act for the 21st century (TEA-21) addressed the distribution of federal highway trust funds, ensuring each state a guaranteed minimum return of 90.5 percent of funds contributed (by states) to the HTF through fuel taxes and other user fees. With the new federal transportation authorization act in 2005, the Safe, Accountable, Flexible, Efficient Transportation Equity Act—A Legacy for Users (SAFETEA-LU) encouraged greater flexibility by states regarding the use of federal funds for transportation services and systems as well as heightened attention to highway safety. The Moving Ahead for Progress in the 21st Century Act (MAP-21) is the most recent federal transportation bill signed into law on July 6, 2012. MAP-21 extended federal highway and transit funding through federal fiscal year 2014, and it consolidated federal surface transportation programs into a streamlined, performance-based program to address many sustainability challenges facing the nation's transportation system.

State Transportation Funding

States provided much of the funding to develop this country's canals and railroads. Also, in response to the good roads movement, states developed road networks, aid systems, and state highway departments (Goetz 2007, 122). In 1892, New Jersey became the first state to establish a state highway department; by 1917, all 48 states had highway departments (Goetz 2007, 122). By 1915, 45 states had aid systems for highway development. In 1919, Oregon, Colorado, and New Mexico became the first states to levy a state gasoline tax for highway building and maintenance. With the creation of the U.S. Department of Transportation in the 1960s, several states reorganized their highway departments into transportation departments (Goetz 2007, 126). Today, state transportation departments are generally responsible for highway, aviation, public transit, rail, water, and intermodal transportation, and in many states, this department is responsible for enacting and maintaining a multiyear transportation plan and the development of transportation-related capital projects.

Currently, states provide nearly half of all highway funding, and about 20 percent of the funding for transit systems. In addition, many states support funding for aviation services and airports. Several states with large seaports, as in California, Louisiana, New York, New Jersey, and Texas, or those with large inland waterway systems, such as Michigan and Mississippi, provide substantial money for port, inland waterway, and intermodal development and improvement. "With the demise of private sector passenger rail service and the difficulties that Amtrak has faced, states become more involved in passenger rail. States began to provide financial assistance to Amtrak to operate service in those states; a few states such as California, Maryland actually began to operate rail service directly" (Goetz 2007, 127).

As of 2010, 19 states earmark transportation revenues into a state trust fund for highways, transit, aviation, or transportation. Some other states use a designated account for such receipts. The use of state transportation funds or accounts is proscribed by constitutional or statutory provision in at least 35 states. The use of state fuel tax revenues exclusively for highway and road purposes has been imposed constitutionally in 23 states and statutorily in 3 others (Rall et al. 2010). All states levy motor fuel taxes, which are the main source of state highway funds in about half of the states; vehicle registration, license, or title fees are charged in 48 states; vehicle or truck weight fees are levied in 37; and 29 states charge motor vehicle or rental car sales taxes. Additionally, toll revenues are collected in 24 states (Rall et al. 2010). General funds are commonly used to complement state highway funds in 34 states. In some states, bond proceeds are a major revenue source used by states for highways. For instance, the major revenue source of state highway funding in seven states from 1994 to 2004 came from bond proceeds (Sundeen and Reed 2006, 17). Some states, such as New York, Massachusetts, and New Jersey, divert significant portions of state fuel tax revenues to fund transit systems.

Local Transportation Funding

Local governments provide about 30 percent of total funding for highways and transit and own 77 percent of the nation's roadway miles (Sundeen and Reed 2006). On average, local governments provide about 25 percent of the funding for airports. Local revenue sources for funding transportation primarily include the property tax, general fund appropriations, and bond proceeds. Given the effects of the Great Recession on federal and state transportation funds, the role of local governments in addressing their own transportation needs has become increasingly important. As one supplement to local transportation revenue sources, local option taxes (such as the general sales tax, income taxes, or motor fuel taxes) have become a popular way to meet growing needs in local transportation (Goldman and Wachs 2003). In 46 states, local option transportation taxes fund a variety of local transportation-related projects (Sundeen and Reed 2006).

Trends in State Transportation Finance

State Transportation Expenditures

From 1955 to 1980, the greatest proportion of transportation expenditures was by state governments, when compared to the federal and local governments. In 1955, states made 45.8 percent of transportation expenditures, local governments made 39.8 percent of these expenditures, and the federal share of transportation spending was 14.5 percent (U.S. Census Bureau 1960; U.S. Office of Management and Budget 2012). Since then, local governments have become the largest spenders on transportation. In 2010, local governments spent 40.8 percent of the total for transportation, while states spent 31.8 percent, and the federal government spent 27.3 percent.

Table 11.1 shows the rate of growth of public spending on transportation. From 1960 to 1990, total transportation expenditures increased at an annual growth rate of about 10 percent, but since 1990, the growth rate has slowed significantly. Regarding each level of government, from 1970 to 1980, federal transportation expenditures grew over 200 percent, but from 1980 to 2000, federal spending growth was slower than both state and local spending. From 1960 to 1990, state transportation expenditures increased at a stable annual growth rate of nearly 9 percent. Since 2000, state transportation spending grew the slowest of all three levels of government. Local transportation spending grew faster than the total during most of these periods.

State Highway Finance

Highways are the most important mode of transportation in the United States, and state governments play the dominant role in financing this mode of transportation.

Table 11.1 Transportation Expenditures by Government Units: 1960–2010

Growth Rate	*Federal*	*State*	*Local*	*Total*
1960–1970	69.8%	84.5%	119.6%	89.7%
1970–1980	204.4%	87.6%	90.8%	119.2%
1980–1990	38.2%	97.9%	194.8%	102.5%
1990–2000	58.9%	69.0%	68.9%	66.4%
2000–2005	44.9%	25.8%	30.9%	32.4%
2005–2010	35.5%	19.1%	32.2%	28.5%
Annual Growth Rate	*Federal*	*State*	*Local*	*Total*
1960–1970	7.0%	8.5%	12.0%	9.0%
1970–1980	20.4%	8.8%	9.1%	11.9%
1980–1990	3.8%	9.8%	19.5%	10.3%
1990–2000	5.9%	6.9%	6.9%	6.6%
2000–2005	4.5%	2.6%	3.1%	3.2%
2005–2010	7.1%	3.8%	6.4%	5.7%

Source: Federal transportation expenditure data are from U.S. Office of Management and Budget, Budget of the United States Government, Fiscal Year 2013, Historical Tables 3.1 and 3.2, 2012; state and local government transportation expenditure data 1960–1990 are from U.S. Census Bureau, *Government Finances;* data 2000–2010 are from U.S. Census Bureau, *State and Local Government Finances.*

On average, 21 percent of public roads are owned by states (USDOT 2008b). Most of these roads are part of the national interstate highway system. States contribute the largest share of revenue to highways, funding over half of all highway spending. They rely heavily on highway user fees in the form of motor fuel taxes, motor vehicle taxes, and tolls. State transportation departments are directly involved in the planning, construction, and maintenance of the network of highways and bridges within their responsibility. About half of state highway expenditure is concentrated on capital outlays.

State Highway Revenues

Table 11.2 shows total state highway revenues since 1921. The early rapid growth of revenues for highways has dropped steadily since the 1960s. In 1921, own-source revenues accounted for 74 percent of total revenues for highways, reaching over

Table 11.2 Total Revenues Used by States for Highways by Source: 1921–2010

	State Own-Source Revenue									*Intergovernmental Transfer*		
(% of total)	*Highway User Revenue*				*Other Revenues*							
Year	*Motor Fuel Taxes*	*Motor Vehicle and Carrier Taxes*	*Tolls*	*Subtotal*	*General Funds*	*Property Taxes and Special Assessments*	*Other State Imposts and Miscellaneous*	*Bonds*	*Total State Own-Source Revenue*	*Federal*	*Local*	*10-Year Growth Rate*
1921	1.0%	28.0%	0	29.0%	8.2%	8.2%	1.6%	27.0%	74.0%	18.3%	7.8%	—
1930	38.1%	26.5%	1.0%	65.5%	2.6%	0.9%	1.1%	17.7%	87.7%	7.5%	4.8%	195.1%
1940	46.5%	23.6%	2.0%	72.1%	0.2%	0.2%	0.8%	13.2%	86.5%	12.8%	0.8%	22.3%
1950	46.8%	22.3%	2.2%	71.3%	0.6%	0	1.4%	12.5%	85.7%	13.0%	1.3%	113.9%
1960	37.6%	16.9%	4.9%	59.3%	0.5%	0	1.8%	8.2%	69.8%	29.1%	1.2%	164.0%
1970	36.9%	16.7%	5.1%	58.6%	1.4%	0	2.7%	7.9%	70.6%	28.7%	0.7%	90.1%
1980	30.0%	17.5%	4.5%	52.0%	4.3%	0	5.3%	3.8%	65.4%	33.8%	0.8%	80.2%
1990	34.0%	17.9%	4.7%	56.6%	2.8%	0	7.1%	6.0%	72.5%	26.2%	1.3%	81.3%
2000	31.4%	17.0%	5.2%	53.6%	4.5%	0	5.6%	8.9%	72.6%	25.7%	1.6%	69.7%
2010	19.6%	14.7%	5.1%	39.4%	4.7%	0	9.6%	18.6%	72.3%	25.6%	2.2%	40.9%

Source: U.S. Department of Transportation, *Highway Statistics*, various issues. Tolls collection began in 1925. States terminated property taxes and special assessments collection in 1952.

85 percent from 1930 to 1950. These revenues declined to 65.4 percent by 1980, given the increasing role of the federal government in subsidizing highways nationwide. Since 1990, the share of state own-source revenues rebounded and then stabilized at slightly over 70 percent. State own-source revenues include motor fuel taxes, motor vehicle taxes, and tolls, as well as a variety of other sources, including general funds, bonds, investment income, and other taxes and fees. The share of motor fuel taxes in state highway revenues declined significantly over a long period, accounting for less than 20 percent of state highway revenues in 2010. Toll receipts as a share of state highway revenue have remained at about 5 percent since 1960. Bonding has recently returned as a significant resource for state highway funding. Since 1980, federal funds comprise about 25 percent of total state highway revenues; local transfers to states are a minor resource for highway spending.

State Motor Fuel Taxes

State tax rates on motor fuel have consistently increased since 1960. The average state motor fuel rate in 1960 of 6.1 cents per gallon doubled by 1985 to 12.1 cents and reached 22 cents in 2010. The minimum state rate rose from 3 cents per gallon in 1960 (Missouri) to 7.5 cents in 2010 (Georgia), while the maximum increased significantly from 7 cents in 1960 (Nebraska) to 37.5 cents in 2010 (North Carolina). Since 1993, the federal gasoline tax rate has been 18.4 cents per gallon. The federal government currently levies 24.4 cents per gallon in excise tax for diesel fuel (USDOT, *Highway Statistics*, various issues). Even though gas tax rates have increased nominally, in real terms, these rates actually have declined since 1960 (O'Connell and Yusuf 2013). For instance, Georgia's state fuel tax rate was 6.5 cents per gallon in 1957. In 2007, its state fuel tax rate was 7.5 cents per gallon, which was the lowest fuel tax rate across the states. However, the real purchasing power of Georgia's state fuel tax rate in 2007 was only 16 percent compared with its rate in 1957.

State Highway Expenditures

Table 11.3 shows the components of state highway expenditures from 1921 to 2010. The growth rate in the early years is higher than in later years, as the system was built out. As with revenues, growth has slowed steadily since 1960. State highway expenditures can be divided into capital and noncapital outlay. Noncapital outlay includes maintenance and traffic services, administration and safety, debt service, and state transfers to local governments. During the build-out of the interstate from 1960 to 1980, state highway capital expenditures made up over half of total spending. Since 1980, the share of capital expenditure has hovered around 50 percent. State highway maintenance and traffic service expenditures have been a relatively stable component of total spending. Expenditures for administration and safety increased significantly from 1930 to 1990, and dipped only slightly since.

Table 11.3 State Expenditures for Highways by Source: 1921–2010

(% of total)	*Capital Outlay*	*Maintenance and Traffic Services*	*Administration and Safety*	*Debt Service*	*Transfers to Local Government*	*Total*	*Average Annual Growth Rate*
1921	69.2%	14.9%	5.7%	3.9%	6.3%	100%	—
1930	57.3%	15.2%	3.3%	9.7%	14.5%	100%	19.5%
1940	41.7%	15.8%	5.8%	16.7%	19.9%	100%	1.1%
1950	50.9%	15.9%	5.9%	8.1%	19.1%	100%	12.6%
1960	59.6%	12.0%	6.3%	7.6%	14.4%	100%	15.8%
1970	56.4%	11.9%	9.2%	7.9%	14.6%	100%	9.8%
1980	51.1%	15.4%	12.8%	7.0%	13.7%	100%	8.2%
1990	48.9%	15.6%	14.1%	6.5%	14.8%	100%	7.8%
2000	53.0%	14.4%	12.5%	7.8%	12.3%	100%	6.8%
2010	49.7%	15.0%	12.0%	12.3%	11.0%	100%	6.3%

Source: U.S. Department of Transportation (1997a, 2000–2010), *Highway Statistics*, various issues (summary to 1995 and 2000–2010).

State debt service expenditures exploded from $17 million in 1921 to $240 million in 1940, growing from 3.9 percent to 16.7 percent of the highway budget. The share of spending on debt decreased until 1990, yet has almost doubled its share since then. States transferred 6.3 percent of their budget for such spending to local governments in 1921, and this rose to 19.9 percent in 1940. Since then, the share has slowly decreased.

State Transit Finance

State governments play an important role in transit finance, even though it is normally thought of as a local activity and responsibility. States fund about one-eighth of transit capital costs and one-fourth of operating costs. States are increasingly reliant on sales and income taxes to pay their share of transit costs. Also, since local governments are creatures of the states, states must ensure that local transit systems have sufficient resources to make repairs, for network expansion, and to cover operating costs.

State Funding of Public Transit

In 1960, there was no federal funding for transit, and state and local funding was very limited. The federal government began to subsidize public transit in 1964, and by the 1970s, state and local transit funding by the federal government more than tripled, increasing at an average annual rate of 20.8 percent. Federal funding grew much more slowly during the 1980s, with transit funding from the federal government growing at an average annual rate of 11.3 percent. In 1960, the state and local share of public funding for transit equaled 100 percent. Since 1990, the share for state and local governments for transit has hovered around 75 percent, with the federal share around 25 percent. Transit systems are capital-intensive, requiring large initial investments. The federal government supported such investments in the 1970s, as many city transit systems transitioned from private to public. After the conversion of many city transit systems to public enterprises, however, tight federal fiscal conditions meant less federal support for transit. The financial responsibility for these systems shifted principally to local governments, with state support that varies across the nation (USDOT 1997b, 1999, 2002, 2004, 2006, 2008a, 2010a).

General funds, dedicated sales taxes, and other dedicated public funds are important sources of revenue for transit at the state level. In 1995, total state funds for transit were $4.6 billion, accounting for 26.7 percent of total public funds. General funds ($2.5 billion) were the largest revenue source for state transit funding, encompassing more than half of this funding in 1995. Dedicated sales taxes and fuel taxes comprised about 8 percent of state transit funding, while income and property taxes made up a smaller portion of total transit funds. By 2008, total state funds for transit rose to over $11 billion, making up 29.3 percent of total public funds. Dedicated sales taxes were now the largest revenue source for state transit funding at 30 percent of the total. General funds were the second largest revenue source for state transit funding at 28 percent, though a much smaller share than in 1995. Fares are an important part of transit revenue. While there has been some variation during this period, they amount to between one-quarter to one-third of total state transit revenue (USDOT 1997b, 1999, 2002, 2004, 2006, 2008a, 2010a).

State Expenditures for Public Transit

Transit capital expenditures generally include the design and construction of new transit systems, extensions of existing systems, and the modernization of existing fixed assets (USDOT 2010a). Table 11.4 shows that in 1988, state transit capital expenditures were $671 million, which accounted for 16.3 percent in total public transit capital expenditures. By 2008, state transit capital expenditures more than tripled. The state share of transit capital expenditures reached a peak of 23 percent in 1993, dropped to 9.3 percent by 2001, then rebounded to 12.4 percent in 2008. From 1988 to 2008, the share of federal transit capital expenditure dropped from 58.3 percent to just shy of 40 percent. Meanwhile, local transit capital expenditures increased to $7.7 billion, and the local share reached 48 percent by 2008, the largest source of funds for transit capital expenditures.

Transit operating expenditures generally include wages, salaries, fuels, preventive maintenance, and lease payments for the provision of transit service (USDOT 2010a). In 1993, state transit operating expenditures were $2.9 billion, which accounted for 18.4 percent in total state spending for transit operations. State transit operating expenditures grew from 1993 to 2008, faster than either federal or local shares for such spending, the state share rising from 18.4 percent to 25.8 percent for this period. By 2008, funds generated by the transit systems (such as fares) made up the greatest share of funding for state transit operating expenditures; the local share is 29.7 percent, the state share is 25.8 percent, and the federal share is 7.1 percent (USDOT 1997b, 1999, 2002, 2004, 2006, 2008a, 2010a).

State Financing for Other Modes of Transportation

Air Transportation Expenditures

Federal and local governments play dominant roles in funding air transportation, while states have a more limited role. In 1960, states spent $26 million on air transportation, accounting for only 2.1 percent in total air transportation expenditures. State air transportation expenditures increased rapidly in the 1960s and 1970s, growing at an average annual rate of 58.5 percent during the 1960s and 10.2 percent in the 1970s. The state share of air transportation expenditures

Table 11.4 Sources of Funds for Transit Capital Expense: 1988–2008[a]

Year	*1988*	*1989*	*1990*	*1991*	*1992*	*1993*	*1994*	*1995*	*1996*	*1997*	*1998*
Federal	2,395	2,667	2,636	2,545	2,599	2,383	2,518	3,314	3,506	4,138	3,680
Federal share	58.3%	56.9%	58.1%	49.9%	49.2%	41.6%	45.0%	47.3%	50.4%	54.2%	49.7%
State	671	790	645	638	778	1,317	1,006	989	895	1,007	875
State share	16.3%	16.9%	14.2%	12.5%	14.7%	23.0%	18.0%	14.1%	12.9%	13.2%	11.8%
Local	1,041	1,226	1,255	1,914	1,906	2,033	2,075	2,706	2,553	2,492	2,856
Local share	25.3%	26.2%	27.7%	37.6%	36.1%	35.5%	37.1%	38.6%	36.7%	32.6%	38.5%
Total	4,108	4,684	4,537	5,097	5,283	5,733	5,599	7,009	6,955	7,636	7,411
Year	*1999*	*2000*	*2001*	*2002*	*2003*	*2004*	*2005*	*2006*	*2007*	*2008*	*Average annual growth (1988–2008)*
Federal	3,726	4,275	5,468	4,994	5,092	4,930	4,612	5,552	5,600	6,400	8.4%
Federal share	44.1%	47.2%	50.5%	40.6%	39.9%	39.0%	39.2%	43.5%	41.2%	39.8%	
State	858	973	1,011	1,433	1,623	1,756	1,494	1,698	1,500	2,000	9.9%
State share	10.2%	10.7%	9.3%	11.7%	12.7%	13.9%	12.7%	13.3%	11.0%	12.4%	
Local	3,860	3,808	4,345	5,874	6,061	5,943	5,654	5,502	6,500	7,700	32.0%
Local share	45.7%	42.1%	40.1%	47.8%	47.4%	47.1%	48.1%	43.1%	47.8%	47.8%	
Total	8,443	9,056	10,825	12,301	12,775	12,629	11,760	12,752	13,600	16,100	14.6%

Source: U.S. Department of Transportation, 1997b, 1999, 2004, 2006, 2008a, 2010a, 2012a; *Status of the National Surface Transportation Condition and Performance*, 1997, 1999; *Status of the Nation's Highways, Bridges, and Transit: Conditions and Performance*, 2002, 2004, 2006, 2008, 2010.

[a] In millions of dollars.

peaked in 1970 at 7.5 percent. The share of spending and rate of growth for state spending have decreased since then. By 2010, state air transportation expenditures stood at $1.7 billion, 3.8 percent of total air transport expenditures.

The federal government has been the largest single funding entity for air transportation in 1960, but this role has receded steadily. The federal share of spending has fallen since 1980, while the local share rose to 50.8 percent in 2000. Following the terrorist attacks in 2001, the federal government greatly increased funds for aviation safety. In 2010, local air transportation expenditures were $22,492 million, which just surpasses federal spending of $21,431 million (U.S. Census Bureau 2010; U.S. Office of Management and Budget 2012).

Water Transportation Expenditures

The federal government dominated public water transportation expenditures in the 1960s and 1970s, though this role has diminished over time while the states' role has been relatively stable. The local role has expanded since the 1960s. In 1960, the federal government share of total water transportation expenditures was nearly 80 percent, while local governments accounted for 13.8 percent, and states just 7 percent. State water transportation expenditures increased rapidly in the two decades of the 1960s and 1970s. State spending grew at a slower rate in the 1980s, and at moderate rates since then. By 2010, the federal share of water transportation spending declined to 63.6 percent, while the local share doubled to 27.9 percent and the state share stood at 8.5 percent (U.S. Census Bureau 2010; U.S. Office of Management and Budget 2012).

Rail Transportation Expenditures

With a few exceptions, railroads are owned and operated by private companies and most investment in them is not subsidized by government. The limited public spending is dominated by federal dollars. Federal spending exceeded $1.5 billion in 2008 for the first time since 1980, still less than 2 percent of total federal transportation expenditures (USDOT 2012b). State spending for rail transport is sporadic, with significant funding arising from federal grants. Since 1985, state spending has not exceeded $50 million, nor has it reached over 4 percent of public spending (USDOT 2003). Local spending for rail transportation is not significant either. Compared with other modes of transportation, all governments play a very limited role in this transportation mode.

Future Challenges in State Transportation Finance

Persistent themes in U.S. transportation are technological innovation, the degree of public versus private sector participation in providing infrastructure and operations, and the division of responsibility among the three levels of government.

States face significant challenges to the funding and provision of transportation infrastructure and service in the future. Demographic and economic changes, traveler behavior, technological innovations, and the fiscal weaknesses brought about by the Great Recession will affect the demand for transportation, system capacity, and financing requirements for the states.

Demographic and Economic Trends

The demand for automobiles has been affected by a series of demographic and economic factors. Table 11.5 shows that while the population of the nation increased by 72 percent from 1960 to 2010, the number of licensed drivers increased by 141 percent for the same period. With greater economic prosperity, automobiles have become more affordable to the majority of Americans—the number of registered vehicles more than tripled from 1960 to 2010. As indicated in Figure 11.1, the average number of vehicles registered per driver increased from less than one (0.85) in 1960 and to more than one by 1980. Population growth, a greater percentage of the population driving, and more vehicles per person are all factors that have contributed to a quadrupling in vehicle miles traveled (VMT) since 1960.

Besides passenger travel, a substantial growth in freight movement will continue to place greater demands on the U.S. transportation network. The deregulation of the trucking industry has contributed to this growth. Decreases in average operating costs (adjusted for inflation) of as much as 75 percent led to an increase in freight traffic (Winston 1998). According to the U.S. Department of Transportation (2010b),

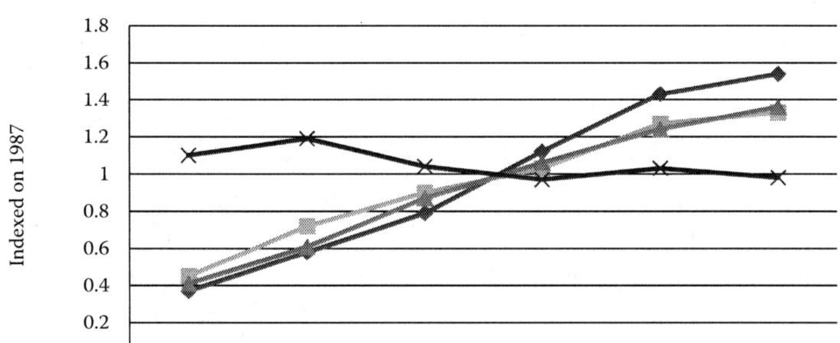

	1960	1970	1980	1990	2000	2010
Vehicle Miles of Travel	0.37	0.58	0.79	1.12	1.43	1.54
Motor Fuel Consumption	0.45	0.72	0.9	1.03	1.27	1.33
Vehicle Registrations	0.41	0.61	0.87	1.06	1.24	1.36
Gallons per Vehicle	1.1	1.19	1.04	0.97	1.03	0.98

Figure 11.1 Vehicle registrations, fuel consumption, vehicle miles of travel as indices (data are indexed to 1987 base). (From U.S. Department of Transportation, *Highway Statistics*, 2010.)

Table 11.5 Vehicle Registrations, Fuel Consumption, and VMT: 1960–2010

	1960	*1970*	*1980*	*1990*	*2000*	*2010*
Population (millions)	180	204	227	248	285	309
Drivers (millions)	87	112	145	167	191	210
Percent of drivers in total population	48.3%	54.9%	63.9%	67.3%	67.0%	68.0%
Vehicles registered (thousands)	73,858	111,242	161,490	193,057	225,821	242,061
Number of vehicles per driver	0.85	0. 99	1.11	1.16	1.18	1.15
Vehicle miles traveled (millions)	718,762	1,109,724	1,527,295	2,144,362	2,746,925	2,966,506
Motor fuel consumption (million gallons)	57,880	92,329	114,960	130,755	162,544	170,776
Average miles traveled per vehicle (thousands)	9.7	10.0	9.5	11.1	12.2	12.3
Average miles traveled per gallon	12.4	12	13.3	16.4	16.9	17.4
Average fuel consumption per vehicle (gallons)	784	830	712	677	720	705

Source: U.S. Department of Transportation, *Highway Statistics*, 2010.

over 16 billion tons of goods at an estimated worth of $14.6 trillion were transported through the U.S. freight systems (including pipelines) in 2009. The Federal Highway Administration (FHWA) estimates that by 2040, the volume of freight movement in the United States may nearly double. Further growth in international trade undoubtedly will contribute to an increase in the volume of traffic as well (Sundee and Reed 2006).

Technological Innovations

The history of transportation in this country is strongly influenced by technological innovation. The invention of the steam engine, the internal combustion engine, and the advent of the airplane brought about great changes in transit and transportation across the nation. Technological changes in the automobile industry, including higher fuel economy standards, alternative fuel vehicles, hybrid engines, and fuel cell technology, will continue to influence the revenues that can be expected from fuel taxes. Table 11.6 shows that the average fuel economy values in cars and trucks increased from 13.1 miles in 1975 to 22.6 miles in 2010, indicative of less fuel consumption per vehicle. As shown in Figure 11.1, the index of motor fuel consumption increased from 0.45 in 1960 to 1.33 in 2010, but the index of gallons per vehicle declined from 1.1 to 0.98. Growing sales of hybrid and alternative fuels vehicles further threaten the fiscal viability of state gas tax revenues. For example, in 2005, the sales of hybrid vehicles reached 205,000. Although such sales

Table 11.6 EPA-Adjusted Fuel Economy Values and Truck Sales Fraction: 1975–2010 (mpg)

Model Years	*Cars*	*Trucks*	*Cars and Trucks*	*Truck Sales (% of total)*
1975	13.5	11.6	13.1	19.2
1980	20.0	15.8	19.2	16.4
1985	23.0	17.5	21.3	24.7
1990	23.3	17.4	21.2	29.6
1995	23.2	17.0	20.5	35.9
2000	22.4	16.9	19.8	40.3
2005	22.9	16.9	19.9	42.8
2010	25.5	18.7	22.6	35.7

Source: U.S. Environmental Protection Agency (EPA), Office of Transportation and Air Quality, 2011, available at http://epa.gov/otaq/cert/mpg/fetrends/2012/420r12001.pdf.

account for a small portion of the new vehicle fleet, the popularity of these types of vehicles is expected to continue to grow, given higher fuel prices and heightened environmental concerns (Sundee and Reed 2006, 20).

Fiscal Challenges

Even accounting for the ups and downs of the business cycle, over the long term, rising transportation construction costs and shrinking state motor fuel tax receipts are more critical to the sustainability of state transportation services and infrastructure. Increasing material and labor prices are evidenced by the fact that the construction price index (Composite Bid Price Index for Federal Aid Highway Construction) grew by 120 percent from 1960 to 2006. Most of this increase is relatively recent—the price index increased by 48 percent from 2003 to 2006. Hurricane Katrina and higher gasoline prices greatly increased the costs of road construction in 2005 (USDOT 2007). Figure 11.2 shows that since 2005, growth in construction costs and factor inputs (Producer Price Index [PPI] for material and supply inputs into highway and street construction) has outpaced general inflation (Consumer Price Index for All Urban Consumers [CPI-U]). Again, these trends pose a challenge to the long-term viability of the highway system.

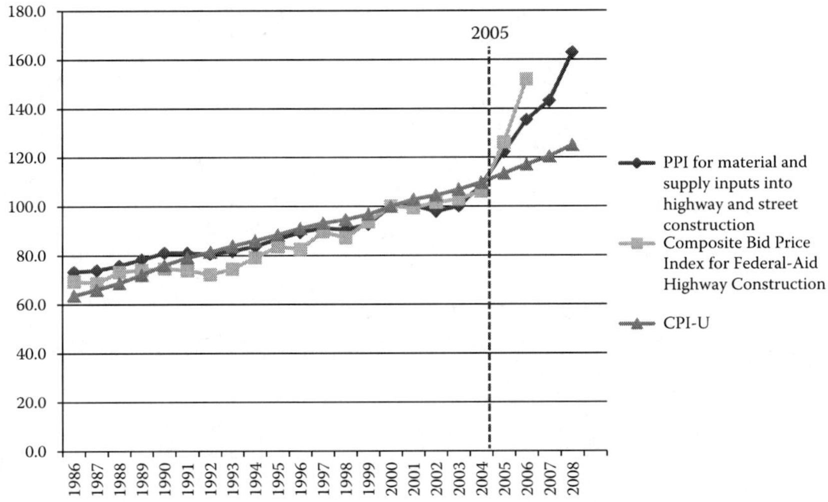

Figure 11.2 Construction-related cost indices (all indices have been rescaled to 2000 as the base year 100). (Consumer price index and producer price index data from the U.S. Bureau of Labor Statistics; Composite Bid Price Index for Federal Aid Highway Construction from U.S. Department of Transportation, *Price Trends for Federal-Aid Highway Construction*, Washington, DC, 2007, available at http://www.fhwa.dot.gov/programadmin/pt2006q4.pdf; since 2007, USDOT has published the National Highway Construction Cost Index [NHCCI].)

Table 11.7 Means of Transportation to Work (Commuting to Work) for the United States: 1960–2010

United States	*Car, Truck, or Van—Driven Alone*	*Car, Truck, or Van—Carpooled*	*Public Transportation (excluding taxicab)*	*Walked*	*Taxicab, Motorcycle, Bicycle, or Other Means*	*Worked at Home*
1960 census	64.0% (combined)		12.1%	9.9%	2.5%	7.2%
1970 census	77.7% (combined)		8.5%	7.4%	2.9%	3.5%
1980 census	64.4%	19.7%	6.2%	5.6%	1.8%	2.3%
1990 census	73.2%	13.4%	5.1%	3.9%	1.5%	3.0%
2000 census	75.7%	12.2%	4.5%	2.9%	1.4%	3.3%
2010 ACF	76.6%	9.7%	4.9%	2.8%	1.7%	4.3%

Source: U.S. Census Bureau, *Decennial Census*, 1960, 1970, 1980, 1990, 2000; U.S. Census Bureau, American Community Survey (ACF), 2010.

Mobility Culture and Traveler Behavior

In 1910, less than 10 percent of the nation's population lived in suburbs, but as automobiles became more affordable and populations migrated to suburbs, more people came to rely on their cars for transportation. By 2010, more than 50 percent of the nation's population lived in suburban communities, increasing the average distances of daily commutes to work (Population Reference Bureau 2011). Table 11.7 shows that in 1960, 64 percent of the working population drove alone in a car, truck, or van or carpooled, while 12.1 percent took public transportation, and nearly 10 percent walked to work. In 2010, people driving to work increased to 76.6 percent, and less than 5 percent took public transportation. The diminished use of transit reduced revenues from fares that cover operating expenses, and increased rush-hour congestion given more cars on roads, and thus contributed to greater travel times to and from work. During this time, the share of people walking to the workplace decreased considerably, too. On the other hand, since 1980, telecommuting (among other things) has boosted the number of people working from home. Nonetheless, an American culture that promotes mobility freedom and driving cars suggests that the automobile will still dominate the means of transportation to work in this country, which means continued and even increasing wear and tear on the nation's highway systems.

Conclusion

State transportation policy is confronting a series of challenges, a fundamental one being the confluence of rising demands for transportation infrastructure and services in an environment of constrained fiscal resources. The ability of states to maintain transportation as a core function is exacerbated by population growth, rising construction costs, and automobile-dependent travel behaviors. As we look for workable solutions to sustainability, three themes are helpful guides. The first theme, technological innovation, has greatly increased the speed, safety, and economy of travel. The potential for technology advancements to help solve our transportation problems remains, yet new technology also presents challenges, as the inventions of the automobile and airplane illustrate. Also, stimulating technological innovations with research and development, whether funded publicly or privately, is critically important. Relatedly, administrative responses to innovations need to facilitate and even incentivize efficient practice. For example, fees or charges should distribute costs to users so as not to encourage overuse of limited-capacity systems.

A second theme regards the balance of public and private involvement in transportation. Governments may be able to mobilize resources quickly and plan transportation systems more effectively than the private sector, but private investment and operations are less subject to political manipulation. The degree of private involvement in public transportation is informed by privatization experiences of the 1980s, when several transportation industries were deregulated. Pricing, entry, and exit from markets in the airline and trucking industries were fully deregulated, and most rail rates have been deregulated. Industry efficiency increased significantly following deregulation, with most of the benefit realized by consumers in the form of lower prices (Winston 1998). Further consideration of privatization is a logical policy option that could be applied to highway and airport investment decisions, and for transit investment and operations. Given the reluctance of taxpayers to pay more in taxes for public transportation services, privatization is a logical option to consider.

The division of responsibility for transportation infrastructure and services among governments is a third theme. It may seem as though states are caught in the middle, but their power should not be underestimated. State sovereignty precedes that of the federal government, and local governments are legal creatures of the state. States have a lot of discretion in policy making, and can delegate responsibility to local governments. However, transportation networks cut across political borders, so without deliberately planned policies and projects, transportation systems can be poorly designed, unsafe, and inefficiently executed. The appropriate balance of power among governments needs to be continually negotiated, especially in a changing environment. State fiscal capacity will be a major determining factor in this decision; if state revenue sources cannot fund desired projects, state authority will diminish. While motor fuel taxes are waning, tolls and bonds present two alternatives for advancing state highway construction and maintenance. The growth of local dedicated sales taxes can also enhance local capacity for transportation services.

Policy Recommendations

Future transportation trends will likely be a continuation of past ones. The demand for mobility will increase, and for most people in the United States, mobility is associated with the personal automobile. Highways will continue to be the dominant mode of transportation, though other methods are likely to expand to accommodate ever-increasing demands for travel. Due to the strained capacity of the nation's highway systems, especially in urban areas, transit and passenger rail travel are likely to increase slowly in the future. High-speed rail is being considered by some states (California, for example). To facilitate intermodal transportation, water transportation in states with ports and larger natural waterway systems may also play a small but increasing role. The significance of motor fuel taxes in funding state highways will likely continue to decrease, presenting perhaps the most pressing problem for transportation financing in the United States. Tolls may become a larger revenue source, and the importance of debt and other innovative financing to support state transportation systems may increase in response to declining federal aid along with decreasing gas tax revenues.

To deal effectively with these issues, it is important for states to better coordinate transportation policy with energy, environmental, and urban development policies.

Policies such as "complete streets" and transit-oriented development are viable solutions that integrate land use and urban planning into the development of sustainable transportation systems and have the potential to reduce the use of personal cars. Second, new technologies in transportation and communication like the intelligent transportation system (ITS) and telecommuting have good potential. These advances can reduce the number of trips, especially during peak hours, relieving stress on congested urban roads. Third, in light of the looming potential changes in vehicle fuel sources, replacing excise taxes on motor fuel with electronic toll charges or mileage-based fees that better reflect the costs associated with road use (including those operating by electricity or hybrid) will improve the long-term economic and fiscal sustainability of current U.S. transportation systems (Bartle 2005; Bartle and Devan 2006; Duncan and Graham 2013). Finally, innovative finance such as state infrastructure banks, federal credit assistance like loans, and credit enhancements offered by the Transportation Infrastructure Finance and Innovation Act (TIFIA) provide more flexibility in financing transportation projects. Given the fiscal constraints on state budgets, it is likely that private participation in transportation investments such as public-private partnerships will be an important ingredient of future transportation finance, too. While the challenges to transportation are great, new technology, innovative thinking, and public-private cooperation offer realistic promise.

References

Bartle, J.R. (2005). Transportation Infrastructure. In *Handbook of Public Sector Economics*, ed. D. Robbins. Boca Raton, FL: Taylor & Francis, pp. 375–405.

Bartle, J.R., and Devan, J. (2006). Sustainable Highways Destination or Mirage? *Public Works Management and Policy*, 10, 1–10.

Dilger, R.J. (2012). *Federalism Issues in Surface Transportation Policy: Past and Present*, technical report. Congressional Research Service. Available at http://www.fas.org/sgp/crs/misc/R40431.pdf.

Duncan, D., and Graham, J. (2013). Road User Fees Instead of Fuel Taxes: The Quest for Political Acceptability. *Public Administration Review*, 73, 415–426.

Fisher, R.C. (2007). *State and Local Public Finance*, 3rd ed. Mason, OH: Thomson.

Goldman, T., and Wachs, M. (2003). A Quiet Revolution in Transportation Finance: The Rise of Local Option Transportation Taxes. *Transportation Quarterly*, 57, 19–32.

Goetz, A.R. (2007). State Departments of Transportation: From Highway Departments to Transportation Agencies. In *Handbook of Transportation Policy and Administration*, ed. J. Plant. New York: Taylor & Francis, pp. 121–144.

Hou, Y., and Duncombe, W.D. (2011). Substantiation of Transportation Infrastructure—Patterns of Governance and Public Finance in Development: An Analytical Comparison of the United States and China. Presented at 1st China-India-US Symposium on Development and Governance. Available at http://papers.ssrn.com/sol3/papers.cfm?abstract_id=1744123.

O'Connell, L., and Yusuf, J. (2013). Improving Revenue Adequacy by Indexing the Gas Tax to Indicators of Need: A Simulation Analysis. *Public Works Management and Policy*, 18, 229–243.

O'Neil, P., and Ebdon, C. (2003). From Canals to Spaceports: Models of Public-Private Cooperation in U.S. Transportation Systems, unpublished book manuscript.

Population Reference Bureau. (2011). *Reports on America*, technical report. Available at http://www.prb.org/pdf11/reports-on-america-2010-census.pdf.

Rall, J., Wheet, A., Farber, N.J., and Reed, J.B. (2010). *Transportation Governance and Finance: A 50-State Review of State Legislatures and Departments of Transportation*, technical report. National Conference of State Legislatures. Available at http://www.ncsl.org/issues-research/transport/transportation-governance-and-finance.aspx.

Sundeen, M., and Reed, J.B. (2006). *Surface Transportation Funding Options for States*, technical report. National Conference of State Legislatures. Available at http://www.ncsl.org/documents/transportation/surfacetranfundrept.pdf.

U.S. Department of Commerce. *Census Bureau: Governmental Finances*, various issues before 1985. Washington, DC.

U.S. Department of Commerce. *Census Bureau: Government Finances*, various issues (1960–2000). Washington, DC.

U.S. Department of Commerce. *Census Bureau: State and Local Government Finances*, 2000–2010. Washington, DC.

U.S. Department of Transportation. *Highway Statistics*, various issues, 1960–2010. Washington, DC.

U.S. Department of Transportation. (1997a). *Highway Statistics Summary*, to 1995, Washington, DC.

U.S. Department of Transportation. (1997b). *Status of the National Surface Transportation Condition and Performance*. Washington, DC.

U.S. Department of Transportation. (1999). *Status of the National Surface Transportation Condition and Performance*. Washington, DC.

U.S. Department of Transportation. (2003). *Government Transportation Financial Statistics*. Washington, DC.

U.S. Department of Transportation. (2004). *2002 Status of the Nation's Highways, Bridges, and Transit: Conditions and Performance*. Washington, DC.

U.S. Department of Transportation. (2006). *2004 Status of the Nation's Highways, Bridges, and Transit: Conditions and Performance*. Washington, DC.

U.S. Department of Transportation. (2007). *Price Trends for Federal-Aid Highway Construction*. Washington, DC. Available at http://www.fhwa.dot.gov/programadmin/pt2006q4.pdf.

U.S. Department of Transportation. (2008a). *2006 Status of the Nation's Highways, Bridges, and Transit: Conditions and Performance*. Washington, DC.

U.S. Department of Transportation. (2008b). *Our Nation's Highways 2008*. Washington, DC.

U.S. Department of Transportation. (2010a). *2008 Status of the Nation's Highways, Bridges, and Transit: Conditions and Performance*. Washington, DC.

U.S. Department of Transportation. (2010b). *Freight Facts and Figures 2010*. Washington, DC.

U.S. Department of Transportation. (2012a). *2010 Status of the Nation's Highways, Bridges, and Transit: Conditions and Performance*. Washington, DC.

U.S. Department of Transportation. (2012b). *National Transportation Statistics 2012*. Washington, DC.

U.S. Environmental Protection Agency, Office of Transportation and Air Quality. (2011). Available at http://epa.gov/otaq/cert/mpg/fetrends/2012/420r12001.pdf.

U.S. Office of Management and Budget. (2012). Budget of the United States Government, Fiscal Year 2013, Historical Tables. Available at http://www.whitehouse.gov/sites/default/files/omb/budget/fy2013/assets/hist.pdf.

Winston, C. (1998). U.S. Industry Adjustment to Economic Deregulation. *Journal of Economic Perspectives*, 12, 89–110.

Chapter 12

Financing Criminal Justice in the States

Michael C. Walker

Passaic County Community College

Contents

Introduction

State governments are facing an increasing demand for criminal justice spending for several reasons, including the need to maintain a post–9/11 homeland security environment, a mounting geriatric and mentally challenged prison population, and the growing trend in mandatory terms of imprisonment for violent and drug-related nonviolent crimes. The increase in the number of local law enforcement officers, resulting in more arrests and subsequent prosecutions, has imposed additional pressures on state criminal justice spending. State own-source revenues to fund criminal justice activities are supplemented by funds from several federal agencies. This chapter discusses the factors that have contributed to the growth of criminal justice spending by the states and analyzes the sources of revenue to fund this spending, with particular focus on federal programs.

Trends in Criminal Justice Expenditures

From 2001 to 2011, spending on criminal justice by the states grew from $48.4 billion (U.S. Census 2002) to $63.4 billion (Lee et al. 2012)—an increase of 31 percent. In a contrasting trend, funding for criminal justice as a percent of total state expenditures decreased from 5.4 percent to 4.3 percent over the 10 years, primarily reflecting growing pressures on state budgets from other areas of spending, especially Medicaid.

The 4.3 percent average, however, masks wide variations across the states. In 2011, criminal justice spending as a percent of total state expenditures varied from a high of 7.1 percent in Maryland to a low of 2.9 percent in Iowa and Hawaii (see Table 12.1). In general, states in the Northeast and Mid-Atlantic regions allocate a higher proportion of total expenditures to criminal justice than do states in other parts of the United States.

Corrections

State spending on criminal justice is divided into two functions, corrections and police services. In 2011, the latest year for which data are available, state spending on corrections stood at $49.1 billion, accounting for 77.5 percent of total criminal justice spending. This significantly overshadowed the $14.3 billion spent on police services (Lee et al. 2012).

Spending by states on corrections "has nearly quadrupled over the past two decades, making it the fastest-growing budget item after Medicaid" (VERA Institute of Justice 2012, 2). Moreover, in addition to direct costs associated with prisons that are borne primarily by state corrections departments, there are other costs above and beyond the corrections budget. In a survey of 40 states, the VERA Institute of Justice (2012, 2) found that "total taxpayer cost of

Table 12.1 U.S. State Government Spending for Criminal Justice

	State	*Expenditures for Criminal Justice ($ in 000)*	*Percent of Total Expenditures*		*State*	*Expenditures for Criminal Justice ($ in 000)*	*Percent of Total Expenditures*
1	Arizona	$1,146,382	10.1%	26	Nebraska	$338,029	5.4%
2	Delaware	$380,736	9.9%	27	Arkansas	$508,822	5.3%
3	Maryland	$1,905,076	9.2%	28	Massachusetts	$1,809,966	5.3%
4	California	$10,396,417	8.8%	29	Rhode Island	$253,498	5.2%
5	Florida	$2,904,311	8.5%	30	Oregon	$871,570	5.1%
6	Colorado	$1,161,603	8.2%	31	Montana	$236,696	5.0%
7	Louisiana	$1,160,086	7.7%	32	Tennessee	$1,018,073	5.0%
8	Virginia	$2,211,272	7.7%	33	New York	$3,948,989	4.9%
9	Georgia	$1,760,094	7.5%	34	Washington	$1,324,540	4.8%
10	Idaho	$271,428	6.6%	35	Iowa	$428,983	4.8%
11	Illinois	$1,954,278	6.5%	36	South Carolina	$637,906	4.8%
12	Indiana	$888,108	6.5%	37	Missouri	$939,281	4.7%
13	North Dakota	$119,290	6.4%	38	North Carolina	$1,957,641	4.6%
14	Nevada	$377,513	6.2%	39	Oklahoma	$747,987	4.5%

Continued

Table 12.1 (*Continued*) U.S. State Government Spending for Criminal Justice

	State	*Expenditures for Criminal Justice ($ in 000)*	*Percent of Total Expenditures*		*State*	*Expenditures for Criminal Justice ($ in 000)*	*Percent of Total Expenditures*
15	Michigan	$1,963,410	6.1%	40	Alaska	$401,918	4.5%
16	Kansas	$440,625	6.0%	41	South Dakota	$144,800	4.4%
17	Connecticut	$899,999	5.9%	42	Minnesota	$904,679	4.2%
18	Texas	$4,647,429	5.9%	43	West Virginia	$351,600	3.9%
19	Wyoming	$186,933	5.7%	44	Alabama	$747,015	3.8%
20	Wisconsin	$1,294,803	5.7%	45	Utah	$441,286	3.8%
21	Vermont	$218,531	5.7%	46	Mississippi	$458,515	3.7%
22	Pennsylvania	$2,794,127	5.7%	47	Maine	$213,878	3.5%
23	New Jersey	$2,074,046	5.5%	48	New Hampshire	$168,663	3.3%
24	New Mexico	$549,646	5.5%	49	Ohio	$1,918,116	3.2%
25	Kentucky	$714,246	5.4%	50	Hawaii	$222,686	3.0%
	Median	$809,799			4.3%		

Source: Lee, C.H., Beleacov, M., and Higgins, N., *Annual Survey of State Government Finances*, Department of Commerce, U.S. Census Bureau, Washington, DC, 2012, available at http://www.census.gov/govs/state/ (accessed September 10, 2013).

prisons in the 40 states that provided data was 13.9 percent higher than the costs represented by their combined corrections budgets."

The Corrections Umbrella

There are three components of criminal justice activity under the state corrections umbrella: (1) state prisons, (2) state probation, which is responsible for persons convicted of a crime but not imprisoned, and (3) state parole, which oversees persons released from prison before the expiration of their sentences. In 2012, an estimated 75 percent of the total $49.1 billion in state expenditures for corrections was for state prisons (Kyckelhahn 2012), the focus of this chapter.

Much like criminal justice spending overall, spending on corrections varies widely across states (see Table 12.2). In 2011, when the state spending on corrections accounted for, on average, 3.2 percent of total expenditures, five states spent over 4.5 percent.[*] This variation is primarily explained by the number of persons under state supervision and the resultant need for correctional personnel to supervise them.

For close to 100 years, the prison population in the United States has grown steadily with three exceptions: (1) during the period leading up to and during the Second World War (1939–1945), (2) during the late 1960s and early 1970s (possibly because of the Vietnam War), and (3) from 2009 to 2011. From 1981 to 2008, the number of persons under the supervision of state adult correctional agencies more than tripled. Several government policies, including the surge in sentences carrying a mandatory minimum sentence, the deinstitutionalization of patients from mental hospitals, and the growth of the number of police officers, contributed to the increase. A discussion of each of these policies follows.

Determinate Sentences

A 2012 study conducted by the Pew Center on the States (Bhati and Warren 2012) showed that the average time served by prisoners rose from 2.1 years in 1990 to 2.9 years in 2009, an increase of 36 percent. Changes in sentencing policy during this period explain much of the growth.

Due to the increase in crime beginning in the 1970s and continuing into the mid-1980s,[†] states began to be "tougher on crime and criminals" and moved to increase time served for many violent and property crimes. At the same time, a surge in the use of heroin and cocaine led to the "war on drugs" and an increase in sentences for drug sales or drug possession. The following sections examine two initiatives to address the surge in crime that are the primary factors explaining the increase in the prison population and rising costs associated with the increase: *three strikes and you're out* and *truth in sentencing.*

---

[*] Colorado, Maryland, Virginia, Delaware, and California.

[†] Crime rose 101.6 percent from 1970 to 1986 (U.S. Department of Justice, Federal Bureau of Investigation, 1970 and 1986).

Table 12.2 U.S. State Government Spending for Corrections

	State	*Expenditures for Corrections ($ in 000)*	*Percent of Total Expenditures*	*Persons under Supervision per 1,000 Population*		*State*	*Expenditures for Corrections ($ in 000)*	*Percent of Total Expenditures*	*Persons under Supervision per 1,000 Population*
1	Colorado	$1,023,871	5.4%	4.4	26	Missouri	$720,834	3.2%	5.1
2	Maryland	$1,383,744	5.1%	3.9	27	Illinois	$1,514,033	3.2%	3.8
3	Virginia	$1,679,294	5.0%	4.7	28	Massachusetts	$1,050,827	3.2%	1.8
4	Delaware	$266,666	4.6%	7.5	29	New Mexico	$406,630	3.2%	3.4
5	California	$8,780,580	4.5%	4.0	30	Ohio	$1,625,282	3.1%	4.4
6	Wisconsin	$1,160,898	4.4%	4.0	31	Oklahoma	$530,853	3.1%	6.9
7	Georgia	$1,462,044	4.4%	5.8	32	Washington	$1,002,442	3.1%	2.6
8	Florida	$2,465,017	4.0%	5.5	33	Pennsylvania	$1,910,065	3.0%	4.1
9	Alaska	$283,764	3.9%	7.5	34	West Virginia	$275,564	2.8%	3.7
10	Connecticut	$698,030	3.9%	5.1	35	Vermont	$128,356	2.8%	3.3
11	Oregon	$711,895	3.9%	3.8	36	Arkansas	$411,436	2.7%	5.5
12	Texas	$3,764,642	3.9%	6.8	37	Kansas	$341,552	2.6%	3.3
13	Montana	$188,537	3.9%	3.7	38	Alabama	$563,058	2.6%	6.7

14	Arizona	$906,213	3.8%	6.2	39	Hawaii	$191,030	2.5%	4.4
15	New Jersey	$1,453,667	3.7%	2.7	40	Indiana	$661,358	2.5%	4.4
16	Michigan	$1,663,416	3.7%	4.3	41	New York	$2,995,539	2.4%	2.9
17	North Carolina	$1,422,868	3.6%	4.1	42	Mississippi	$354,626	2.4%	7.2
18	Rhode Island	$181,796	3.6%	3.2	43	Kentucky	$518,890	2.4%	5.0
19	Wyoming	$137,518	3.6%	3.8	44	South Carolina	$445,612	2.3%	4.9
20	Nevada	$275,865	3.5%	4.7	45	Utah	$297,609	2.3%	2.5
21	Idaho	$219,042	3.4%	4.9	46	New Hampshire	$112,666	2.2%	2.0
22	Louisiana	$757,363	3.4%	8.7	47	Iowa	$332,291	2.2%	3.0
23	Nebraska	$241,829	3.3%	2.5	48	North Dakota	$88,475	2.2%	2.1
24	Tennessee	$796,449	3.3%	4.5	49	Maine	$142,410	2.1%	1.6
25	South Dakota	$112,316	3.2%	4.3	50	Minnesota	$508,237	1.8%	1.8
	Median	$546,956	3.2%	4.2					

Source: Lee, C.H., Beleacov, M., and Higgins, N., *Annual Survey of State Government Finances*, Department of Commerce, U.S. Census Bureau, Washington, DC, 2012, available at http://www.census.gov/govs/state (accessed September 10, 2013).

Three Strikes and You're Out

Three-strikes legislation is an anticrime initiative that imposes increasingly longer sentences on recidivist offenders.* The first push in the states toward a three-strikes policy, the Persistent Offender Accountability Act, was passed in 1994 by the State of Washington. The law required that a defendant convicted of a violent crime for the third time be committed to life imprisonment without the possibility of parole (Austin et al. 2000). The same year the federal government adopted the Violent Crime Control and Law Enforcement Act with similar provisions. By 1997, there were 24 more states† with three-strikes laws (Austin et al. 2000). These policies greatly added to the prison populations at both the state and federal levels.

Unintended consequences of the three-strikes laws spread to the courts. Defendants, facing the possibility of enhanced sentences, would refuse to plead guilty hoping that the judge or jury would find a reasonable doubt as to their guilt. The likelihood of a plea bargain, where a prosecutor with a weaker case would negotiate with a defense attorney for a guilty plea in exchange for a lesser penalty, was also greatly reduced when the law required a life sentence.

Two provisions in California's policy took the three-strikes law a step further than any other state. The first called for the initial two strikes to be for a conviction for a serious or violent felony‡; the third strike could be a conviction for any other felony, even one not involving violence. The second provision called for a two-strikes sentence in which offenders committing any felony are sentenced to an extended term when they were previously convicted of a "strikeable" offense. The California Department of Corrections estimated that correctional costs were expected to increase by over $2 billion as a result of the three-strikes law (Austin et al. 2000).

Truth in Sentencing

Truth in sentencing policies require that persons sentenced for certain crimes serve a predetermined percentage of their sentence (typically 85 percent) prior to being eligible for early release. Rehabilitation of the offender or good behavior on their part cannot be used to reduce a determinate sentence. The federal Truth in Sentencing Act that served as a model for the states was also part of

---

* A recidivist is a criminal who commits more criminal acts after being punished for the first offense.

† The following states had some version of a three-strikes policy: Arkansas (2 strikes needed for an extremely violent offense/3 strikes for other enumerated offenses), California (2/3), Colorado (3), Connecticut (3), Florida (3), Georgia (2/4), Indiana (3), Kansas (2/3), Louisiana (3/4), Maryland (4), Montana (2/3), Nevada (3), New Jersey (3), New Mexico (3), North Carolina (3), North Dakota (2), Pennsylvania (2/3), South Carolina (2), Tennessee (2/3), Utah (3), Vermont (3), Virginia (3), Washington (3), and Wisconsin (3) (Austin et al. 2000, 9–11).

‡ The California statute (Penal Code §667 et seq.) enumerates 25 strikeable offenses, ranging from murder to residential burglary, grand theft with a firearm, any felony with a firearm, and any attempts to commit any of the enumerated crimes (Austin et al. 2000, 22).

the 1994 Violent Crime Control and Law Enforcement Act referred to earlier that created the federal three-strikes policy.

The federal Truth in Sentencing Act encouraged states to adopt similar laws and provided grants to states that adopted the 85 percent minimum sentence (Bhati and Warren 2012). Missouri is an example of a state that implemented the federal model. The state expanded its prison population by 30 percent after the new sentencing standard was established (Bhati and Warren 2012).

An Aging and Mentally Challenged Prison Population

One result of three-strikes laws and other enhanced sentencing initiatives is that many prisoners remain incarcerated for longer periods of time than in the past. An examination of data from 1992 to 2011 shows that the number of federal and state inmates over the age of 50 increased from 41,586 in 1992 (Anno et al. 2004) to 239,800 in 2011 (Carson and Sabol 2012)—an astonishing 476.6 percent increase.

An older prison population carries with it an increasing health care price tag as well as added costs related to (1) the construction of facilities to accommodate inmates with restricted mobility and (2) the protection of elderly inmates from predatory attacks. Results of a recent survey conducted by the National Institute of Justice (NIJ) showed that inmate medical expenses grew at an average of 48.8 percent between 2001 and 2008. Thirty-six of the 44 states that responded to the survey had an increase in per capita medical expenses in 2008, with seven reporting an increase of over 100 percent. Two states, Oregon and New Hampshire, reported increases of more than 300 percent (Kyckelhahn 2012).

Prisons are also becoming a haven for mentally challenged persons. In the 1960s, after a series of exposés in the media revealed the warehousing and maltreatment of the mentally ill in state mental health facilities, a move toward deinstitutionalization of the population housed in mental hospitals began. This movement, combined with the development of psychotropic medications* intended to better control symptoms of mental illness, resulted in the release of large numbers of mentally ill persons from state institutions. Many ended up in state prison systems.

The Treatment Advocacy Center has estimated that approximately 16 percent of the prison population suffers from a serious mental illness,† a number that has

* Medications used to treat the symptoms of mental disorders such as schizophrenia, depression, bipolar disorder (sometimes called manic-depressive illness), anxiety disorders, and attention deficit-hyperactivity disorder (ADHD). Sometimes medications are used with other treatments, such as psychotherapy.

† In 2013 *The Wall Street Journal* conducted a survey of state Departments of Corrections concerning inmates with mental illness. Of the 23 states that responded, 11 reported that over 20 percent of their prison population was mentally ill: Iowa (51 percent), Oregon (50 percent), South Dakota (35 percent), Vermont (33 percent), Montana (30 percent), Idaho (29 percent), California (27 percent), Kentucky and Massachusetts (24 percent), and Pennsylvania and Illinois (21 percent) (Fields and Phillips 2013).

tripled in the past three decades (Torrey et al. 2010). Inmates with a mental illness cost more to house. In Texas, for example, the average prisoner costs $22,000 a year, while those with a mental illness cost from $30,000 to $50,000 per year (Sentencing Project 2002).

The Growing Number of Police Officers

The previously mentioned Federal Violent Crime Control and Law Enforcement Act of 1994 had one more effect on the number of persons under correctional supervision. The act provided funding for police hiring under the Community Oriented Policing Services (COPS) Program (to be discussed later in the chapter). It greatly increased the number of police officers across the states. Under COPS, from 1994 to 2010, more than $11.4 billion flowed to over 14,000 law enforcement agencies in the United States, funding the hiring of more than 114,000 officers (James 2011). A great majority of these newly hired officers were young, new to their profession, and eager to do their jobs. As a result of their deployment, many additional arrests were made that probably would not have occurred absent COPS funding.

The increase in the number of arrests started a domino effect on criminal justice agencies at all levels, including agencies that did not directly benefit from the COPS funding. For instance, an increased demand was placed on county, state, and federal prosecutors that in turn increased the demand for legal aid assistance for those arrested. Courts at all three levels of government experienced increased criminal cases, and corrections institutions at all levels had to deal with more convicted and sentenced offenders. In the 10-year period following passage of the COPS Program, state correctional institutions experienced a growth in their inmate populations of 30 percent (Stephan 1997, 2008). This increase was reflected in the costs of correctional services.

Recent Trends in State Corrections

An examination of data from the Bureau of Justice Statistics from 2008 (Sabol and West 2011), the year with the largest number of persons under state correctional supervision[*], to 2012[†] (Carson and Golinelli 2013), the latest year available, show that the population declined by 6.6 percent nationwide and that seven states had their supervised population decrease by over 20 percent over the five year period (2008–2012), including Rhode Island (down 50.6 percent) and

[*] Persons under state correctional supervision include the prison population and persons under the supervision of either probation or parole.

[†] 2012 data for Illinois, Nevada, and Washington were not submitted in time to be published by the Bureau of Justice Statistics; the author used 2011 data in those cases and it didn't appear to substantially affect the analysis.

Connecticut (down 42.1 percent).* California1†,‡ (–39,459) and Texas§ (–14,606) had the largest absolute declines in populations under supervision during that period. The release of persons under correctional supervision by California, Rhode Island, and Connecticut may be attributed to the budgetary problems that the states encountered since 2008.

Policing

The police function accounts for a smaller percentage of criminal justice spending by the states than does corrections. However, spending on policing rose by 40 percent from 2001 to 2011, compared with the 29 percent increase in spending on corrections (Lee et al. 2012).

As with corrections, state spending on policing varies across states, with those located in the Northeast and Mid-Atlantic regions generally spending more on state policing operations than states in other parts of the country. In 2012, Massachusetts allocated the highest percentage of its total spending to policing, and Hawaii the lowest (see Table 12.3).

Funding Criminal Justice: Intergovernmental Aid

State and local criminal justice agencies receive support from the federal government primarily through the U.S. Department of Homeland Security (DHS), the U.S. Department of Justice (DOJ), and the U.S. Department of the Treasury. For DHS and DOJ, support to the states consists of specific grant programs and funding for joint task forces. For the Treasury, support to the states is related to joint task forces. The task forces result from agreements between a federal agency and a subnational law enforcement agency as a way to utilize local personnel to investigate criminal behavior. The state or local agency pays the officers' salaries and benefits; the federal partner reimburses the agency for overtime and other expenses related to officers' duties. As an added incentive to participate

---

* The seven states were Rhode Island (–50.6%), Connecticut (–42.1%), Delaware (– 41.6%), Alaska (–41.4%), Hawaii (–35.9%), Vermont (–28.4%), and California (–22.7%).

† In the case of Brown v. Plata (563 U.S. ___, ___ (2011)), the U.S. Supreme Court upheld a lower court decision ordering that the State of California reduce its prison population from almost 200% to 137.5% of its capacity within two years in order to alleviate overcrowding. As a result, the State implemented the Public Safety Realignment (PSR) policy which was "designed to reduce the prison population through normal attrition of the existing population while placing new nonviolent, nonserious, nonsexual offenders under county jurisdiction for incarceration in local jail facilities" (Carson & Sabol, 2012, p. 4).

‡ From 2008 to 2012 California had a 22.7% decrease in its prison population.

§ From 2008 to 2012 Texas had an 8.5% decrease in its prison population.

Table 12.3 U.S. State Government Spending for Police Purposes

	State	Expenditures for Police Purposes ($ in 000)	Percent of Total Expenditures	State Police Sworn per 1,000 Population		State	Expenditures for Police Purposes ($ in 000)	Percent of Total Expenditures	State Police Sworn per 1,000 Population
1	Massachusetts	$759,139	2.3%	0.29	26	Missouri	$218,447	1.0%	0.18
2	Delaware	$114,070	2.0%	0.73	27	South Dakota	$32,484	0.9%	0.20
3	Vermont	$90,175	1.9%	0.52	28	Illinois	$440,245	0.9%	0.15
4	Maryland	$521,332	1.9%	0.24	29	Texas	$882,787	0.9%	0.14
5	Louisiana	$402,723	1.8%	0.26	30	Tennessee	$221,624	0.9%	0.13
6	Alaska	$118,154	1.6%	0.46	31	Georgia	$298,050	0.9%	0.11
7	Virginia	$531,978	1.6%	0.23	32	Kentucky	$195,356	0.9%	0.26
8	New Jersey	$620,379	1.6%	0.33	33	Oregon	$159,675	0.9%	0.16
9	Rhode Island	$71,702	1.4%	0.22	34	Indiana	$226,750	0.8%	0.20
10	Minnesota	$396,442	1.4%	0.10	35	Alabama	$183,957	0.8%	0.11
11	Pennsylvania	$884,062	1.4%	0.29	36	California	$1,615,837	0.8%	0.21
12	North Carolina	$534,773	1.4%	0.18	37	Idaho	$52,386	0.8%	0.16
13	Nebraska	$96,200	1.3%	0.26	38	New York	$953,450	0.8%	0.24

14	Wyoming	$49,415	1.3%	0.35	39	West Virginia	$76,036	0.8%	0.35
15	Nevada	$101,648	1.3%	0.20	40	North Dakota	$30,815	0.8%	0.21
16	Oklahoma	$217,134	1.3%	0.22	41	Kansas	$99,073	0.8%	0.19
17	Connecticut	$201,969	1.1%	0.33	42	Colorado	$137,732	0.7%	0.14
18	New Hampshire	$55,997	1.1%	0.26	43	Florida	$439,294	0.7%	0.08
19	New Mexico	$143,016	1.1%	0.24	44	Mississippi	$103,889	0.7%	0.18
20	Utah	$143,677	1.1%	0.15	45	Michigan	$299,994	0.7%	0.17
21	Maine	$71,468	1.1%	0.23	46	Iowa	$96,692	0.6%	0.21
22	Arizona	$240,169	1.0%	0.18	47	Arkansas	$97,386	0.6%	0.18
23	Washington	$322,098	1.0%	0.16	48	Ohio	$292,834	0.6%	0.12
24	Montana	$48,159	1.0%	0.23	49	Wisconsin	$133,915	0.5%	0.09
25	South Carolina	$192,294	1.0%	0.18	50	Hawaii	$31,656	0.4%	0.00
	Median Spending	$ 188,126	1.0%	0.20					

Source: Lee, C.H., Beleacov, M., and Higgins, N., *Annual Survey of State Government Finances*, Department of Commerce, U.S. Census Bureau, Washington, DC, 2012, available at http://www.census.gov/govs/state (accessed September 10, 2013).

in task forces, the subnational law enforcement agency can receive a percentage of any money or property seized from the defendant and subjected to forfeiture proceedings.* This can result in millions of dollars flowing to the state or local government.

Department of Homeland Security

Since the terrorist attacks in New York City in September 2001, the DHS has eclipsed the DOJ as the primary federal source of funding for state and local law enforcement activities. Prior to 2001, state and local governments were eligible to apply for three federal grants associated with homeland security: the State Domestic Preparedness Program, administered by the DOJ through the Office for Domestic Preparedness†; the Emergency Management Performance Grant Program, administered by the Federal Emergency Management Agency (FEMA); and the Metropolitan Medical Resource System, administered by the U.S. Department of Health and Human Services (DHHS).

After the 2001 attacks, these three programs were placed under the jurisdiction of the newly created DHS‡; by 2003, there were another four homeland security-related grant programs offered to the states, bringing the total to seven. Of the seven, the four directly related to criminal justice activities are the State Homeland Security Grant Program (SHSGP),§ the Law Enforcement Terrorism Prevention Program (LETPP), the Urban Areas Security Initiative (UASI), and the Critical Infrastructure Protection (CIP) Program.¶ In 2010, DHS added a fifth program related to criminal justice activities, Operation Stonegarden (OPSG).

State Homeland Security Grant Program

The State Homeland Security Grant Program (SHSGP) is the longest running of the five DHS grants that fund criminal justice activities at subnational levels. The purpose of the SHSGP is to provide assistance to state and local government

---

* If it can be proven that some of a defendants' property is criminally possessed or came under their control as a result of criminal behavior, that property could be subject to forfeiture, seized and used, or sold by the law enforcement entities involved in the investigation. The proceeds can then be used to fund police operations at the local agency.

† The Office of Domestic Preparedness was transferred to the DHS in FY2003 (P.L. 107-296) and renamed the Office of Grants and Training in FY2006.

‡ DHS combined 22 different federal departments and agencies into a unified, integrated cabinet-level department.

§ This program was formerly called the State Domestic Preparedness Program.

¶ The Critical Infrastructure Program was intended to strengthen railroads, dams, and utility plants at the outset of the wars in Afghanistan and Iraq. The funding was discontinued after one year.

in their preparations for terrorist attacks involving weapons of mass destruction (WMD). The program funds the purchase of specialized equipment to enhance the capabilities of subnational agencies in responding to WMD attacks and other terrorist-related incidents. Funds are also available to train first responders and to assess the readiness of state and local agencies to prevent and respond to terrorist attacks. The SHSGP provided $401.3 million to the states (and territories) in FY2014 (U.S. Department of Homeland Security 2014).

Urban Areas Security Initiative (UASI)

The UASI is currently the largest DHS source of funding for criminal justice activities at state and local levels. It provides funding to high-risk, high-threat urban areas to prepare for, prevent, and respond to terrorist incidents (Maguire and Reese 2006). These funds allow the designated UASI areas to purchase specialized WMD equipment, plan and execute exercises, pay first responder overtime costs associated with Homeland Security threat levels, and train first responders. UASI funds may also be used to finance mass transit and port security, radiological defense systems, and for technical assistance (Maguire and Reese 2006). In FY2014, the UASI program provided $587.0 million to urban areas (U.S. Department of Homeland Security 2014).

Operation Stonegarden (OPSG)

OPSG "funds are intended to enhance cooperation and coordination among local, tribal, territorial, state, and federal law enforcement agencies in a joint mission to secure the United States' borders along routes of ingress from international borders to include travel corridors in States bordering Mexico and Canada, as well as states and territories with international water borders" (U.S. Department of Homeland Security 2013, 7). In FY2014, OPSG provided $55.0 million to the border states (U.S. Department of Homeland Security 2014).

Most states received less than 0.05 percent of the total funding distributed by the Department of Homeland Security; five states received more than 5 percent, with New York accounting for over 25 percent of total funds distributed to the states (see Table 12.4).

Department of Justice

The DOJ is the second largest provider of intergovernmental funds to state and local governments. For the past several decades, it has provided billions of dollars in funding for hiring police officers and civilian personnel and for financial support through funding of law enforcement initiatives and technological innovations.

Table 12.4 Distribution of FY2014 Homeland Security Grants by State[a]

State	*FY2014 SHSP Funding*	*FY2014 UASI Funding*	*FY2013 OPSG Funding*	*Total*	*State Share as % of Distribution to States*
New York	$76,742,000	$178,926,000	$1,707,382	$257,375,382	26.3%
California	$60,035,000	$119,274,000	$9,425,732	$188,734,732	19.3%
Illinois	$16,357,000	$69,500,000	$–	$85,857,000	8.8%
Texas	$21,448,000	$40,500,000	$19,422,318	$81,370,318	8.3%
Pennsylvania	$10,026,000	$21,500,000	$177,396	$31,703,396	3.2%
New Jersey	$8,354,000	$21,800,000	$–	$30,154,000	3.1%
Massachusetts	$5,622,000	$18,000,000	$–	$23,622,000	2.4%
Arizona	$4,568,000	$5,500,000	$12,005,449	$22,073,449	2.3%
Florida	$11,010,000	$9,500,000	$954,977	$21,464,977	2.2%
Washington	$6,493,000	$5,500,000	$1,711,305	$13,704,305	1.4%
Michigan	$6,658,000	$5,500,000	$766,193	$12,924,193	1.3%
Georgia	$6,807,000	$5,500,000	$–	$12,307,000	1.3%
Maryland	$6,125,000	$5,500,000	$–	$11,625,000	1.2%
Ohio	$7,698,000	$3,000,000	$754,422	$11,452,422	1.2%
Minnesota	$3,978,000	$5,500,000	$596,623	$10,074,623	1.0%

North Carolina	$5,489,000	$3,000,000	$–	$8,489,000	0.9%
Virginia	$7,414,000	$1,000,000	$–	$8,414,000	0.9%
Kansas	$3,733,000	$–	$–	$3,733,000	0.4%
Louisiana	$3,978,000	$3,000,000	$96,538	$7,074,538	0.7%
Colorado	$3,979,000	$3,000,000	$–	$6,979,000	0.7%
Missouri	$3,978,000	$4,000,000	$–	$7,978,000	0.8%
New Mexico	$3,733,000	$–	$3,146,501	$6,879,501	0.7%
Indiana	$3,978,000	$1,000,000	$–	$4,978,000	0.5%
Oregon	$3,837,000	$1,000,000	$–	$4,837,000	0.5%
Hawaii	$3,733,000	$1,000,000	$–	$4,733,000	0.5%
Nevada	$3,733,000	$1,000,000	$–	$4,733,000	0.5%
Utah	$3,733,000	$1,000,000	$–	$4,733,000	0.5%
Montana	$3,733,000	$–	$960,059	$4,693,059	0.5%
Maine	$3,733,000	$–	$924,422	$4,657,422	0.5%
North Dakota	$3,733,000	$–	$637,406	$4,370,406	0.4%
Vermont	$3,733,000	$–	$491,358	$4,224,358	0.4%

Continued

Table 12.4 (*Continued*) Distribution of FY2014 Homeland Security Grants by State*

State	*FY2014 SHSP Funding*	*FY2014 UASI Funding*	*FY2013 OPSG Funding*	*Total*	*State Share as % of Distribution to States*
Connecticut	$3,979,000	$–	$–	$3,979,000	0.4%
Kentucky	$3,978,000	$–	$–	$3,978,000	0.4%
Tennessee	$3,978,000	$–	$–	$3,978,000	0.4%
Wisconsin	$3,978,000	$–	$–	$3,978,000	0.4%
New Hampshire	$3,733,000	$–	$182,333	$3,915,333	0.4%
Alabama	$3,733,000	$–	$155,206	$3,888,206	0.4%
Idaho	$3,733,000	$–	$49,121	$3,782,121	0.4%
Alaska	$3,733,000	$–	$–	$3,733,000	0.4%
Arkansas	$3,733,000	$–	$–	$3,733,000	0.4%
Delaware	$3,733,000	$–	$–	$3,733,000	0.4%
Iowa	$3,733,000	$–	$–	$3,733,000	0.4%
Mississippi	$3,733,000	$–	$–	$3,733,000	0.4%
Nebraska	$3,733,000	$–	$–	$3,733,000	0.4%

Oklahoma	$3,733,000	$–	$–	$3,733,000	0.4%
Rhode Island	$3,733,000	$–	$–	$3,733,000	0.4%
South Carolina	$3,733,000	$–		$3,733,000	0.4%
South Dakota	$3,733,000	$–	$–	$3,733,000	0.4%
West Virginia	$3,733,000	$–	$–	$3,733,000	0.4%
Wyoming	$3,733,000	$–	$–	$3,733,000	0.4%
Total Distributed to States	**$390,079,000**	**$534,000,000**	**$54,164,741**	**$978,243,741**	
Total to Territories and District of Columbia	**$11,267,000**	**$53,000,000**	**$835,259**	**$65,102,259**	
TOTAL	**$401,346,000**	**$587,000,000**	**$55,000,000**	**$1,043,346,000**	

Source: U.S. Department of Homeland Security, Federal Emergency Management Agency, 2014; U.S. Department of Homeland Security, Funding Opportunity Announcement (FOA), FY2014 Homeland Security Grant Program (HSGP), http://www.fema.gov/media-library-data/1395161200285-5b07ed0456056217175fbdee28d2b06e/FY_2014_HSGP_FOA_Final.pdf (accessed April 10, 2014).

[a] FY2014 Funding for Operation Stonegarden (OPSG) has not been allocated at the time of this analysis. The total amount funded ($55.0 million) is the same as in FY2013 and the FY2013 distribution has been used.

Community Oriented Policing Services (COPS) Program

As discussed earlier, the Violent Crime Control and Law Enforcement Act of 1994 created the Community Oriented Policing Services (COPS) Program. The objective of the program was to provide funding to state, local, and tribal law enforcement agencies to hire additional police officers. In the first nine years of funding (FY1995–2003), COPS provided more than $11.3 billion to states and localities to fund new police officers. After FY2003, funding began to decrease, and by FY2006 it was less than $500 million a year. However, under the American Reinvestment and Recovery Act (ARRA), subnational governments received $1.6 billion in additional COPS hiring grants in 2009; funding has decreased since then.

Conclusion

Although own-source spending by state governments on criminal justice has been increasing for decades, it now accounts for a smaller part of total state budgets than in previous years. Federal funding to the states for criminal justice has also been declining. The U.S. Department of Homeland Security grants to subnational governments amounted to $2.9 billion in FY2003; by 2013, the grants amounted to $968 million—a 66 percent decrease. U.S. Department of Justice COPS grants, which in FY1995 sent $1.3 billion to states and localities, were reduced to $127 million in FY2013—a 90 percent decline. If the decline in the prison population that began in 2009 continues, there may be less pressure on the states to increase funding for correctional institutions. However, the ability to maintain adequate levels of criminal justice services in light of reduced federal support is a critical factor in the fiscal sustainability of the states.

References

Anno, B.J., Graham, C., Lawrence, J.E., and Shansky, R. (2004). *Correctional Health Care: Addressing the Needs of Elderly, Chronically Ill and Terminally Ill Inmates.* Washington, DC: U.S. Department of Justice, National Institute of Justice.

Austin, J., Clark, J., Hardyman, P., and Henry, D.A. (2000). *Three Strikes and You're Out: The Implementation and Impact of Strike Laws.* Washington, DC: U.S. Department of Justice, National Institute of Justice. Available at https://www.ncjrs.gov/pdffiles1/nij/grants/181297.pdf (accessed September 2013).

Bhati, A., and Warren, J. (2012). *Time Served: The High Cost, Low Return of Longer Prison Terms.* Available at http://www.pewstates.org/uploadedFiles/PCS_Assets/2012/Pew_Time_Served_report.pdf (accessed November 2, 2013).

Carson, E.A., and Golinelli, D. (2013, July 25). *Prisoners in 2012—Advance Counts.* U.S. Department of Justice, Bureau of Justice Statistics. Available at http://www.bjs.gov/index.cfm?ty=pbdetail&iid=4737 (accessed September 11, 2013).

Carson, E.A., and Sabol, W.J. (2012, December). *Prisoners in 2011.* Washington, DC: U.S Department of Justice, Bureau of Justice Statistics. Available at http://www.bjs.gov/content/pub/pdf/p11.pdf (accessed September 10, 2013).

Fields, G., and Phillips, E.E. (2013, September 25). The New Asylums: Jails Swell with Mentally Ill. *The Wall Street Journal.* Available at http://online.wsj.com/news/articles/SB10001424127887323455104579012664245550546?KEYWORDS=the+new+asylums (accessed October 3, 2013).

James, N. (2011, June 2). *Community Oriented Policing Services (COPS): Background and Funding.* Federation of American Scientists. Available at http://www.fas.org/sgp/crs/misc/RL33308.pdf (accessed August 2013).

Kyckelhahn, T. (2012). *State Correction Expenditures, FY1982–2010.* Washington, DC: U.S. Department of Justice, Bureau of Justice Statistics. Available at http://www.bjs.gov/index.cfm?ty=pbdetail&iid=4556 (accessed September 10, 2013).

Lee, C.H., Beleacov, M., and Higgins, N. (2012). *Annual Survey of State Government Finances.* Washington, DC: Department of Commerce, U.S. Census Bureau. Available at http://www.census.gov/govs/state/ (accessed September 10, 2013).

Maguire, S., and Reese, S. (2006). *CRS Report for Congress: Department of Homeland Security Grants to State and Local Governments: FY2003 to FY2006.* Available at http://www.fas.org/sgp/crs/homesec/RL33770.pdf (accessed August 21, 2013).

Sabol, W.J., and West, H.C. (2011, December 15). *Prisoners in 2009 (Revised).* U.S. Department of Justice, Bureau of Justice Statistics. Available at http://www.bjs.gov/index.cfm?ty=pbdetail&iid=2232 (accesed September 13, 2013).

Sentencing Project. (2002). *Mentally Ill Offenders in the Criminal Justice System: An Analysis and Prescription.* The Sentencing Project. Available at http://www.sentencingproject.org/doc/publications/sl_mentallyilloffenders.pdf (accessed October 11, 2013).

Stephan, J. (1997). *Census of State and Federal Correctional Facilities, 1995.* Washington, DC: Bureau of Justice Statistics. Available at http://www.bjs.gov/index.cfm?ty=pbdetail&iid=535 (accessed September 10, 2013).

Stephan, J.J. (2008). *Census of State and Federal Correctional Facilities, 2005.* Washington, DC: Bureau of Justice Statistics. Available at http://www.bjs.gov/index.cfm?ty=pbdetail&iid=530 (accessed September 10, 2013).

Torrey, E.F., Kennard, A.D., Eslinger, D., Lamb, R., and Pavle, J. (2010). *More Mentally Ill Persons Are in Jails and Prisons Than Hospitals: A Survey of the States.* Treatment Advocacy Center. Available at http://www.prisonpolicy.org/scans/treatment/final_jails_v_hospitals_study.pdf (accessed October 14, 2013).

U.S. Department of Commerce, U.S. Census Bureau. (2002). *Annual Survey of State Government Finances.* Available at http://www.census.gov/govs/state/historical_data_2001.html (accessed September 10, 2013).

U.S. Department of Homeland Security, Federal Emergency Management Agency. (2013). *FY 2013 Homeland Security Grant Program (HSGP).* Available at www.fema.gov: http://www.fema.gov/fy-2013-homeland-security-grant-program-hsgp-0 (accessed August 3, 2013).

U.S. Department of Homeland Security, Federal Emergency Management Agency. (2014). FY2014 Homeland Security Grant Program (HSGP). Available at http://www.fema.gov/fy-2014-homeland-security-grant-program-hsgp (accessed April 10, 2014).

U.S. Department of Homeland Security, Federal Emergency Management Agency. (2014). U.S. Department of Homeland Security, Funding Opportunity Announcement (FOA),

FY2014 Homeland Security Grant Program (HSGP). Available at http://www.fema.gov/media-library-data/1395161200285-5b07ed0456056217175fbdee28d2bo6e/FY_2014_HSGP_FOA_Final.pdf (accessed April 10, 2014).

U.S. Department of Justice, Federal Bureau of Investigation. (1970). *Crime in the United States 1970*. Washington, DC: Government Printing Office.

U.S. Department of Justice, Federal Bureau of Investigation. (1986). *Crime in the United States 1986*. Washington, DC: Government Printing Office.

VERA Institute of Justice. (2012). *The Price of Prisons: What Incarceration Costs Taxpayers.* Available at http://www.vera.org/sites/default/files/resources/downloads/Price_of_Prisons_updated_version_072512.pdf (accessed November 17, 2013).

Chapter 13

State Government Workforces of the Future*

Sally Coleman Selden
Lynchburg College

Contents

Introduction

Since the Great Recession began in December 2007, state government workforces have experienced pressure to cut their budgets and reduce their workforce. Government jobs have traditionally been the most stable. However, states have

* Produced by Sally Selden in partnership with the Pew Center on the States. The views expressed here are those of the author and do not necessarily reflect the views of the Pew Center on the States.

experienced significant job losses due to employee layoffs and hiring freezes that have occurred in the last five years (Duggan et al. 2010). Between 2009 and 2012, the American states collectively have lost almost half a million jobs (Council of State Governments 2013). During this same period, states have witnessed a surge in civil service reforms with an emerging trend of limiting employee protections and moving toward employment-at-will. Do these changes signal that the implicit social contract for state government employees is shifting?

State government employees have long worked in "internal labor markets" characterized by long-term employment protected by civil service rules, internal promotional opportunities, well-defined jobs linked progressively to form a career, and compensation based upon merit, seniority, or a combination of the two. These components have been essential to state government personnel systems. The private sector had a similar model, excluding the civil service protections, until the late 1970s, when the economy changed. Subsequently, the employment relationship between private firms and their employees shifted from an internal labor market focused on tenure, internal promotion, and workforce stability to a model that is "market mediated" and able to respond more rapidly to environmental changes by hiring from the outside—that is, new employees from the external labor market (Cappelli 1999).

While states have faced considerable constraints in the past five years that have resulted in smaller workforces and less employment security, the future promises even more changes. State labor forces will become more diverse and older. By the early 2040s, racial and ethnic minorities are projected to become a majority of the nation's population and whites will become a minority population (Levit 2012). During this same time period, the number of multiracial citizens will increase threefold, and the number of persons over 65 will increase twofold (Levit 2012). Not only is the future workforce of the United States more diverse and older, but also it may shrink (Brenner 2010; NASPO 2008). Several factors contribute to this possibility: Since the 1970s, birth rates have declined, with significant dips occurring after the Great Recession. Finally, the percentage of the workforce expected to leave in the next 20 years will rise as baby boomers retire.

This chapter addresses seven trends in and projections about the United States and state government workforces. The chapter considers how current trends are likely to impact state personnel or civil service systems. Observations and findings are based upon data collected by the Department of Labor, U.S. Census Bureau, and surveys of state human resource management (HRM) department directors in 1999, 2007, and 2012.*

* As part of the Government Performance Project, in partnership with the Pew Center of the States, the author surveyed states in 1999, 2003, and 2007. The author also surveyed states in 2010 and 2012.

Trend 1: Leaner State Workforces in the Northeast and Midwest

Since the recession began in 2007, many state governments have laid off employees or implemented hiring freezes. As a result, the state government workforce in the United States has had its largest reduction in more than 30 years. Without federal aid, even more jobs may have been lost in state governments (Council of State Governments 2013). As shown in Table 13.1, between 2009 and 2011, state government employment decreased in 33 states. Five states, Connecticut, Idaho, Louisiana, Oklahoma, and New York, lost more than 5 percent of their state government workforces. On the other hand, between 2009 and 2011, 27 states increased the percentage of employees, with Texas and North Dakota increasing the percentage of state employees by more than 5 percent each. Overall, the net decrease in employees across state governments between 2009 and 2011 was –0.90 percent. The impact of the Great Recession on state government employment differed across regions, with states in the East and Midwest losing, on average, more employees than states located in the South and West. Between 2009 and 2011, government workforces in northeastern states contracted by 2.4 percent, slightly more than in midwestern states.

The expansion and contraction of government positions are consistent with the general regional population trend in the country. The population grew almost 9.7 percent between 2000 and 2010, which was lower than the 13.2 percent increase in the 1990s (U.S. Census 2011b). There was more population growth in the southern (14.3 percent) and western (13.8 percent) regions than in the northeastern (3.2 percent) and midwestern (3.9 percent) regions (Center for Public Education 2013). States with the most significant population gains included Nevada (35 percent), Arizona (25 percent), Utah (23.8 percent), and Idaho (21 percent).

Trend 2: More Part-Time State Workers

During the Great Recession, many states increased their reliance on part-time workers to compensate for the loss of full-time employees, given the continued demand for state services (Maciag 2012). In 2011, part-time employees comprised approximately 29 percent of state workforces (see Table 13.2). States varied, however, in their reliance on part-time employees, with three states employing more than 40 percent of their workforce part-time: Colorado, New Hampshire, and Wisconsin. Table 13.3 presents a comparison of the percent of state government employees who worked part-time in 1997, 2007, and 2011. Between 2007 and 2011, 39 states increased the percentage of employees who were part-time. Seven states increased the percentage of part-time workers by 3 or more percent: Colorado, Indiana, Maine, New Hampshire, Oklahoma, Pennsylvania, and South Dakota.

Table 13.1 State Government Full-Time Equivalent (FTE) Employment: 2009–2011

	2009 FTE	*2010 FTE*	*Percent Change 2009–2010*	*2011 FTE*	*Percent Change 2010–2011*	*Percent Change 2009–2011*
Texas	300,112	317,912	5.90%	318,370	0.14%	6.08%
North Dakota	17,667	18,139	2.70%	18,592	2.50%	5.24%
North Carolina	147,895	152,229	2.90%	154,364	1.40%	4.37%
Oregon	63,086	65,369	3.60%	65,542	0.26%	3.89%
Utah	51,606	51,291	–0.60%	53,501	4.31%	3.67%
South Dakota	14,053	14,310	1.80%	14,458	1.03%	2.88%
Pennsylvania	163,903	168,268	2.70%	168,548	0.17%	2.83%
Tennessee	84,387	82,871	–1.80%	86,215	4.04%	2.17%
Alaska	26,183	26,689	1.90%	26,747	0.22%	2.15%
Arkansas	61,337	63,484	3.50%	62,562	–1.45%	2.00%
Michigan	142,924	145,606	1.90%	144,921	–0.47%	1.40%
Montana	20,590	20,375	–1.00%	20,795	2.06%	1.00%
West Virginia	39,505	39,375	–0.30%	39,882	1.29%	0.95%
Georgia	122,582	124,115	1.30%	123,627	–0.39%	0.85%
Wisconsin	70,457	72,428	2.80%	70,891	–2.12%	0.62%
Kentucky	81,117	80,714	–0.50%	81,493	0.97%	0.46%
Alabama	89,467	89,632	0.20%	89,768	0.15%	0.34%
South Carolina	77,261	77,071	–0.20%	77,342	0.35%	0.10%
Mississippi	57,773	56,858	–1.60%	57,656	1.40%	–0.20%
Arizona	68,972	66,807	–3.10%	68,786	2.96%	–0.27%
Virginia	125,570	124,709	–0.70%	124,930	0.18%	–0.51%
Maine	21,497	21,130	–1.70%	21,354	1.06%	–0.67%
Florida	185,630	184,465	–0.60%	184,237	–0.12%	–0.75%
Nebraska	32,333	32,560	0.70%	32,065	–1.52%	–0.83%

Table 13.1 (*Continued*) State Government Full-Time Equivalent (FTE) Employment: 2009–2011

	2009 FTE	*2010 FTE*	*Percent Change 2009–2010*	*2011 FTE*	*Percent Change 2010–2011*	*Percent Change 2009–2011*
Colorado	72,778	71,064	–2.40%	72,113	1.48%	–0.91%
California	411,142	410,653	–0.10%	407,321	–0.81%	–0.93%
New Hampshire	19,591	19,470	–0.60%	19,394	–0.39%	–1.01%
Minnesota	80,536	79,941	–0.70%	79,672	–0.34%	–1.07%
Delaware	26,510	26,022	–1.80%	26,215	0.74%	–1.11%
Vermont	14,598	14,408	–1.30%	14,419	0.08%	–1.23%
Wyoming	13,628	13,577	–0.40%	13,416	–1.19%	–1.56%
Ohio	142,945	139,907	–2.10%	139,049	–0.61%	–2.73%
Indiana	92,484	89,549	–3.20%	89,796	0.28%	–2.91%
Missouri	90,092	88,818	–1.40%	87,361	–1.64%	–3.03%
Maryland	89,511	88,318	–1.30%	86,714	–1.82%	–3.12%
Hawaii	60,041	58,121	–3.20%	58,142	0.04%	–3.16%
Washington	125,423	122,772	–2.10%	121,136	–1.33%	–3.42%
Kansas	45,163	43,824	–3.00%	43,555	–0.61%	–3.56%
Iowa	52,288	51,328	–1.80%	50,378	–1.85%	–3.65%
New Mexico	48,680	48,160	–1.10%	46,794	–2.84%	–3.87%
Rhode Island	19,669	18,694	–5.00%	18,900	1.10%	–3.91%
Illinois	136,542	131,352	–3.80%	131,153	–0.15%	–3.95%
Nevada	29,517	28,345	–4.00%	28,121	–0.79%	–4.73%
New Jersey	154,106	152,003	–1.40%	146,801	–3.42%	–4.74%
Massachusetts	96,865	95,354	–1.60%	92,033	–3.48%	–4.99%
Oklahoma	72,198	70,501	–2.40%	68,339	–3.07%	–5.35%
New York	257,490	251,150	–2.50%	243,647	–2.99%	–5.38%

Continued

Table 13.1 (*Continued*) State Government Full-Time Equivalent (FTE) Employment: 2009–2011

	2009 FTE	*2010 FTE*	*Percent Change 2009–2010*	*2011 FTE*	*Percent Change 2010–2011*	*Percent Change 2009–2011*
Idaho	23,179	21,940	–5.30%	21,773	–0.76%	–6.07%
Connecticut	66,498	63,199	–5.00%	62,090	–1.75%	–6.63%
Louisiana	91,809	88,720	–3.40%	84,402	–4.87%	–8.07%
	4,399,190	4,383,597		4,359,380	–0.55%	–0.90%

Source: U.S. Census Bureau, Government Employment and Payroll, available at http://www.census.gov/govs/apes.

The impact of part-time work on employees long term is not known. Allowing for a larger part-time workforce may attract some individuals to work in state government who were not interested in working full-time or who may have retired. For example, some women have elected to work part-time so that they can continue to be involved in the workforce while being able to be at home more, particularly when they have children. For some older individuals, part-time work provides an avenue for them to shift more slowly toward full-time retirement. For others who have been out of the workforce for different reasons, part-time work can be a stepping stone to full-time employment. A potential negative impact for individuals interested in full-time employment is that some part-time positions offer little opportunity for career progression within the state government and may negatively impact a person's career in the long term if it is difficult to transition from part-time to full-time status within a state (O'Reilly and Bothfeld 2002).

Some of these part-time workers may also be temporary workers who are working in a position as a short-term assignment. Going forward, states will have to consider the potential hidden costs associated with contingent workers, which may include the erosion of employee commitment and the loss of government-specific skills that permanent employees are able to develop over a longer-term working relationship. Still, research shows that with proper planning, training, and supervision, organizations can utilize a contingent workforce—part-time, temporary, and contract workers—to efficiently reach organizational work goals (Lautsch 2002). States will need to help managers develop plans for supervising part-time workers and building positive working relationships between full-time and part-time employees who work together in state agencies and departments. Moreover, with the implementation of the federal Affordable Care Act (ACA) and the requirement to provide health insurance to employees who work,

Table 13.2 Full-Time and Part-Time Employment in the States: 2011

State	*Full-Time Employees*	*Part-Time Employees*	*Full-Time Equivalent*	*Total Employees*	*Percent Part-Time*
Wisconsin	56,068	47,421	70,891	103,489	45.82%
Colorado	54,882	44,008	72,113	98,890	44.50%
New Hampshire	15,548	10,684	19,394	26,232	40.73%
Iowa	40,561	26,190	50,378	66,751	39.24%
Ohio	113,917	72,171	139,049	186,088	38.78%
Maine	17,665	10,872	21,354	28,537	38.10%
Montana	16,780	10,051	20,795	26,831	37.46%
Indiana	73,874	44,219	89,796	118,093	37.44%
Utah	44,529	25,727	53,501	70,256	36.62%
Michigan	118,740	67,433	144,921	186,173	36.22%
North Dakota	15,843	8,917	18,592	24,760	36.01%
Idaho	18,318	10,023	21,773	28,341	35.37%
Washington	100,371	54,414	121,136	154,785	35.15%
Virginia	105,953	54,075	124,930	160,028	33.79%
Minnesota	66,208	33,196	79,672	99,404	33.40%
Illinois	105,892	52,604	131,153	158,496	33.19%
South Dakota	12,594	6,237	14,458	18,831	33.12%
Arizona	57,907	27,280	68,786	85,187	32.02%
Pennsylvania	142,206	66,664	168,548	208,870	31.92%
California	335,971	155,149	407,321	491,120	31.59%
Oklahoma	59,833	27,060	68,339	86,893	31.14%
Connecticut	53,305	23,519	62,090	76,824	30.61%
Kansas	38,293	16,448	43,555	54,741	30.05%
Oregon	58,091	24,557	65,542	82,648	29.71%
Massachusetts	81,246	32,858	92,033	114,104	28.80%

Continued

Table 13.2 (*Continued*) Full-Time and Part-Time Employment in the States: 2011

State	*Full-Time Employees*	*Part-Time Employees*	*Full-Time Equivalent*	*Total Employees*	*Percent Part-Time*
Georgia	110,625	43,755	123,627	154,380	28.34%
Nevada	24,963	9,862	28,121	34,825	28.32%
Rhode Island	17,056	6,727	18,900	23,783	28.28%
Nebraska	26,659	10,401	32,065	37,060	28.07%
Hawaii	53,574	19,409	58,142	72,983	26.59%
Alabama	80,409	28,418	89,768	108,827	26.11%
Tennessee	76,872	26,995	86,215	103,867	25.99%
Delaware	23,182	8,112	26,215	31,294	25.92%
Kentucky	71,863	24,912	81,493	96,775	25.74%
West Virginia	36,210	12,124	39,882	48,334	25.08%
New Mexico	41,240	13,776	46,794	55,016	25.04%
North Carolina	135,171	43,317	154,364	178,488	24.27%
Missouri	77,797	23,938	87,361	101,735	23.53%
Louisiana	76,775	23,012	84,402	99,787	23.06%
South Carolina	70,147	19,938	77,342	90,085	22.13%
Arkansas	57,093	16,146	62,562	73,239	22.05%
New Jersey	134,410	37,287	146,801	171,697	21.72%
Texas	284,729	78,804	318,370	363,533	21.68%
Wyoming	12,522	3,446	13,416	15,968	21.58%
Florida	168,583	45,079	184,237	213,662	21.10%
Mississippi	52,474	12,431	57,656	64,905	19.15%
New York	226,662	52,343	243,647	279,005	18.76%
Alaska	24,633	5,603	26,747	30,236	18.53%
Vermont	13,236	2,610	14,419	15,846	16.47%
Maryland	77,778	14,045	86,714	91,823	15.30%
	3,779,258	1,534,267	4,359,380	5,313,525	28.87%

Source: U.S. Census Bureau, Government Employment and Payroll, 2011 Annual Survey of Public Employment and Payroll.

Table 13.3 Percent of Part-Time Employees: 1997, 2007, and 2011

State	*Percent Part-Time 1997*	*Percent Part-Time 2007*	*Percent Part-Time 2011*	*Change in Percent Part-Time 2011–2007*
Maine	27.14%	28.33%	38.10%	9.77%
Pennsylvania	26.68%	26.14%	31.92%	5.78%
South Dakota	31.47%	27.45%	33.12%	5.67%
Indiana	33.30%	32.38%	37.44%	5.06%
New Hampshire	33.82%	36.25%	40.73%	4.48%
Colorado	44.71%	40.90%	44.50%	3.60%
Oklahoma	23.88%	27.86%	31.14%	3.28%
Iowa	35.55%	36.57%	39.24%	2.67%
South Carolina	18.26%	19.52%	22.13%	2.61%
Illinois	26.97%	30.62%	33.19%	2.57%
Rhode Island	25.01%	25.71%	28.28%	2.57%
Arkansas	19.49%	19.54%	22.05%	2.51%
Maryland	25.86%	12.80%	15.30%	2.50%
Virginia	30.92%	31.45%	33.79%	2.34%
New Jersey	17.24%	19.41%	21.72%	2.31%
Montana	36.88%	35.40%	37.46%	2.06%
New York	16.59%	16.96%	18.76%	1.80%
Minnesota	38.97%	31.64%	33.40%	1.76%
Massachusetts	26.76%	27.08%	28.80%	1.72%
Ohio	34.31%	37.18%	38.78%	1.60%
Wisconsin	32.31%	44.36%	45.82%	1.46%
Oregon	33.99%	28.31%	29.71%	1.40%
California	30.05%	30.27%	31.59%	1.32%
Connecticut	21.42%	29.31%	30.61%	1.30%
Georgia	24.75%	27.04%	28.34%	1.30%
Tennessee	23.79%	24.76%	25.99%	1.23%

Continued

Table 13.3 (*Continued*) Percent of Part-Time Employees: 1997, 2007, and 2011

State	*Percent Part-Time 1997*	*Percent Part-Time 2007*	*Percent Part-Time 2011*	*Change in Percent Part-Time 2011–2007*
Louisiana	22.54%	21.85%	23.06%	1.21%
Michigan	37.26%	35.03%	36.22%	1.19%
West Virginia	22.06%	24.06%	25.08%	1.02%
Washington	36.14%	34.15%	35.15%	1.00%
Wyoming	24.27%	20.73%	21.58%	0.85%
North Carolina	22.48%	23.53%	24.27%	0.74%
New Mexico	26.40%	24.34%	25.04%	0.70%
Utah	24.68%	36.19%	36.62%	0.43%
Florida	25.04%	20.82%	21.10%	0.28%
Vermont	20.14%	16.30%	16.47%	0.17%
Idaho	27.61%	35.22%	35.37%	0.15%
Kansas	32.29%	29.96%	30.05%	0.09%
Alabama	23.99%	26.05%	26.11%	0.06%
Arizona	29.44%	32.42%	32.02%	–0.40%
Nebraska	26.58%	28.53%	28.07%	–0.46%
Alaska	18.73%	19.01%	18.53%	–0.48%
Nevada	22.24%	28.87%	28.32%	–0.55%
Hawaii	28.43%	27.16%	26.59%	–0.57%
Texas	17.35%	22.37%	21.68%	–0.69%
Kentucky	27.81%	26.60%	25.74%	–0.86%
Delaware	26.31%	26.94%	25.92%	–1.02%
Missouri	25.19%	24.69%	23.53%	–1.16%
Mississippi	17.88%	21.61%	19.15%	–2.46%
North Dakota	38.41%	39.75%	36.01%	–3.74%
United States	26.74%	27.40%	28.87%	1.47%

Source: United States Census Bureau, Build-a-Table, available at https://harvester.census.gov/datadissem/Results.aspx.

on average, 30 hours per week, states will have to consider carefully how they structure part-time positions or incur the costs of providing benefits if they do not currently offer them to part-time employees.

Trend 3: Older State Workforces

Over the next decade, scholars anticipate that there will be increased participation of persons 65 years and older in the labor force as the baby boomer generation, those born between 1946 and 1954, move toward retirement and as the average age of retirement increases (Eyster et al. 2008). The trend of individuals working past the traditional retirement age can be attributed, at least in part, to changes in employee retirement plans, increased cost of health insurance, and increased life expectancy (Tishman et al. 2012). Some older workers have opted to stay in the workforce because they want to continue to be engaged in their work, are committed to their organizations, or are satisfied with their careers (Tishman et al. 2012). The U.S. Census Bureau data suggest that rates of participation of persons over 55 years in the labor force will grow, and by 2016, one-third of the total workforce in the United States will be over 55 years of age (U.S. Census Bureau 2011b). In 2003, this age group comprised only 13 percent of the labor force. Research demonstrates that the proportion of older workers is increasing more rapidly in the public sector than in the private sector, and that the effects of the aging population will impact public sector organizations more significantly (Abbey and Boyd 2002; Deloitte 2007). According to U.S. Census data, older workers are more likely to work in occupations that require specialized skills and education, and over 50 percent of government workers are in such occupations (Abbey and Boyd 2002).

State government workforces are aging. In 1999, the average age of the state government employee was 43.7 years of age (Government Performance Project 1999). By 2012, the average age had increased to 45.7 years.[*] This demographic shift in state governments may be associated with several factors. First, states tend to hire older workers; the average age of new hires has hovered around 37 years since 2007. Second, while approximately one-fourth of state employees are eligible to retire, most state government employees do not retire when eligible. For example, on average, 2.88 percent of classified state employees retired in fiscal year 2009, 4.32 percent in fiscal year 2010, 3.46 percent in fiscal year 2011, and 3.37 percent in fiscal year 2012.[†] As more employees retire, states will have to grapple with how to replace employees in positions that require specialized skills and education. A recent study finds that 54 percent of state and local governments reported that they require higher education requirements of those they employ today than they did 10 years ago (Achieve 2012). Fifty-three percent reported that they had more

[*] Results from author survey of states in 1999, 2003, 2007, 2010, and 2012.

[†] Author survey.

jobs with specific technical requirements or skills than they did 10 years ago (Achieve 2012). Looking forward and as discussed in more detail later in this chapter, 33 percent of state and local governments expect their demand for employees with advanced degrees to increase, and 52 percent of governments expect their demand for employees with a bachelor's degree to increase (Achieve 2012). This may present challenges to states if the educational levels of the labor force decline as predicted (National Center for Public Policy and Higher Education 2005).

Trend 4: More Diverse State Workforces

Demographic shifts will continue over the next 25 years as the population and labor force become increasingly more diverse. According to the National Center for Public Policy and Higher Education (2005), the white working age population is expected to decline from 82 percent to 63 percent between the years 1980 and 2020. During this same time period, the percent of the nation's workforce comprised of minorities is projected to increase twofold, from 18 percent to 37 percent, with the fastest rate of growth for Hispanics and Latinos. The demographic changes are being driven by several factors: The number of ethnic and racial minorities between the ages of 0 and 44 years are growing, although birth rates for all groups have dropped recently; the number of white workers in the labor force reaching retirement age is growing; and the white population in this country is declining (National Center for Public Policy and Higher Education 2005).

Figure 13.1 shows that birth rates have fallen significantly for all women since 1991, with the largest declines observed for African American women (7 less births per 1,000 African American women) and Hispanics (9 less births per 1,000 Hispanic women). Declining birth rates will contribute to smaller future workforces. However, birth rates for ethnic and racial minorities still exceed those for whites. The declining birth rates will impact the overall size of the future workforce in the United States, but the extent of that impact will depend upon how many individuals immigrate to this country.

The number of persons obtaining legal permanent resident status did not decline immediately after the Great Recession started in 2007, although a slight decline occurred in 2010 (see Figure 13.2). Given the current birth and immigration rates, the Pew Research Center concludes that immigrants will continue to play a significant role in the growth of population in the United States. Pew's projections "indicate that immigrants arriving since 2005 and their descendants will account for fully 82 percent of U.S. population growth by 2050" (Livingston and Cohn 2012, 4).

As noted above, the white population has been declining in many states and is expected to decrease from 64.7 percent in 2010 to 46.3 percent in 2050 (Center for Public Education 2013). In contrast, the Hispanic population has grown considerably in parts of the United States, particularly in the western and southern regions. North Carolina and South Carolina had more than a 100 percent increase in their

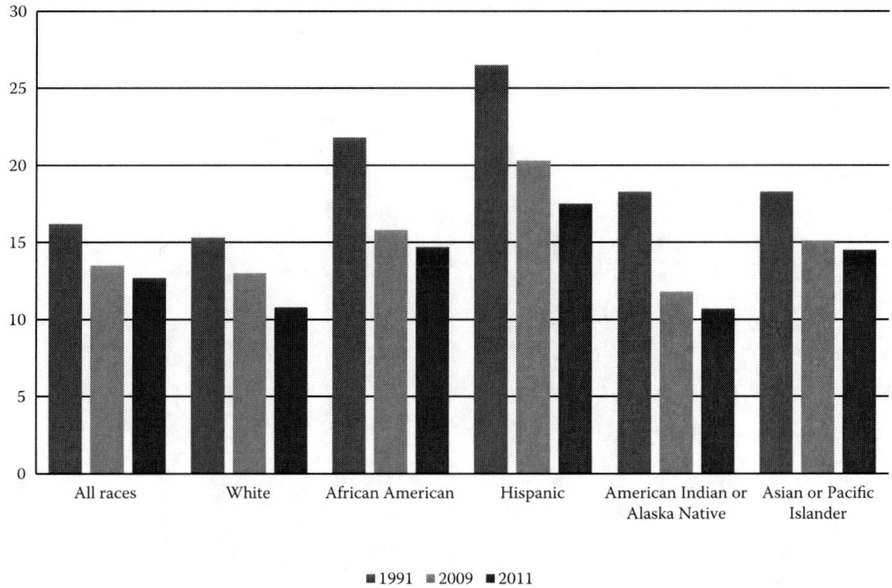

Figure 13.1 Birth rates by race and ethnicity, 1991, 2007, 2009, and 2011 (per 1,000 women in specified group). (From U.S. Health and Human Services, Centers for Disease Control and Prevention, National Center for Health Statistics, National Vital Statistics Systems, 2012, available at http://www.cdc.gov/nchs/data/nvsr/nvsr61/nvsr61_01.pdf.)

Hispanic population between 2000 and 2010 (Center for Public Education 2013). The Census Bureau predicts that between 2010 and 2050 the Hispanic population will increase from 49.7 million to 132.8 million, or 167 percent (Center for Public Education 2013). The Hispanic share of the population is expected to almost double from 16 percent in 2010 to 30 percent in 2050 (Center for Public Education 2013).

Between 2000 and 2010, the African American population grew by 15.4 percent (U.S. Census 2011a). However, looking forward, the African American share of the population is expected to remain constant between 2010 and 2050 (Center for Public Education 2013). In 2011, African Americans comprised 11.6 percent of the labor market (U.S. Department of Labor 2013a). African Americans were more likely to be employed in the public sector than were whites or Asian Americans (U.S. Department of Labor 2013a). Approximately 50 percent of African Americans over the age of 16 years were employed, and 18 percent of the African Americans employed worked part-time. Of African Americans employed, approximately 25 percent had at least their bachelor's degree. While the percentage of African Americans with a college degree was less than that for whites, the rate has been growing steadily over the past two decades (U.S. Department of Labor 2013a).

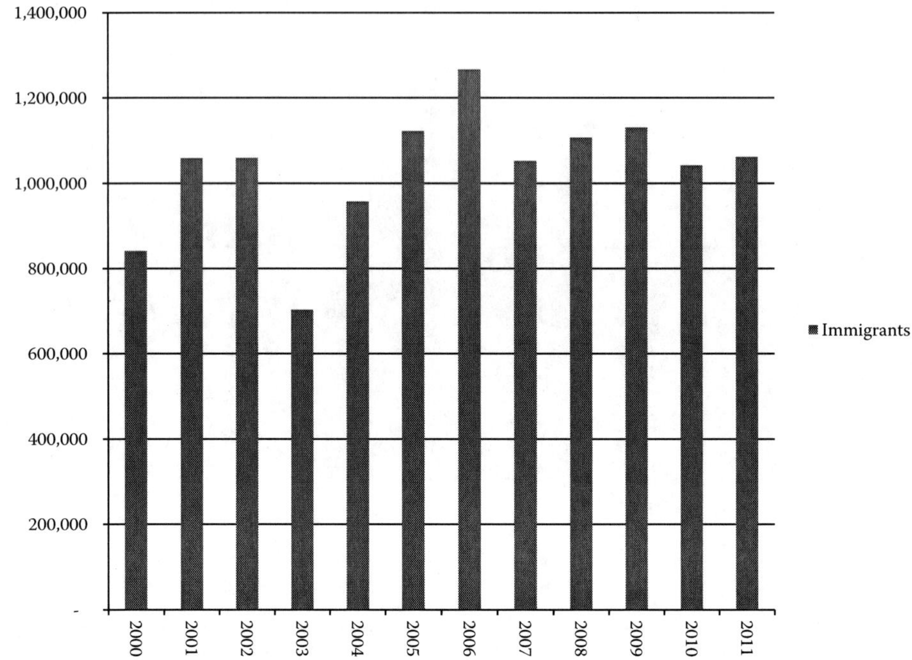

Figure 13.2 Persons obtaining legal permanent resident status, 2000–2011. (From Office of Immigration Statistics, Department of Homeland Security, 2012, available at http://www.dhs.gov/sites/default/files/publications/immigration-statistics/yearbook/2011/ois_yb_2011.pdf.)

Asian Americans, which include Hawaiians and Pacific Islanders, are a growing share of the nation's labor market and currently represent approximately 5 percent of the labor force (U.S. Department of Labor 2013b). The Asian share of the population is expected to increase slightly from 4.7 percent to 7.8 percent by 2050 (Center for Public Education 2013). In 2010, almost 60 percent of Asian Americans over 16 were employed in the labor force (U.S. Department of Labor 2013b). Asian Americans were less likely than women and African Americans to work in the public sector. Just over 11 percent of Asian Americans were employed in the public sector compared to 19.8 percent of African Americans and 18.2 percent of women (U.S. Department of Labor 2013a, 2013b, 2013c). Asian Americans were significantly more likely to have a college degree than were whites, African Americans, or Hispanics (U.S. Department of Labor 2013b). Almost 60 percent of employed Asians over 25 have a bachelor's degree (U.S. Department of Labor 2013b).

In 2010, women comprised 46.7 percent of this country's labor force; 13.1 percent of women in the workforce were African American, 12.8 percent were Hispanic, and 4.7 percent were Asian. Women were almost twice as likely as men to work part-time, with about 26.6 percent of women working part-time in 2010 (U.S. Department of Labor 2013d). In 2010, 57 percent of women with children under six years of age were employed, and 71 percent of these women held a full-time job (U.S. Department of Labor 2013d). Almost 71 percent of women with children between the ages of 6 and 17 worked, and the majority of these women worked full-time (U.S. Department of Labor 2013d). Women were more likely to work in the public sector than men. About 18 percent of women in the labor market worked in the public sector compared to 12.4 percent of men (U.S. Department of Labor 2013d).

In 2012, approximately 155 million persons, or 63.8 percent, were in the labor force out of the total U.S. working age population of 244 million. Approximately, 83.5 percent of the people in the labor market worked in the private sector and 16.5 percent work in the public sector. About 3.8 percent of persons in the labor market worked for state government (Burns et al. 2012). Historically, public organizations, including state governments, have provided more equitable employment opportunities for women and minorities. Looking at data collected by the Equal Employment Opportunity Commission (EEOC 2013), in 2011, 51.7 percent of full-time positions in state government were held by women and 53.9 percent of part-time positions (see Table 13.4). Approximately 53.2 percent of new hires were women. In 2011, African Americans held 19.6 percent of full-time positions and 14.5 percent of part-time state government positions. African Americans comprised a larger share of new hires—22.2 percent—in 2011.

One consequence of greater participation of women and minorities in the public sector is that these groups were impacted more significantly by recent job losses in government, especially at the state and local levels (Cooper et al. 2012). One study showed that in state and local governments "about 70.5 percent of jobs lost were held by women" (Cooper et al. 2012, 8). African Americans represented about 19.8 percent of the job losses in state and local government, which resulted in an overall 7.6 percent decrease in African American representation in state and local government (Cooper et al. 2012).

Trend 5: More Educated and Skilled State Workforces

As discussed previously, governments and other employers will increasingly need employees with more education and skills (Carnevale et al. 2010). While opportunities for workers with fewer skills exist across all sectors, Carnevale et al. (2010) expect opportunities for less skilled workers to decrease in the future. This may create a dilemma in the country—according to the National Center for Public Policy and Higher Education (2005, 1), "if current trends continue, the proportion of workers with high school diplomas and college degrees will decrease … over the next 15 years." One reason is that the most significant population growth in the nation's labor force is occurring among the racial and ethnic groups with the lowest levels of education. "About 50 percent of African

Table 13.4 State Government Representation by Gender, Race, and Ethnicity for Full-Time Employees, Part-Time Employees, and New Hires: 2011

Full-Time Employees						
	State Employment	*White*	*Black*	*Hispanic*	*Asian*	*Indian*
Male	48.3	35.9	6.8	3.6	1.6	0.4
Female	51.7	32.5	12.8	4.2	1.8	0.4
Total	100	68.4	19.6	7.8	3.5	0.8
Part-Time Employees						
	State Employment	*White*	*Black*	*Hispanic*	*Asian*	*Indian*
Male	46.1	35.3	5.3	3.1	1.8	0.7
Female	53.9	38.1	9.3	4	2	0.6
Total	100	73.4	14.5	7.1	3.8	1.3
New Hires						
	State Employment	*White*	*Black*	*Hispanic*	*Asian*	*Indian*
Male	46.8	32.9	8.2	4	1.3	0.5
Female	53.2	32.5	14	4.8	1.4	0.6
Total	100	65.4	22.1	8.8	2.7	1.1

Source: Data from Equal Employment Opportunity Commission (EEOC), *State and Local Government Information (EEO-4), 2011 National Employment Summary*, 2013, available at http://www.eeoc.gov/eeoc/statistics/employment/jobpat-eeo4/2011/table3/table3_1_state (accessed March 9, 2013).

Americans and Hispanic/Latino 9th graders do not become eligible to enter college after four years of high school because they have not completed high school" (National Center for Public Policy and Higher Education 2005, 4). Thus, unless declines in educational levels can be altered by state educational systems, employers, including state government, will face a gap between the skill level of individuals in the labor market and the skill levels required for open positions. Also, some states will be impacted more than other states because 90 percent of Hispanics/Latinos in the United States live in 16 states and 90 percent of African Americans reside in 21 states (National Center for Public Policy and Higher Education 2005).

The projections about declining levels of education in the United States are not evident when reviewing census data about the nation's education levels by states in 1990, 2000, and 2009. As shown in Table 13.5, the percent of the population holding a bachelor's degree increased from 20.3 percent in 1990 to 24.4 percent in 2000 to 27.9 percent in 2009. Similarly, the percent of the population with at least an advanced degree was 7.2 percent in 1990, 8.9 percent in 2000, and 10.3 percent in 2009. If the education levels in the United States decline as projected, it will coincide with the growth of a knowledge-based economy that requires many workers to have higher levels of education (National Center for Public Policy and Higher Education 2005). As a result, competition for skilled workers will increase, which may make it more difficult for state governments to hire, since state wages often lag those of the private sector.

Based upon interviews with directors of state personnel offices in 2012 and 2013, states are particularly concerned about their ability to hire people for top-level information technology positions, engineers, computer programmers, medical doctors, and other highly skilled positions. To grapple with this problem, some states are implementing various strategies. Pennsylvania is anticipating losing key employees in the next 10 years and has implemented the Keystone Academy for Learning to address potential skill gaps in its workforce. The academy offers state government employees training for soft skills, technical skills, management development, and leadership development.

Trend 6: Changes in Employment Security

For many years, public personnel systems, often referred to as civil service systems, have been built upon merit principles and providing employment security for public employees (Ingraham 1995). Public employees expected the employment relationship to be long term and that their employment would be protected by a set of due process rules. Traditional personnel systems relied on centralized oversight of the personnel function and numerous rules to provide discipline in state decision making and to ensure political noninterference and equity in the treatment of all applicants and employees. The employment relationship provided benefits both to the employee and to the state. State governments benefit because when political administrations and political appointees change, there is a cadre of civil service employees with government and job-specific knowledge and skills to assist during the leadership transition.

Over the past 20 years, reforms of state personnel systems have been advanced that would eliminate or reduce employee job protections and create more flexible selection, reward, and termination procedures by dismantling civil service and adopting employment-at-will. Many of these changes mirror changes in the employment relationship that occurred in private sector organizations in the 1980s and 1990s. For example, companies, such as IBM, AT&T, and Lucent Technologies,

Table 13.5 Educational Attainment by State

State	*1990*				*2000*			*2009*		
	Not a High School Graduate	*High School Graduate or More*	*Bachelor's Degree or More*	*Advanced Degree or More*	*High School Graduate or More*	*Bachelor's Degree or More*	*Advanced Degree or More*	*High School Graduate or More*	*Bachelor's Degree or More*	*Advanced Degree or More*
United States	24.8	75.2	20.3	7.2	80.4	24.4	8.9	85.3	27.9	10.3
Massachusetts	20	80	27.2	10.6	84.8	33.2	13.7	89	38.2	16.4
Maryland	21.6	78.4	26.5	10.9	83.8	31.4	13.4	88.2	35.7	16
Connecticut	20.8	79.2	27.2	11	84	31.4	13.3	88.6	35.6	15.5
Virginia	24.8	75.2	24.5	9.1	81.5	29.5	11.6	86.6	34	14.1
New York	25.2	74.8	23.1	9.9	79.1	27.4	11.8	84.7	32.4	14
Vermont	19.2	80.8	24.3	8.9	86.4	29.4	11.1	91	33.1	13.3
New Jersey	23.3	76.7	24.9	8.8	82.1	29.8	11	87.4	34.5	12.9
Colorado	15.6	84.4	27	9	86.9	32.7	11.1	89.3	35.9	12.7
Illinois	23.8	76.2	21	7.5	81.4	26.1	9.5	86.4	30.6	11.7
Rhode Island	28	72	21.3	7.8	78	25.6	9.7	84.7	30.5	11.7
Delaware	22.5	77.5	21.4	7.7	82.6	25	9.4	87.4	28.7	11.4
New Hampshire	17.8	82.2	24.4	7.9	87.4	28.7	10	91.3	32	11.2

Washington	16.2	83.8	22.9	7	87.1	27.7	9.3	89.7	31	11.1
California	23.8	76.2	23.4	8.1	76.8	26.6	9.5	80.6	29.9	10.7
New Mexico	24.9	75.1	20.4	8.3	78.9	23.5	9.8	82.8	25.3	10.4
Oregon	18.5	81.5	20.6	7	85.1	25.1	8.7	89.1	29.2	10.4
Minnesota	17.6	82.4	21.8	6.3	87.9	27.4	8.3	91.5	31.5	10.3
Kansas	18.7	81.3	21.1	7	86	25.8	8.7	89.7	29.5	10.2
Pennsylvania	25.3	74.7	17.9	6.6	81.9	22.4	8.4	87.9	26.4	10.2
Georgia	29.1	70.9	19.3	6.4	78.6	24.3	8.3	83.9	27.5	9.9
Hawaii	19.9	80.1	22.9	7.1	84.6	26.2	8.4	90.4	29.6	9.9
Maine	21.2	78.8	18.8	6.1	85.4	22.9	7.9	90.2	26.9	9.6
Missouri	26.1	73.9	17.8	6.1	81.3	21.6	7.6	86.8	25.2	9.5
Michigan	23.2	76.8	17.4	6.4	83.4	21.8	8.1	87.9	24.6	9.4
Arizona	21.3	78.7	20.3	7	81	23.5	8.4	84.2	25.6	9.3
Utah	14.9	85.1	22.3	6.8	87.7	26.1	8.3	90.4	28.5	9.1
Alaska	13.4	86.6	23	8	88.3	24.7	8.6	91.4	26.6	9
Florida	25.6	74.4	18.3	6.3	79.9	22.3	8.1	85.3	25.3	9
Nebraska	18.2	81.8	18.9	5.9	86.6	23.7	7.3	89.8	27.4	8.8

Continued

Table 13.5 (*Continued*) Educational Attainment by State

State	1990				2000			2009		
	Not a High School Graduate	*High School Graduate or More*	*Bachelor's Degree or More*	*Advanced Degree or More*	*High School Graduate or More*	*Bachelor's Degree or More*	*Advanced Degree or More*	*High School Graduate or More*	*Bachelor's Degree or More*	*Advanced Degree or More*
Ohio	24.3	75.7	17	5.9	83	21.1	7.4	87.6	24.1	8.8
Kentucky	35.4	64.6	13.6	5.5	74.1	17.1	6.9	81.7	21	8.5
Texas	27.9	72.1	20.3	6.5	75.7	23.2	7.6	79.9	25.5	8.5
South Carolina	31.7	68.3	16.6	5.4	76.3	20.4	6.9	83.6	24.3	8.4
Wisconsin	21.4	78.6	17.7	5.6	85.1	22.4	7.2	89.8	25.7	8.4
Montana	19	81	19.8	5.7	87.2	24.4	7.2	90.8	27.4	8.3
Indiana	24.4	75.6	15.6	6.4	82.1	19.4	7.2	86.6	22.5	8.1
Tennessee	32.9	67.1	16	5.4	75.9	19.6	6.8	83.1	23	7.9
Wyoming	17	83	18.8	5.7	87.9	21.9	7	91.8	23.8	7.9

Alabama	33.1	66.9	15.7	5.5	75.3	19	6.9	82.1	22	7.7
Nevada	21.2	78.8	15.3	5.2	80.7	18.2	6.1	83.9	21.8	7.6
Idaho	20.3	79.7	17.7	5.3	84.7	21.7	6.8	88.4	23.9	7.5
Iowa	19.9	80.1	16.9	5.2	86.1	21.2	6.5	90.5	25.1	7.4
Oklahoma	25.4	74.6	17.8	6	80.6	20.3	6.8	85.6	22.7	7.4
South Dakota	22.9	77.1	17.2	4.9	84.6	21.5	6	89.9	25.1	7.3
Mississippi	35.7	64.3	14.7	5.1	72.9	16.9	5.8	80.4	19.6	7.1
Louisiana	31.7	68.3	16.1	5.6	74.8	18.7	6.5	82.2	21.4	6.9
North Dakota	23.3	76.7	18.1	4.5	83.9	22	5.5	90.1	25.8	6.7
West Virginia	34	66	12.3	4.8	75.2	14.8	5.9	82.8	17.3	6.7
Arkansas	33.7	66.3	13.3	4.5	75.3	16.7	5.7	82.4	18.9	6.1

Source: U.S. Census Bureau, Educational Attainment, available at http://www.census.gov/population/www/socdemo/educ-attn.html.

known for providing lifelong careers and employment security for their employees, began to lay off employees. Some firms were hiring new employees at the same time they were laying off other employees. The implicit contract between employer and employees in these firms moved from being long term to short term (Cappelli 1999). A number of factors have contributed to the changing employee-employer relationship across sectors, including, but not limited to, globalization and international competition promoted by firms that sought to have work completed less expensively in developing countries, changing technologies that increased demand for employees with new technical skills, and increased need for organizations to do more with fewer employees (Cappelli 1999). Moreover, the power of unions in the private sector has been declining, making it increasingly more challenging for employees to exercise a collective voice and bargain for employment security (U.S. Bureau of Labor Statistics 2013; Cappelli 1999).

In the 1990s, reformers began to push for civil service changes across all levels of state employees, with a primary focus on removing civil service protections from a critical mass of state employees (e.g., Coggburn 2006; Crowell and Guy 2010; Goodman and Mann 2010; Hays and Sowa 2006; Kellough and Nigro 2006). These reforms sought to redefine the relationship between public employees and their employers by allowing for at-will termination without the protection of procedural due process (Kellough and Nigro 2006). In 1996, civil service protections were eliminated in Georgia for all new employees, and then in 2001, civil service protections for managers were stricken in Florida (e.g., Battaglio and Condrey 2009; Bowman et al. 2003; Condrey and Maranto 2001; Condrey and Battaglio 2007; Goodman and Mann 2010; Kellough and Nigro 2006; Nigro and Kellough 2000, 2008). While there had been lots of activity and dialogue around adopting employment-at-will systems in other states, no other similar large-scale changes were passed until 2011. Since then, three states, Arizona, Indiana, and Tennessee, have adopted employment-at-will to replace their civil service system. Other states, such as Colorado and Louisiana, have considered but have not passed systemwide changes to their civil service system. Many of the recent state government reforms have been driven by activist governors, because of the fiscal stress brought about by the Great Recession, and in light of the American political climate.

Even in states that have maintained civil service, the nature and form of service protections, including due process protections, can vary from state to state. Moreover, due process procedures may vary across nonclassified or at-will personnel systems. The underlying assumption of reformers is that employees serving in nonclassified personnel systems have few, if any, due process protections. Since reformers often focus on how difficult it is to terminate tenured state employees serving in the classified service, this chapter presents information on variations in due process procedures for disciplinary actions for both classified and nonclassified employees.

Table 13.6 presents results from a recent survey of state personnel directors about due process protections provided by the state to all persons serving in either

Table 13.6 Employment Security Classified and Nonclassified Systems

Employment Security Measure	*Classified Service*	*Nonclassified Service*	*N*
Employment security index (additive index of the following five measures)	3.7	1.4	42
1. Allow employees to appeal disciplinary actions?	98%	43%	42
2. Require pretermination hearings?	74%	14%	42
3. Have an external source review all termination requests?	21%	10%	42
4. Have an external source review termination requests when appealed by the employee?	83%	26%	42
5. Require notification of termination?	93%	45%	42

Source: Survey of State Government Personnel Directors, 2007.

the classified or nonclassified service.* The data do not indicate the share of agencies that provided each of the aforementioned protections when the response was "varies by agency." The five items included in the survey were summed to create an index from 0 to 5. As shown in Table 13.7 and as expected, employees serving in the classified service, on average, had more procedural due process protections (3.7) than employees serving in the nonclassified service (1.4). However, states varied in the extent to which they provided protections to employees in both the classified and the nonclassified service. Given this, expect that state government employees will realize fewer protections and less employment security in the future.

* Based upon the recommendations of a focus group of state personnel directors, a set of five questions was developed and included on a survey administered to directors of state HRM departments in 2007. States were asked: "For employees in the classified system, does your state: allow employees to appeal disciplinary actions; require pre-termination hearings; have an external review of all termination requests; have an external source review termination requests when appealed by the employee; and require notification of termination?" States responded: yes, no, or varies by agency. These same questions were posed to state personnel executives for the nonclassified service.

Table 13.7 Availability of Flexible Work Arrangement for State Employees

	Not Available to State Employees	*Available to Some State Employees*	*Available to Most State Employees*	*Available to All State Employees*
Flex time	7.7%	23.1%	38.5%	30.8%
Compressed workweek	15.4	38.5	23.1	23.1
Telecommuting	25.6	38.5	10.3	25.6
Job sharing	33.3	33.3	12.8	20.5

Source: Survey of State Government Personnel Directors, 2007.

Trend 7: Increasing Use of Employment Flexibility

The demand for flexibility in work organizations has been traced to the increased proportion of women in the workforce, especially women with children (Subramaniam et al. 2011). As noted above, in 2010, 57 percent of women with children under 6 years of age were employed, and 71 percent of women with children between the ages of 6 and 17 years of age worked. The rise of white, middle-class women into higher management and leadership positions in organizations elicited increased dialogue about ways to balance work and family. More recently, the dialogue about work-life balance has expanded beyond women to include men and addresses other topics, such as adoption, caring for aging parents, and caring for sick family members. As a result, the number of organizations offering flexible work arrangements increased in the late 1990s and early 2000s. A 2011 report prepared by the U.S. Department of Commerce's Economics and Statistics Administration and the Executive Office of the President, Office of Management and Budget, for the White House Council on Women and Girls (2011, 31) found that in 2004, 30 percent of wage and salary employees could opt to work flexible schedules. The study found no differences between men and women, or mothers and fathers. States may offer more flexible work arrangements than employers in the private sector. That is, as shown in Table 13.7, all employees in 30.8 percent of states had access to flex time, and most employees in another 38.5 percent of states had an option to use flex time. Both compressed workweeks and telecommuting were offered to at least some employees in most state governments.

Flexible work arrangements can take different forms. Flex time typically offers employees some flexibility in their hours "on the job." For example, employees may be given a choice in their start and end work times, and sometimes choice regarding what days of the week they will work. The basic nature of the position typically is not altered in this case. Flex time is a commonly accepted practice in state governments, with only 7.7 percent of states not allowing it. Job sharing, on the other hand, deals with the allocation of job tasks between two employees who share responsibilities that have been typically associated with one job description and position. Job sharing requires that employees sharing a position communicate across their roles. Twenty percent of states offer employees the option of sharing a position.

Another form of flexibility offered in states is flexible space. Telecommuting allows employees to work at home or off-site at a different location. Usually, telecommuting employees are connected electronically to the central agency or department office by Internet and telephone, and are expected to be available at certain hours or to report to work online at certain times. They often do the same job, and sometimes work longer hours, but they do it in a different location. The capacity to telecommute has grown as new and less expensive technologies, including tele- and videoconferencing, have evolved. However, telecommuting has not diffused across states as much as flex time. A quarter of states offer the option to request to telecommute for a part of their time to all of their employees, while a quarter of states do not allow their employees to telecommute. The capacity to telecommute, however, continues to change rapidly as new and less expensive technologies are introduced into the market.

As competition for skilled employees increases, states may be able to attract talented people by providing greater flexibility in time, tasks, and space. Thus, a challenge for states will be how to prepare managers and leaders to think about and manage employee flexibility in state government.

Conclusion

Given the above analyses, it is predicted that future state government workforces will have more part-time workers who are older, more ethnically diverse, and more educated. These workers should expect to have fewer job protections, but more flexible working arrangements. The question remains whether or not the state workforces of the future will be more or less committed to a career in state government. The social contract that has been implicit in public employment is no longer a norm in all American state governments. While many state employees approaching retirement have often spent a significant part of their career with the state, new state employees are much less likely to do so, even those workers in positions with civil service protections. This is particularly challenging given that a recent study showed that the highest rates of turnover in states are among new hires (Selden et al. 2013).

On the other hand, states have done well in advancing the diversity of their workforces—a primary strength of state governments. Yet, both women and African Americans in state governments were impacted significantly by layoffs over the past four to five years. As the economy recovers, states may have to work hard to communicate their commitment to diversity and inclusion to attract women and minorities to return to state government. If states are able to do so, they will be well poised to attract the workforce of the future.

Another challenge facing state governments that directors of state personnel offices point out is employee morale, which may impact states' abilities to retain employees. Many states have not awarded consistent or meaningful pay increases since 2007, and employee benefits have been reduced, in some cases significantly, in many states. Some states have not provided pay increases, including cost of living adjustments, for four, five, or even six years. On the other hand, during this same period, states have been able to hire highly qualified individuals because alternative employment options were not as plentiful. The question remains whether or not states will be able to retain their highly skilled employees as the economy continues to improve. Ultimately, states will need to grapple with compensation systems that have been thwarted by the Great Recession.

States will also need to consider what they will do if larger shares of their employees, who are eligible to retire, decide to do so, leaving many jobs to be filled. Older state workers often hold senior positions and their retirement represents a significant loss of institutional knowledge (NASPO 2008). States may be able to use workplace flexibility as an incentive to retain highly skilled older employees, offering flexible schedules and work options, such as part-time employment and telecommuting.

Finally, in today's environment, state governments must continue to evaluate the nature of the work to be done, and how this work translates into needed workforce skills sets and education. States must understand the nature of their workplaces, as well as the composition of their workforces, and question whether existing personnel rules and practices best meet their current and future workforce needs. States should think strategically about how their personnel systems can be developed to accommodate changes in their internal workforce as well as the external labor market.

References

Abbey, C.W., and Boyd, D.J. (2002). *The Aging Government Workforce*, technical report. Nelson Rockefeller Institute of Government. Available at http://www.rockinst.org/pdf/workforce_welfare_and_social_services/2002-07-the_aging_government_workforce.pdf (accessed November 24, 2013).

Achieve, Inc. (2012). *The Future of the U.S. Workforce: A Survey of Hiring Practices across Industries*. Achieve, Inc., ERIC, EBSCOhost (accessed March 15, 2013).

Battaglio Jr., R., and Condrey, S.E. (2009). Reforming Public Management: Analyzing the Impact of Public Service Reform on Organizational and Managerial Trust. *Journal of Public Administration Research and Theory*, 19(4), 689–707.

Bowman, J., Gertz, M.G., Gertz, S.C., and Williams, R.L. (2003). Civil Service Reform in Florida State Government: Employee Attitudes 1 Year Later. *Review of Public Personnel Administration*, 23(4), 286–304.

Brenner, B.K. (2010). Using Employee Benefits Can Help Recruit, Attract, and Retain the Workforce of the Future: The Mature Employee. *Journal of Financial Service Professionals*, 64(3), 24–28.

Burns, C., Barton, K., and Kerby, S. (2012). *The State of Diversity in Today's Workforce: As Our Nation Becomes More Diverse So Too Does Our Workforce*. Washington, DC: Center for American Progress. available at http://www.americanprogress.org/issues/labor/report/2012/07/12/11938/the-state-of-diversity-in-todays-workforce/ (accessed February 23, 2013).

Cappelli, P. (1999). *The New Deal at Work: Managing the Market-Based Employment Relationship*. Boston: Harvard Business School Press.

Carnevale, A.P., Smith, N., and Strohl, J. (2010). *Help Wanted: Projections of Jobs and Education Requirements through 2018*, technical report. Center on Education and the Workforce, Georgetown University. Available at http://www9.georgetown.edu/grad/gppi/hpi/cew/pdfs/FullReport.pdf (accessed March 2, 2013).

Center for Public Education. (2013). *The United States of Education: The Changing Demographics of the United States and Their Schools*. Alexandria, VA: National School Board Association. Available at http://www.centerforpubliceducation.org/You-May-Also-Be-Interested-In-landing-page-level/Organizing-a-School-YMABI/The-United-States-of-education-The-changing-demographics-of-the-United-States-and-their-schools.html (accessed March 9, 2013).

Coggburn, J.D. (2006). At-Will Employment in Government: Insights from the State of Texas. *Review of Public Personnel Administration*, 26(2), 158–177.

Condrey, S.E., and Battaglio Jr., P. (2007). A Return to Spoils? Revisiting Radical Civil Service Reform in the United States. *Public Administration Review*, 67(3), 424–436.

Condrey, S.E., and Maranto, R., eds. (2001). *Radical Reform of the Civil Service*. Lanham, MD: Lexington Books.

Cooper, D., Gable, M., and Austin, A. (2012). *The Public Sector Job Crisis: Women and African Americans Hit Hardest by Job Losses in State Government*, technical report. Economic Policy Institute. Available at http://www.epi.org/publication/bp339-public-sector-jobs-crisis/ (accessed February 1, 2013).

Council of State Governments. (2013). *Book of the States*. Lexington, KY: Council of State Governments.

Crowell, E., and Guy, M. (2010). Florida's HR Reforms: Service First, Service Worst, or Something in Between? *Public Personnel Management*, 39(1), 15–46.

Deloitte. (2007). *The Graying Government Workforce*. Available at http://www.deloitte.com/assets/Dcom-Shared%20Assets/Documents/dtt_publicsector_snapshot_greygovt_113007.pdf.

Duggan, M., Lewis, J., and Milluzzi, M. (2010). Labor Relations in Hard Times. *Illinois Public Employee Relations Report*, 27(2), 1–8.

Equal Employment Opportunity Commission (EEOC). (2013). *State and Local Government Information (EEO-4), 2011 National Employment Summary*. Available at www.eeoc.gov/eeoc/statistics/employment/jobpat-eeo4/2011/table3/table3_1_state (accessed March 9, 2013).

Eyster, L., Johnson, R., and Toder, E. (2008). *Current Strategies to Employ and Retain Older Workers*. Urban Institute. Available at http://www.urban.org/publications/411626.html (accessed February 19, 2013).

Goodman, D., and Mann, S. (2010). Reorganization or Political Smokescreen: The Incremental and Temporary Use of At-Will Employment in Mississippi State Government. *Public Personnel Management*, 39(3), 183–209.

Hays, S.W., and Sowa, J.E. (2006). A Broader Look at the "Accountability" Movement: Some Grim Realities in State Civil Service Systems. *Review of Public Personnel Administration*, 26(2), 102–117.

Ingraham, P.W. (1995). *Foundations of Merit: Public Service in American Democracy*. Baltimore: Johns Hopkins.

Kellough, J.E., and Nigro, L.G. (2006). Dramatic Reform in the Public Service: At-Will Employment and the Creation of a New Public Workforce. *Journal of Public Administration Research and Theory*, 16(3), 447–466.

Kellough, J.E., and Nigro, L.G. (2008). Personnel Reform in the States: A Look at Progress Fifteen Years after the Winter Commission. *Public Administrative Review*, 68 (Suppl., December), S50 –S57.

Lautsch, B. (2002). Uncovering and Explaining Variance in the Features and Outcomes of Contingent Work. *Industrial and Labor Relations Review*, 56, 23–43.

Levit, N. (2012). Changing Workforce Demographics and the Future of the Protected Class Approach. *Lewis and Clark Law Review*, 16(2), 463–498.

Livingston, G., and Cohn, D. (2012). *U.S. Birth Rate Falls to a Record Low; Decline Is Greatest among Immigrants*, technical report. Pew Center on Research. Available at http://www.pewsocialtrends.org/files/2012/11/Birth_Rate_Final.pdf (accessed January 11, 2013).

Maciag, M. (2012). Full-Time Government Jobs Down, Part-Time Employment Up. *Governing*, August 23. Available at http://www.governing.com/blogs/by-the-numbers/state-local-full-time-part-time-jobs-data.html (accessed January 23, 2013).

National Association of State Procurement Officials (NASPO). (2008). *Responding to an Aging and Changing Workforce: Attracting, Retaining and Developing New Procurement Professional*. Available at http://www.naspo.org/documents/Responding_to_an_Aging_and_Changing_Workforce_-_FINAL_compressed.pdf (accessed January 3, 2013).

National Center for Public Policy and Higher Education. (2005). *Income of U.S. Workforce Projected to Decline if Education Doesn't Improve*, technical report. Available at http://www.highereducation.org/reports/pa_decline/pa_decline.pdf (accessed December 13, 2012).

Nigro, L.G., and Kellough, J. (2000). Civil Service Reform in Georgia. *Review of Public Personnel Administration*, 20(4), 41–54.

Office of Immigration Statistics, Department of Homeland Security. (2012). *Yearbook of Immigration Statistics*. Washington, DC: Department of Homeland Security. Available at http://www.dhs.gov/sites/default/files/publications/immigration-statistics/yearbook/2011/ois_yb_2011.pdf (accessed January 23, 2013).

O'Reilly, J., and Bothfeld, S. (2002). What Happens after Working Part-Time? Integration, Maintenance or Exclusionary Transitions in Britain and Western Germany. *Cambridge Journal of Economics*, 26(4), 409–439.

Selden, S., Schimmoeller, L., and Thompson, R. (2013). The Influence of Human Resource Management Practices on Voluntary Turnover of New Hires in U.S. State Governments. *Personnel Review*, 42(3), 300–323.

Subramaniam, G., Balasundram M., and Ershad, A. (2011). Can Workforce Flexibility Have an Effect on Women's Lifestyles and Work-Life Balance? *International Journal of Business Research*, 11(4), 168–173.

Tishman, F.M., Van Looy, S., and Bruyere, S.M. (2012). *Employer Strategies for Responding to an Aging Workforce*. New Brunswick, NJ: NTAR Leadership Center.

U.S. Bureau of Labor Statistics (BLS). (2013). *Union Members—2012*. Washington, DC. Available at www.bls.gov/news.release/union2.nr0.htm (accessed March 15, 2013).

U.S. Census Bureau. (2011a). *The Black Population 2010*. U.S. Department of Commerce, Economics and Statistics Administration. Available at http://www.census.gov/prod/cen2010/briefs/c2010br-06.pdf (accessed January 21, 2013).

U.S. Census Bureau. (2011b). *Population Distribution and Change: 2000 to 2010*. U.S. Department of Commerce, Economics and Statistics Administration.

U.S. Department of Commerce, Economics and Statistics Administration and the Executive Office of the President, Office of Management and Budget. (2011). *Women in America: Indicators of Social and Economic Well-Being*. U.S. Department of Commerce. Available at http://www.whitehouse.gov/sites/default/files/rss_viewer/Women_in_America.pdf (accessed February 23, 2013).

U.S. Department of Labor (DOL). (2013a). *African-American Labor Force in the Recovery*. Available at http://www.dol.gov/_sec/media/reports/blacklaborforce/ (accessed February 19, 2013).

U.S. Department of Labor (DOL). (2013b). *Asian-American Labor Force in the Recovery*. Available at http://www.dol.gov/_sec/media/reports/asianlaborforce/ (accessed February 19, 2013).

U.S. Department of Labor (DOL). (2013c). *Hispanic Labor Force in the Recovery*. Available at http://www.dol.gov/_sec/media/reports/hispaniclaborforce2011/ (accessed February 19, 2013).

U.S. Department of Labor (DOL). (2013d). *Women's Employment during the Recovery*. Available at http://www.dol.gov/_sec/media/reports/femalelaborforce/ (accessed February 19, 2013).

U.S. Health and Human Services, Centers for Disease Control and Prevention, National Center for Health Statistics, National Vital Statistics Systems. (2012). *Births: Preliminary Data for 2011*. Available at http://www.cdc.gov/nchs/data/nvsr/nvsr61/nvsr61_01.pdf (accessed January 23, 2013).

Chapter 14

A Vision of the Future Sustainability of the States

Robert D. Ebel
World Bank

Marilyn Marks Rubin
City University of New York

Contents

Converging Challenges

Four challenges are converging that will frame state government finance as the United States approaches the 2020s. The first is the growing vulnerability of state (and local) fiscal systems to economic recessions and to a slow-growth national economy. The second is the increasing federal fiscal austerity that will reinforce the dominant role of subnational governments in providing essential public services. The third challenge is the obsolescence of state revenue structures that have not been adapted to reflect changing demographic, economic, institutional, and technological trends that frame the "fiscal architecture" of spending and tax policies (Wallace 2012). The fourth is the continuing movement toward a "coercive" system of federalism as evidenced by increasing federal regulations, unfunded spending mandates, and preemption of state revenue and regulatory authority (Conlan and Posner 2012; Kincaid 2012).

These four challenges move from the low-priority "problems to be addressed" stage to high-priority concerns when subnational governments face economic and political shocks that are beyond their control. Just such an external shock occurred when the financial crisis of the late 2000s sparked the Great Recession that took hold at the end of 2007 and remained until the middle of 2009. And what a shock it was that "40 to 90 percent of one year's output … was foregone due to the 2007–2009 recession" (Atkinson et al. 2013, 1).

As discussed in Chapter 1, similar shocks have occurred throughout the history of this nation. Each time, the resiliency and built-in flexibility of the U.S. system of fiscal federalism and subnational financial continuity have allowed the states and the nation to regain momentum and move on. Yet this system will continue to be tested. While most states are recovering from the Great Recession, many were facing long-term structural problems before it began and continue to operate under fiscal stress. How the four challenges materialize will, to a large degree, determine the future fiscal sustainability of the states and the nation.

Vulnerability of the States to Economic Recessions

The 1980s ended with robust fiscal performance by the states, many of which experienced increased revenue flows following the recessions in the early years of the decade. The relatively brief recession of 1991–1992 caused a minor downswing in state revenues but was generally seen as a cyclical occurrence rather than a harbinger of longer-term structural imbalance. By 1993, federal, state, and local governments had entered into a phase of prolonged financial health.

The strong national economy in the latter half of the 1990s boosted the growth of government revenues, enabling states to cut taxes, initiate new programs, and increase spending for existing activities at the same time that they were building reserves. But, the deep stock market slump of 2000 and the recession that began in 2001 reduced the growth of state revenues, raising the prospect of substantial budget deficits. Faced with impending shortfalls, states responded with a variety of actions to maintain their mandated balanced budgets. These included raising taxes, cutting expenditures, drawing down accumulated reserves, and shifting special fund surpluses to balance general funds.

At about the same time, another long-term problem was gathering steam, the condition of state and local public pension plans. As described earlier in Chapter 7, for several years, state pension plans had largely moved from a pay-as-you-go basis to advanced funding for their liabilities.* States had also invested heavily in the stock market and had been rewarded with strong returns as the markets moved ahead. As a result, pension systems were in unusually good shape by the end of the 1990s, and state governments had begun to skip employer contributions and enrich employee benefits with their surpluses.

Then came the "dot-com bust" of the early 2000s that resulted in widespread losses in pension portfolio values due to declines in the stock market. States thus had to increase their pension fund contributions to keep them actuarially sound. This should have led to reconsideration of the rates of return assumptions that were being used to calculate pension fund assets and liabilities. Instead, most states continued to assume that their pension fund investments would earn at the elevated historic rates of return. Such an assumption effectively amounted to a bet that the spectacular growth in the nation's economy and financial markets in the last half of 20th century would be repeated in the next one. This turned out to be a very bad bet (Listokin-Smith 2012).

The Great Recession

Most states slowly recovered after the recession of the early 2000s, increasing their surpluses and rainy-day reserves. However, given the size of the deficits that emerged as a result of the Great Recession that ran from 2007 to 2009,† these reserves would provide little protection.

The recession began at the end of 2007 in the wake of the rupture of the "housing bubble" that had created a run-up in consumer spending fueled by newfound housing wealth. The woes caused by the bursting bubble quickly spread throughout financial markets. Institutional practices, such as "liar loans," often combined with subprime mortgage lending to individuals who did not qualify for

---

* Advanced funding refers to setting up a trust fund to prefund obligations. The trust fund can be separate from a pension fund or pooled together with other funds, such as one established for employer contributions to health care.

† The National Bureau of Economic Research (NBER) dates the recession as December 2007–June 2009. According to the NBER, a recession "is a significant decline in economic activity spread across the economy, lasting more than a few months, normally visible in real GDP, real income, employment, industrial production, and wholesale-retail sales" (http://www.nber.org/cycles.html).

prime loans led to a wave of foreclosures.* Making matters worse, many subprime loans had been packaged into Mortgage Backed Securities that were sold to investors worldwide. Inflation in capital values in the markets and, consequently, in the balance sheets of households and businesses, evaporated as deleveraging took place.†

Nationwide, unemployment climbed and businesses cut back production or closed their doors. Clamor for the federal government to intervene increased and culminated in February 2009 with the passage of the American Recovery and Reinvestment Act (ARRA), generally referred to as the stimulus package or the recovery act. The primary objective of the ARRA was to quickly infuse funds into flailing national and subnational economies by providing funds for infrastructure improvements.

The evidence shows that there was a payoff from ARRA in terms of higher output and employment than would have occurred in its absence. By substituting federal for state borrowing, a deep decline in capital spending—"a pragmatic but economically unwise strategy that ... distorts broader economic development goals"—was softened (Marlow 2012, 668). From 2008 to 2010, annual gross capital spending decreased by $115 billion; without ARRA the decline would have been closer to $177 billion—a decrease of about 15 percent (Marlow 2012). In addition, because of its huge presence and even its paperwork requirements, ARRA may have brought top-down pressure for reforming the subnational capital budgeting process. As Marlow (2012, 668) writes, "unlike in past recessions, efficiency became a key consideration for many capital-planning decisions." Thus, while the countercyclical impact of ARRA has largely run its course, it may have resulted in improvements in subnational capital budgeting and at the same time preserved debt capacity for future borrowing. The consequences of ARRA, even if unintended, have important implications not only for the robustness of the post–Great Recession recovery, but also for the structure of subnational fiscal policy into the future.

Although generally seen as an infrastructure program, ARRA also provided funds to the states to shore up the "social safety net" that protects the nation's most economically vulnerable residents (Gais et al. 2012). ARRA funds focused on maintaining the safety net by

- Directing resources to state cash assistance and social service programs
- Enhancing the availability of the Supplemental Nutrition Assistance Program (SNAP) (food stamps)
- Providing state aid to deal with a recession-induced increase in demand for Medicaid as people who lost jobs also lost employer-sponsored health insurance

* The "liar loan" refers to a loan made without clear measures of the borrower's (individual homeowner and investor alike) ability to repay and without equity protections to cushion against defaults. In addition, multiple risks were often layered into many subprime loans, for example, subprime mortgages that started at initial rates that reset after two to three years, leaving borrowers subject to payment shock, and in some cases, a home value that had fallen below the market (and refinancing) value (Joint Center for Housing Studies, 2008).

† Moore and Palumbo (2009).

- Giving states incentives to redefine their unemployment insurance (UI) programs, e.g., qualifying people with part-time work experience
- Increasing grants to several child-related programs, such as Head Start and the Child Care Development Block Grant
- Providing grants to the states to maintain funding for K–12 education
- Providing fiscal stability grants to the states

Troubled Asset Relief Program

ARRA was not the only federal program that helped to mitigate the recession's impact on states (Petersen and Ciccarone 2012). Congressional enactment in 2008 of the Troubled Asset Relief Program (TARP) that "bailed out" financial institutions played an important role with respect to municipal bonds secured by local property taxes. TARP enabled a vast majority of banks to stay healthy enough to pay taxes due on properties that the banks took over as a result of subprime delinquent loans. Federal assistance through TARP thus helped local government to maintain high property tax collection rates from 2007 to 2010. This in turn put less pressure on states to provide assistance to local jurisdictions (Petersen and Ciccarone 2012).

Federal Fiscal Austerity

ARRA was designed as a countercyclical stimulus program to revive a flailing economy. The evidence shows that although it increased the federal deficit as expected, there was a payoff in higher output and employment than would have occurred absent the stimulus (U.S Congressional Budget Office 2009–2013). While the overall impact of ARRA has been questioned (Jones and Rothfield 2011), the economic recovery in the states would have taken longer without the ARRA infusion of funding.

But the days of ARRA funds flowing to subnational governments are over and the federal government is back in a deficit reduction mode. The 2011 Budget Control Act (BCA) adopted by Congress in August 2011 to increase the federal debt ceiling and to reduce the federal deficit meant less funding for state and local governments. BCA established what is called sequestration, an automatic spending reduction process that was scheduled to begin in 2013 if Congress and the president did not agree to $1.2 trillion in deficit reduction. After months of failed negotiations within Congress and between Congress and the president, sequestration was triggered in March 2013.* The impact of sequestration on the states, particularly those relying on defense spending either directly or via defense contracting, was significant.

Certain federal programs that provide funding to the states, including Medicaid and the Children's Health Insurance Program (discussed in Chapter 10), were

* The sequestration was originally set to begin by January 2, 2013. It was delayed by the "fiscal cliff" legislation, and Congress moved the date of implementation to March 1, 2013.

exempt from the cuts. But, the sequester meant fewer federal dollars for a wide range of intergovernmental services, including public housing assistance, schools for low income students, and law enforcement. A second round of sequestration was averted as a result of the bipartisan budget agreement reached in December 2013, although there will still be federal cutbacks in funds to the states. While these 2014 reductions may be less in dollar terms than the previous round of cuts, they may hurt more since they will come on top of fiscal year 2013 reductions.

In addition to fiscal austerity, the change in the mix of federal assistance to the states, especially with regard to Medicaid, will have budgetary impacts. Medicaid increased from 12 percent of total federal assistance to the states in 1978 to 20 percent in 2008. This repositioning of the federal-state mix will likely accelerate as a result of the Patient Protection and Affordable Health Care Act (ACA) of 2010. If fully implemented, by 2015, ACA will make about an additional 15 million people eligible for the jointly funded federal-state Medicaid program (Scheppach 2012; U.S. Congressional Budget Office 2012).

States could, however, be "financial winners" due to the ACA's Medicaid expansion. According to a study done by Ohio's Health Policy Institute (2012), higher costs associated with increased eligibility are more than offset by a combination of several factors. These include (1) certain categories of current Medicaid spending will qualify for a higher federal matching rate, (2) some state spending for the uninsured and the mentally ill will be supplanted by Medicaid, and (3) new revenues to be generated through growth in the state's managed care and insurance taxes.

What's Next?

Some states have experienced a revenue rebound to prerecession levels. However, the slow-growth national economy accompanied by increases in Medicaid costs for most states and growing income inequality suggests a subnational fiscal system under continuing pressure. One way to look ahead for a way to relieve this pressure is to look back to 1982 when President Ronald Reagan proposed the "big swap" that would have had the federal government take over Medicaid in a trade for state takeover of the Aid to Families with Dependent Children (AFDC) and Food Stamp programs and dozens of categorical grant programs. Had the swap been made, it would have allowed the states to concentrate on providing other services, including education and infrastructure maintenance and development (Scheppach 2012). The time has come to reconsider the trade.

Obsolescence of State Revenue Systems

With the exception of assigning exclusive authority for the federal government to tax foreign imports, the U.S. Constitution provides revenue autonomy to the states that possess inherent, plenary taxing powers. The question is whether the states are using that power to structure revenue systems that capture changing demographic, economic, institutional, and technological trends. On that score, state revenue systems are in need of review and reform so that they do not become obsolete.

As discussed in Chapters 3 and 4, states are primarily reliant on two taxes, the individual income and general sales taxes. Taken together, these taxes accounted for close to two-thirds of state tax revenues in 2012 (U.S. Bureau of the Census 2013).

Individual Income Tax

The individual or personal income tax (PIT) is a primary revenue source for 41 states and accounted for a third of total state tax collections in 2012.* The PIT will become increasingly obsolete if states do not reform the tax to take account of changing demographic trends (Wallace 2012). Recognizing, but for this discussion setting aside, the impact of changing demographics on state expenditures, what are the revenue implications? The cohort of persons 65 and older moving out of their earning years and into retirement is expected to increase into the second decade of this century, making a jump between 2010 and 2025 from 13.0 to 17.9 percent of the total population (Wallace 2012). As the country's population ages, so too does the composition of income change, and thus the amount of resources that states can extract through taxes. Taxable income becomes fully or partially tax-exempt. For example, 33 states that have broad-based PITs make some adjustment for social security income (Commerce Clearing House 2013).†

In addition, some states give preferential treatment to income from pensions, including in-state systems, the federal retirement system, private pensions, and IRAs. Even for those who remain in the workforce, income generally declines with age. When the effect of non-means-tested senior citizen PIT tax credits is added in, it becomes even more evident that there is a demographic effect that must be addressed to counteract the erosion in the state personal income tax base (Fisher 2010).

The needed policy response is clear, but it will take political leadership and citizen consensus to make it happen. The possibilities range from sweeping changes, such as taxing transfer payments as ordinary income, to more targeted reforms, such as means testing tax credits to seniors. The payoff comes in enhanced horizontal and vertical equity and having a tax that reflects rather than trails behind the nation's changing demographics. In addition, with a broader base, tax rates could be reduced to provide for fiscal space if and when rate adjustment is needed, as it was during the Great Recession.

* Alaska, Florida, Nevada, South Dakota, Texas, Washington, and Wyoming do not collect the tax; New Hampshire and Tennessee impose the tax on only interest and dividend income. D.C. also levies a PIT, but the U.S. Census classifies D.C. as a local government. When one adds in selective sales tax collections, the sales tax share goes to 48.9 percent (U.S. Bureau of the Census, *State Government Tax Collections Summary Report, 2010*, 2011a). For a full discussion, see also Cordes and Juffras (2012, 333–351).

† Includes the District of Columbia.

Sales Tax

The general retail sales tax that is levied in 45 of the 50 states is based on consumption, which is a function of income.* With the post–Great Recession recovery, it follows that the sales tax should be a good producer of state tax revenues. But, as pointed out in several previous chapters, sales tax revenues are declining as a share of total state tax revenues despite rising rates.

The erosion of the sales tax base is primarily explained by three factors. The first is the profusion of legislated exemptions for individual taxpayers (e.g., clothing and food for home consumption) and exemptions accorded to some businesses and nonprofit organizations. Although politically justified on the grounds of reducing the regressivity of the sales tax and economic development, there is generally agreement in the public finance literature that sales tax exemptions are inefficient in accomplishing either objective (Lav 2012; Eckl and Perez 2005).

The second factor is the shift in consumption away from the goods component of the sales tax base to services. Household consumption of services as a percent of total personal consumption expenditures increased from 49 percent in 1973 to 64 percent in 2011 (U.S. Bureau of Economic Analysis 2013). It follows, or would seem to, that to keep the retail sales tax "up with the times," states would expand the sales tax base to include more services. A recommendation to expand the sales tax to services may, however, be bad advice. Many untaxed services are intermediate (business to business) in the production-to-distribution chain. Unless the transaction is taxable as a final sale at retail, it ought to remain untaxed to minimize tax pyramiding.

While there is diversity among the states (Ring 1999), on average, about 45 percent of retail sales taxes are collected on intermediate transactions (Fox 2012). Moreover, professional services are more mobile across jurisdictional borders than are goods. A tax on them may result in reduced local employment. The reality, however, is that although the United States is moving from a goods-based to a services-based economy, many states have already done about as much as they can with their retail sales taxes to capture this change. What merits further attention is a national sales (value-added) tax that addresses state border wars and tax pyramiding problems. Such a tax could be collected by the federal government and apportioned among states choosing to piggyback on the federal base and at the same time preserve a high degree of tax autonomy (Duncan 2012).

A third source of sales tax base erosion is the growth in remote shopping. Remote sales happen in four ways: e-commerce, catalogue sales, telephone orders, and consumers physically crossing borders (Maguire 2011). Of these, it is e-commerce that presents the most vexing issue with respect to the ability of state sales taxes to capture changing shopping modalities. It has been estimated that in 2012 e-transactions totaled $4 trillion, nearly double the 2005 level (Fox 2012). The estimated revenue lost on e-commerce increased from $2.7 billion in 2000 to more than $11.0 billion in 2012 (Fox 2012). Given the anticipated trends in e-commerce, not only will the revenue

* The non-sales tax states are Alaska, Delaware, Montana, New Hampshire, and Oregon.

losses to subnational governments continue to grow, but so too will the excess burden of the tax whereby an efficiency loss occurs when a tax treatment interferes with taxpayers' economic decisions at no gain to collections (Watson 2005; Fox 2012).

Toward a Coercive System of Federalism

The U.S. federal system has always been tested, starting from the 18th century when it transitioned from a confederation to a federation and to the "cooperative federalism" phase in place from the 1930s through the early 1960s. Since then, this system has again been tested as it has moved from a system of cooperation across levels of government to one of coercion, in which the federal government has increasingly turned to unfunded mandates on the states and preemption of state regulatory and revenue policies (Conlan and Posner 2012; Eads 2012).

The National Conference of State Legislatures (NCSL) estimates that Congress imposed as least $131 billion in unfunded mandates on the states from 2004 to 2008 (NCSL 2013).* Examples range from sweeping cost shifting to the states in the Real ID Act requiring states to standardize driver's licenses to the No Child Left Behind mandate requiring states to establish K–12 standardized tests (Ravitch 2010). Mandates are typically enforced (perhaps *incentivized* is a better term) by requiring states to assume these costs as a condition for receiving federal grant funds.

The federal government has also acted in a coercive manner through preemption, whereby federal laws take precedence over state laws. Preemption in its various forms has been growing since the 1970s with the current federal preemption on state taxation of e-commerce transactions a good example (Eads 2012). In his catalogue of federal preemption of revenue and regulatory authority, Eads opines that Alexander Hamilton would have likely regarded such preemption as a "usurpation of power not granted by the constitution" (Eads 2012).

There are several reasons to expect continuation of "coercive federalism." One is the growing federal fiscal austerity that tempts Congress to increasingly "shift the deficit down" to subnational governments. Another is that the increasingly globalized business sector has morphed from a traditional position of supporting decentralization policy to that of seeking national legislation to standardize, restrict, and prohibit state initiatives (Conlan and Posner 2012).

Conclusions

The Great Recession was the worst contraction in the U.S. economy since the Great Depression. It started with a dramatic financial shock that led to a downturn that was long, deep, and economy-wide. But as bad as the recession was, it was

* The NCSL maintains a catalogue of mandates on the states. NCSL uses a broader definition of *unfunded mandate* than the one included in the Unfunded Mandate Reform Act (UMRA) enacted in 1995.

not the depression. This country in the 2000s had learned from the 1930s of the importance of bold countercyclical action and the need to build subnational human, institutional, and organizational capacity.

What also came out of the 1930s was a revolution in fiscal policy as subnational governments laid the foundations of government finance that has carried the nation to the present time. On the revenue side, states adopted general sales taxes and personal and corporate income taxes that are the current backbone of state revenue systems.* On the spending side, states moved from being the "backwaters" of expenditure management to the forefront of leadership in adopting management and performance systems (Snell 2004; Mann 1985).

But what can we expect of the American states in the future? The preceding chapters have presented the past, current status of, and prospects for the fiscal activities and capacities of these governments. Considering this, it is certainly evident that just as government policy makers in the 1930s were faced with an obsolete fiscal system, so too are those of today. The future fiscal sustainability of states thus rests on policy reforms that move the four challenges discussed here from problems to be addressed to high-priority concerns. And, the path is not all that opaque. Though deficiencies in the system are clear, so too are the options for getting subnational government finance on track for this still new century. There may not be many politically easy answers to the challenges facing the states, but there are solutions. The question is whether policy makers at all levels of government as well as voters are up to the task of their Great Depression predecessors. History suggests that they are. But, for now, the country waits.

References

Atkinson, T., Luttrell, D., and Rosenblum, H. (2013). *How Bad Was It? The Costs and Consequences of the 2007–09 Financial Crisis*. Federal Reserve Bank of Dallas.

Baer, D. (2007). *State Taxation of Social Security and Pensions in 2006*, Issue Brief 84. Washington, DC: AAPR Public Policy Institute, pp. 1–7. Available at www.research.aarp.org/ppi (accessed September 2013).

Bruce, D., and Fox, W.F. (2005). Cross-Border Shopping. In *The Encyclopedia of Taxation and Tax Policy*, ed. J.C. Cordes, R.D. Ebel, and J.G. Gravelle. Washington, DC: Urban Institute Press, pp. 72–73.

Commerce Clearing House. (2012). *2013 State Tax Handbook*. Chicago: Commerce Clearing House.

Conlan, T.J., and Posner, P.L. (2012). Federalism, Trends, Tensions and Outlook. In *The Oxford Handbook of State and Local Government Finance*, ed. R.D. Ebel and J.E. Petersen. New York: Oxford University Press, pp. 83–104.

Cordes, J.J., and Juffras, J.N. (2012). State Personal Income Taxes. In *The Oxford Handbook of State and Local Government Finance*, ed. R.D. Ebel and J.E. Petersen. New York: Oxford University Press, pp. 300–332.

* For example, two dozen states that use sales taxes today established them in the 1930s.

Duncan, H.T. (2012). Implications of a Federal Value Added Tax for State and Local Governments. In *The Oxford Handbook of State and Local Government Finance*, ed. R.D. Ebel and J.E. Petersen. New York: Oxford University Press, pp. 380–405.

Eads Jr., J.R. (2012). Federal Preemption of Revenue Authority. In *The Oxford Handbook of State and Local Government Finance*, ed. R.D. Ebel and J.E. Petersen. New York: Oxford University Press, pp. 198–213.

Ebel, R.D., Petersen, J., and Vu, T.T. (2012). *The Oxford Handbook on State and Local Government Finance*, ed. R.D. Ebel and J.E. Petersen. New York: Oxford University Press, pp. 1–9.

Eckl, C., and Perez, A. (2005). State Sales Tax Relief Programs. In *The Encyclopedia of Taxation and Tax Policy*, ed. J.J. Cordes, R.D. Ebel, and J.G. Gravelle. Washington, DC: Urban Institute Press, pp. 351–352.

Federal Funds Information for the States. (2013). Available at http://www.ffis.org/ (accessed October 2013).

Fisher, R.C. (2010). The State of State and Local Government Finance. *St. Louis Regional Economic Development*, Federal Reserve Bank of St. Louis, 2010, 4-22. Available at http://research.stlouisfed.org/publications/red/2010/01/Fisher.pdf (accessed October 2013).

Fox, W.F. (2012). Retail Sales and Use Taxation. In *The Oxford Handbook of State and Local Government Finance*, ed. R.D. Ebel and J.E. Petersen. New York: Oxford University Press, pp. 406–428.

Gais, T., Boyd, D., and Dadayan, L. (2012). The Social Safety Net, Health Care and the Great Recession. In *The Oxford Handbook of State and Local Government Finance*, ed. R.D. Ebel and J.E. Petersen. New York: Oxford University Press, pp. 543–593.

Health Policy Institute in Ohio. (2013, March). *Expanding Medicaid in Ohio*. Columbus, OH: Health Policy Institute.

Joint Center for Housing Studies of Harvard University. (2008). *The State of the Nation's Housing*. Cambridge, MA: Harvard Kennedy Shook, 44 pp.

Jones, G., and Rothfield, D.M. (2011). *No Such Thing as Shovel Ready: The Supply Side of the Recovery Act*, Working Paper 11-34. Mercatus Center, George Mason University. Available at http://mercatus.org/sites/default/files/publication/Did_Stimulus_Dollars_Hire_The_Unemployed_Jones_Rothschild_WP34.pdf (accessed September 2013).

Kincaid, J. (2012). The Constitutional Frameworks of State and Local Government Finance. In *The Oxford Handbook of State and Local Government Finance*, ed. R.D. Ebel and J.E. Petersen. New York: Oxford University Press, pp. 45–82.

Lav, I.J. (2012). Accomplishing State Budget Policy and Process Reforms. In *The Oxford Handbook of State and Local Government Finance*, ed. R.D. Ebel and J.E. Petersen. New York: Oxford University Press, pp. 871–893.

Maguire, S. (2011). *State Taxation of Internet Transactions*, CRS Report for Congress (R41-853). Washington, DC: Congressional Research Service. Available at http://www.fas.org/sgp/crs/misc/R41853.pdf www.crs.gov (accessed September 2013).

Mann, M.R. (1985). *The Question of State Government Capability*. Washington, DC: U.S. Advisory Commission on Intergovernmental Relations. Available at www.library.unt.edu/gpo/acir (accessed September 2013).

Marlow, J. (2012). Capital Budgeting. In *The Oxford Handbook of State and Local Government Finance*, ed. R.D. Ebel and J.E. Petersen. New York: Oxford University Press, pp. 658–681.

Mazerov, M. (2012). *States Should Embrace 21st Century Economy by Extending Sales Taxes to Digital Goods and Services.* Washington, DC: Center on Budget and Policy Priorities. Available at www.cbpp.org (accessed August 2013).

Moore, K.B., and Palumbo, M.G. (2009). *The Finances of American Households in the Past Three Recessions: Evidence from the Survey of Consumer Finances.* Working paper 2010–6. Washington, DC: Federal Reserve Board, 40 pp.

National Bureau of Economic Research (NBER). (2013). *Business Cycle (Recession and Recovery).* Available at www.nber.org (accessed September 2–13, 2013).

National Conference of State Legislatures (NCSL). (2013). *Mandate Monitor of the Standing Committee on Budgets and Review.* Denver, CO: National Conference of State Legislatures. Available at www.ncsl.org/ncsl-in-dc.standing-committees (accessed September 2013).

Petersen, J.E., and Ciccarone, R. (2012). Financial Markets and State and Local Governments. In *The Oxford Handbook of State and Local Government Finance*, ed. R.D. Ebel and J.E. Petersen. New York: Oxford University Press, pp. 682–726.

Ravitch, D. (2010). *The Death of the Great American School System: How Testing and Choice Are Undermining Education.* New York: Basic Books.

Ring Jr., R.R. (1999). The Proportion of Consumers' and Producers' Goods in the General Sales Tax. *National Tax Journal*, 52, 79–80.

Scheppach, R.C. (2012). The Intergovernmental Grant System. In *The Oxford Handbook of State and Local Government Finance*, ed. R.D. Ebel and J.E. Petersen. New York: Oxford University Press, pp. 937–957.

Snell, R. (2004). *New Realities in State Finance.* Boulder, CO: National Conference of State Legislatures.

U.S. Bureau of the Census. (2002, April). *State and Local Government Finances Summary, 1988–99.* Washington, DC: Governments Division. Available at www.census.gov.

U.S. Bureau of the Census. (2011a, March). *State Government Tax Collections Summary Report, 2010.* Washington, DC: Governments Division. Available at www.census.gov.

U.S. Bureau of the Census. (2011b, October). *State and Local Government Finances Summary, 2009.* Washington, DC: Governments Division. Available at www.census.gov.

U.S. Bureau of the Census. (2012, September). *State and Local Government Finances Summary, 2010*, Washington, DC: Governments Division. Available at www.census.gov.

U.S. Bureau of Economic Analysis. (2013). *National Income and Product Tables, Interactive Data Base.* Washington, DC: U.S Department of Commerce. Available at www.bea.gov.

U.S. Congressional Budget Office. (2009–2013, quarterly). *Estimated Impact of the American Recovery and Reinvestment Act on Employment and Economic Output.* Washington, DC: U.S. Congress.

U.S. Congressional Budget Office. (2012). *An Update to the Budget and Economic Outlook: Fiscal Years 2012–2020.* Congressional Budget Office. Washington, DC: U.S. Congress.

U.S. Congressional Budget Office. (2013, May). *Updated Budget Projections: 2013–2023.* Congress of the United States, Congressional Budget Office. Available at www.cbo.gov.

Wallace, S. (2012). The Evolving Financial Architecture of State and Local Governments. In *The Oxford Handbook of State and Local Government Finance*, ed. R.D. Ebel and J.E. Petersen. New York: Oxford University Press, pp. 156–175.

Watson, H. (2005). Excess Burden. In *The Encyclopedia of Taxation and Tax Policy*, ed. C. Cordes, R.D. Ebel, and J.G. Gravelle. Washington, DC: Urban Institute Press, pp. 121–122.

Zodrow, G.R. (1999). *State Sales and Income Taxes: An Economic Analysis.* College Station: Texas A&M University Press.

Index

V

W

Z